WETLAND AND RIPARIAN AREAS
OF THE INTERMOUNTAIN WEST

NUMBER FOUR

Peter T. Flawn Series in Natural Resource Management and Conservation

Wetland and Riparian Areas of the Intermountain West

Ecology and Management

EDITED BY MARK C. MCKINSTRY,
WAYNE A. HUBERT, AND
STANLEY H. ANDERSON

UNIVERSITY OF TEXAS PRESS, AUSTIN

COPYRIGHT © 2004 BY THE UNIVERSITY OF TEXAS PRESS

All rights reserved

Printed in the United States of America

First edition, 2004

Requests for permission to reproduce material from this work should be sent to Permissions, University of Texas Press, P.O. Box 7819, Austin, TX 78713-7819.

♾ The paper used in this book meets the minimum requirements of ANSI/NISO Z39.48-1992 (R1997) (Permanence of Paper).

LIBRARY OF CONGRESS CATALOGING-IN-PUBLICATION DATA

Wetland and riparian areas of the intermountain West : ecology and management / edited by Mark C. McKinstry, Wayne A. Hubert, and Stanley H. Anderson.— 1st ed.
     p.   cm.—(Peter T. Flawn series in natural resource management and conservation ; no. 4)
Includes bibliographical references and index.
ISBN 0-292-70248-5 (cloth : alk. paper)
1. Wetland ecology—Great Basin.   2. Wetland management—Great Basin.   3. Wetlands—Great Basin.   4. Riparian ecology—Great Basin.
5. Riparian areas—Great Basin—Management.   6. Riparian areas—Great Basin.   I. McKinstry, Mark C. (Mark Calvert), 1960–   II. Hubert, Wayne A.
III. Anderson, Stanley H.   IV. Series.
QH104.5.G68W48   2004
577.68'0979—dc22

                                                                      2003023047

CONTENTS

Figures

Tables

ACKNOWLEDGMENTS

Any book requires the dedicated assistance of many individuals and organizations. We are especially grateful for the help and assistance from several individuals within the Wyoming Game and Fish Department, including Gary Butler, Harry Harju, Jay Lawson, and Reg Rothwell. These individuals suggested a need for the book and helped push it along conceptually and administratively. The Wyoming Cooperative Fish and Wildlife Research Unit and the University of Wyoming provided much of the logistical support for this project. Kelly Gordon, Regan Plumb, Jason Herreman, Christina Schmidt, and Tamasin Schroeder provided invaluable assistance with editorial and formatting changes. Elizabeth Rahel created several of the figures. We thank not only the authors who contributed manuscripts for this volume, but also the reviewers of this book for improving the text and helping it become an important addition to the science and management of western wetland and riparian areas. Our thanks are also extended to William Bishel, Leslie Tingle, and Jan McInroy at the University of Texas Press and the managing editorial staff for their help and support. Finally, we thank the many researchers and others whose excellent work has been reviewed in these pages. Without their commitment to furthering science and natural resource management, a volume such as this would not be possible.

INTRODUCTION

Water in the western United States has been referred to as "liquid gold." The overappropriation of most streams is a testament to the value of water and a source of conflict. Water flowing from a typical mountain range in the Rocky Mountains is often used for multiple purposes: for fish and wildlife habitat, for irrigation and stock watering, for municipal and industrial purposes, and even for ornamental displays. The Intermountain West is an incredibly diverse area that occupies a large portion of the United States (Figure I.1). The area varies from mountains where snow and summer rains feed high-elevation wetlands to arid basins where natural systems depend upon mountain runoff and spring storms. Throughout the Intermountain West, wetlands and riparian areas perform functions far out of proportion to the area that they cover. As an example, wetland and riparian areas in Wyoming, Nevada, and Montana comprise less than 2% of the surface area, yet more than 80% of wildlife species in those states depend on these areas to fulfill life requirements. Wetlands in the Intermountain West are no less important than estuarine wetlands, prairie potholes, or forested wetlands of the Midwest, and yet scant attention has been focused on them. Part of the problem has been the relatively sparse human population and its associated impacts that usually drive research and information needs. However, this is rapidly changing in the Intermountain West, where many towns and cities have expanded within the past two decades. For example, Denver, Boise, and Phoenix have doubled in population since 1985. This population boom is not restricted to large metropolitan areas but extends also to towns like Buffalo, Wyoming; Durango, Colorado; and Moab, Utah. As conflicts involving wetland and riparian areas of the Intermountain West increase, so will the need for information about them.

We believe there is a need for a book that reviews these unique habitats and identifies areas on which future research should focus. With that goal in mind, we have organized this book to encompass legal issues, a

FIGURE I.I. Map of Intermountain West covered within this book

description of the region, riverine habitats, natural palustrine habitats, created palustrine habitats, and evaluation.

The first chapter covers laws and regulations that apply to wetland and riparian areas of the western United States. Important case law is reviewed with respect to its impacts on current and future regulations and management issues. While some may find legal issues difficult to follow and out of their realm of interest, we feel that they are critical in understanding how management decisions are made regarding wetland and riparian habitats in the West. In this regard, the authors have done an excellent job of putting the legal concerns into laymen's terms.

The second chapter offers an in-depth description of the area that is called the Intermountain West. Throughout the development of the book we struggled with defining our area of coverage and the research that pertains to wetlands and riparian areas within this region. In several instances throughout the volume, authors discuss research in areas out-side of the Intermountain West. We allowed this only where we felt that the work was applicable to areas within the Intermountain West. Mur-ray Laubhan's chapter helped to define our focus and gives the reader in-sight into the formative geological, meteorological, and ecological forces that shape wetland and riparian habitats in the Intermountain West.

The third section, chapters 3–5, encompasses the ecology and man-agement of riverine wetlands. We recognize that riparian/riverine sys-tems are actually wetlands and are considered as such under many clas-sification schemes. However, we have kept them separate because of their importance and the influence they have on politics, management, and ecology in the Intermountain West. In this section, as in the follow-ing two sections, we have included chapters that cover ecosystem func-tion, important taxa associated with these habitats, and issues that are important when managing these areas.

The fourth section, chapters 6–8, covers natural palustrine habitats, areas that traditionally have been the mainstay of wetland habitat and management. Palustrine wetlands are those areas that can support rooted aquatic vegetation, have anaerobic soils, and are flooded during portions of the year. While the Intermountian West is considered a dry region, it has a surprisingly large number of natural wetlands, especially in basins between the mountain ranges. This section not only assists the manager in identifying techniques to manage these areas but also helps the ecol-ogist gain understanding of how they function.

The fifth section, chapters 9–11, covers created palustrine habitats, a subject that has been neglected in most wetland texts. Wetland creation in the Intermountain West is often associated with other activities (e.g., stock pond construction, mining, irrigation), and these habitats can be very valuable. Created wetlands in the western United States number in the hundreds of thousands, and little is known about their function or value. The authors in this section provide excellent descriptions of the many types of created wetlands and suggest various management prac-tices that can assist in making them more productive.

Finally, chapter 12 leads the reader through the many classification and evaluation techniques that can be used for wetlands and riparian areas of the Intermountain West.

While commendable work has been conducted on wetland and ripar-ian areas within the Intermountain West, we believe that much more needs to be done. Areas of importance that are particularly lacking in re-search and understanding include vegetative community structure and function; the role of salinity in structuring wetland communities; the importance of hydrologic regimes and hydrology in general; nutrient cy-cling in wetlands (especially as it pertains to contaminants); impacts of dams on structure and function of adjacent wetlands; and development of successful techniques for wetland and riparian restoration. A considerable information gap exists with regard to created wetlands and the role they play ecologically, biologically, socially, and economically. It is our wish that this text will stimulate agencies and individuals to devote more time and resources to studying these issues.

This book serves as a good starting point for managers and researchers working with wetland and riparian areas in the Intermountain West. No single body of work, the present volume included, is the end point in any discipline. The Intermountain West is an incredibly diverse area, and to attempt to cover the ecology and management of all of its wetland and riparian areas would have been a mistake. If we have brought to light more management options and identified topics for future research, we will have accomplished our goal. Good luck in your endeavors.

MARK C. MCKINSTRY
WAYNE A. HUBERT
STANLEY R. ANDERSON

WETLAND AND RIPARIAN AREAS
OF THE INTERMOUNTAIN WEST

CHAPTER I

Laws and Regulations Pertaining to Wetland Areas in the Intermountain West

MAUREEN RYAN AND MARK SQUILLACE

Introduction

In recent years, the federal government has grown to understand the important ecological value of wetlands. Wetlands act as natural water purification filters, flood control mechanisms, and important wildlife habitat. Federal laws designed to preserve and protect wetlands have proliferated as a result of this growing appreciation for these resources. All federal wetlands legislation shares a central premise: promoting preservation by mitigating the environmental impact of development on the nation's wetlands. While the goal of this legislation may be simple, the means for achieving that goal are not. Federal wetlands legislation presents a complex web of requirements and options through which proponents of any significant project affecting wetlands must navigate. Thus, to facilitate planning, managers of projects that could affect wetlands should have a firm understanding of the federal requirements and available options.

Overview of Western Water Law

The climate throughout most of the Intermountain West is arid, but wetlands are still commonplace, especially near streams and in mountain areas. The limited surface water resources in the Intermountain West and the release of much of that water from melting snow in the mountains during the spring and early summer have prompted states throughout this region to adhere to the prior appropriation doctrine for allocating water resources.[1] This means that water is allocated to persons with the earliest water rights in order of priority until all of the water rights in a stream system are exhausted. Beneficial use is the basis, the measure, and the limit of the water right in a prior appropriation state.[2] This doctrine limits a person's water rights to the amount of water that can reasonably be put to beneficial use without waste. Moreover, any person holding a water right who repeatedly fails to apply the water to the beneficial use for which it was appropriated may lose the water to abandonment or forfeiture.[3]

Irrigated agriculture accounts for 78% of water withdrawals and 90% of water consumption in the western United States.[4] Moreover, most of the senior water rights in the Intermountain West are held by farmers. Thus, water allocation decisions for agricultural use will likely have the greatest impact on wetlands.

Western farmers and ranchers grow a wide variety of crops and use a wide variety of irrigation techniques. Although agriculturists are increasingly turning to more efficient irrigation technologies, flood irrigation remains the most common irrigation method, especially for growing low-value crops on marginal lands.[5] Flood irrigation frequently creates or enhances wetland areas, although sometimes at the expense of natural stream flows. Wetlands are also formed along leaky, unlined ditches that deliver water to farmers and ranchers who hold water rights. Although most western states now encourage farmers and ranchers to use water conservation practices, few states require such measures. As a result, the current water allocation laws followed in the Intermountain West tend to have a salutary effect on wetlands protection. This protection could expand over time as pressure to improve water conservation practices mounts.

Substantive Regulatory Programs
The Clean Water Act

Congress enacted the Clean Water Act (CWA)[6] to "restore and maintain the chemical, physical and biological integrity" of the waters of the United States.[7] Section 301 prohibits any person from discharging pollutants from a point source without a permit.[8] Congress specifically designed section 404 to target wetland conversions. Section 404 prohibits any unauthorized discharge of dredged or fill materials, the primary pollutants implicated in wetland conversions, from a point source into the navigable waters of the United States.[9] Possible ramifications of section 404 violations include injunctive relief, civil and criminal penalties, and citizen suits.[10]

The Army Corps of Engineers (Corps) and the Environmental Protection Agency (EPA) share responsibility for administering section 404,[11] and each agency has promulgated regulations to permit dredge and fill programs.[12] Section 404 authorizes the Corps to issue permits for the discharge of dredged or fill materials into a jurisdictional wetland after public notice and comment.[13] The EPA establishes (in conjunction with the Corps) the substantive environmental criteria—known as section 404(b)(1) guidelines[14]—that the Corps must examine when issuing dredged and fill permits. These guidelines identify a special concern for wetlands. The EPA treats wetlands as special aquatic sites subject to greater protection than other waters because of their importance to "the general overall environmental health or vitality of the entire ecosystem of a region."[15] The Corps and the EPA also share section 404 enforcement responsibilities. While the Corps polices violations of *existing* section 404 permits, the EPA takes enforcement action against those who discharge dredged materials into the navigable waters of the United States *without* a permit.[16]

THE SECTION 404 PERMIT PROCESS

Regulations establishing the procedure for filing an application for a section 404 permit[17] require, among other things, that applicants describe the purpose and need for the proposed project, its location, and the names and addresses of adjoining landowners.[18] An applicant should also include preliminary drawings, sketches, and maps of the vicinity of the project area. A sample application form is reproduced in the Corps' regulations.[19] The applicant must pay a modest application fee. Because the cost of processing section 404 applications is generally much higher than the fee, and because the federal government is increasingly concerned about asserting its cost recovery authority, fees for section 404 applications will likely rise in coming years.

Within 15 days from receipt of an application, the district engineer must either determine that the application is incomplete and request additional information or notify the public that the application is complete.[20] The Corps must inform the applicant if a nationwide permit[21] might encompass the activities proposed in the application.

Because section 404 revolves around the goal of preservation and mitigation to compensate for lost wetland values and functions, the Corps is directed to make permit determinations with the goal of no net loss of wetlands. Almost by definition, a request to discharge dredged and fill materials on wetlands involves the destruction of wetlands. Consequently, section 404 and its implementing guidelines require a land manager seeking a section 404 permit to submit a plan for mitigating adverse environmental impacts resulting from the project.[22] Such mitigation, which typically must occur in the same watershed, requires both proper management of the project itself and compensation for any wetlands destroyed by the conversion, including on-site and off-site restoration or creation of wetlands.[23]

Mitigation involves measures to minimize the impacts from development and replaces those ecological resources that are inevitably damaged. Under a Memorandum of Agreement (MOA) between the Corps and EPA,[24] the Corps must seek to avoid or minimize impacts from the proposed activities. Only after such efforts are made will compensatory mitigation be considered. The MOA sets a policy of no net loss of wetlands, but it does not require that an applicant meet that goal in every application. It also takes a functional approach to wetlands mitigation, favoring wetland values over equality of area. And it establishes preferences for wetland restoration over wetland creation, on-site mitigation over off-site, and in-kind compensatory mitigation.

To facilitate compensatory mitigation where it may be necessary, the federal government has promulgated guidance on the use of mitigation banks.[25] This policy allows applicants to receive credits for the restoration, creation, or enhancement of wetlands that can be used as compensatory mitigation in appropriate cases.

Section 404 also requires an applicant to show that a proposed wetland activity is the least environmentally damaging alternative in a particular project after surveying all practical alternatives. Under the Corps' regulations, an alternative is practical if it is "available and capable of being done after taking into consideration cost, existing technology, and logistics, in light of the overall project purposes."[26] The applicant must show that no upland areas can accommodate the proposed project. A project that is not dependent on access or proximity to or sitting within a wetland is presumed to have upland alternatives unless the applicant can clearly demonstrate otherwise.[27] The Corps then reviews the applicant's proposal under section 404(b)(1) guidelines to determine whether any practical alternatives to the proposed activity exist.

Pursuant to section 404(c), the EPA retains but rarely uses veto authority over the Corps' decision to issue a section 404 permit.[28] If the EPA decides that the dredged or fill material will "have an unacceptable effect on municipal water supplies, shellfish beds and fishery areas,"[29] the EPA may veto the permit issued by the Corps.[30] The EPA uses this veto power to police compliance with the section 401(b)(1) guidelines. The threat of a veto motivates the Corps to consider and accommodate the EPA's concerns in the permitting process.

When considering a section 404 dredged and fill permit application, the Corps must comply with the requirements set out in other federal environmental legislation. In particular, the Corps must consider the effect of proposed activities on endangered species. Section 7 of the Endangered Species Act (ESA) requires federal agencies to "insure that any action authorized, funded or carried out by such agency . . . is not likely to jeopardize . . . any endangered or threatened species" or to adversely affect such species' critical habitat.[31] Pursuant to this authority, the

Corps must consider how any listed species may be impacted by issuance of a section 404 permit.

The most significant and expensive part of processing a section 404 application is the environmental review required by the National Environmental Policy Act (NEPA).[32] NEPA's primary function is to assure that all federal agencies make informed, environmentally responsible decisions when considering federal actions that may have a significant impact on the environment. Thus, NEPA requires the Corps to evaluate potential environmental consequences of a proposed project when making decisions on section 404 permit applications.

The NEPA review is conducted in accordance with the Corps' own NEPA regulations,[33] as well as regulations promulgated by the Council on Environmental Quality (CEQ).[34] The CEQ exercises the federal government's primary responsibility for setting NEPA standards. Under NEPA and CEQ regulations, the Corps must prepare an environmental impact statement (EIS) on any "major federal action significantly affecting the quality of the human environment" before it can approve a section 404 permit.[35] For projects that do not appear to meet this threshold, the CEQ rules require the Corps to prepare a less expensive environmental assessment (EA).[36] The EA procedure accounts for the vast majority of the environmental reviews carried out for section 404 permit applications.

Another key issue that may arise during the NEPA process concerns the scope of a project. The CEQ rules define the scope of an EIS to encompass connected actions, which are defined to include actions that: (1) automatically trigger other actions that may require an EIS; (2) cannot or will not proceed unless other actions are taken previously or simultaneously; or (3) are interdependent parts of a larger action and depend on the larger action for their justification.[37] Furthermore, those rules require that the EIS address all cumulative impacts, which are defined to include the impacts on the environment that result from the incremental impact of the action when added to past, present, and reasonably foreseeable future actions, regardless of what agency or person undertakes the actions.[38] However, the Corps' rules appear to limit the scope of a NEPA document to "those portions of the entire project over which the district engineer has sufficient control and responsibility."[39] In *Sylvester v. U.S. Army Corps of Engineers,* the Corps issued a section 404 permit to a developer who wanted to fill lands for the construction of a golf course.[40] The golf course was part of a larger resort complex in Squaw Valley, California, that included a resort village and ski runs. All components of the resort were being built by the same developer. On the basis of its rules, the Corps limited its environmental inquiry to the impacts associated with construction of the golf course. The U.S. Court of Appeals for the Ninth Circuit upheld the Corps' decision against a claim that the Corps' rules were inconsistent with the CEQ rules. In particular, the court found that the Corps' rules were entitled to deference from the court, notwithstanding that the agency primarily responsible for establishing NEPA guidance is the CEQ and not the Corps.[41]

NATIONWIDE GENERAL PERMITS

One way in which the CWA eases the burden of section 404 permits on applicants and the Corps is through the use of nationwide general permits (NWPs), which authorize specified kinds of wetlands activities without requiring an applicant to obtain an individual permit. These permits are reserved for certain categories of dredged and fill activities that pose only minimal adverse environmental effects.[42] NWPs, which are established through a formal rule-making process, may be issued on a nationwide, regional, or statewide basis. Before a wetland manager may use a NWP in any state, the state must make water quality certifications in accordance with section 401 of the CWA and, for coastal states, coastal zone consistency determinations under the Coastal Zone Management Act.[43] If a state fails to take these actions for the NWP itself, individual certifications and determinations must be obtained. However, the Corps' rules establish a presumption that the necessary state decisions have been made when a state fails to act in a timely manner.[44]

Generally, if a wetlands manager can operate under the scope of a NWP, the manager need only give the Corps advance notice, or in some instances a report after the fact, of wetland activities. However, to take advantage of a general permit, the permittee must comply with certain conditions. For example, the permittee generally must conduct activities in a manner that controls erosion and avoids significant disruptions of aquatic species.[45] Even when an activity otherwise would fall under a NWP, an individual permit is required when such an activity might adversely affect a species listed or proposed for listing under the ESA or cause adverse modification to critical habitat.[46] Likewise, a NWP will not authorize activities that could affect historic properties listed or eligible for listing under the National Historic Preservation Act.

DEFINING REGULATED WETLANDS

Section 404 prohibits unpermitted discharges of dredged or fill material into waters within the scope of the Corps' jurisdiction. The Corps' jurisdiction, and thus the reach of section 404, extends to all "waters of the United States."[47] These include navigable waters and their tributaries, interstate waters and their tributaries, and non-navigable intrastate waters whose use could affect interstate or foreign commerce.[48] The Corps has defined "waters of the United States" specifically to encompass wetlands,[49] and as a result, section 404 has evolved principally into a wetlands protection program. The Corps' authority to regulate isolated wetlands that are not connected to navigable waters, however, is very much in doubt.

In *United States v. Riverside Bayview Homes*,[50] the U.S. Supreme Court upheld the Corps' jurisdiction over all wetlands adjacent to navigable or interstate waters, even where the adjacent water is not the source of the water held in the wetland. According to the Court, "Congress evidently intended to repudiate limits that had been placed on federal regulation by earlier water pollution control statutes and to exercise its power under the Commerce Clause to regulate at least some waters that would not be deemed navigable under the classical definition of the term."[51]

But in *Solid Waste Agency of Northern Cook County v. United States Army Corps of Engineers* (SWANCC),[52] in a 5-4 decision, the Court refused to accept the full breadth of the Corps' claim to jurisdiction over isolated wetlands. The SWANCC case involved an attempt by the Corps to require a section 404 permit at an abandoned sand and gravel pit that was slated for use as a solid waste disposal site. The site had permanent and seasonal ponds, and several migratory bird species had been observed there. The Corps had based its jurisdictional claim primarily on migratory bird use. According to the Corps, such use brought the Corps regulations within the scope of the Commerce Clause of the U.S. Constitution.[53] However, the five prevailing justices held that congressional intent in the Clean Water Act was not sufficiently clear to warrant an extension of federal authority over isolated wetlands, given the possibility that the exercise of such authority might be beyond the scope of the Commerce Clause and thus be unconstitutional.

A strong dissenting opinion took issue with the majority's claim that congressional intent was not clear. In particular, the dissent noted that Congress had expressly stated its intent that the phrase "navigable waters," defined in the CWA as "waters of the United States,"[54] "be given the broadest possible constitutional interpretation."[55] On the related question of Congress' constitutional authority to assert jurisdiction over isolated wetlands, the dissent had no trouble supporting such authority on the basis of migratory bird use.[56] Nonetheless, the upshot of the SWANCC decision was to deny the Corps' authority over isolated wetlands, which comprise as much as 79% of the nation's wetlands,[57] at least until the Congress decides to clarify its intentions under section 404 of the Clean Water Act. Should Congress ultimately choose to grant the Corps such authority, the Court will likely have to face the constitutional issue upon which the majority demurred.

For those wetlands over which the Corps does have authority, wetlands are defined as "those areas that are inundated or saturated by surface or ground water at a frequency and duration sufficient to support, and the under normal circumstances do support, a prevalence of vegetation typically adapted for life in saturated soil conditions. Wetlands generally include swamps, marshes, bogs, and similar areas."[58] This regulatory definition was embellished in the 1987 Corps of Engineers Wetland Delineation Manual (1987 Manual), which is used by all federal agencies responsible for making wetland delineations.[59] The 1987 Manual directs agencies to examine an area at issue for hydric soils, hydrology, and hydrophytic vegetation.

Many applicants choose to have a consulting firm, rather than the Corps, perform wetland delineations. Because of delineation backlogs in many Corps districts, this approach can expedite the wetland delineation review process.[60] In a Regulatory Guidance Letter promulgated in 1988, the Corps actively encouraged landowners to provide their own preliminary jurisdictional determination (PJD). At least one commentator has suggested that in the less complex cases, where an applicant provides a PJD prepared by a qualified consultant, the Corps will often approve the determination without even making a site visit.[61] Conversely, applicants who submit a request without a PJD may wait a long time before the Corps is able to begin the delineation process.

DEFINING REGULATED WETLAND ACTIVITIES

Section 404 prohibits unpermitted discharges of pollutants into jurisdictional wetlands from a point source.[62] A point source is defined as a "discernable, confined or discrete conveyance,"[63] and a discharge is defined as "any addition of any pollutant to navigable waters from any point source."[64] The point source pollutant at issue in most wetland conversions consists of the actual dredged or fill materials used in converting wetlands to dry lands. Such materials generally eliminate the aquatic resources in wetland areas and may pollute downstream waters.

In *Avoyelles Sportsmen's League v. Marsh*,[65] the U.S. Fifth Circuit Court held that equipment used to clear land was a point source and that conversion of timbered wetlands into agricultural land involved the discharge of fill, if not dredged, materials from that point source. Consequently, converting a wetland to agricultural production generally requires a section 404 permit. Certain agricultural activities, such as established and ongoing farming, ranching, or silviculture,[66] are exempt from the section 404 permit requirement.[67] However, this exemption does not apply to new conversion operations even when implemented in the context of ongoing agricultural enterprises.

Section 404 does not regulate wetland activities that do not involve the discharge of dredged and fill materials. Nonetheless, most wetland activities usually implicate the deposit of some dredged or fill material, so the Corps can often assert regulatory authority over dredging and draining activities. Historically, the Corps has not claimed the power to regulate dredging activities alone,[68] but in regulations promulgated by the Corps in 1993, the agency appeared to take a broad view, requiring permits for "any addition, including redeposit, including excavation material, into waters of the United States which is incidental to any activity, including . . . ditching, channelization, or other excavation."[69] In 1998 the Court of Appeals for the District of Columbia Circuit struck down the Corps' 1993 rules on the grounds that they were intended to regulate certain activities that did not result in the addition of new material to the regulated water body.[70] In particular, the Court held that the Corps could not regulate incidental fallback that occurs, for example, "when a bucket used to excavate material from the bottom of a river, stream or wetlands is raised and soil or sediments fall from the bucket back into the water."[71]

Simple removal of vegetation has been a subject of section 404 debate. In *Save Our Wetlands v. Sands,*[72] the plaintiffs claimed that the Louisiana Power and Light Company was required to obtain a section 404 permit before cutting timber and vegetation in preparation for construction of a transmission line. The court found that the trees and vegetation would be cut with chainsaws and allowed to deteriorate naturally and that the wooded swampland would be changed to swampland vegetation with shrubs, grasses, and other low growth. Moreover, the lands would not be drained or converted through the discharge of dredged or fill materials. Accordingly, no permit was required.

In line with the decision in *Save Our Wetlands,* the Corps' current regulations limit the Corps' authority to regulate vegetation removal activities under section 404. Those rules provide that the discharge of dredged materials does not include "activities that involve only the cutting or removing of vegetation above the ground (e.g., mowing, rotary cutting, and chainsawing) where the activity neither substantially disturbs the root system nor involves mechanized pushing, dragging, or other similar activities that redeposit soil material."[73]

Although draining activities frequently destroy wetlands, such activities do not require section 404 permits.[74] However, if draining activities are accompanied by dredging activities and if those dredging activities cause the addition of dredged materials, then the Corps may claim regulatory authority.

THE "TAKINGS" PROBLEM

The Fifth Amendment to the U.S. Constitution prohibits the taking of private property by a public agency for a public use without just compensation. At least since Justice Holmes' seminal opinion in *Pennsylvania Coal Co. v. Mahon*,[75] the courts have recognized that a Fifth Amendment taking can occur as a result of government regulation that precludes all reasonable use of property, even where no physical invasion of that property has occurred. Justice Holmes wrote that "if regulation goes 'too far' it will be recognized as a taking."[76] Just how far is too far remains a subject of debate among judges and scholars throughout the United States. However, whatever the answer, the principle that government regulation can effect a taking has important consequences in wetlands cases under section 404, especially when the Corps denies a permit application that effectively precludes all private property development.

As suggested above, the law of regulatory takings is a morass that cannot fully be described here. But four important Supreme Court cases since the time of *Pennsylvania Coal* help shed light on how the takings doctrine might affect wetlands cases. In *Penn Central Transportation Co. v. New York City*,[77] local historic preservation laws prevented a developer from building a high-rise office building over Penn Central Station in New York City. The Supreme Court denied the developer's taking claim on the grounds that the building restrictions did not interfere with reasonable, investment-backed expectations. However, the Court implied that a regulation that interferes with such expectations goes "too far."[78]

Subsequently, in *Keystone Bituminous Association v. DeBenedictis*, the plaintiff challenged a State of Pennsylvania rule that required that coal owners leave 50% of the coal in the ground below surface structures to protect those structures from damage that might otherwise be caused by surface subsidence.[79] The plaintiff claimed that this resulted in a total taking of the coal the owner was required to leave in the ground. However, the Court held that the coal owner could not treat the coal left in the ground as a separate property segment for takings law purposes.[80] Justice Stevens suggested that a rule that allowed segmentation would allow a property owner to claim a taking where a zoning law precluded development a certain distance from the property line.[81]

Five years later, in *Lucas v. South Carolina Coastal Commission*,[82] the U.S. Supreme Court reviewed a decision by South Carolina's Coastal

Commission that denied a development permit to a landowner whose property fell within a coastal protection zone. The Court held that where a total taking occurs as a result of government regulation, that regulation usually results in an unlawful taking, unless the government agency can show that the failure to enforce the regulation would cause a nuisance as defined under state law.[83]

Finally, in *Palazzolo v. Rhode Island*, 533 U.S. 606 (2001), the Supreme Court considered a takings claim that arose as a direct result of a decision denying development on a wetland in Rhode Island. The Rhode Island Supreme Court had concluded: (1) that the case was not ripe for judicial review because the petitioner had not been denied all development rights; (2) that the petitioner had no right to challenge regulations adopted before acquiring the property because such regulations could not have interfered with any of the petitioner's reasonable, investment-backed expectations; and (3) that the petitioner had not suffered a "total taking" because the right was retained to develop a tract of land on the parcel with a development value of $200,000.

The U.S. Supreme Court overturned the Rhode Island Court's decision of the first two grounds but sustained the third holding. The Court held that the case was ripe because it was clear that the petitioner's application to develop the wetlands portion of his property would not be approved. The Court had a more difficult time with the second issue. If investment-backed expectations were truly necessary to show a taking, then a person's right to compensation might depend on when the person acquired the property, before or after the regulation at issue. This was too much for a majority of justices, and although the Court was split, the prevailing view seemed to be that while investment-backed expectations must be considered, the date on which title transferred should not necessarily control the outcome. Although the Supreme Court ultimately sustained the Rhode Island court's finding that no total taking had occurred, this did not necessarily require a denial of the petitioner's takings claim. Rather, it denied him the benefit of the more generous formula articulated in *Lucas*.

Although the Court was too fractured in *Palazzolo* to offer a definitive view of the takings clause in wetland cases, it does suggest that such cases can generally be analyzed using the basic principles from the other takings law cases. Thus, when the Corps denies a section 404 permit, the court can ask whether the permit denial interferes with the reasonable, investment-backed expectations of the property owner regardless of when the property was acquired and whether the owner retains a substantial portion of property on which development can go forward. If denial of a permit does not interfere with a property owner's reasonable expectations and if the owner retains the right to develop a substantial portion of the property, then no taking should be found. If, however, the court finds that a total taking has occurred, then compensation is owed unless the court finds that the activity that the applicant seeks to permit would constitute a nuisance under state law.[84] If so, no taking has occurred.

Despite the hurdles that a private landowner must overcome to show a Fifth Amendment taking, several wetlands owners have successfully pursued such claims after section 404 permits were denied. Perhaps the most celebrated example is *Loveladies Harbor Inc. v. United States*.[85] In that case, the plaintiff originally owned a 250-acre tract of land. After the application to fill 11.5 acres was filed but before the application was denied, the plaintiff sold all but 57.4 acres of the parcel. With the exception of 1 acre, which was probably not wetlands, the remainder of the 57.4 acres was either other wetlands on which development would not likely be approved or land not adjacent to the 11.5-acre tract. The Court of Federal Claims found that the denial of the permit resulted in a 99% reduction in the value of the tract of land on which development was sought and that such a diminution in value amounted to an unlawful taking.[86] Relying on the *Lucas* decision, the Court of Appeals for the Federal Circuit affirmed.[87]

The Rivers and Harbors Act

Even before the Clean Water Act was enacted in 1972, the Corps asserted regulatory authority over wetlands under section 10 of the Rivers and Harbors Act of 1899 (RHA).[88] That provision requires the Secretary of the Army to issue permits for the construction of any structure in the navigable waters of the United States and for excavating from or depositing material into such waters.[89] The Corps' claim of authority to regulate wetlands under this statute was precipitated by language in the Fish and Wildlife Coordination Act,[90] which provides in relevant part that "whenever the waters of any stream or other body of water are proposed or authorized to be impounded, diverted, the channel deepened, or the stream or other body of water otherwise controlled or modified for any purpose whatever, including navigation or drainage, by any department of the United States, or by any public or private agency under Federal permit or license, such department or agency first shall consult with the United States Fish and Wildlife Service . . . with a view to the conservation of wildlife resources by preventing loss of and damage to such resources as well as providing for the development and improvement thereof in connection with such water resource development."[91]

In 1967 the Secretaries of Army and Interior entered into a MOA in which the Corps agreed to consider the views of the Interior Department before issuing RHA permits.[92] Furthermore, the Corps itself decided to undertake a public interest review in conjunction with RHA permits that would include ecological impacts of issuing permits.[93] The Corps' authority to consider such impacts was upheld in *Zabel v. Tabb*.[94]

The Corps' authority to regulate wetlands under the RHA has been substantially superseded by section 404 of the CWA. Moreover, since jurisdiction under RHA is limited by a fairly narrow definition of navigable waters,[95] the Corps' authority to regulate discharges is much broader under section 404 of the CWA, even with the significant limits imposed by the SWANCC decision. However, the RHA covers more than just discharges. In particular, the RHA covers the excavation or removal of materials from navigable waters, matters specifically not encompassed by the CWA.[96] Moreover, there may be a few other areas in which the Corps has permitting authority under the RHA, even when it lacks such authority under the CWA. One example is lands behind dikes. These fall within RHA jurisdiction because they are below the mean high water mark but may not be subject to the Corps' authority under section 404 of the CWA.[97] Likewise, mooring a houseboat on navigable waters requires a Section 10 RHA permit but no permit under the CWA.[98]

Incentive-based Programs

Unlike wetlands regulation under the CWA and the RHA, which make unauthorized conversions of wetlands illegal, compliance with the balance of federal wetlands legislation is voluntary. For example, the Swampbuster Law (Swampbuster)[99] and Internal Revenue Code regulate certain wetland-damaging activities by applying substantive disincentives to such activities. The Wetlands Reserve Program (WRP)[100] offers an outright incentive to preserve wetlands by authorizing the federal government to pay farmers and ranchers who agree to hold previously cropped wetlands out of agricultural production.

Swampbuster

Congress enacted Swampbuster as part of the Food Security Act of 1985 in response to increasing concern over agriculture's contribution to the nation's soil erosion and water pollution problems. Swampbuster is the primary federal regulatory program designed to combat the disappearance of wetlands caused by their conversion to agricultural use. Two highly decentralized agencies of the U.S. Department of Agriculture (USDA)—the Farm Service Agency (FSA) and the Natural Resources Conservation Service (NRCS)—administer Swampbuster.

Swampbuster operates by denying federal farm assistance benefits to any person who "converts a wetland by draining, dredging, filling, leveling, or any other means for the purpose, or to have the effect, of making the production of an agricultural commodity possible on such converted wetland . . . for that crop year and all subsequent crop years."[101] Landowners must certify eligibility to the NRCS to participate in federal farm assistance benefits programs. As a part of this process, the NRCS determines whether the land for which a farmer or rancher seeks benefits contains wetlands that have been converted for agricultural purposes. A landowner who has converted a wetland to agricultural use without the authorization of the NRCS forfeits eligibility for many benefits, even if the manager has never actually produced an agricultural product on the converted wetland. The NRCS performs wetland delineations to establish wetlands subject to Swampbuster.[102] Wetland determinations must be made in accordance with delineation procedures agreed to by the Corps, EPA, U.S. Fish and Wildlife Service (FWS), and NRCS.[103] Persons affected by the NRCS determinations must be afforded an opportunity to appeal the decision before it becomes final.[104]

A converted wetland for Swampbuster purposes is any wetland area that has been drained, dredged, filled, leveled, or otherwise manipulated to make the production of an agricultural commodity viable.[105] Thus, Swampbuster applies to wetland conversions that involve simple drainage or dredging of wetlands.[106] Prior to 1996, wetland managers who obtained a section 404 permit to fill a wetland had to comply with Swampbuster if they wanted to remain eligible for farm program benefits. Amendments in 1996 changed this interplay by exempting wetland conversions authorized by a section 404 permit from Swampbuster requirements if such conversion is accompanied by an adequate mitigation plan.

Some agricultural wetlands may be excluded from Swampbuster regulation under several possible exemptions.[107] Moreover, Swampbuster exempts any wetland conversion commenced prior to December 23, 1985, as a prior converted wetland. Conversion has commenced if a wetland manager has made physical efforts to convert the wetland or has committed funds to the conversion prior to that date.[108] Furthermore, if economic hardship forced the producer to convert a wetland to cropland due to a debt incurred prior to December 23, 1985, the conversion will be exempted as a prior converted wetland.[109] In order to meet the exemption for commenced conversions, a person must have submitted a request for a determination of commencement to the FSA by September 19, 1988, and the conversion must have been completed by January 1, 1995.[110]

If significant wetland characteristics remain on land manipulated prior to the given date, the land is not considered a prior converted wetland. A manager may farm such land without forfeiting federal benefits only if the farming does not involve significantly improving upon the previously accomplished drainage or manipulation so as to further degrade remaining wetland characteristics.[111] Thus, even if some drainage has taken place prior to the given date, the land does not become exempt from Swampbuster altogether with respect to further manipulation.

Prior to 1996, converted wetlands that had reverted to official wetland status through neglect were subject to Swampbuster regulation. However, as of 1996, prior converted wetlands can be permanently exempted from Swampbuster subject to certain conditions. To preserve an exclusion from Swampbuster regulation, a landowner must notify the NRCS of an intent to allow the land to return to a wetland and that the land should remain excluded.

The NRCS may grant a wetland manager permission to convert a wetland to cropland if the wetland manager mitigates the adverse environmental impacts of the project by meeting required wetland conservation standards. A wetland manager must mitigate the loss of the wetland by restoring, enhancing, or creating a new wetland with equivalent wetland values and functions.[112] Once a regulated wetland is identified, the NRSC and FWS undertake a biological assessment of the wetland to be converted and determine whether the proposed mitigation plan will adequately replace the converted wetland. The two agencies must agree on all technical determinations regarding the restoration of converted wetlands and plans implementing such restoration.

Swampbuster authorizes some administrative exemptions that have challenged the effectiveness of the Swampbuster program. If a wetland manager violates in good faith the terms of Swampbuster by relying on misrepresentations made by a federal Swampbuster administrator, the land manager will not lose eligibility for farm program benefits if the manager begins restoration of the wetland within one year of the violation.[113] Also, the NRCS may grant an exemption if it determines the wetland conversion will have minimal environmental impacts.[114]

Wetlands Reserve Program

The Wetlands Reserve Program (WRP) was the product of a 1990 expansion of the Conservation Reserve Program (CRP). Congress created the CRP in the Food Security Act of 1985 to "reduce water and wind erosion, protect our long term capability to produce food and fiber, reduce sedimentation, improve water quality, create better habitat for fish and wildlife through improved food and cover, and curb production of surplus commodities." The CRP encourages the preservation of fragile cropland by reimbursing land managers who remove highly erodible land from agricultural production for periods of 10–15 years.

The WRP operates as the wetland corollary to the CRP. The WRP authorizes the federal government to purchase long-term easements from landowners who agree to restore wetlands converted to cropland prior to 1985.[115] Participants may choose between permanent easements, 30-year conservation easements, or restoration cost-share agreements. Nonpermanent easement status is typically reserved for wetlands least likely to be reconverted to farmland, and the statute gives a priority to obtaining permanent easements.[116] Restoration plans must be developed with the local NRCS representative in consultation with the state technical committee.[117] The eligible wetland manager's duties vary according to the classification of the participant. In return, participants receive annual rental payments and cost-sharing assistance. The federal government contributes 50–75% of the restoration cost if a participant chooses a cost-share agreement.[118]

In 1997 the USDA promulgated regulations revising the terms and conditions of the CRP and the WRP,[119] seeking in part to target more environmentally sensitive acreage.[120] While the WRP initially included geographic restrictions and limited coverage, the USDA indicated its willingness to expand the provisions to include more areas. Specific to this project, the new regulations recognize the contribution of wetlands in mountain regions to the health of the national environment.[121]

Pursuant to the revised regulations, persons eligible to participate must own, operate, or lease land qualifying as a wetland that has been planted annually for at least two of the five years spanning 1992 through 1996 and that is plantable in a normal manner at the time of enrollment. Other requirements of land eligibility vary according to geographic and environmental factors.

Inclusion in the WRP requires a participant to comply with the terms of the WRP contract as well as to implement a conservation plan to manage the subject wetland. A WRP participant consults with the NRCS and the local conservation district or a NRCS-approved substitute to develop a conservation plan for an eligible wetland. Regulations define some universally accepted practices on WRP land, and the contract and the conservation plan set out the particular acceptable practices that apply. To protect the integrity of the wetland system, the contract forbids the participant from producing an agricultural commodity on the land or allowing grazing or harvesting of any kind. Participants who violate the conditions of their wetlands conservation plans may have to refund any payments received for the conservation easements. However, the easements remain in effect.

Internal Revenue Code

Section 1257 of the Internal Revenue Code is another example of federal legislation designed to inhibit the conversion of wetlands. This section provides tax disincentives to anyone who converts wetlands and then sells or otherwise disposes of the converted wetlands. Pursuant to section 1257(a), any gain from the disposition of such converted wetlands receives ordinary income treatment as opposed to the generally more favorable capital gains treatment.[122] Section 1257(b) provides that any loss on the disposition of converted wetlands receives only long-term capital loss treatment rather than the more favorable ordinary loss treatment.[123]

Conclusion

The federal government's authority to regulate wetlands falls predominantly under the dredged and fill permitting program of section 404 of the Clean Water Act. Thus, private landowners who may be engaged in activities affecting wetlands would be wise to consider the possible application of that provision and the ways in which the burden of compliance with section 404 can be minimized. For certain limited activities on waters subject to interstate or foreign waters, the application of the Rivers and Harbors Act must also be addressed. Finally, wetlands owners should be aware of incentive programs, including Swampbuster, the Wetlands Reserve Program, and section 1257 of the Internal Revenue Code, established to encourage wetlands preservation and discourage wetlands destruction.

Notes

1. For a detailed discussion of the prior appropriation doctrine and other schemes for water allocation see DAVID H. GETCHES, WATER LAW IN A NUTSHELL (2d ed. 1990), 74–190. Alaska, Arizona, Colorado, Idaho, Montana, Nevada, New Mexico, Utah, and Wyoming have historically followed the prior appropriation system. *Id.* at 6. The states along the West coast, and those in the middle of the country through which the 100th meridian passes, including California, Kansas, Nebraska, North Dakota, Oklahoma, Oregon, South Dakota, Texas, and Washington, began as riparian states but have now effectively shifted to a prior appropriation system. Remnants of the riparian system remain in these states to varying degrees. *Id.* at 7.

2. *See e.g.,* ARIZ. REV. STAT. ANN. § 45–131; NEV. REV. STAT. § 533.035; N.M. STAT. ANN. § 72–1–2; WYO. STAT. ANN. § 41–3–101.

3. D. GETCHES, *supra,* note 1 at 178–180.

4. WATER IN THE WEST: CHALLENGE FOR THE NEXT CENTURY, Report of the Western Water Policy Review Advisory Commission, 2–24 (June 1998).

5. *Id.* at 2–24 to 2–26.

6. 33 U.S.C. §§ 1251 *et seq.* (2000).

7. 33 U.S.C. § 1251(a) (2000).

8. 33 U.S.C. §§ 1311(a); 1342(a); 1344(a) (2000).

9. 33 U.S.C. § 1344(a) (2000).

10. 33 U.S.C. § 1344(n) (2000).

11. The CWA authorizes states to assume regulatory jurisdiction over most aspects of the section 404 program. See 33 U.S.C. § 1344 (g)(1) (2000). However, only two states—Michigan and New Jersey—have thus far taken advantage of this opportunity. States wishing to assume regulatory authority must obtain EPA approval. EPA may withdraw approval from states not complying with their legal responsibilities under the approved program. Id. at § 1344(i).

12. The Corps' regulations are found generally at 33 C.F.R. parts 320–330, and the EPA's regulations are found generally at 40 C.F.R. parts 230–233.

13. 33 U.S.C. § 1344(a) (2000).

14. 33 U.S.C. § 1344(b) (2000). Although generally referred to as § 404(b)(1) guidelines, the EPA has promulgated these standards as binding regulations. 40 C.F.R. part 230 (2000).

15. 40 C.F.R. § 230.3(q-1) (2000).

16. Compare 33 U.S.C. §§ 1311(a), 1319, and 1344(n) with 33 U.S.C. § 1344(s) (2000).

17. Set forth at 33 C.F.R. part 325 (2000).

18. 33 C.F.R. § 325.1(d)(1) (2000).

19. 33 C.F.R. § 325, Appendix (2000).

20. 33 C.F.R. § 325.2(a)(2) (2000).

21. See infra text accompanying notes 33–37.

22. 40 C.F.R. § 230.10(d) (2000).

23. Supplementary Information, 60 Fed. Reg. 58, 605–606 (Nov. 28, 1995).

24. Memorandum of Agreement Between the Environmental Protection Agency and the Department of Army Concerning the Determination of Mitigation under the Clean Water Act section 404 Guidelines (MOA) (Nov. 15, 1989). For commentary on the MOA see OLIVER A. HOUCK, MORE NET LOSS FOR WETLANDS, 20 ENVTL. L. REP. 10212 (June 1990); WILLIAM L. WANT, THE ARMY-EPA AGREEMENT ON WETLANDS MITIGATION, 20 ENVTL. L. REP. 10209 (June 1990).

25. 60 Fed. Reg. 58,605 (Nov. 28, 1995).

26. 40 C.F.R. § 230.10(a)(2) (2000). See also THEDA BRADDOCK, WETLANDS: AN INTRODUCTION TO ECOLOGY, THE LAW AND PERMITTING 98–100 (1995).

27. 40 C.F.R. § 230.10(d) (2000).

28. On the basis of section 404(c), the Attorney General has determined that the EPA and not the Corps holds the ultimate authority over the issuance of section 404 permits. 43 Op. Att'y Gen. No. 15 (1979). This opinion was affirmed in Avoyelles Sportsmen League v. Marsh, 715 F.2d 897, 903 n. 12 (5th Cir. 1983).

29. 40 C.F.R. § 231.1(a) (2000).

30. 33 U.S.C. § 1344(c) (2000). General permit requirements are set out in 33 U.S.C. § 1344(e).

31. 16 U.S.C. § 1536(a) (2000).

32. 42 U.S.C. §§ 4321 et seq. (2000).

33. 33 C.F.R. pt. 230 (2000).

34. 40 C.F.R. pt. 1500 (2000).

35. 42 U.S.C. § 4332(2)(C) (2000).

36. 40 C.F.R. § 1501.4 (2000). An EA generally leads to a "finding of no significant impact" (FONSI), although it can also lead to a decision to prepare an EIS. Id.

37. 40 C.F.R. § 1508.25(a) (2000).

38. *Id.* at § 1508.7.

39. 33 C.F.R. pt. 325, App. B, § 7(b) (2000).

40. Sylvester v. United States Army Corps of Engineers, 871 F.2d 817 (9th Cir. 1989), opinion amended and superseded on denial of rehearing (on other grounds) by Sylvester v. United States Army Corps of Engineers, 882 F.2d 407 (9th Cir. 1989).

41. *Id.* at 822.

42. On March 9, 2000, the Corps issued five new nationwide permits (NWP) and modified six others to replace NWP 26, which authorizes discharges of dredged and fill material into headwaters and isolated waters of the United States. 65 Fed. Reg. 12818 (2000). The new NWPs are activity-specific and establish more stringent conditions to minimize impacts to aquatic environments. Perhaps more importantly, the new and modified NWPs are generally limited to no more than ½ acre in size, and notice to the Corps is required for any activities that result in the loss of more than ¹⁄₁₀ of an acre of "waters of the United States." In 1984 NWP had a 10-acre limit; this limit was changed to 3 acres in 1996. The new policy was announced in a final "notice" and was issued following an earlier notice and opportunity for public comment. The new NWPs will also limit development in floodplains. Under the final notice, development activities are also precluded in any 100-year floodplain where the flow is 5 cubic feet per second (cfs) or greater. *Id.* Other changes to the NWP program were announced in a 1996 notice found at 61 Fed. Reg. 65,874 (Dec. 13, 1996).

43. Certification under the Coastal Zone Management Act is required by 16 U.S.C. § 1456(c) (2000); certification under the CWA is required by 33 U.S.C. § 1341(a) (2000).

44. See e.g., 33 C.F.R. §§ 330.4(c)(6); 330.4(d)(6) (2000).

45. 61 Fed. Reg. 65,920 (Dec. 13, 1996).

46. *Id.* See also Riverside Irrigation District v. Andrews, 758 F.2d 508 (10th Cir. 1985).

47. 33 U.S.C. § 1362 (7) (2000).

48. The Corps' rules (33 C.F.R. § 328.3(a) (2000)) provide as follows:
The term waters of the United States means:

(1) All waters which are currently used, or were used in the past, or may be susceptible to use in interstate or foreign commerce, including all waters which are subject to the ebb and flow of the tide;

(2) All interstate waters including interstate wetlands;

(3) All other waters such as intrastate lakes, rivers, streams (including intermittent streams), mudflats, sandflats, wetlands, sloughs, prairie potholes, wet meadows, playa lakes, or natural ponds, the use, degradation or destruction of which could affect interstate or foreign commerce including any such waters:

(i) Which are or could be used by interstate or foreign travelers for recreational or other purposes; or

(ii) From which fish or shellfish are or could be taken and sold in interstate or foreign commerce; or

(iii) Which are used or could be used for industrial purpose by industries in interstate commerce;

(4) All impoundments of waters otherwise defined as waters of the United States under the definition;

(5) Tributaries of waters identified in paragraphs (a) (1) through (4) of this section;

(6) The territorial seas;

(7) Wetlands adjacent to waters (other than waters that are themselves wetlands) identified in paragraphs (a) (1) through (6) of this section.

(8) Waters of the United States do not include prior converted cropland . . .

As noted in the text, however, this definition was struck down, in part at least, as a result of the Supreme Court's decision in *Solid Waste Agency of Northern Cook County v. United States Army Corps of Engineers*, 121 S. Ct. 675 (2001). See *infra* text accompanying notes 52–56.

49. The Corps' rules define "wetlands" as "those areas that are inundated or saturated by surface or ground water at a frequency and duration sufficient to support, and that under normal circumstances do support, a prevalence of vegetation typically adapted for life in saturated soil conditions. Wetlands generally include swamps, marshes, bogs, and similar areas." 33 C.F.R. § 328.3(b) (2000).

50. United States v. Riverside Bayview Homes, 474 U.S.121 (1985).

51. *Id.* at 133.

52. 121 S. Ct. 675 (2001).

53. U.S. CONST. art. I, § 8, cl.3.

54. 33 U.S.C. § 1362(7) (2000).

55. 121 S. Ct. 675, 687 (2001).

56. *Id.* at 694–695. The area that was proposed for filling included the second-largest breeding colony of great blue herons in northeastern Illinois and several species of waterfowl protected by international treaty and Illinois endangered species law. The dissent found that this was adequate to support commerce clause authority given the intrinsic value of migratory birds as well as the commercial activities that such birds support including hunting and birdwatching. *Id.* at 695. See JON KUSLER, THE SWANCC DECISION AND STATE REGULATION OF WETLANDS, SG 096 ALI-ABA 79 (2002); reprinted at http://www.aswm.org/fwp/swancc/aswm-int.pdf.

57. *See* Kusler, *supra* note 56. Kusler notes that the percentage of wetlands that remain subject to the Clean Water Act's section 404 program will depend upon how narrowly the SWANCC decision is construed. He indicates, however, that the Association of State Wetlands Managers has received "[t]entative state estimates . . . [which] suggest 30–79% of total wetlands acreage may be affected." *Id.*

58. 33 C.F.R. 328.3(b) (2000).

59. Although the Corps developed the 1987 Manual specifically for identifying and delineating wetlands for purposes of section 404 of the CWA, the agencies responsible for administering the federal wetlands programs described *infra* have been directed to use the 1987 Manual as well.

60. See 60 Fed. Reg. at 13,655 (March 14, 1995).

61. WILLIAM L. WANT, LAW OF WETLANDS REGULATION § 4.02[1] (1989; updated by release No. 9, 5/98).

62. 33 U.S.C. §§ 1311(a); 1344(a) (2000).

63. 33 U.S.C. § 1362(14) (2000).

64. 33 U.S.C. § 1362(12) (2000).

65. Avoyelles Sportsmen's League v. Marsh, 715 F.2d 897 (5th Cir. 1983).

66. Silviculture is the "art of producing and tending a forest." DAVID M. SMITH, PRACTICE OF SILVICULTURE (8th ed. 1986).

67. 33 U.S.C. § 1344(f)(1)(A) (2000).

68. See 51 Fed. Reg. 41,210 (Nov. 13, 1986).

69. 33 C.F.R. § 323.2(d)(1)(iii) (2000).

70. National Mining Association v. U.S. Army Corps of Engineers, 145 F.3d 1399 (D.C. Cir. 1998). The *National Mining Association* opinion also describes the litigation that led to the promulgation of the 1993 rule.

71. *Id.* at 1404. The rules were amended in 1999 to address the incidental fallback problem. 63 Fed. Reg. 25123 (May 6, 1998); 33 C.F.R. § 323.2(d) (2000).

72. Save Our Wetlands v. Sands, 711 F.2d 634 (5th Cir. 1983).

73. 33 C.F.R. § 323.3 (d)(2)(ii) (2000).

74. Save Our Community v. EPA, 971 F.2d 1155, 1167 (5th Cir. 1992).

75. Pennsylvania Coal Co. v. Mahon, 260 U.S. 393 (1922).

76. *Id.* at 415.

77. Penn Central Transport Co. v. New York, 438 U.S. 104 (1978).

78. *Id.* at 124–25. In *Penn Central*, however, the Court held that the historic preservation restrictions on building a multistory office complex over the Grand Central Terminal did not interfere with the owner's reasonable investment-backed expectations.

79. Keystone Bituminous Ass'n v. DeBenedictis, 480 U.S. 470 (1987).

80. *Id.* at 498.

81. *Id.*

82. Lucas v. South Carolina Coastal Comm'n, 505 U.S. 1003 (1992).

83. *Id.* at 1031.

84. The Restatement of Torts defines a private nuisance as "a nontrespassory of another's interest in the private use and enjoyment of land." Rest. 2d. of Torts, § 821D (1997).

85. 28 F. 3d 1171 (Fed. Cir. 1994).

86. Loveladies Harbor Inc. v. United States, 21 Cl. Ct. 153 (1990), aff'd 28 F. 3d 1171 (Fed. Cir. 1994). Other cases in which courts have found takings following a denial of a section 404 permit include *Formanek v. United States,* 26 Cl. Ct. 332 (1992) and *Bowles v. United States,* 31 Fed. Cl. 37 (1994). Other significant cases in which takings determinations may have been found at some stage during the proceedings include *Broadwater Farms Joint Venture v. United States,* 27 Envtl L. Rep. 21516 (Fed. Cir. 1997), and *Florida Rock Industries Inc. v. United States,* 18 F.3d 1560 (Fed. Cir. 1994).

87. Loveladies Harbor Inc. v. United States, 28 F3d 1171 (Fed. Cir. 1994). The result in *Loveladies Harbor* is arguably inconsistent with the Supreme Court's decision in *Keystone Bituminous,* described above, since the court failed to consider the impact of the denial on the full 250-acre tract of land held by the applicant at the time of the application.

88. 33 U.S.C. § 403 (2000).

89. See 33 C.F.R. § 320.2(b) (2000).

90. 16 U.S.C. §§ 661–667 (2000).

91. *Id.* at § 662(a).

92. Reprinted at 33 Fed. Reg. 18,672–73 (1968).

93. 33 Fed. Reg. 18672–73, formerly codified at 33 C.F.R. § 209.120(d)(11) and now superseded by 33 C.F.R. § 320.4 (2000).

94. Zabel v. Tabb, 430 F.2d 199 (5th Cir. 1970), cert. denied, 401 U.S. 910 (1971).

95. See 33 C.F.R. 329.4 (2000), which generally defines "navigable waters" to include waters that are "subject to the ebb and flow of the tide and/or are presently used, or have been used in the past, or may be susceptible for use to transport interstate or foreign commerce." By its terms, this definition does not apply to the Corps' jurisdiction under the CWA. 33 C.F.R. § 329.1 (2000). See National Mining Association v. U.S.

Army Corps of Engineers, 145 F.3d 1399, 1404 (D.C. Cir. 1998). A Section 10 permit is required, however, not only for activities in navigable waters, but for those that "affect" navigable waters as well. 33 C.F.R. § 322.3(a) (2000).

96. National Mining Association v. U.S. Army Corps of Engineers, 145 F.3d 1399, 1404 (D.C. Cir. 1998). See also CHARLES D. ABLARD AND BRIAN B. O'NEILL, WETLAND PROTECTION AND SECTION 404 OF THE FEDERAL WATER POLLUTION CONTROL ACT AMENDMENTS OF 1972: A CORPS OF ENGINEERS RENAISSANCE, 1 VT. L. REV. 51, 93 (1976).

97. See Leslie Salt Co. v. Froehlke, 578 F.2d 742 (9th Cir. 1978).

98. United States v. Estate of Boothby, 16 F.3d 19 (1st Cir. 1994).

99. 16 U.S.C. §§ 3801, 3821–24 (1994 & Supp. 1996). Swampbuster falls under the Erodible Land and Wetlands Conservation and Reserve Program. 16 U.S.C. Chapter 58 (2000). Key regulations implementing Swampbuster are at 7 C.F.R. § 12.2 and § 12.5 (2000).

100. 16 U.S.C. § 3837 (2000); 7 C.F.R. § 703 (2000).

101. 16 U.S.C. § 3821(c) (Supp. 1996).

102. 7 C.F.R. § 12.30 (2000). The Food Security Act's definition of a wetland, which applies to both Swampbuster and the WRP, is found at 16 U.S.C. § 3801(a)(18) (Supp. 1996). It is very similar to the definition used under the CWA.

103. 7 C.F.R. § 12.30(c) (2000).

104. Id.

105. 16 U.S.C. § 3801(a)(6)(A) (2000). If production is possible without manipulation of the wetland, such as in periods of drought, the wetland is not considered "converted" so long as farming does not "permanently alter or destroy natural wetland characteristics." 16 U.S.C. § 3801(a)(6)(B) (2000); 7 C.F.R. § 12.32(b) (2000).

106. 7 C.F.R. § 12.32(a)(2) (2000) lists factors to be considered, such as whether woody hydrophytic vegetation has been removed, in designating a "converted" wetland.

107. These exemptions are described at 7 C.F.R. § 12.5 (2000).

108. 7 C.F.R. § 12.2(a)(6), 12.5(b)(2)(i) and (ii) (2000).

109. 7 C.F.R. § 12.5(b)(2)(iv) (2000).

110. 7 C.F.R. § 12.5(b)(2)(ii), (iii) (2000).

111. See Gunn v. United States Department of Agriculture, 118 F.3d 1233 (8th Cir. 1997).

112. 7 C.F.R. § 12.5(b)(4)(i) (2000).

113. 7 C.F.R. § 12.5(b)(5)(i)(A), (B) (2000).

114. 7 C.F.R. § 12.5(b)(v) (2000).

115. 16 U.S.C. § 3837 (1994 & Supp. 1996).

116. 16 U.S.C. § 3837c(d) (1994 & Supp. 1996).

117. 16 U.S.C. § 3837a(c) (Supp. 1996).

118. 16 U.S.C. § 3837(c)(b)(2) (Supp. 1996).

119. See generally 7 C.F.R. § 1410 (2000).

120. 62 Fed. Reg. 7,602 (Feb. 19, 1997).

121. See 62 Fed. Reg. 7,602 (1997) ("Mountain regions are extremely important to waterfowl and grassland bird species, both of which have experienced significant reductions in numbers until recent years.").

122. 26 U.S.C. § 1257(a) (1994).

123. 26 U.S.C. § 1257(b) (1994). A long-term capital loss is worth only half as much in tax savings as an ordinary loss. See Marilyn Cohen, "Tax Savvy for Bondholders," *Forbes*, April 4, 1999.

CHAPTER 2

Variation in Hydrology, Soils, and Vegetation of Natural Palustrine Wetlands among Geologic Provinces

MURRAY K. LAUBHAN

Introduction

Although considered vital to wildlife, natural wetlands are not a common feature of the landscape throughout the Intermountain West (Brown et al. 1977, Williams and Dodd 1979, Ratti and Kadlec 1992). Exact estimates of wetland area are not available for this region, but in the 1780s only 7.9% of the more than 82 million ha of wetlands in what is now the coterminous 48 United States occurred in the 10 westernmost states (Dahl 1990). By the mid-1980s, only 46.5% of the original wetland area in these 10 western states remained (Dahl 1990). The exact percentages for the Intermountain West are even smaller because most of the wetlands in California occur west of the Sierra Nevada, and a portion of the wetland area included for Colorado, Wyoming, and Montana occurs east of the Rocky Mountains, outside the Intermountain West. States exhibiting the most substantial wetland losses during the past 200 years include California, Colorado, and Idaho (Figure 2.1). Further, few remaining wetlands in the Intermountain West have retained their native structure and function since settlement by Europeans began because of extensive modification of both wetlands and surrounding uplands to advance agricultural interests and promote settlement. The most common cause of degradation is altered hydrology, including channelization (Ohmart and Anderson 1979), diversion of surface water, and excessive withdrawal of groundwater (Goodwin and Niering 1975). Thus, "natural" has been broadly defined to include wetlands that were historically part of the landscape although they may currently exist in modified states.

Of critical importance to understanding wetlands in the Intermountain West is the recognition that landforms and many functional attributes of wetlands differ considerably across the region. Shimer (1972) identified 4 geologic provinces in the Intermountain West: (1) Columbia Plateau, (2) Basin and Range, (3) Rocky Mountain (subdivided into northern, central, and southern), and (4) Colorado Plateau (Figure 2.2).

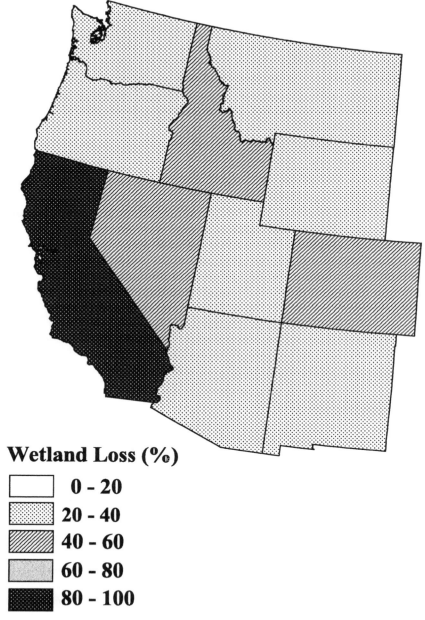

Wetland Loss (%)

- [ ] 0 - 20
- [ ] 20 - 40
- [ ] 40 - 60
- [ ] 60 - 80
- [ ] 80 - 100

FIGURE 2.1. Percentage of wetland loss occurring in the 10 states composing the Intermountain West (Source: Dahl 1990)

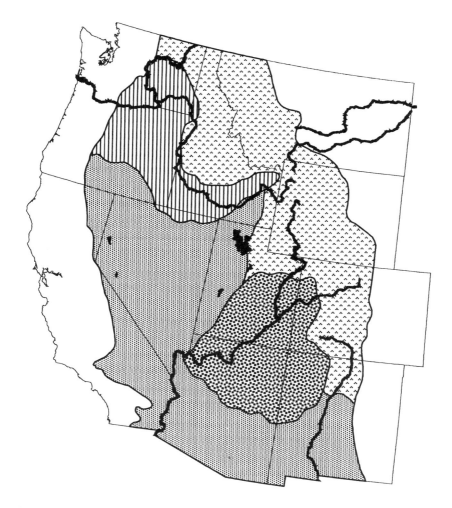

Geologic Provinces

 **Basin and Range**

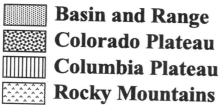 **Colorado Plateau**

Columbia Plateau

Rocky Mountains

 **Lakes**

Rivers

FIGURE 2.2. Location of geologic provinces, major rivers, and lakes occurring in the Intermountain West

Processes leading to the formation of wetlands, as well as abiotic factors (e.g., climate, soils, hydrology) that determine wetland plant and invertebrate community composition, differ within each province. Information on these subjects is presented collectively for wetlands within each province to facilitate comparisons.

Formative Processes
Columbia Plateau

The Columbia Plateau is a lava sheet that encompasses more than 250,000 km^2 between the Rocky and Cascade Mountains. The lavas are commonly basalt, although there are areas of andesites and rhyolites (Shimer 1972). A region of highlands in the central part of the province divides it into 3 sections: (1) the Columbia Basin on the north, (2) the Highlands in the middle, and (3) the Lava Plains on the south (Shimer 1972). In the Columbia Basin section, rolling topography has developed in a structurally broad basin. As the basalt decomposed in this section, the residual material became loessal and was distributed by southwest winds toward the eastern edge of the plateau, resulting in rich Palouse soils (Daubenmire 1942, Shimer 1972) that cover basalt tablelands ranging in elevation from 370 to 1,800 m above mean sea level (Bailey 1995). In the center of the Columbia Basin section are the Channeled Scablands, which were formed by glaciation (Bretz 1923, Daubenmire 1942). Scouring action of water resulted in 725,200 ha of land being eroded to bedrock and an additional 233,100 ha being buried by glacial debris (Bretz 1923). Surrounding the Channeled Scablands are deposits of loess that overlie basalt (Busacca 1991). The Highland section is deeply dissected and faulted with basins filled with sediments, including volcanic ash (Shimer 1972). The Lava Plains section has younger, less deformed flows that are interbedded with lake and stream deposits (Shimer 1972).

Basin and Range

The Basin and Range province encompasses about 518,000 km^2 and includes the Great Basin (70% of province) and portions of the Mojave, Sonoran, and Chihuahuan Deserts (Eakin et al. 1976, Dobrowolski et al. 1990). The entire province is characterized by isolated mountain ranges paralleled by valleys underlain by alluvial and lacustrine sedimentary deposits (Burkham 1988). Mountain ranges occupy about 20% and 35% of the landscape in the southern and northern portions of the province, respectively. Intermountain valleys dominate the remainder of the area (Snyder 1962). Mountain ranges commonly are 80–120 km long and 8–

24 km wide, and they reach elevations of 610–3,050 m (Burkham 1988). Rocks forming the mountains have provided a floor for sediment accumulation in valleys of the Great Basin region. In general, the sediment regime of valleys can be described as occurring in 3 zones (Duffy and Al-Hassan 1988). First, alluvial fan deposits of Quarternary age occur along the margin of basins, and in many cases, individual fans coalesce to form a piedmont plain or a bajada. Second, basins occur that are filled with deposits of mixed fluvial and lacustrine origin. Third, pluvial (rain-formed) lakes influenced near-surface deposits and the exposed playas, nearly flat areas where fine-grained deposits accumulate and surface water may temporarily occur. Elevation of valley floors ranges from about 640 m in the Amargosa Desert to about 2,130 m in central Nevada (Eakin et al. 1976).

During the Pleistocene, pluvial lakes covered vast areas of the province (West 1983). Lake Lahontan covered about 20,700 km^2 in Nevada and Lake Bonneville about 52,000 km^2 in Utah (Eakin et al. 1976). As conditions became drier and hotter, evaporation resulted in saline lakes and playas. Notable lakes include Walker Lake and Pyramid Lake, which are remnants of Lake Lahontan, and the Great Salt Lake, Sevier Lake, and Utah Lake, which are remnants of Lake Bonneville (Fiero 1986). Additional wetlands were formed as erosional material was transported by streams and deposited as alluvial fans at the base of mountains or farther out in the basins (Snyder 1962). An alluvial fan from a mountain may extend outward and merge with a fan from an adjacent range (Lamke and Moore 1965). Generally, this results in playas (Mabbutt 1979, Burkham 1988). Even larger rivers, although having well-defined channels, terminate at a lake or playa (Burkham 1988). For example, Mono Lake, a remnant of pluvial Lake Russell, has no surface outlet but is fed by 5 major tributaries originating on the east slope of the Sierra Nevada (Brotherson and Rushforth 1985).

Colorado Plateau

The Colorado Plateau (336,000 km^2) is characterized by an extensive area of sedimentary rocks that are generally flat-lying and dissected by the Colorado River drainage system (May et al. 1995). Elevation varies from about 1,200 to 4,600 m (West 1983), with local relief from 150 to 900 m in some of the deeper canyons that dissect plateaus (Bailey 1995). Seven structural features are found in the province: (1) basins, (2) uplifts, (3) upwarps, (4) monoclines, (5) fault blocks, (6) salt structures, and (7) igneous domal uplifts (Kelley 1955). A number of plateau levels occur and are separated by narrow monoclines, the most common structural feature of the plateau (Kelley 1955).

Rocky Mountains

The portion of the Rocky Mountain province occurring in the United States encompasses an area about 2,000 km north to south and 200–800 km east to west (Wright 1983) and includes 108 mountain ranges and 33 intermountain basins (Windell et al. 1986). Elevations range from 970 to 4,399 m (Windell et al. 1986). The general geologic history consists of folding and faulting of rock layers at the end of the Mesozoic era to create a major mountain range. Erosion followed this uplift, creating basins in the mountains. A late-Tertiary arching of the whole province initiated more erosion and was followed by glaciation that steepened slopes (Shimer 1972). Granite and metamorphic rocks generally outcrop in the cores of the mountain ranges where uplift and resulting erosion have been greatest, and valleys are prominent in areas that contain less resistant layers.

The province can be separated into the southern, middle, and northern Rocky Mountain sections (Shimer 1972). The southern Rocky Mountains extend from southeast Wyoming into southern New Mexico and Arizona. There are 5 major basins (North Park, Middle Park, South Park, Arkansas River Valley, and San Luis Valley) and several minor basins (Windell et al. 1986). The central Rocky Mountains in Wyoming and Utah consist of asymmetric basins separated by uplifted anticlinal mountain structures that have been largely buried under a thick covering of Tertiary sediments (Shimer 1972). The central and southern Rocky Mountains are separated by the Wyoming Basin, a large intermountain tectonic basin with gently rolling topography and a few low ridges. The northern Rockies have diverse origins (Windell et al. 1986). Mountain ranges in western and central Idaho are formed of granite, whereas mountains in southwest Montana are fault-block types. Intermountain basins that are much narrower and more valleylike than those in the central and southern Rocky Mountains separate the ranges in Montana (Windell et al. 1986).

Although formation of the mountains was a result of large-scale forces associated with plate tectonics, glaciation was a major factor in creating the wide variety of wetland habitats in the Rocky Mountains. Glaciation was more extensive in the northern than the southern Rocky Mountains (Richmond 1960). Individual glaciers were small (<15 km long), but large glacier complexes formed in several regions, including mountain ranges in Colorado, Wyoming, Utah, northwestern Montana, and central Idaho (Wright 1983). The direct influence of glaciers has largely been restricted to high mountain valleys (Price 1981). Landforms in the province have also been greatly altered by the erosional forces of water (Thornbury 1965, Windell et al. 1986).

Climate
Columbia Plateau

The climate of the Columbia Plateau is characterized as semiarid and cool (Bailey 1995). However, there is a gradient in climatic conditions; the eastern edge is subhumid, whereas the southwest is arid. Winters are cold and dry, and summers are warm to hot (Harris 1954, Bailey 1995). Because the Cascade Mountains create a rain-shadow effect, annual precipitation in the plateau varies from 150 mm in the southwest to 510 mm in the northeast (Whittaker and Fairbanks 1958, Bailey 1995). Most precipitation (65–70%) occurs between October and March (Daubenmire 1942), but annual evaporation usually exceeds precipitation (Bailey 1995).

Basin and Range

The province is classified as a high-elevation, mountainous, arid to semiarid, cool desert (Irwin-Williams et al. 1990, Hidy and Klieforth 1990). However, the complex terrain, including large differences in elevation, aspect, and relief, can result in highly variable climatic patterns in time and space (Duffy and Al-Hassan 1988). The average annual precipitation is 229 mm but can range from 38–100 mm at lower elevations to 635–1,270 mm at higher elevations (Houghton 1969). Total precipitation generally increases from south to north (Beatley 1975, Neilson 1987), but widely different seasonal rainfall regimes often occur in adjacent valleys (Beatley 1974). Temporal variability of precipitation is great (Burkham 1970) and typically increases as annual precipitation decreases (Fogel 1981). Further, the importance of an early spring growing season increases as the amount of annual precipitation decreases because early spring is often the only time when available soil moisture approaches evaporative demand (Comstock and Ehleringer 1992).

Average annual temperatures range from about −1° C in some high northern valleys to about 16° C in the extreme southern valleys (Ehleringer 1985). Diurnal temperature fluxes tend to be great, with daily temperature ranges exceeding 17° C in most valleys and approaching 28° C in some valleys of western Nevada (Eakin et al. 1976). Soil surface temperatures >60° C are common during summer in the warm deserts; thus plants growing close to the surface are exposed to air temperatures of 45–55° C (Ehleringer 1985). The growing season ranges from less than 30 days in some high mountain valleys to more than 200 days in the extreme south (Eakin et al. 1976, Smith and Nowak 1990). Low humidity (average of 30–40%), coupled with abundant sunshine and light to moderate winds, results in very rapid evaporation (Kohler et al. 1959, Flaschka et al. 1987).

Colorado Plateau

The climate is arid to semiarid, with average annual temperatures of 4–13° C decreasing with rising elevation (Bailey 1995). Average annual precipitation is about 510 mm (Bailey 1995) but varies considerably depending on elevation and aspect (Comstock and Ehleringer 1992). The temporal pattern of precipitation is bimodal, with peaks during summer and winter. Summer precipitation accounts for 35–50% of annual precipitation (Comstock and Ehleringer 1992), but winter precipitation is important to ensure soil moisture recharge and a reliable spring growing season (West 1983, Caldwell 1985). The growing season on the plateau is determined largely by a combination of temperature and soil moisture. Soil moisture is typically greatest during winter, but low temperatures prohibit photosynthesis, and plants may experience shoot desiccation due to exposure to dry winds and frozen soils (Nelson and Tiernan 1983). In contrast, plant growth usually is restricted beginning in early or mid-summer by low soil moisture and high temperatures (Comstock and Ehleringer 1992).

Rocky Mountains

The climate of the Rocky Mountains is semiarid and is influenced by prevailing west winds. Depending on elevation, average annual temperatures range from 2° to 10° C in the southern Rocky Mountains, whereas mean monthly temperatures in the central and northern Rocky Mountains range from 0° to 22° C (Shimer 1972). The average annual growing season ranges from 87 days in subalpine zones to 137 days in the lower montane zone (Marr 1967). Annual precipitation ranges from 260–510 mm at the base of mountains to 1,020 mm at higher elevations in the southern and northern Rocky Mountains. Pacific air masses are the primary source of precipitation on the western slope, and winter is the period of greatest precipitation, with as much as 80% of annual precipitation occurring as snow at higher elevations (Shimer 1972, Johnston and Brown 1979, Rink and Kiladis 1986). In the central Rocky Mountains, snowmelt begins in late May and June at montane elevations (Despain 1973) and occurs about 3–4 weeks later in subalpine and alpine regions (Johnston and Brown 1979). Snowmelt is 2–3 weeks earlier in the southern Rocky Mountains (Marr 1967). Evaporation typically exceeds precipitation in lower montane areas and intermountain basins, but at higher elevations the trend is reversed because of increased precipitation coupled with lower air temperatures. However, other factors, such as to-pography and exposure to solar radiation, often moderate general temperature and precipitation trends related to elevation (Geiger 1959, Marr 1967, Baldwin 1973, Rink and Kiladis 1986).

Soils
Columbia Plateau

Soils vary from alluvial and eolian (wind-caused) deposits to areas that technically do not have soil. Alluvium dominates the floodplains of streams and bajadas near the mountains, whereas extensive eolian deposits, including dune sand and loess, predominate at other sites (Bailey 1995). In some areas of the Snake River Plain, lava flows are so recent that there is no soil (Shimer 1972). Soil depths vary depending on how long the materials have weathered and how much loess has been deposited or removed (West 1983). In the Columbia River Basin, loess deposits are up to 46 m thick and soils are complex. Aridisols dominate basin and lowland areas, and mollisols are found at higher elevations (Bailey 1995). The dominant soil-forming process is calcification, but salinization is common on poorly drained sites. Soils contain excess precipitated calcium carbonate and are rich in bases, and humus content is low (Bailey 1995). In the Pothole area of the Channeled Scablands, agricultural cultivation has reduced the porosity of the upper horizons, causing serious erosion of loessal soils (Daubenmire 1942).

Basin and Range

Soil in wetland basins ranges from histosols in marshes to aridisols in playas (West 1983). Soils in valleys usually derive either from flat, deep lacustrine deposits or badlands. Soil development on lacustrine deposits depends largely on salt content, texture, and depth of the water table (West 1983). Most marshes are relics of pluvial lakes that were veneered and leveled with fine-textured, stratified sediments (Peterson 1981). In contrast, the soils of most playas develop from shale outcrops in desert to semidesert climates and are fine-textured and easily eroded (Young and Evans 1986, Dobrowolski et al. 1990). Aridisols are distinguishable by the lack of development (Steila 1976, Ehleringer 1985) and are characterized by low concentrations of nitrogen and phosphorus (West 1981). Soil salinities vary within playas depending on topography because both water and salts accumulate in the lowest portion of a basin. In wet playas, leaching is rarely sufficient to remove ions that cause salinization, alkalization, and calcification of soils. Further, evaporation causes many elements to move upward in the soil profile, causing accumulations of calcium carbonate and calcium sulfate that form petrocalcic or gypsic (caliche) layers (Whitford 1986). As a result, soils containing high levels of neutral or alkaline salts often develop at the terminus of closed drainage basins (Caldwell 1985). In contrast, the soil in dry playas tends to have lower concentrations of evaporites such as salts (Snyder 1962).

Location relative to relief and hydrology also influences soil properties (Peterson 1981). Soils on slopes and bajadas tend to be rocky, while those on flat plains are high in clay particles and often have caliche layers 1–2 m below the surface (Ehleringer 1985). In addition, nonvascular microphytes and a network of shrinkage cracks often cover spaces between plants within a basin. These microphytic crusts may functionally substitute for the organic mulch layer common in mesic systems (Friedman and Galun 1974, Wagner 1980), whereas shrinkage cracks are considered preferential pathways for water infiltration, percolation, and root growth (Hugie and Passey 1964, Eckert et al. 1986).

Colorado Plateau

The Colorado Plateau has extensive areas of bedrock and limited soil cover (Shimer 1972, Welsh 1978). Plateaus are composed of aridisols and badlands, whereas aridisols predominate on older terraces and alluvial fans (Bailey 1995). In many areas, weathering of marine shales has resulted in the formation of clays that inhibit water infiltration or soils with high concentrations of sodium sulfate that restrict plant diversity and total cover (Welsh 1978, Potter et al. 1985). In some areas, massive sandstone outcrops dominate the landscape. Soils are shallow and rocky, whereas deeper soils are generally aeolian deposits forming sands or sandy loams (Comstock and Ehleringer 1992). These sandy soils exhibit faster infiltration of water, are less prone to anoxic conditions, and allow deeper water penetration with less water movement to the surface via capillary action and evaporation. The combination of much sandier soils and more summer rainfall in the Colorado Plateau is largely responsible for its major floristic and ecological differences from the Great Basin (Comstock and Ehleringer 1992).

Rocky Mountains

Different rock types, in combination with widely varying climatic regimes and formative processes (e.g., glaciation, erosion), have resulted in a complex mosaic of heterogeneous, discontinuous soil types (Retzer 1962, Price 1981). Wetlands in the Rocky Mountains can be underlain by either organic or mineral soils. In the southern and central sections, inceptisols occur on steep slopes in glaciated areas, alfisols and mollisols occur above 600 m elevations, mollisols dominate valley floors and fans at elevations less than 600 m, and aridisols occur in the foothills (Bailey 1995). Thick alluvial deposits lying on bedrock underlie intermountain basins (Shimer 1972). The floors of these basins are composed of Tertiary sediments and some lava (Windell et al. 1986). Soils in these basins are very different physically and chemically from soils on surrounding mountains (Windell et al. 1986). Soils in the Wyoming Basin are composed of shales and marlstones formed when large lakes occupied the basin in the Eocene (Hunt 1974). Soils in the northern Rocky Mountains are mostly inceptisols, but the foothills and areas south of the primary glacial activity exhibit loess and volcanic ash deposits that greatly increase fertility (Bailey 1995).

Inceptisols are young soils that have formed quickly due to alteration of parent material, and they are relatively unproductive. Aridisols, which are mineral soils typically low in organic matter, are characterized by a layer of accumulated calcic, gypsic, or salic salts and are considered unproductive (Brady 1974). In contrast, alfisols and mollisols are considered among the most productive mineral soils. Relatively undeveloped soils, or entisols, are common in areas dominated by fragmented bedrock, talus, or recent glacial moraine deposits (Rink and Kiladis 1986). In addition, histosols occur where drainage and oxidation are poor, and spodosols occur in subalpine areas where organic input and accumulation are relatively high (Price 1981).

Hydrology and Vegetation
Columbia Plateau

The distribution of wetlands within the Columbia Plateau is varied. The Snake River Plain contains few wetlands (Shimer 1972). Similarly, natural wetlands are largely absent in the Palouse region (Whittaker and Fairbanks 1958). In contrast, the Columbia Basin section contains numerous natural wetlands.

Playas are scattered throughout the province but primarily near mountains where winter precipitation and discharge from mountain streams result in ephemeral or intermittent periods of surface flows into shallow basins (Bailey 1995). Playas with saline soils support 3 plant associations that typically occur in concentric zones: inland saltgrass at the lowest elevations, black greasewood and inland saltgrass at intermediate elevations, and spiny hopsage at the highest elevations (Daubenmire 1942). Big sagebrush typically defines the wetland-upland margin of playas. The width of each zone is determined by soil moisture and salinity (Daubenmire 1942). In the most saline basins, salinity at the lowest elevation is so extreme that vegetation establishment is precluded.

In contrast, wildrye and occasionally inland saltgrass typically dominate playas with nonsaline or weakly saline soils. Compared to saline
playas, the soil is fine-textured, and soil horizons deeper than 50 cm often contain water available for plant growth throughout the summer
(Daubenmire 1942).

The density of beaver-created wetlands varies depending on food supplies, stream gradient and cross-sectional area, stream depth and width,
past trapping pressure, and stability of water levels (Williams 1965,
Slough and Sadlier 1977, Howard and Larson 1985, Beier and Barrett
1987, McComb et al. 1990). Vegetation composition of beaver wetlands
is determined by site conditions such as elevation (and therefore climatic variables such as precipitation, temperature, etc.) and geographic
location. In general, perennial herbaceous species such as sedges typically occur in the seasonally flooded zone around the periphery of the
wetlands, as do woody species such as alder, willow, hawthorn, pine, and
cottonwood.

Within the Columbia Basin region, the Channeled Scablands contain
numerous wetlands termed "potholes" (Johnsgard 1955). Sand deposited
by impounded glacial waters formed dunes, and a high water table between dunes resulted in potholes (Johnsgard 1956). Most potholes range
from <1 ha to 32 ha, occur in basalt depressions, are shallow and eutrophic, and have hydroperiods that range from intermittently to permanently flooded (Harris 1954, Whittaker and Fairbanks 1958). Historically, hydroperiods were determined by precipitation and evaporation
cycles (Whittaker and Fairbanks 1958). However, a few potholes derive
water from springs and exhibit permanent or semipermanent hydroperiods. This region also contains relatively deep, often oligotrophic lakes
with shores of vertical or steeply sloped basalt and vernal pools that are
mostly associated with interrupted channels (Whittaker and Fairbanks
1958, Crowe et al. 1994).

Historically, salinity conditions varied widely (155–88,030 ppm total
salts) even within small geographic areas but generally tended to increase
toward the more arid western part of the area (Whittaker and Fairbanks
1958). However, the creation of reservoirs, lakes, and ditches has resulted
in the loss of potholes and in some cases has lengthened hydroperiods and
lowered salinities in remaining potholes due to the elevation of groundwater levels (Johnsgard 1956, Foster et al. 1984, Ball et al. 1989).

Wetland vegetation in the Channeled Scablands is varied and rich,
with composition determined by salinity, hydroperiod, and depth of water (Daubenmire 1942). In areas that remain relatively unaltered by human developments, the dominant species on the driest sites (sand dunes)
include Douglas rabbitbrush, rubber rabbitbrush, sagebrush, spiny hop-
sage, cheatgrass, Indian ricegrass, and alkali cordgrass. At lower eleva-

tions nearer the water table, sand dunes surrounding potholes support species such as lemon scurfpea, willow, and veiny dock. As soil moisture increases below this zone, an extensive inland saltgrass–Nevada club rush community often develops. This zone grades into an area that is moist or shallowly flooded that is often dominated by Baltic rush, Douglas sedge, and occasionally American bulrush, longspike spikerush, sedge, and Torrey's rush (Harris 1954). In semipermanently and permanently flooded potholes, tule bulrush or common cattail occurs in areas flooded to depths <1 m. Water deeper than 1 m supports submersed aquatic plants, including fennelleaf pondweed, common hornwort, spiked watermilfoil, and occasionally common bladderwort, musk grass, common widgeonweed, and floating knotweed. Semipermanent potholes that are not deep enough to support submersed aquatic plants and robust emergent vegetation are typically dominated by Baltic rush and sedges (Johnsgard 1956). In contrast, the Columbia Basin Irrigation Project has altered the hydrology of a large portion of the channeled scablands in Washington. Many of the wetlands described by Johnsgard (1956) and Harris (1954) no longer exist or have been degraded by high densities of carp or extensive stands of purple loosestrife and common reed.

Basin and Range

Physiography, climate, and soil properties determine wetland hydrology. Physiography can be used to characterize valleys as topographically closed or open. In topographically closed valleys, the outlet may be either above or below the valley floor. If the outlet is above the valley floor, no groundwater outlet exists and water accumulates until it reaches the surface, where discharge occurs by evaporation (Snyder 1962). Playas occurring in these valleys remain wet throughout the year or have water within a few centimeters of the surface during the dry summer season (Snyder 1962). In contrast, if the outlet of the valley is below the soil surface and has sufficient capacity to export all precipitation inflow, the water table remains at or slightly above the subsurface outlet. Consequently, soil does not become saturated, and playas, if present, remain dry throughout most of the year (Snyder 1962). Closed valleys with wet playas are common in Nevada, western Utah, and eastern California (Snyder 1962).

Topographically open valleys typically are tributaries of large streams, and surface drainage is generally continuous. In the Great Basin, these open valleys drain via 8 major river systems (Bear, Weber, Jordan, Sevier, Humboldt, Carson, Truckee, and Walker) into 5 major terminal lakes or sinks (Great Salt Lake and Sevier Lake in Utah and the Humboldt-Carson Sink, Pyramid Lake, and Walker Lake in Nevada). Water draining to these internal basins primarily evaporates, often leaving extensive salt flats in the bottom of the basins (Irwin-Williams et al. 1990). However, the continuity of drainage may be interrupted locally by barriers such as alluvial fans that result in the development of small playas. In some cases, groundwater in a topographically open valley may drain through subsurface channels without reappearing at the surface (Snyder 1962).

Most valleys in the Great Basin region have groundwater reservoirs, but comparatively few valleys have abundant surface water supplies (Eakin et al. 1976). Thus, temporary wetlands are widespread, and permanently flooded wetlands are uncommon (Williams 1985, Duffy and Al-Hassan 1988). Precipitation is the source of virtually all groundwater recharge (Eakin et al. 1976). Thus, precipitation is of primary importance in determining the timing and frequency of hydroperiods in natural wetlands. In general, spring represents the primary, and often the only, soil moisture recharge period (Caldwell 1985, Ehleringer et al. 1991). Thus, most playas receive surface water inflow during spring. Similarly, water levels in terminal sinks and marshes in topographically open valleys also increase in spring as a result of increased stream flows. However, precipitation patterns in the province are highly variable within and among years. Consequently, the hydrology of playas is extremely dynamic. A dry playa may become moist or wet by a slight increase in the water table, a moist playa may form an ephemeral lake following a single summer thunderstorm, or a lake may appear during winter when groundwater discharge exceeds evaporation (Duffy and Al-Hassan 1988). Similar fluctuations in water levels occur in some terminal sinks and marshes, whereas others (primarily in the eastern Great Basin) remain relatively stable due to artesian wells (Eakin et al. 1976).

Evaporation rates affect the duration of flooding. The dry atmosphere, coupled with high wind velocities and low relative humidity, results in moderately high evaporation rates (Fautin 1946). About half the annual precipitation is lost via evaporation from the soil surface or sublimation from the snowpack in the Great Basin region (West 1983, Caldwell 1985).

The salinity of wetlands varies within and among individual basins, wetland types, and seasons. In arid regions, salinity is second only to water as the most crucial factor limiting plant growth (Chapman 1966). In closed basins, salinity varies inversely with lake volume (Eardley et al. 1957), and concentrations may exceed that of ocean water (Eakin et al. 1976, Wurtsbaugh 1992). Further, salinities in bays that have been diked to facilitate management vary greatly among seasons (Kadlec 1982). In playas, salinity varies depending on physiography and the resulting hydroperiod. In valleys with a groundwater outlet, the groundwater table is not near the surface, and the surface soils of playas typically accumulate only small amounts of salt (Eakin et al. 1976). In contrast, the ground-

water table remains near the surface in valleys with no groundwater outlet, and evaporation often results in accumulation of soluble salts on the
soil surface during the dry season (Eardley et al. 1957, Mabbutt 1979,
Dobrowolski et al. 1990). Differences in salinity can also occur within a
single wet playa basin. The ratio of precipitated salt to surface sediments
increases from the outer margin to the lowest elevations and is related
to the changing hydrologic regime (Line 1979, Duffy and Al-Hassan
1988). Along the margin of the playa, a thin salt crust develops at the
highest elevations during summer in response to evaporation from the
shallow water table and capillary fringe. However, as the evaporation
rate decreases during winter, salts are redissolved by the rising groundwater and transported to the lowest portion of the basin (Duffy and Al-
Hassan 1988). As conditions permit, standing water in the central playa
evaporates and contributes to the perennial salt crust. Following complete evaporation, the depth of salt is approximately 25% of the depth of
the standing water (Mabbutt 1979).

Vegetation composition is determined largely by landform and climatic features, the most important being low and variable precipitation
(as it relates to hydroperiod), low atmospheric humidity, high diurnal air
temperature, great daily range of temperature, soil properties (e.g., salinity), and active erosion (Shreve and Mallery 1933, Shreve 1942, Beatley
1974). Vegetation distribution in playas exhibits zonal patterns that reflect salinity gradients (Ungar et al. 1969, Skougard and Brotherson
1979, Comstock and Ehleringer 1992). Although extreme environmental conditions limit vegetation composition to a few dominant plants,
more than 19 species have been identified (Skougard and Brotherson
1979, Brotherson 1987). In general, the lowest elevations of wet playas
in closed and undrained valleys are so saline that only the most salt-
tolerant species, such as inland saltgrass, iodine bush, and pickleweeds,
can become established (Snyder 1962, Skougard and Brotherson 1979,
Comstock and Ehleringer 1992, Trent et al. 1997). Inland saltgrass tends
to be least restricted by salt concentrations, exhibiting tolerances from
1,000 to 27,000 ppm (Ungar 1974, Hansen et al. 1976, Skougard and
Brotherson 1979). Less salt-tolerant phreatophytes occur around the margin of playas where salinities are less extreme and depth to the groundwater table is not excessive (Snyder 1962). Phreatophytes are replaced by
xerophytes as the depth to groundwater increases (Snyder 1962). In contrast, soil properties (e.g., moisture, oxygen) seem more important than
climatic factors in determining plant composition in dry playas (Snyder
1962, MacMahon 1988). Dry playas support predominantly xerophytic
vegetation (Snyder 1962), including common winterfat and shadscale on
sites with moderately saline soils and a groundwater table that remains
deeper than the root zone (Comstock and Ehleringer 1992). These spe-

cies are replaced by sagebrush, rabbitbrush, bitterbrush, and spiny hop-sage at higher elevations and on moister, nonsaline soils.

Vegetation of more permanently flooded wetlands also is influenced by salinity and water regimes. In general, salinity limits macrophyte communities in most lakes to a few species. The most common growth forms include erect aquatics (e.g., fennelleaf pondweed, curlyleaf pond-weed, common widgeonweed), low aquatics (e.g., musk grass, benthic mats of filamentous algae), thin-stemmed emergents (e.g., tule bulrush), and other erect aquatics such as watermilfoil (Rawson and Moore 1944, Hammer and Heseltine 1988). However, many of the erect aquatics are rare or absent at higher salinities (Stewart and Kantrud 1972, Kantrud et al. 1989). Further, most saline lakes exhibit low cover and biomass (Hammer 1981, Lancaster and Scudder 1987), although a few salt-tolerant species may be abundant (Tones 1976). The shore of Great Salt Lake is characterized by bare salt flats interspersed with sparse stands of species that can tolerate high soil salinities, including pickleweed, fireweed summercypress, mentzelia, evening primrose, and inland saltgrass (Kad-lec 1982, Kadlec and Smith 1984, Brotherson and Rushforth 1985). In or-der of increasing depth to groundwater, dominant species include Baltic rush, inland saltgrass, shrubby cinquefoil, basin wildrye, black grease-wood, and rubber rabbitbrush. Dominant species in order of increasing water-retention capacity of soils are black sagebrush, Douglas rabbit-brush, common winterfat, big sagebrush, Nuttall saltbush, and shadscale (Miller et al. 1982). Similarly, Bolen (1964) characterized plant commu-nity composition at Fish Springs National Wildlife Refuge, Utah, into 4 emersed soil communities (inland saltgrass, rush meadows, rush borders, and common reed) and 6 submersed-soil communities (spike-rush meadows, olney bulrush, cattail, tule bulrush, alkali bulrush, and musk grass/common widgeonweed). Although these associations ap-pear monospecific, close examination reveals that each association is floristically diverse (Bolen 1964, Brotherson 1981).

In contrast, species diversity and total plant biomass are often higher in managed marshes that surround large, saline lakes (Cox and Kadlec 1995). Plant species in managed marshes include cattail, tule bulrush, alkali bulrush, river bulrush, common reed, lambsquarters goosefoot, dwarf spikerush, common spikerush, foxtail barley, rice cutgrass, arrow-head, giant burreed, and rabbitfoot grass in addition to pondweeds and inland saltgrass (Duebbert 1969, Kadlec 1982, Kadlec and Smith 1984, Smith and Kadlec 1985a).

Water-level manipulations directed toward changing salinity can be used to selectively alter the extent of established vegetation. For ex-ample, reduced water levels (Smith and Kadlec 1983) or extended draw-downs in combination with mowing (Nelson and Dietz 1966) may lead to increased salinity that favors alkali bulrush and discourages cattail. However, efforts to establish or control species such as cattail or bulrush by lowering water levels to expose mudflats (Kadlec and Wentz 1974) may fail if seedlings are subjected to salt buildup at the mud surface (Kadlec 1982). Other methods (e.g., haying, burning) have been marginally successful in controlling dense stands of emergent vegetation (Nelson and Dietz 1966; Ward 1968; Smith and Kadlec 1984, 1985a,b).

Colorado Plateau

About 90% of the Colorado Plateau is drained by the Colorado River and its tributaries (Thornbury 1965). Movement of groundwater in the Colorado Plateau is controlled by broad dip planes and extensive joint systems within sedimentary strata (Heath 1988). Several permeable sandstone formations on the plateau are underlain by relatively impermeable strata and function as aquifers (Taylor and Hood 1988). Although the sandstone can retain an immense volume of water, the primary permeability of these sandstones is minimal due to fine grain size, overburden loading, and secondary infilling of fractures (Hood and Patterson 1984).

Natural marshes are uncommon on the Colorado Plateau (Harper et al. 1994). In Arizona, most natural marshes are seasonal, and hydroperiod is determined primarily by precipitation and snowmelt rather than groundwater (Brown 1985). Typically these wetlands have steep littoral zones, and vegetation exhibits distinct patterns of zonation (Judd 1972). In the permanently flooded zone, the dominant plants include spiked watermilfoil, watercrowfoot buttercup, beaked sedge, water ladysthumb, and bullwhip. Areas frequently inundated along the shore are dominated by pale sedge, longspike spikerush, northern mannagrass, and Baltic rush, whereas shortawn foxtail, needle spikerush, and watercress are prevalent as soil moisture decreases. Redtop bentgrass and inland rush occur in slightly drier sites, and northern meadow barley and curly dock are often among the dominant species in the driest zone, adjacent to the forest edge.

Playas exist in low-elevation areas with shallow water tables or areas with fine-textured soils. The upper soil profile remains sufficiently moist or groundwater is available within the rooting zone in these areas to allow establishment of halophytic plants, such as black greasewood, iodine bush, pickleweed, and inland saltgrass, that can tolerate moist and extremely saline soils (Detling 1969). The hydroperiod of these wetlands is determined by local precipitation patterns and varies among seasons and years.

Unique wetland types occurring on the Colorado Plateau are hanging gardens and tinajas. Hanging gardens occur at seeps and springs along

xeric canyon walls and support hydrophytic, herbaceous plant communities (Fowler and Stanton 1995). This wetland type is common within
the Colorado River drainage system from Zion National Park, Utah, to
the canyons of the Green and Yampa Rivers in the northeast portion of
the province. Hanging gardens are isolated mesophytic habitats (May
et al. 1995) that form as water percolates along impervious bedding
planes and emerge as seeps and springs where canyons cut through the
strata (Spence and Henderson 1993). Additional requirements for the formation of hanging gardens include the absence of significant fluvial processes and protection from excessive sun and wind, which ensures the
presence of water. Geologic (e.g., aquifer sandstones) and hydrologic parameters (e.g., number of seep lines, hydraulic pressure, discharge rate)
control the location, distribution, and physical attributes of hanging gardens (May et al. 1995).

There are 3 types of microhabitats in hanging gardens: seep line, wet
wall, and colluvial soil (May et al. 1995). Seep-line habitats, by definition, occur in all hanging gardens and support vegetation that can tolerate the driest conditions. Wet-wall habitat is characterized by water
slowly flowing across bare rock and the absence of colluvium. Although
sparsely colonized, wet walls can support algae, bacteria, bryophytes,
and vascular plants. Colluvial-soil habitats develop on deposits that
accumulate by gravitational downslope movement of material that has
been mechanically or chemically weathered in the seep zone (Brady
1974, May et al. 1995). Colluvial-soil habitats support the greatest
abundance and diversity of vascular plants, including forbs, grasses,
sedges, and woody vegetation that are obligate wetland species (Malanson and Kay 1980, Spence and Henderson 1993, Fowler and Stanton 1995).
Species found on seep lines and wet walls also occur on colluvial soil
with the exception of the least mesophytic plants. Factors controlling
plant assemblages include the time available for colonization between
disturbances (Malanson and Kay 1980) and plant dispersal type (Malanson 1980).

Tinajas, also called potholes or weathering pits, are depressions that
have been eroded out of bedrock (Spence and Henderson 1993). Tinajas
are common on gently sloping outcrops of weathered granite and sandstone and are so abundant on friable sandstones of the Colorado Plateau
that they locally create a distinctive dome-and-pit landscape. Most theories on formation include a combination of physical, chemical, and biological weathering processes that promote mineral decomposition followed by removal of the resulting decomposed material by wind or
water (Twidale and Bourne 1975, Godfrey 1980, Goudie 1991).

Tinajas are commonly flat-floored, circular to elliptical, 0.5–4.0 m in
width, 5–60 cm deep, with width-depth ratios of 6:1 to 10:1 (Twidale

1982). Bedrock floors are covered with sandy sediments or alternating layers of materials that vary in organic content (Netoff et al. 1995). Pit walls, floors, and rims have a fine-grained arkosic sandstone that is weakly cemented with calcium carbonate and lesser amounts of clay. The annual hydroperiod of tinajas varies depending on dimensions and climate. In general, relatively shallow (<1 m) pools dry frequently, whereas deeper (>2 m) or more protected pools retain water much longer. Many of the deeper pits retain water from months to years. However, local variations in precipitation often result in shallow tinajas containing more water in areas that receive greater rainfall than larger and deeper tinajas (Netoff et al. 1995).

Tinajas with the thickest sediment tend to have the densest cover, and pools exhibiting longer hydroperiods (deeper or more protected) support species that do not tolerate extensive drying, such as cottonwood, willow, and cattail (Netoff et al. 1995). In contrast, shallow exposed tinajas tend to support dense populations of grasses that tolerate drying. Tinajas are often classified according to riparian vegetation (e.g., willow, cottonwood). However, several facultative and obligate herbaceous species also occur, including Baltic rush, muhly, few-flowered panicum, rosette grass, common reed, evening primrose, plantain, and inland saltgrass (Spence and Henderson 1993).

Rocky Mountains

Natural wetlands are found at all elevations throughout the Rocky Mountain region. Wetlands of mountain valleys are often distinguished from those of intermountain basins on the basis of distinctly different geological origins, weather, and resulting soil types (Windell et al. 1986). Mountain valleys are relatively young topographical forms, shaped by erosional forces of water and, at higher elevations, by glacial movements. Direct or indirect effects of glaciers have resulted in the formation of many different types of palustrine wetlands, including cirque basins; spring, seep, and snowbed wetlands; tarns; kettles; and terminal or lateral moraine lakes (Windell et al. 1986). In the Uinta Mountains, most wetlands are located at the head of glaciated valleys (Briggs and MacMahon 1983). In addition, hanging garden wetlands are evident on some cliff faces, and beavers have created large wetland regions in many Rocky Mountain areas (Brayton 1983). The northern Rocky Mountains also contain several large, mostly freshwater, natural lakes that were formed by morainal dams (Shimer 1972, Windell et al. 1986). Wetlands in intermountain basins are composed of playas, alkali flats, marshes, and lakes associated with tectonic disruption of drainage. In many basins, the original types and extent of wetlands are not known, and current wetland distribution and type are determined by canals, irrigation seeps, return flows, and artesian wells (Windell et al. 1986).

Wetland hydrology is complex because the relative contribution of surface (direct and indirect) and groundwater components varies depending on numerous physical and climatic factors. The majority of surface water input results from indirect precipitation occurring in the watershed. Five major river systems (Columbia, Colorado, Missouri, Red, and Rio Grande) and numerous tributaries arise in the Rocky Mountains and influence the hydroperiod of wetlands regardless of elevation. Direct precipitation is probably the least significant source of water (Knud-Hansen 1986), except in terrain depressions (Willard 1979) and bogs (Cooper 1986). Groundwater hydrology varies greatly depending on geology, watershed topography, soil characteristics, and season (Leaf 1975, Rink and Kiladis 1986). Snowmelt at higher elevations supplies a large volume of water that can contribute to groundwater dynamics and indirectly affect wetland hydroperiods. In mountain valleys, a high water table is maintained by accumulation of water from melting snow and summer storms, and the water table interacts with variable depth of bedrock and permeable materials (e.g., moraines) that contain either surface or subsurface water (Rink and Kiladis 1986). The frequency, time, depth, and duration of flooding are determined by several factors, including the renewal rate of water and the timing, regularity, and predictability of daily and seasonal water input (Gosselink and Turner 1978, Mitsch and Gosselink 1993). These factors, in turn, are influenced by physical (e.g., soil, topography) and climatic (e.g., temperature, humidity) properties. Historically, frequency of flooding varied among wetland types depending on location relative to water source. Wetlands associated with river systems (e.g., moraine lakes) or those that act as catchment basins for snowmelt runoff (e.g., snowbeds) typically received some water every year, whereas wetlands not associated with water courses (e.g., playas and meadows) were less frequently flooded. Today, however, wetland hydroperiods in valleys and basins are significantly influenced by the direct and indirect effects of wells, canals, and irrigation patterns (Ramaley 1942, Windell et al. 1986; also see Chapter 6 of this volume).

Rocky Mountain wetlands support numerous vegetation types, from floating aquatic and emergent species to halomorphic shrubs. Permanently flooded basins support floating aquatics, which tend to be most abundant in areas that are too deep or turbid to support rooted species. However, these species are largely absent from oligotrophic basins, such as newly formed wetlands or wetlands in the subalpine and alpine zones, due to limited dissolved organic and inorganic nutrients and/or low water temperatures (Windell et al. 1986). At lower elevations, eutrophication may result from increased wetland productivity, which leads to an accumulation of nutrients that enable establishment of floating aquatics (Wetzel 1983). Dominant species primarily include common duckweed and star duckweed (Cooper 1986).

Basins characterized by shallow (<3 m), permanent flooding with light penetration to the bottom often support communities of rooted, submersed, and, if wave action is minimal, floating-leaved plants. Dominant submersed species include quillwort, stonewort, pondweeds, slender naiad, common marestail, white buttercup, spiked watermilfoil, bladderwort, musk grass, and common widgeonweed (Cooper 1986, Wollheim and Lovvorn 1996). Prevalent rooted, floating-leaved species include yellow pondlily, painted cowlily, waterlily, narrowleaf burreed, and some species of pondweeds (Cooper 1986). Geographically, most rooted, submersed macrophytes appear limited to the upper and lower montane zones and intermountain basins; however, some species (e.g., marestail, spiked watermilfoil) exhibit a cosmopolitan distribution (Hulten 1968). Rooted, floating-leaved communities dominated by burreed occur throughout boreal and mountain regions of North America (Cooper 1986), whereas cowlily is most abundant in low subalpine and high montane ponds (Weber 1976). Although many rooted submersed plants exhibit broad salinity tolerance, species capable of establishment and growth in extremely saline waters include only common widgeonweed and fennelleaf pondweed (Bolen 1964, Hammer and Heseltine 1988).

Rooted emergent species occur in numerous wetland types, including temporary and seasonally flooded wetlands, as well as around the margins of permanently flooded basins. Typical species are perennials, including sedges, spikerushes, rushes, mannagrass, common reed, arrowhead, bulrushes, cattail, foxtail barley, field horsetail, hairgrass, reedgrass, burreed, and goosefoot (see Cooper 1986 for a detailed list). Establishment from seed requires bare and exposed mudflats, moist to saturated soils, and salinities from <4,000 ppm to 15,000 ppm. Thus, floristics is determined by abiotic factors (e.g., soil type, water source, precipitation-evapotranspiration ratios, elevation) that influence soil moisture and salinity gradients (Cooper 1986).

Playas often support perennial vegetation that is tolerant of saline conditions or, if salinities are extreme, remain unvegetated. Dominant species include inland saltgrass, alkali sacaton, foxtail barley, sedges, grasses, and various shrubs, including black greasewood, saltbush, rabbitbrush, mesquite, and various species of sagebrush (Cooper 1986, Windell et al. 1986). Hydroperiod (e.g., depth, duration, frequency), water chemistry (e.g., salinity, pH), substrate type (organic, mineral), and source of water are important determinants of floristics (Ramaley 1942, Windell et al. 1986).

Literature Cited

Bailey, R. G. 1995. Description of the ecoregions of the United States. Second edition. U.S. Department of Agriculture, Forest Service, Washington, D.C., USA.

Baldwin, J. L. 1973. Climates of the United States. U.S. Department of Commerce, Washington, D.C., USA.

Ball, I. J., R. D. Bauer, K. Vermeer, and M. J. Rabenberg. 1989. Northwest riverine and Pacific coast. Pages 429–449 in L. M. Smith, R. L. Pederson, and R. M. Kaminski, editors. Habitat management for migrating and winterfowl in North America. Texas Tech University Press, Lubbock, Texas, USA.

Beatley, J. C. 1974. Phenological events and their environmental triggers in Mojave Desert ecosystems. Ecology 55:856–863.

———. 1975. Climates and vegetation patterns across the Mojave/Great Basin desert transition of southern Nevada. American Midland Naturalist 93:53–70.

Beier, P., and R. H. Barrett. 1987. Beaver habitat use and impact in the Truckee River Basin, California. Journal of Wildlife Management 51:794–799.

Bolen, E. G. 1964. Plant ecology of spring-fed salt marshes in western Utah. Ecological Monographs 34:143–166.

Brady, N. C. 1974. The nature and properties of soils. Eighth edition. Macmillan, New York, New York, USA.

Brayton, S. 1983. Eager beavers improve stream habitats in Wyoming. Wyoming Horizons 8:1.

Bretz, J. H. 1923. The channeled scablands of the Columbia Plateau. Journal of Geology 31:617–649.

Briggs, G. M., and J. A. MacMahon. 1983. Alpine and subalpine wetland plant communities of the Uinta Mountains, Utah. Great Basin Naturalist 43:523–530.

Brotherson, J. D. 1981. Aquatic and semiaquatic vegetation of Utah Lake and its bays. Great Basin Naturalist Memoirs 5:68–84.

———. 1987. Plant community zonation in response to soil gradients in a saline meadow near Utah Lake, Utah County, Utah. Great Basin Naturalist 47:322–333.

———, and S. R. Rushforth. 1985. Invasion and stabilization of recent beaches by salt grass (Distichlis spicata) at Mono Lake, Mono County, California. Great Basin Naturalist 45:542–545.

Brown, D. E. 1985. Arizona wetlands and waterfowl. University of Arizona Press, Tucson, Arizona, USA.

———, C. H. Lowe, and J. F. Hausler. 1977. Southwestern riparian communities: their biotic importance and management in Arizona. Pages 201–211 in R. R. Johnson and D. A. Jones, coordinators. Importance, preservation and management of riparian habitat: a symposium. U.S. Department of Agriculture, Forest Service General Technical Report RM-43.

Burkham, D. E. 1970. Precipitation, streamflow, and major floods at selected sites in the Gila River drainage basin above Coolidge Dam, Arizona. U.S. Geological Survey Professional Paper 655-B.

———. 1988. Methods for delineating flood-prone areas in the Great Basin of Nevada and adjacent sites. U.S. Geological Survey Water Supply Paper 2316.

Busacca, A. J. 1991. Loess deposits and soils of the Palouse and vicinity. Pages 216–228 in R. B. Morrison, editor. Quaternary non-glacial geology of the United States. Geology of North America. Volume K-2. Geological Society of America, Boulder, Colorado, USA.

Caldwell, M. M. 1985. Cold desert. Pages 198–212 *in* B. F. Chabot and H. Mooney, editors. Physiological ecology of North American Plant Communities. Chapman and Hall, London, England.

Chapman, V. J. 1966. Vegetation and salinity. Pages 110–130 *in* H. Boyko, editor. Salinity and aridity: new approaches to old problems. Dr. W. Junk Publishers, The Hague.

Comstock, J. P., and J. R. Ehleringer. 1992. Plant adaptation in the Great Basin and Colorado Plateau. Great Basin Naturalist 52:195–215.

Cooper, D. J. 1986. Community structure and classification of Rocky Mountain wetland ecosystems. Pages 66–147 *in* J. T. Windell, B. E. Willard, D. J. Cooper, S. Q. Foster, C. F. Knud-Hansen, L. P. Rink, and G. N. Kiladis, editors. An ecological characterization of Rocky Mountain montane and subalpine wetlands. U.S. Fish and Wildlife Service, Biological Report 86.

Cox, R. R. Jr., and J. A. Kadlec. 1995. Dynamics of potential waterfowl foods in Great Salt Lake marshes during summer. Wetlands 15:1–8.

Crowe, E. A., A. J. Busacca, J. P. Reganold, and B. A. Zamora. 1994. Vegetation zones and soil characteristics in vernal pools in the channeled scabland of eastern Washington. Great Basin Naturalist 54:234–247.

Dahl, T. E. 1990. Wetlands losses in the United States 1780's to 1980's. U.S. Department of Interior, Fish and Wildlife Service, Washington, D.C., USA.

Daubenmire, R. F. 1942. An ecological study of the vegetation of southeastern Washington and adjacent Idaho. Ecological Monograph 12:55–79.

Despain, D. G. 1973. Vegetation of the Big Horn Mountains, Wyoming, in relation to substrate and climate. Ecological Monograph 43:329–355.

Detling, J. K. 1969. Photosynthetic and respiratory response of several halophytes to moisture stress. Dissertation, University of Utah, Salt Lake City, Utah, USA.

Dobrowolski J. P., M. M. Caldwell, and J. H. Richards. 1990. Basin hydrology and plant root systems. Ecological Studies 80:243–292.

Duebbert, H. F. 1969. The ecology of Malheur Lake and management implications. Bureau of Sport Fisheries and Wildlife, U.S. Fish and Wildlife Service, Refuge Leaflet Number 412.

Duffy, C. J., and S. Al-Hassan. 1988. Groundwater circulation in a closed desert basin: topographic scaling and climatic forcing. Water Resources Research 24:1675–1678.

Eakin, T. E., D. Price, and J. R. Harrill. 1976. Summary appraisals of the nation's groundwater resources—Great Basin Region. U.S. Geological Survey Professional Paper 813-G.

Eardley, A. J., V. Gvosdetsky, and R. E. Marsell. 1957. Hydrology of Lake Bonneville and sediments and soils of its basin. Bulletin of the Geological Society of America 68:1141–1201.

Eckert, R. E. Jr., F. F. Peterson, and J. T. Belton. 1986. Relation between ecological range condition and proportion of soil surface types. Journal of Range Management 39:409–414.

Ehleringer, J. 1985. Annuals and perennials of warm deserts. Pages 162–180 *in* B. F. Chabot and H. A. Mooney, editors. Physiological ecology of North American plant communities. Chapman and Hall, New York, New York, USA.

———, S. L. Phillips, W. S. F. Schuster, and D. R. Sandquist. 1991. Differential utilization of summer rains by desert plants. Oecologia 88:430–434.

Fautin, R. W. 1946. Biotic communities of the northern desert shrub biome in western Utah. Ecological Monograph 16:251–310.

Fiero, B. 1986. Geology of the Great Basin. University of Nevada Press, Reno, Nevada, USA.

Flaschka, I., C. W. Stockton, and W. R. Bogess. 1987. Climatic variation and surface water resources in the Great Basin region. Water Resources Bulletin 23:47–57.

Fogel, M. M. 1981. Precipitation in the desert. Pages 219–234 in D. D. Evans and J. L. Thames, editors. Water in desert ecosystems. Dowden, Hutchinson and Ross, Stroudsburg, Pennsylvania, USA.

Foster, J. H., W. E. Tillett, W. L. Myers, and J. C. Hoag. 1984. Columbia Basin wildlife/irrigation development study. Bureau of Reclamation Report Number REC-ERC-83–86.

Fowler, J. F., and N. L. Stanton. 1995. Level of endemism in hanging gardens of the Colorado Plateau. Pages 215–223 in Proceedings of the second biennial conference on research in Colorado Plateau national parks. Transactions and Proceedings Series NPS/NRAU/NRTP-95/11. U.S. Department of the Interior, National Park Service.

Friedman, E. I., and M. Galun. 1974. Desert algae, lichens, and fungi. Pages 165–212 in G. W. Brown, editor. Desert Biology. Volume 2. Academic Press, New York, New York, USA.

Geiger, R. 1959. The climate near the ground. Harvard University Press, Cambridge, Massachusetts, USA.

Godfrey, A. E. 1980. Porphyry weathering in a desert climate. Pages 189–196 in M. D. Picard, editor. Henry Mountains symposium. Utah Geological Association, Salt Lake City, Utah, USA.

Goodwin, R. H., and W. A. Niering. 1975. Inland wetlands of the United States evaluated as potential registered natural landmarks. U.S. Department of Interior, National Park Service, Natural History Theme Study Number 2. Washington, D.C., USA.

Gosselink, J. G., and R. E. Turner. 1978. The role of hydrology in freshwater wetland ecosystems. Pages 63–78 in R. E. Good, editor. Freshwater wetlands: ecological processes and management potential. Academic Press, New York, New York, USA.

Goudie, A. S. 1991. Pans. Progress in Physical Geography 15:221–237.

Hammer, U. T. 1981. Primary production in saline lakes. Hydrobiologia 81:47–57.

———, and J. M. Heseltine. 1988. Aquatic macrophytes in saline lakes of the Canadian prairies. Hydrobiologia 158:101–116.

Hansen, D. J., P. Dayanandan, P. B. Kaufman, and J. D. Brotherson. 1976. Ecological adaptations of the salt marsh grass, Distichlis spicata (Gramineae), and environmental factors affecting its growth and distribution. American Journal of Botany 63:635–650.

Harper, K. T., L. L. St. Clair, K. H. Thorne, and W. M. Hess. 1994. Geologic contrasts of the Great Basin and Colorado Plateau. Pages 1–7 in K. T. Harper, L. L. St. Clair, K. H. Thorne, and W. M. Hess, editors. Natural history of the Colorado Plateau and Great Basin. University Press of Colorado, Niwot, Colorado, USA.

Harris, S. W. 1954. An ecological study of the waterfowl of the potholes area, Grant County, Washington. American Midland Naturalist 52:403–432.

Heath, R. C. 1988. Hydrogeologic setting of regions. Pages 15–23 in W. Back, J. S. Rosenshein, and P. R. Seaber, editors. Volume o-2, Hydrogeology. Geological Society of America, Boulder, Colorado, USA.

Hidy, G. M., and H. E. Klieforth. 1990. Atmospheric processes and the climates of the basin and range. Ecological Studies 80:17–45.

Hood, J. W., and D. J. Patterson. 1984. Bedrock aquifers in the northern San Rafael Swell area, Utah, with special emphasis on the Navajo Sandstone. Utah Department of Natural Resources Technical Publication 78:1–28.

Houghton, J. G. 1969. Characteristics of rainfall in the Great Basin. University of Nevada Desert Research Institute Report, Reno, Nevada, USA.

Howard, R. J., and J. S. Larson. 1985. A stream habitat classification system for beaver. Journal of Wildlife Management 49:19–25.

Hugie, V. K., and H. B. Passey. 1964. Soil surface patterns of some semiarid soils in northern Utah, southern Idaho, and northeastern Nevada. Soil Science Society of America Proceedings 28:786–792.

Hulten, E. 1968. A flora of Alaska and neighboring territories: a manual of the vascular plants. Stanford University Press, Stanford, California, USA.

Hunt, C. B. 1974. Natural regions of the United States and Canada. W. H. Freeman, San Francisco, California, USA.

Irwin-Williams, C. C., C. B. Osmond, A. J. Dansi, and L. F. Pitelka. 1990. Man and plants in the Great Basin. Ecological Studies 80:1–15.

Johnsgard, P. A. 1955. The relation of water level and vegetational change to avian populations, particularly waterfowl. Thesis, Washington State University, Pullman, Washington, USA.

———. 1956. Effects of water fluctuation and vegetation change on bird populations, particularly waterfowl. Ecology 37:689–701.

Johnston, R. S., and R. W. Brown. 1979. Hydrologic aspects related to the management of alpine areas: special management needs of alpine ecosystems. U.S. Department of Agriculture, Forest Service General Technical Report R672.

Judd, B. I. 1972. Vegetation zones around a small pond in the White Mountains of Arizona. Great Basin Naturalist 32:91–96.

Kadlec, J. A. 1982. Mechanisms affecting salinity of Great Salt Lake marshes. American Midland Naturalist 107:82–94.

———, and L. M. Smith. 1984. Marsh plant establishment on newly flooded salt flats. Wildlife Society Bulletin 12:388–394.

———, and W. A. Wentz. 1974. State-of-the-art survey and evaluation of marsh plant establishment techniques: induced and natural. Volume I, Report of Research. USA Coastal Engineering Research Center Final Report.

Kantrud, H. A., J. B. Millar, and A. G. van der Valk. 1989. Vegetation of wetlands of the prairie pothole region. Pages 132–187 in A. G. van der Valk, editor. Northern prairie wetlands. Iowa State University Press, Ames, Iowa, USA.

Kelley, V. C. 1955. Monoclines of the Colorado Plateau. Geological Society of America Bulletin 66:789–804.

Knud-Hansen, C. F. 1986. Ecological processes in Rocky Mountain wetlands. Pages 148–176 in J. T. Windell, B. E. Willard, D. J. Cooper, S. Q. Foster, C. F. Knud-Hansen, L. P. Rink, and G. N. Kiladis, editors. An ecological characterization of Rocky Mountain montane and subalpine wetlands. U.S. Fish and Wildlife Service, Biological Report 86.

Kohler, M. A., T. J. Nordenson, and D. R. Baker. 1959. Evaporation maps for the United States. U.S. Department of Commerce, Weather Bureau Technical Paper 37.

Lamke, R. D., and D. O. Moore. 1965. Interim inventory of surface-water resources of Nevada. Nevada Department of Conservation and Natural Resources Water Resources Bulletin 30:1–49.

Lancaster, J., and G. G. E. Scudder. 1987. Aquatic coleoptera and hemiptera in some Canadian saline lakes: patterns in community structure. Canadian Journal of Zoology 65:1383–1390.

Leaf, C. F. 1975. Watershed management in the Central and Southern Rocky Mountains: a summary of the status of our knowledge by vegetation types. U.S. Department of Agriculture, Forest Service Research Paper RM-142.

Line, G. C. 1979. Hydrology and surface morphology of the Bonneville Salt Flats and Pilot Valley playa, Utah. U.S. Geological Survey Water Supply Paper 2057.

Mabbutt, J. 1979. Desert landforms. Massachusetts Institute of Technology Press, Cambridge, Massachusetts, USA.

MacMahon, J. A. 1988. Warm deserts. Pages 209–230 in M. G. Barbour and D. W. Billings, editors. North American terrestrial vegetation. Cambridge University Press, New York, New York, USA.

Malanson, G. P. 1980. Habitat and plant distributions in hanging gardens of the Narrows, Zion National Park. Great Basin Naturalist 40:178–182.

———, and J. Kay. 1980. Flood frequency and the assemblage of dispersal types in hanging gardens of the Narrows, Zion National Park, Utah. Great Basin Naturalist 40:365–371.

Marr, J. 1967. Ecosystems of the east slope of the Front Range in Colorado. University of Colorado Studies, Biological Series Number 8. University of Colorado Press, Boulder, Colorado, USA.

May, C. L., J. F. Fowler, and N. L. Stanton. 1995. Geomorphology of the hanging gardens of the Colorado Plateau. Proceedings of the second biennial conference on research in Colorado Plateau National Parks. U.S. Department of Interior, National Park Service, Washington, D.C., USA.

McComb, W. C., J. R. Sedell, and T. D. Buchholz. 1990. Dam-site selection by beavers in an eastern Oregon basin. Great Basin Naturalist 50:273–281.

Miller, R. F., F. A. Branson, I. S. McQueen, and C. T. Snyder. 1982. Water relations in soils as related to plant communities in Ruby Valley, Nevada. Journal of Range Management 35:462–468.

Mitsch, W. J., and J. G. Gosselink. 1993. Wetlands. Second edition. Van Nostrand Reinhold, New York, New York, USA.

Neilson, R. P. 1987. Biotic regionalization and climatic controls in western North America. Vegetatio 70:135–147.

Nelson, D. L., and C. F. Tiernan. 1983. Winter injury of sagebrush and other wildland shrubs in the western United States. U.S. Department of Agriculture, Intermountain Forest and Range Experiment Station, Forest Service Research Paper IMT-314.

Nelson, N. F., and R. A. Dietz. 1966. Cattail control methods in Utah. Utah Department of Fish Game Publication 66-2.

Netoff, D. I., B. J. Cooper, and R. R. Shroba. 1995. Giant sandstone weathering pits near Cookie Jar Butte, southeastern Utah. Proceedings of the second biennial conference on research in Colorado Plateau National Parks. U.S. Department of Interior, National Park Service, Washington, D.C., USA.

Ohmart, R. D., and B. W. Anderson. 1979. Wildlife use values of wetlands in the arid southwestern United States. Pages 278–295 in P. E. Greeson, J. R. Clark, and J. E. Clark, editors. Wetland functions and values: the state of our understanding. American Water Resources Association Publication, Minneapolis, Minnesota, USA.

Peterson, F. F. 1981. Landforms of the Basin and Range Province defined for soil survey. Nevada Agricultural Experiment Station Technical Bulletin 28.

Potter, L. D., R. C. Reynolds Jr., and E. T. Louderbough. 1985. Mancos shale and plant community relationships: field observations. Journal of Arid Environment 9: 137–145.

Price, L. W. 1981. Mountains and man: a study of processes and environment. University of California Press, Los Angeles, California, USA.

Ramaley, F. 1942. Vegetation of the San Luis Valley in southern Colorado. University of Colorado Studies, Series D, Volume 1. University of Colorado Press, Boulder, Colorado, USA.

Ratti, J. T., and J. A. Kadlec. 1992. Concept plan for the preservation of wetland habitat of the intermountain west. U.S. Department of Interior, Fish and Wildlife Service, Portland, Oregon, USA.

Rawson, D. S., and J. E. Moore. 1944. The saline lakes of Saskatchewan. Canadian Journal of Research 22:141–201.

Retzer, J. L. 1962. Soil survey of the Fraser alpine area, Colorado. U.S. Forest Service and Soil Conservation Service Serial Paper 20.

Richmond, G. M. 1960. Glaciation of the east slope of Rocky Mountain National Park, Colorado. Geological Society of America Bulletin 71:1371–1382.

Rink, L. P., and G. N. Kiladis. 1986. Geology, hydrology, climate, and soils of the Rocky Mountains. Pages 42–65 in J. T. Windell, B. E. Willard, D. J. Cooper, S. Q. Foster, C. F. Knud-Hansen, L. P. Rink, and G. N. Kiladis, editors. An ecological characterization of Rocky Mountain montane and subalpine wetlands. U.S. Fish and Wildlife Service, Biological Report 86.

Shimer, J. A. 1972. Field guide to landforms in the United States. Macmillan, New York, New York, USA.

Shreve, F. 1942. The desert vegetation of North America. Botanical Review 8: 195–246.

———, and T. D. Mallery. 1933. The relation of caliche to desert plants. Soil Science 35:99–113.

Skougard, M. G., and J. D. Brotherson. 1979. Vegetational response to three environmental gradients in the salt playa near Goshen, Utah County, Utah. Great Basin Naturalist 39:44–58.

Slough, B. G., and R. M. F. S. Sadlier. 1977. A land capability classification system for beaver (Castor canadensis Kuhl). Canadian Journal of Zoology 55:1324–1335.

Smith, L. M., and J. A. Kadlec. 1983. Seed banks and their role during drawdown of a North American marsh. Journal of Applied Ecology 20:673–684.

———, and———. 1984. Effects of prescribed burning on nutritive quality of marsh plants in Utah. Journal of Wildlife Management 48:285–288.

———, and———. 1985a. Predictions of vegetation change following fire in a Great Salt Lake marsh. Aquatic Botany 21:43–51.

———, and———. 1985b. Fire and herbivory in a Great Salt Lake marsh. Ecology 66: 259–265.

Smith, S. D., and R. S. Nowak. 1990. Ecophysiology of plants in the intermountain lowlands. Ecological Studies 80:179–241.

Snyder, C. T. 1962. A hydrologic classification of valleys in the Great Basin, western United States. Bulletin of the International Association of Scientific Hydrology 7:53–59.

Spence, J. R., and N. R. Henderson. 1993. Tinaja and hanging garden vegetation of Capitol Reef National Park, southern Utah, USA. Journal of Arid Environment 24: 21–36.

Steila, D. 1976. The geography of soils. Prentice Hall, Englewood Cliffs, New Jersey, USA.

Stewart, R. E., and H. A. Kantrud. 1972. Vegetation of prairie potholes, North Dakota, in relation to quality of water and other environmental factors. U.S. Geological Survey Professional Paper 585-D.

Taylor, O. J., and J. W. Hood. 1988. Region 3, Colorado Plateau and Wyoming basins. Pages 51–58 in W. Back, J. S. Rosenshein, and P. R. Seaber, editors. Hydrogeology. Volume 0-2. Geological Society of America, Boulder, Colorado, USA.

Thornbury, W. D. 1965. Regional geomorphology of the United States. John Wiley and Sons, New York, New York, USA.

Tones, P. I. 1976. Factors influencing selected littoral fauna in saline lakes in Saskatchewan. Thesis, University of Saskatchewan, Saskatoon, Canada.

Trent, J. D., R. R. Blank, and J. A. Young. 1997. Ecophysiology of the temperate desert halophytes: *Allenrolfea occidentalis* and *Sarcobatus vermiculatus*. Great Basin Naturalist 57:57–65.

Twidale, C. R. 1982. Granite landforms. Elsevier Scientific, New York, New York, USA.

―――, and J. A. Bourne. 1975. Episodic exposure of inselbergs. Geological Society of America Bulletin 86:1473–1481.

Ungar, I. A. 1974. Halophyte communities of Park County, Colorado. Bulletin of the Torrey Botanical Club 101:145–152.

―――, W. Hogan, and M. McClelland. 1969. Plant communities of saline soils at Lincoln, Nebraska. American Midland Naturalist 82:564–577.

Wagner, F. H. 1980. Integrating and control mechanisms in arid and semi-arid ecosystems—considerations for impact assessment. Proceedings of a symposium on the biological evaluation of environmental impact. Council on Environmental Quality and U.S. Department of Interior, FWS-OBS 80/26.

Ward, P. 1968. Fire in relation to waterfowl habitat of Delta marshes. Proceedings of the Tall Timbers fire ecology conference 8:255–267.

Weber, W. A. 1976. Rocky Mountain flora. Colorado University Press, Boulder, Colorado, USA.

Welsh, S. L. 1978. Problems in plant endemism on the Colorado Plateau. Great Basin Naturalist Memoirs 2:191–195.

West, N. E. 1981. Nutrient cycling in desert ecosystems. Pages 301–324 in D. A. Goodall and R. A. Perry, editors. Arid land ecosystems: structure functioning and management. Volume 2. Cambridge University Press, New York, New York, USA.

―――, editor. 1983. Temperate deserts and semi-deserts. Volume 5 of Ecosystems of the world. Volume 5. Elsevier Scientific, New York, New York, USA.

Wetzel, R. G. 1983. Limnology. W. B. Saunders, New York, New York, USA.

Whitford, W. G. 1986. Decomposition and nutrient cycling in deserts. Pages 93–116 in W. G. Whitford, editor. Pattern and process in desert ecosystems. University of New Mexico Press, Albuquerque, New Mexico, USA.

Whittaker, R. H., and C. W. Fairbanks. 1958. A study of plankton copepod communities in the Columbia Basin, southeastern Washington. Ecology 39:46–65.

Willard, B. E. 1979. Plant sociology of alpine tundra, Trail Ridge, Rocky Mountain National Park, Colorado. Colorado School of Mines Quarterly 74:1–119.

Williams, J. D., and C. K. Dodd Jr. 1979. Importance of wetlands to endangered and threatened species. Pages 565–575 in P. E. Greeson, J. R. Clark, and J. E. Clark, editors. Wetland functions and values: the state of our understanding. American Water Resources Association Publication, Minneapolis, Minnesota, USA.

Williams, R. M. 1965. Beaver habitat and management. Idaho Wildlife Review 17: 3–17.

Williams, W. D. 1985. Biotic adaptations in temporary lentic waters, with special reference to those in semi-arid and arid regions. Hydrobiologia 125:85–110.

Windell, J. T., B. E. Willard, and S. Q. Foster. 1986. Introduction to Rocky Mountain wetlands. Pages 1–41 in J. T. Windell, B. E. Willard, D. J. Cooper, S. Q. Foster, C. F. Knud-Hansen, L. P. Rink, and G. N. Kiladis, editors. An ecological characterization of Rocky Mountain montane and subalpine wetlands. U.S. Fish and Wildlife Service, Biological Report 86.

Wollheim, W. M., and J. R. Lovvorn. 1996. Effects of macrophyte growth forms on invertebrate communities in saline lakes of the Wyoming High Plains. Hydrobiologia 323:83–96.

Wright, H. E. Jr. 1983. The Late Pleistocene. Volume 1 of Late-Quaternary environments of the United States. S. C. Porter, editor. University of Minnesota Press, Minneapolis, Minnesota, USA.

Wurtsbaugh, W. A. 1992. Food-web modification by an invertebrate predator in the Great Salt Lake (USA). Oecologia 89:168–175.

Young, J. A., and R. A. Evans. 1986. Erosion and deposition of fine sediments from playas. Journal of Arid Environment 10:103–115.

CHAPTER 3

Ecological Processes of Riverine Wetland Habitats

WAYNE A. HUBERT

Introduction

Riparian and wetland habitats of riverine systems are links between terrestrial and aquatic systems (Malanson 1993). They have high water tables because of their proximity to streams (Allen-Diaz 1991, Stromberg and Tiller 1996), but downhill and lateral movements of surface and subsurface water are the main forces that organize and regulate the functioning of riverine riparian and wetland habitats (Brown et al. 1979, Graf 1988). Riverine riparian habitats have been viewed as ecotones, or environmental gradients, between terrestrial and aquatic habitats. Over time, these habitats have features of both terrestrial and aquatic systems. Overall, riverine riparian habitats are flooded frequently, but the soil is seldom saturated with water for long periods of time. Wetlands adjacent to streams are also flooded frequently, but they remain flooded for longer periods and soils remain saturated most of the time. Occasionally flooded riparian habitats and frequently flooded wetlands are not markedly different because they are on a continuum. Understanding the hydrology of riverine systems and interrelated erosion, sediment transport, sediment deposition, and channel movement is necessary in comprehending the dynamics of riverine riparian areas and associated wetlands in the Intermountain West.

Water

Riparian and wetland habitats along riverine systems are substantially influenced by the hydrologic cycle, the evaporation of water from oceans, lakes, and streams, accumulation and movement of the water in the atmosphere, and subsequent return of water to the surface of the earth as precipitation. The hydrologic cycle can be modeled (Wesche 1993) as

$$P = R + E_T + S$$

where P = precipitation, R = streamflow or total water yield, E_T = water loss by evaporation, and S = change in storage or that portion of the precipitation that is retained or lost from storage in the earth's mantle. This equation can be rearranged to represent the factors affecting streamflow as

$$R = P - E_T - S$$

This model is applicable to understanding factors affecting riverine riparian and wetland habitats in the Intermountain West.

Throughout the Intermountain West there is substantial variation in the amount and form of precipitation that reaches the earth's surface as a result of variation in the topography of the land. Elevation varies from mountain peaks >3,000 m above sea level to intermountain basins and plains with elevations <1,000 m. Annual precipitation tends to increase with elevation, while temperature declines. Mountains can receive >100 cm of precipitation each year, mostly in the form of snow. High-elevation mountain streams are influenced by relatively high amounts of precipitation, but water loss by evaporation is relatively low, and there is little soil within the floodplain in which water can be stored, so streamflows are high relative to the area of the watersheds.

Despite the abundance of mountains in the Intermountain West, most of the region lies in basins where precipitation is limited by the rain-shadow effect of the nearby mountains. These basins are generally arid, with <15 cm of annual precipitation, or semiarid, with 15–30 cm. The precipitation that does occur is often the result of monsoonal airflow from the Gulf of California and comes as afternoon thundershowers during the summer. Intermountain basins and plains also tend to have low humidity due to low precipitation, so annual evapotranspiration rates are high, exceeding annual precipitation rates. Additionally, relatively constant and strong winds over most basins increase the effects of the dryness. Consequently, streams in arid to semiarid basins receive relatively low amounts of precipitation and lose much water to evaporation and percolation into sedimentary soils of the floodplain; thus, streamflows are low relative to the areas of the watersheds. Because of the limited number of streams that maintain relatively continuous or perennial flows in intermountain basins, riparian and wetland habitats are widely dispersed across the landscape.

Most river systems in the Intermountain West originate in mountains where there is heavy snow accumulation, but they flow from the mountains onto dryland areas. Consequently, these rivers are allogenic, rising in well-watered areas and flowing for long distances through arid or semiarid basins that contribute little runoff (Walker et al. 1995). As a result, the annual hydrograph or pattern of streamflow (discharge) is

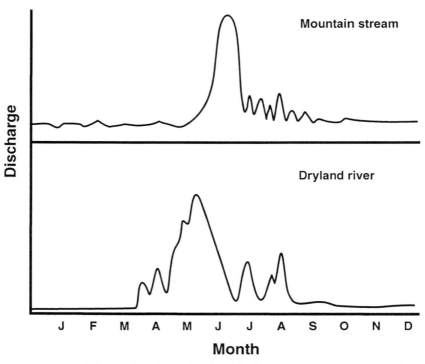

FIGURE 3.1. Typical annual hydrographs of a high-elevation mountain stream and an allogenic basin (dryland) river

greatly affected by melting snow in spring and early summer, with peak annual flows at that time (Figure 3.1). Allogenic dryland rivers are hydrologically distinct in several ways (Molles et al. 1992): (1) responses to variations in precipitation tend to be nonlinear, compared with near-linear responses in well-watered (mesic) watersheds; (2) annual discharge may decrease with basin area, whereas it increases in mesic watersheds; (3) seasonal and long-term flow is strongly influenced by climatic variation, such as El Niño–Southern Oscillation (ENSO); and (4) there may be little or no correlation between summer precipitation and runoff. Flow regimes of dryland rivers do not tend to exhibit regular annual patterns, but trends appear at longer scales corresponding with climate variations such as ENSO. Nevertheless, recurring flood and drought events occur among dryland rivers and affect associated riparian areas.

In mountainous headwater streams, watersheds are small, slopes are steep, and the channels have high gradients that are constrained by bedrock (Brinson 1990). This results in predominantly V-shaped valleys with shallow soils and little or no stream-deposited or alluvial material.

Where floodplains are narrow and alluvium is not abundant, there is little capacity for the floodplain to store water overflowing from the channel during high water. Orographic, or mountain-induced, rains or snow result in short, intense precipitation events that contribute pulses of higher streamflow during the summer (Figure 3.1). As a result of the limited water storage and orographic precipitation events, hydrographs of small mountain streams show sharp and frequent peaks, particularly during the summer. Because floodplain inundation is irregular, adaptive strategies of plants in these riparian systems are not coupled to the flood regime (Junk et al. 1989).

At the foot of the mountains where steep mountain streams begin to flow onto flat basins, depositional areas of gravel and cobble form. These reaches are characterized by multiple channels flowing among unstable islands and bars formed from alluvium. In the most unstable upstream sections, the islands and bars are transient, lacking permanent vegetation. More downstream sections tend to be stabilized by vegetation. Due to the location of these reaches in the watershed and the porous channel substrate, surface flows are quite variable.

In the basins beyond the foot of the mountains, streams occur on floodplains formed from deep alluvial deposits. These reaches are often characterized by single, meandering channels with riparian vegetation in the floodplain. Where alluvium is deep and wide, it serves as a recipient of water from the channel at high flows and, subsequently, stores water for release into the channel at low flows (Figure 3.2). Prolonged runoff from melting snow in the mountains often results in hydrographs with peak flows of a relatively long duration from spring through early summer (Figure 3.1). Storage of water in the floodplain contributes to flow throughout the rest of the year.

In areas of the Intermountain West where streams originate in relatively low mountain ranges or within intermountain basins, there is little snow accumulation in headwater areas to provide high spring flows and water for storage in the floodplain for later release into the channel during low-flow periods. Consequently, surface flows in these streams may occur when snow melts or following summer thunderstorms, but flows tend to be relatively low and generally disappear by mid- to late summer, except when thunderstorms provide periods of brief runoff.

These differing patterns of streamflow and storage of water in floodplains affect the extent and composition of riparian habitats that occur over the Intermountain West, with the most extensive habitats in areas with the most consistent flows. Patches of riparian habitats occur along streams where flows are less consistent.

The river continuum concept (Vannote et al. 1980, Minshall et al. 1985) is useful in defining physical and biological changes over the length

Flood flows

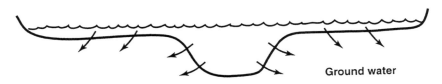

Ground water

Low flows

Water table

FIGURE 3.2. Cross section of a river channel and alluvial floodplain illustrating movement of water between the surface and ground at flood flows and low flows

of a river system. Systematic changes in the influence of riparian vegetation on biological productivity, relative contributions of allochthonous and autochthonous sources of energy, and invertebrate and fish assemblages occur with downstream progression in stream systems. The insight into connectivity over the length of a river system, as well as the connection between the river and floodplain, that this concept provides currently governs most of the theory on the dynamics of riparian and wetland habitats of riverine systems (Poff et al. 1997, Miranda and Raborn 2000).

Sediment

Erosion is a natural process whereby upland areas are gradually worn away by wind and water. Eroded material is moved downhill and eventually becomes deposited as sediment in intermountain basins, lakes, or oceans. The process of erosion, sediment transport, and sediment deposition has substantial bearing on the formation of riverine riparian habitats in the Intermountain West.

Most of the movement of eroded material into intermountain basins is the result of the movement of water, and this process is accelerated by the arid and semiarid climate over much of the Intermountain West. Vegetation serves to slow the movement of water and to anchor soil, but the lack of precipitation leads to sparse vegetative cover and accelerated erosion rates when precipitation events occur. Most of the erosion occurs in association with runoff from melting snow or afternoon thundershowers during the summer.

Within stream channels, most erosion, sediment transport, and deposition of sediment occur during high-flow events when stream power is the highest. Stream power is the rate at which a stream does work (Wesche 1993). It is usually defined in English units as

$$\omega = \gamma \, D \, V \, S$$

where ω = stream power (pounds per foot of channel width per second), γ = specific weight of water (62.4 lb/ft^3), D = mean depth of the water (ft), V = mean velocity of the water (ft/sec), and S = channel slope (ft of drop/ft of channel length). As streamflow increases, both stream power and sediment carrying capacity increase. Stream power is also a function of channel slope, with sediment-carrying capacity increasing with channel slope. Since streamflow varies over time, there is temporal variation in stream power and sediment transport. Material is eroded and transported primarily on the rising limb of the hydrograph, and sediment is deposited on the falling limb. Banks erode and pools are scoured as discharge increases, and sediment accumulates in slow-moving areas, such as the inside of bends, as discharge decreases.

Since water depth, water velocity, and channel slope vary over the length of a stream, stream power varies spatially. Consequently, some locations in a stream (sites with faster water or higher channel slope) can more readily move sediment, whereas other locations (sites with slower water or lower channel slope) do not have as high a capability and tend to be the locations of sediment deposition.

The ability to transport sediment is evident among streams in the Intermountain West. High-gradient mountain streams have the capability to move a large amount of sediment, in terms of both volume and size of the sediment particles, because of their high stream power. Low-gradient basin streams do not have sufficient stream power to move much of the sediment carried to them from upstream high-gradient reaches, so these reaches become locations for sediment deposition (Lyons et al. 1992).

Given the dynamics of sediment movement and deposition, streams generally establish a state of dynamic equilibrium. At any specific location in a stream with a given discharge and channel slope, sediment movement becomes balanced so the channel form is relatively constant over time. This dynamic equilibrium is illustrated by Lane's mass balance model (Figure 3.3, derived from Lane 1955). With a given sediment load and water discharge, a constant size of sediment particles in the system, and a specific channel slope, the stream remains in balance with no

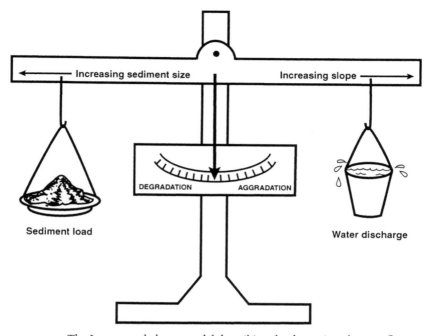

FIGURE 3.3. The Lane mass balance model describing the dynamics of streamflow, sediment movements, and channel slope associated with stream channels (after Lane 1955)

degradation or aggradation of the channel. However, if any of these parameters changes, the dynamic equilibrium is upset, and channel changes will result. A variety of human alterations to a watershed (dams, cattle grazing, irrigation, etc.) can alter the dynamic equilibrium and affect the dynamics of riverine riparian habitats (Kellerhals et al. 1979, Miller et al. 1985, Gribb and Brosz 1990, Henszey et al. 1991, Davies et al. 1992, Kearsley et al. 1994).

Suspended sediments settle from water when the velocity declines. Under flood conditions, the discharge frequently exceeds the capacity of the stream channel, and water flows across a portion of the valley known as the floodplain (Figure 3.2). As the water spreads out across the floodplain, it slows down and releases suspended sediments relatively evenly to form a somewhat flat surface of fine material (Allen 1965). This process of floodplain building contributes to the dynamics of riparian habitats. Floodplain building fills in existing wetlands but at the same time contributes nutrients that enhance plant productivity. The rate of deposition of material on the floodplain is a function of the frequency and magnitude of flooding as well as the concentration of suspended sediments in floodwaters. The relatively frequent inundation of floodplains and large amounts of sediment transported by many rivers in the Intermountain West cause relatively rapid changes in riparian habitats.

Meander Process

Most stream channels are continually changing position and shape as a consequence of hydraulic forces acting on the stream beds and banks (Langbein and Leopold 1966, Leopold and Wolman 1966, Hasfurther 1985). Stream channels tend to be straight, braided, meandering, or a combination of these classes (Figure 3.4). The type of channel is determined by channel slope, sediment loads and movements, and discharge. Straight channels tend to occur in mountains or narrow valleys where the channel slope is high and bedrock confines the movement of the channel. Braided channels tend to occur where the channel slope declines downstream from high-gradient reaches, such as at the base of a mountain. Transported sediments are deposited in these areas, causing the streambed to aggrade and form many small channels. Meandering channels tend to occur in low-gradient reaches flowing across valleys or basins filled with alluvial deposits. In low-gradient stream reaches where the valley is relatively wide and a substantial floodplain occurs, the meander process is pronounced (Gay et al. 1998). The most extensive riverine riparian habitats of the Intermountain West are associated with perennially flowing streams that exhibit meandering channels. The meander process is a major, common causative agent in the formation of riverine riparian habitats.

A meandering channel is a single channel that curves in an S-shaped waveform when viewed from the air, occurs on a floodplain formed by alluvial deposits, and is able to move without the constraints of geological controls in the form of bedrock or rock outcroppings (Figure 3.4). The S-shaped meanders tend to move laterally back and forth across the floodplain and to migrate down the valley over geologic time. Where the downstream movement of floodplain deposits are in balance with the transport and deposition of alluvium from upstream, stream channels continue to meander and the morphological features of the floodplain change as a result. The meander rate varies with stream size and the extent of riparian vegetation that stabilizes the stream bank (Gay et al. 1998). In mountain meadows where streams are small and extensive growths of willows and sedges stabilize the banks, the meander process is slow, with movements of only a few centimeters each year. However, along larger streams in arid basins where there may be little riparian vegetation to stabilize the outside of meander bends, the meander process can be quite rapid, with the stream bank moving several meters in a year. Wolman and Miller

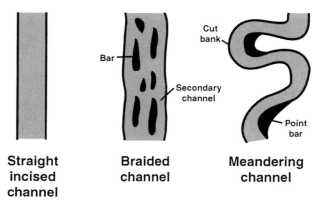

Straight   **Braided**   **Meandering**
incised   **channel**   **channel**
channel

FIGURE 3.4. Examples of straight, braided, and meandering
stream channels and their associated stability

(1960) found that bankfull discharge was the most effective discharge
level controlling the meander process. Bankfull discharge is the maximum streamflow that can be accommodated within the channel without overtopping the banks and spreading onto the floodplain (Armantrout 1998). Bankfull discharge is attained every 2–3 years on average in
mesic regions and less frequently in dryland areas. Nevertheless, channel shape and the floodplain are influenced by a force of moderate magnitude that occurs relatively frequently.

The meander process leads to the formation of topographic features
important to the formation of diverse riparian habitats. Some typical
topographic features include natural levees adjacent to the channel that
contain coarser materials deposited during flooding, ridges and swales
created by abandoned point bar deposits as the channel migrates (Figure 3.5), point bars on the inside of river bends where deposition is rapid,
and oxbow lakes that are relict meander bends that have been cut off
(Brinson 1990). Levees support riparian vegetation because they flood
frequently but drain rapidly. Ridges and swales support different types
of riparian vegetation because of the relative distance between the soil
surface and the water table. Because of the rapid deposition of sediment
and wet conditions on point bars, they are colonized by invading species
such as cottonwoods and initiate successional development of riparian
vegetation. Oxbow depressions are frequently or continually flooded and
have saturated soils, so they support wetland vegetation.

Over geologic time, the meander process causes the stream channel
to migrate back and forth across the floodplain, forming a diverse array
of riparian habitats within the floodplain. For example, as cottonwood

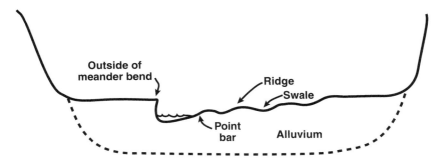

FIGURE 3.5. Cross section of a river channel and alluvial floodplain at the location of a point bar illustrating ridge-and-swale topography

forests growing on concave banks are undercut and lost to erosion, primary succession is initiated on point bars formed in increments on the inside of bends (Johnson et al. 1976, Reily and Johnson 1982, Bradley and Smith 1986, Rood and Mahoney 1990). Deposited seeds of annual and woody plants germinate on the point bars, and seedlings grow to stabilize the bars. With the next flood cycle, additional late-succession mature forest is lost to erosion, but more rejuvenation occurs on newly created point bars. As the elevation of point bars is raised by sediment deposition, the surviving saplings are less likely to be adversely affected by flooding. Patches of riparian plants at numerous stages of development subsequently occur on floodplains, creating multiple successional stages and a mosaic of riparian habitat types across the alluvial floodplain.

In the Intermountain West, variation in climate as well as tectonic activity has led to nonsteady-state conditions in many watersheds over geologic time, causing periodic aggradation or degradation of alluvial valleys and basins. For example, following cold glacial periods, erosion was enhanced when the glaciers melted. Eroded material from upland areas was frequently deposited in valleys at a rapid rate, and the material built up to raise the elevation of the stream channel and floodplain. As conditions stabilized, less material was deposited and sediment was exported from the valley, leading to downcutting of the channel. Eventually a dynamic equilibrium returned. As a result of repeated episodes of this nature, many rivers in the Intermountain West have a modern floodplain and a series of terraces representing the remnants of ancient floodplains. The terraces play a role in maintaining modern streamflows and riparian areas by trapping water that eventually returns to streams via the ground.

Meander dynamics create an array of habitats on the floodplain (Ward and Stanford 1995a). The valley of a typical alluvial river reach consists of the following topographic features (Leopold et al. 1964; Welcomme 1979, 1985; Mitsch and Gosselink 1993): (1) hillslopes forming the sides of the valley; (2) 1 or more levels of terraces, remnants of abandoned floodplains at higher elevations; (3) active floodplains (inundated frequently); (4) natural levees that form along the river channel from coarser sediment deposited as water velocity abruptly decreases when the river overtops its banks; (5) meander scrolls, the ridge-and-swale topography on the floodplain surface, that are formed by a series of progressively older levees (ridges) of abandoned meander bends and the depressions (swales) between them (levees and therefore ridges are usually the highest points on the active floodplain and are composed of coarse, well-drained soils); (6) natural drainage channels that breach the levees, forming connections between the floodplain and the river channel; and (7) permanent and temporary floodplain water bodies in various stages of hydrarch succession (Mitsch and Gosselink 1993).

Meander dynamics create an array of lotic and lentic habitats on the floodplain (Ward and Stanford 1995a). These include the main river and its side channels, cut-off side channels, and oxbows that retain connection to the active channel throughout the year, as well as cut-off side channels and oxbows that are disconnected from surface flows in the main channel much of the time. The extent of connectedness to surface flows in the river channel and the frequencies of inundation affect the dynamics of the various habitats.

Floodplains

Floodplain habitats are differentially influenced by groundwater dynamics (Marmonier et al. 1992, Stanford and Ward 1993, Ward and Palmer 1994, Ward and Stanford 1995a). Throughout an alluvial floodplain, the relatively porous soils can become saturated with water during flood events or during high flows when water moves laterally from the river channel into the soil of the floodplain (Figure 3.2). During low streamflows the stored groundwater moves laterally and down the valley, with some return to the river channel to maintain streamflows. The availability and movement of groundwater within a floodplain enables riparian and wetland vegetation to thrive. However, the level of the water table varies temporally and spatially as a function of distance from the stream channel, time elapsed since the stream has risen or fallen, geometry of the river meander and valley walls, and composition of the alluvium (Granneman and Sharp 1979). Groundwater flows and the temporal and spatial variation in groundwater are very important in structuring riparian and wetland habitats of the Intermountain West.

Lateral water movement is an important force that organizes and regulates the function of riparian habitats, including their biogeochemical cycles and their role in the landscape (Brown et al. 1979). Flows of rivers in the Intermountain West are generally maintained by precipitation in the mountains outside of the area where the river flows, so their relation with groundwater generally is influent, i.e., water moves from the surface flow of the river into the ground (Figure 3.2). Many streams with intermittent or ephemeral surface flows can provide groundwater needed to maintain riparian vegetation.

Floods

Infrequent, catastrophic floods are very important in changing channel and floodplain morphometry through massive erosion and deposition of sediment (Brinson 1990, Poff et al. 1997, Gray 1998, Sparks and Spink 1998). However, more frequent floods do not have the power to alter the structural features of most floodplains. Flood power and frequency of inundation are inversely proportional and exist in a continuum from high-power, low-frequency floods that affect the whole floodplain to low-power, high-frequency floods that influence only lower elevations of the floodplain. High-power, low-frequency floods determine patterns of the large geomorphic features that persist on the order of hundreds to thousands of years. Medium-power, intermediate-frequency floods determine patterns of ecosystem structure that have lifetimes of tens to hundreds of years. Low-power, high-frequency floods that occur almost annually determine short-term patterns such as seed germination and seedling survival. Wolman and Leopold (1957) reported that floodplains of rivers flowing through diverse physiographic and climatic regions are typically inundated by channel overspill about once each year. However, predictable flood patterns are less evident in arid and semiarid regions of the Intermountain West.

Nutrient-rich alluvial soils result from inundation of the floodplain and seasonal flooding. Nutrients and water availability contribute to high rates of biological productivity common among riparian habitats. Nutrient limitations have not been demonstrated in riparian areas of arid regions where water stress commonly occurs (Brinson 1990).

Vegetation growing on a floodplain contributes to sediment deposition and dynamics of the floodplain. Vegetation reduces the water velocity, allowing sediment to be deposited and water to infiltrate the soil (Abt et al. 1994, Pearce et al. 1997), and it increases resistance to erosion (Dunaway et al. 1994, Swanson and Myer 1994).

Six soil features are critical in determining suitability of a site for a particular plant species: water infiltration rate, soil depth, water-holding capacity, salinity, fertility, and aeration. Infiltration rate is the rate at which water percolates into the soil; it is important where evaporation is high. Coarse-textured soils, such as those deposited at the edge of the channel on natural levees, have high infiltration capacities (Noy-Meyer 1973, Sala et al. 1988). Soil conditions can also range to highly organic silts with low infiltration capacity (Ward and Stanford 1995a). Soil depth is the depth of alluvial soils accumulated on a floodplain. Water-holding capacity is a function of soil depth, soil texture, and the amount of organic matter. Fine-textured soils, such as silts and clays, hold more water per unit volume than coarse-textured soils. Soil aeration is determined by soil texture and the depth of the water table. Aeration is important to riparian plants because air spaces in the soil determine oxygen availability for root transportation; however, obligate wetland plants thrive in saturated, anaerobic soil. Saline soils have concentrations of soluble salts that produce an electrical conductivity of 4 dS/m or more (Branson et al. 1967, 1970, 1976) and are common in the Intermountain West. All of these dynamics produce patches of aerobic and anaerobic soils on the floodplain that differ in nutrient dynamics.

Junk et al. (1989) developed the flood pulse concept, which provides a theoretical framework for analyzing predictable flooding patterns on floodplains of large rivers. The concept refers to the floodplain surface as an aquatic/terrestrial transition zone (ATTZ) to emphasize the importance of alternating dry and wet phases in driving productivity and habitat diversity. Inundation of the floodplain results in a moving littoral zone that traverses the floodplain from the river channel to the uplands, affecting sediment deposition and nutrient cycling. The role of this natural disturbance in maintaining ecological integrity of the floodplain is evident (Junk et al. 1989, Duncan 1993, Ward and Stanford 1995a).

In arid and semiarid drainages of the Intermountain West where river flows are highly variable, the flood pulse concept may be more complex due to variations in flood magnitude, timing, duration, and rates of rise and fall (Walker et al. 1995). The dynamics of the ATTZ differ from floodplain streams with more predictable hydrological patterns in humid tropical and temporal regions, but the flood pulse concept can be a useful model for dryland rivers. Because dryland rivers experience less frequent flooding, their dynamics are slower, but they still exhibit similar patterns to more flood-prone rivers. Floodplain topography is still a function of meander processes and severe flood frequencies. Riparian plant dynamics are still dependent on deposition of sediment, nutrients, organic material, and maintenance of the water table that are the result of more frequent, less severe flood events. The flood pulse concept still accounts for the lateral linkages within the floodplain, but flood pulses on dryland streams are not as regular as in mesic watersheds.

Vegetation

In arid drainages of the Intermountain West, riparian vegetation provides a stark contrast to the water-stressed desert, chaparral, and grassland communities of upland areas. Species in riparian habitats include those that are confined to moist areas, as well as some that can survive under drier upland conditions (Campbell and Green 1968). Riparian habitats constitute a small portion of the total land area in watersheds of the Intermountain West, but they are generally the most productive habitats due to the availability of water (Brinson et al. 1981). As a result of hydrologic processes, disturbance and environmental gradients structure riverine riparian and wetland communities in the Intermountain West.

Longitudinal gradients

Variation in riparian community structure occurs with progression from high-elevation mountain streams to low-elevation rivers. For example, among streams in Wyoming (Knight 1994) high-elevation riparian areas adjacent to small streams are dominated by several species of willows and sedges. At lower elevations where streams are wider, they tend to have a slightly different and more diverse array of willow species and other shrubs. In riparian areas further downstream within the mountains, alder and tall willow species become dominant. With progression into the foothills, narrowleaf cottonwood becomes the predominant woody plant, with willows, aspens, and a variety of conifers along the riparian area. Riparian habitats along streams and rivers on the plains are generally tree-dominated woodlands. In the eastern lowlands of Wyoming, plains cottonwoods predominate, but ash, boxelder, lanceleaf cottonwood, and peachleaf willow commonly occur along with a variety of shrubs. Similar patterns occur throughout the Intermountain West, with variation in species over the region (Brinson 1990).

Among streams of similar size at similar elevations, the extent of streamflow affects riparian plant community structure. Differences in riparian vegetation occur between perennial and ephemeral streams as well as among ephemeral streams in arid regions (Zimmerman 1969). Floodplain vegetation ranges from canopy forests of deciduous trees along perennial streams to scattered shrubs or no vegetation along some ephemeral streams. Among ephemeral streams there can be a wide range of vegetation, depending on the amount and timing of water delivered to a particular site along a stream.

Lateral gradients

The major distinction between riparian and wetland habitats is based on the extent and duration of water-saturated soils. For example, in plains grassland regions, 3 forest types have been distinguished in floodplains based on the frequency of flooding (Keammerer et al. 1975, Johnson et al. 1976). The lowest and most frequently flooded areas have few tree species other than cottonwoods and willows, and the trees are small (6–12 m tall). In higher, less frequently flooded areas, older cottonwoods form a canopy over boxelder and oak. At the highest elevations, the community is dominated by a mix of boxelder, oak, ash, and elm. A similar pattern has been described in eastern Colorado along the Arkansas and South Platte Rivers (Lindauer 1983). Cottonwoods are common throughout, but willows dominate in areas that remain moist throughout the year.

On floodplains in arid regions, plants that can tolerate periods of drought and withstand flooding by extending roots to the water table (phreatophytes) are most likely to survive. Evapotranspiration by phreatophytes in arid areas during summer and early fall can frequently exceed infiltration of water into the soil from the stream and uplands (Bell and Johnson 1974). Seedlings of most flood-tolerant species grow best under saturated soil conditions, so they are susceptible to water stress when low soil moisture occurs seasonally or during droughts (Hosner et al. 1965). Treeless areas are commonly found on floodplains where there is insufficient soil moisture. The frequency and duration of droughts affect the composition of plant communities in riverine riparian and wetland habitats. Depending on their life history characteristics and degree of flood tolerance, specific species are distributed within boundaries delineated by hydroperiod, which includes flood frequency, duration, magnitude, and timing (Yin 1998).

Kusler and Kentula (1990) noted that a gap in our knowledge of wetland dynamics is the hydrologic needs of plants, particularly minimum groundwater depths and duration of the period of groundwater availability needed for individual species. While this has been recognized for some time (Bryan 1928), little work has been done (Auble et al. 1994, Stromberg and Tiller 1996). Recently, Henszey et al. (1994) defined depth-to-groundwater needs of riparian species in mountain meadows to serve as measures of groundwater needs and the influence of groundwater on community structure. Similarly, Yeager (1996) identified different critical groundwater hydroperiods for different species from mountain meadows.

The dynamic nature of alluvial floodplain rivers is a function of flow and sediment regimes interacting with the physiographic features and vegetation cover across the landscape (Ward and Stanford 1995a). During periodic or seasonal inundation of the floodplain, a moving littoral zone transverses and interconnects habitat patches. The extent of flooding and connectivity determines successional patterns and habitat hetero-geneity. These dynamics are responsible for maintaining the ecological processes of floodplain river systems and their associated riparian habi-tats. Flow regulation and other anthropogenic impacts (flood-control lev-ees, channelization, river training structures, etc.) alter flood frequency and duration, sediment transport and deposition, channel migration, water table dynamics, rejuvenation and succession of plant communi-ties, and the mosaic of riparian habitat patches across the floodplain (Si-mons 1979; Williams and Wolman 1984; Snyder and Miller 1991, 1992; Bray 1996).

Floodplain plant communities are disturbance-dependent, relying on flooding and fluvial dynamics to maintain them (Ward and Stanford 1995a). Pinay et al. (1990) stated that such instability maintains the overall stability of a riparian system. To survive in a floodplain envi-ronment, plant species must be able to tolerate periods of anaerobic con-ditions caused by inundation during the growing season. Three inter-acting processes—sediment deposition, plant community succession, and river meandering—form the mosaic patterns of vegetation on flood-plains.

Fire is another factor causing variation in plant community structure along riparian corridors of low-elevation rivers. Though more moist than uplands, the dense herbaceous biomass along streams is flammable in the fall (Knight 1994). Trees are often killed by inevitable fires, lead-ing to formation of shrublands.

Exotic species

Numerous exotic species of riparian and wetland plants have been in-troduced by humans. Salt cedar and Russian olive are most notewor-thy in the Intermountain West. These species are causing substantial changes in riparian communities, especially those naturally dominated by cottonwoods and willows (Akashi 1988). Exotic plants often do not do well when the hydrologic regime has strong interannual variation (Stromberg 1993, Decamps et al. 1995), as was common among dryland streams of the Intermountain West. However, alterations in hydrologic regime that are the common result of dams and water development contribute to the establishment of invading exotic plants (Bergmann and Sullivan 1963, Shafroth et al. 1995).

Conclusion

Because fluvial disturbance and connectivity are critical attributes that maintain ecological integrity of floodplain rivers and associated riparian and wetland habitats, reestablishment of these processes serves as the focus of restoration efforts (Ward and Stanford 1995a,b; Poff et al. 1997; Norris and Thoms 1999). Bayley (1991) noted that more than a century ago Stephen Forbes (1895) recognized the importance of the floodplain when he stated that "the point of direction towards which all studies shall tend is the effect on the aquatic plant and animal life of a region produced by the periodic overflow and gradual recession of the waters of a great river." Since Forbes' observations, most temperate river systems have undergone multiple modifications that have affected the hydrograph, topography, and water quality. These modifications include dam building; land clearing (establishment of agriculture, deforestation, channelization, drainage of wetlands) with accelerated watershed drainage and erosion; construction of high, artificial levees to isolate floodplain habitat from the river system; and development of river training structures to hinder meander processes. Restoration of riparian systems requires reestablishment of river-floodplain dynamics, as well as watershed-scale management of land uses (Rosgen 1993).

Literature Cited

Abt, S. R., W. P. Clary, and C. I. Thornton. 1994. Sediment deposition and entrapment in vegetated streambeds. Journal of Irrigation and Drainage Engineering 120:1098–1111.

Akashi, Y. 1988. Riparian vegetation dynamics along the Big Horn River, Wyoming. Thesis, University of Wyoming, Laramie, Wyoming, USA.

Allen, J. R. L. 1965. A review of the origin and characteristics of recent alluvial sediments. Sedimentology 5:89–191.

Allen-Diaz, B. H. 1991. Water table and plant species relationships in Sierra Nevada meadows. American Midland Naturalist 126:30–43.

Armantrout, N. B. 1998. Glossary of aquatic habitat inventory terminology. American Fisheries Society, Bethesda, Maryland, USA.

Auble, G. F., J. M. Friedman, and M. L. Scott. 1994. Relating riparian vegetation to present and future streamflows. Ecological Applications 4:544–554.

Bayley, P. B. 1991. The flood pulse advantage and the restoration of river-floodplain systems. Regulated Rivers: Research and Management 6:75–86.

Bell, D. T., and F. L. Johnson. 1974. Ground-water level in the floodplain and adjacent uplands of the Sangamon River. Transactions of the Illinois State Academy of Science 67:376–383.

Bergmann, D. L., and C. W. Sullivan. 1963. Channel changes in Sandstone Creek near Cheyenne, Oklahoma. Article 97. U.S. Geological Survey Professional Paper 475–C.

Bradley, C. E., and D. G. Smith. 1986. Plains cottonwood recruitment and survival on a prairie meandering river floodplain, Milk River, southern Alberta and northern Montana. Canadian Journal of Botany 64:1433–1442.

Branson, F. A., R. F. Miller, and I. S. McQueen. 1967. Geographic distribution of salt desert shrubs in the United States. Journal of Range Management 20:287–296.

———,———, and———. 1970. Plant communities and associated soil and water factors on shale-derived soils in northeastern Montana. Ecology 51:391–407.

———,———, and———. 1976. Moisture relationships in twelve northern desert shrub communities near Grand Junction, Colorado. Ecology 57:1104–1124.

Bray, T. J. 1996. Changes in channel morphology and riparian mosaic on the Big Horn River, Wyoming. Thesis, University of Wyoming, Laramie, Wyoming, USA.

Brinson, M. M. 1990. Riverine forests. Pages 87–141 in A. E. Lugo, M. Brinson, and S. Brown, editors. Forested wetlands. Volume 15 of Ecosystems of the world. Elsevier, Amsterdam, The Netherlands.

———, A. E. Lugo, and S. Brown. 1981. Primary production, decomposition, and consumer activity in freshwater wetlands. Annual Review of Ecological Systems 12:123–161.

Brown, S., M. M. Brinson, and A. E. Lugo. 1979. Structure and function of riparian wetlands. Pages 17–31 in R. R. Johnson and J. F. McCormick, editors. Strategies for protection and management of floodplain wetlands and other riparian ecosystems. U.S. Forest Service General Technical Report WO-12.

Bryan, K. 1928. Change in plant associations by change in ground water level. Ecology 9:474–478.

Campbell, C. J., and W. Green. 1968. Perpetual succession of stream-channel vegetation in a semi-arid region. Arizona Academy of Science Journal 5:86–98.

Davies, B. R., M. C. Thoms, and M. Meador. 1992. The ecological impact of inter-basin water transfers and their threats to river basin integrity and conservation. Aquatic Conservation of Marine and Freshwater Ecosystems 2:325–349.

Decamps, H., A. M. Planty-Tabacchi, and E. Tabacchi. 1995. Changes in the hydrological regime and invasions by plant species along riparian systems of the Adour River, France. Regulated Rivers: Research and Management 11:23–33.

Dunaway, D., S. Swanson, J. Wendel, and W. Clary. 1994. Effect of herbaceous plant communities and soil textures on particle erosion of alluvial streambanks. Geomorphology 9:47–56.

Duncan, R. P. 1993. Flood disturbance and the coexistence of species in a lowland podocarp forest, South Westland, New Zealand. Journal of Ecology 81:403–416.

Forbes, S. A. 1895. Illinois Fish Commission Report for 1892–1894. Illinois State Laboratory of Natural History, Champaign, Illinois, USA.

Gay, G. R., H. H, Gay, W. H. Gay, H. A. Martinson, R. H. Meade, and J. A. Moody. 1998. Evolution of cutoffs across meander necks in Powder River, Montana, USA. Earth Surface Processes and Landforms 23:61–662.

Graf, W. L. 1988. Fluvial processes in dryland rivers. Springer-Verlag, New York, New York, USA.

Grannemann, N. G., and J. M. Sharp Jr. 1979. Alluvial hydrogeology of the lower Mississippi River valley. Journal of Hydrology 40:85–99.

Gray, C. L. 1998. The effects of three residual vegetation heights on streambank sediment deposition and vegetation production: A continuation. Thesis, University of Wyoming, Laramie, Wyoming, USA.

Gribb, W. J., and D. J. Brosz. 1990. Irrigated acreage. Pages 38–39 in L. M. Ostresh, R. A. Marston, and W. M. Hudson, editors. Wyoming water atlas. Wyoming Water Development Commission, Cheyenne, Wyoming, USA.

Hasfurther, V. R. 1985. The use of meander parameters in restoring hydrologic balance to reclaimed stream beds. Pages 21–40 in J. A. Gore, editor. The restoration of rivers and streams. Butterworty, Boston, Massachusetts, USA.

Henszey, R. J., Q. D. Skinner, and T. A. Wesche. 1991. Response of montane meadow vegetation after two years of streamflow augmentation. Regulated Rivers: Research and Management 6:29–38.

———, T. A. Wesche, and Q. D. Skinner. 1994. Riparian zone changes caused by streamflow augmentation. Wyoming Water Resources Center Publication WWRC-94–02. University of Wyoming, Laramie, Wyoming, USA.

Hosner, J. F., A. L. Leaf, R. E. Dickson, and J. B. Hart Jr. 1965. Effects of varying soil moisture upon nutrient uptake of four bottomland tree species. Proceedings of the Soil Science Society of America 29:313–316.

Johnson, W. C., R. L. Burgess, and W. R. Keammerer. 1976. Forest overstory vegetation on the Missouri River floodplain in North Dakota. Ecological Monographs 46:59–84.

Junk, W. J., P. B. Bayley, and R. E. Sparks. 1989. The flood pulse concept in river-floodplain systems. Canadian Special Publication of Fisheries and Aquatic Sciences 106:110–127.

Keammerer, W. R., W. C. Johnson, and R. L. Burgess. 1975. Floristic analyses of the Missouri River bottomland forests in North Dakota. Canadian Field-Naturalist 89:5–19.

Kearsley, L. H., J. C. Schmidt, and K. D. Warren. 1994. Effects of Glen Canyon Dam on Colorado River sand deposits used as campsites in Grand Canyon National Park. Regulated Rivers: Research and Management 9:137–149.

Kellerhals, R., M. Church, and L. B. Davies. 1979. Morphological effects of interbasin river diversions. Canadian Journal of Civil Engineering 6:18–31.

Knight, D. H. 1994. Mountains and plains. The ecology of Wyoming landscapes. Yale University Press, New Haven, Connecticut, USA.

Kusler, J. A., and M. E. Kentula, editors. 1990. Wetland creation and restoration: the state of the science. Island Press, Washington, D.C., USA.

Lane, E. W. 1955. The importance of fluvial geomorphology in hydraulic engineering. Proceedings of the American Society of Civil Engineers 81:1–17.

Langbein, W. B., and L. B. Leopold. 1966. River meanders—theory of minimum variance. Pages H1–H45 in U.S. Geological Survey Professional Paper 422–H.

Leopold, L. B., and M. G. Wolman. 1966. River meanders. Bulletin of the Geological Society of America 71:769–794.

———, ———, and J. P. Miller. 1964. Fluvial processes in geomorphology. Freeman, San Francisco, California, USA.

Lindauer, I. E. 1983. A comparison of the plant communities of the South Platte and Arkansas River drainages in eastern Colorado. Southwestern Naturalist 28:249–259.

Lyons, J. K., M. J. Pucherelli, and R. C. Clark. 1992. Sediment transport and channel characteristics of a sand-bed portion of the Green River below Flaming Gorge Dam, Utah, USA. Regulated Rivers: Research and Management 7:219–232.

Malanson, G. P. 1993. Riparian landscapes. Cambridge University Press, Cambridge, England.

Marmonier, P., M.-J. Dole-Olivier, and M. Crueze des Chatelliers. 1992. Spatial distribution of interstitial assemblages in the floodplain of the Rhone River. Regulated Rivers: Research and Management 7:75–82.

Miller, J. R., T. T. Schultz, N. T. Hobbs, K. R. Wilson, D. L. Schrupp, and W. L. Baker. 1985. Changes in the landscape structure of a southeastern Wyoming riparian zone following shifts in stream dynamics. Biological Conservation 72:371–379.

Minshall, G. W., K. W. Cummins, R. C. Petersen, C. E. Cushing, D. A. Bruns, J. R. Sedell, and R. L. Vannote. 1985. Developments in stream ecosystem theory. Canadian Journal of Fisheries and Aquatic Science 42:1045–1055.

Miranda, L. E., and S. W. Raborn. 2000. From zonation to connectivity: fluvial ecology paradigms of the 20th century. Polskie Archiwum Hydrobiologii 47:5–19.

Mitsch, W. J., and J. G. Gosselink. 1993. Wetlands. Second edition. Van Nostrand Reinhold, New York, New York, USA.

Molles, M. C. Jr., C. N. Dahm, and M. T. Crocker. 1992. Climatic variability and streams and rivers in semiarid regions. Pages 197–202 in R. D. Robarts and M. L. Bothwell, editors. Aquatic ecosystems in semiarid regions: implications for resource management. NHRI Symposium Series 7, Environment Canada, Saskatoon, Canada.

Norris, R. H., and M. C. Thoms. 1999. What is river health? Freshwater Biology 41: 197–209.

Noy-Meyer, I. 1973. Desert ecosystems: Environment and producers. Annual Review of Ecological Systems 4:25–51.

Pearce, R. A., M. J. Trlica, W. C. Leininger, J. L. Smith, and G. W. Frasier. 1997. Efficiency of grass buffer strips and vegetation height on sediment filtration in laboratory rainfall simulations. Journal of Environmental Quality 26:139–144.

Pinay, G., H. Decamps, E. Chauvet, and E. Fustec. 1990. Functions of ecotones in fluvial systems. Pages 141–169 in R. J. Naiman and H. Decamps, editors. The ecology and management of aquatic-terrestrial ecotones. CRC, London, England.

Poff, N. L., J. D. Allan, M. B. Bain, J. R. Karr, K. L. Prestegaard, B. D. Richter, R. E. Sparks, and J. C. Stromberg. 1997. The natural flow regime. BioScience 47: 769–784.

Reily, P. W., and W. C. Johnson. 1982. The effects of altered hydrologic regime on tree growth along the Missouri River in North Dakota. Canadian Journal of Botany 60: 2410–2423.

Rood, S. B., and J. M. Mahoney. 1990. Collapse of riparian poplar forests downstream from dams in western prairies: probable causes and prospects for mitigation. Environmental Management 14:451–464.

Rosgen, D. L. 1993. Overview of the rivers in the West. Pages 8–15 in Riparian management: common threads and shared interests. U.S. Forest Service General Technical Report RM-226.

Sala, O. E., W. J. Parton, L. A. Joyce, and W. K. Lauenroth. 1988. Primary production of the central grassland region of the United States. Ecology 69:40–45.

Shafroth, P. B., G. T. Auble, and M. L. Scott. 1995. Germination and establishment of the native plains cottonwood (*Populus deltoides* Marshall subsp. *Monilifera*) and the exotic Russian-olive (*Elaeagnus angustifolia* L.). Conservation Biology 9: 1169–1175.

Simons, D. B. 1979. Effects of stream regulation on channel morphology. Pages 95–111 in J. V. Ward and J. A. Stanford, editors. The ecology of regulated rivers. Plenum Press, New York, New York, USA.

Snyder, W. D., and G. C. Miller. 1991. Changes in plains cottonwoods along the Arkansas and South Platte Rivers—eastern Colorado. Prairie Naturalist 23: 165–176.

———, and ———. 1992. Changes in riparian vegetation along the Colorado River and Rio Grande, Colorado. Great Basin Naturalist 52:357–363.

Sparks, R. E., and A. Spink. 1998. Disturbance, succession, and ecosystem processes in rivers and estuaries: effects of extreme hydrologic events. Regulated Rivers: Research and Management 14:155–160.

Stanford, J. A., and J. V. Ward. 1993. An ecosystem perspective of alluvial rivers: connectivity and the hyporheic corridor. Journal of the North American Benthological Society 12:48–60.

Stromberg, J. C. 1993. Fremont cottonwood–Goodding willow riparian forests: a review of their ecology, threats, and recovery potential. Arizona-Nevada Academy of Science 26:97–110.

———, and R. Tiller. 1996. Effects of groundwater decline on riparian vegetation of semiarid regions: the San Pedro, Arizona. Ecological Applications 6:113–131.

Swanson, S., and T. Myers. 1994. Streams, geomorphology, riparian vegetation, livestock, and feedback loops: thoughts for riparian grazing management by objectives. Pages 255–264 in Effects of human-induced changes on hydrologic systems, proceedings of American Water Resources symposium, June 25–29, Jackson Hole, Wyoming, USA.

Vannote, R. L., G. W. Minshall, K. W. Cummins, J. R. Sedell, and C. E. Cushing. 1980. The river continuum concept. Canadian Journal of Fisheries and Aquatic Science 37:130–137.

Walker, K. F., F. Sheldon, and J. T. Puckridge. 1995. A perspective on dryland river ecosystems. Regulated Rivers: Research and Management 11:85–104.

Ward, J. V., and M. A. Palmer. 1994. Distribution patterns of interstitial freshwater meiofauna over a range of spatial scales, with emphasis on alluvial river-aquifer systems. Hydrobiologia 287:147–156.

———, and J. A. Stanford. 1995a. Ecological connectivity in alluvial river ecosystems and its disruption by flow regulation. Regulated Rivers: Research and Management 11:105–119.

———, and J. A. Stanford. 1995b. The serial discontinuity concept: extending the model to floodplain rivers. Regulated Rivers: Research and Management 10: 159–168.

Welcomme, R. L. 1979. Fisheries ecology of floodplain rivers. Longman, London.

———. 1985. River fisheries. Food and Agricultural Organization Fisheries Technical Paper 262. Food and Agriculture Organization of the United Nations, Rome, Italy.

Wesche, T. A. 1993. Watershed management and land-use practices. Pages 181–204 in C. C. Kohler and W. A. Hubert, editors. Inland fisheries management in North America. American Fisheries Society, Bethesda, Maryland, USA.

Williams, G. P., and M. G. Wolman. 1984. Downstream effects of dams on alluvial rivers. U.S. Geological Survey Professional Paper 1286.

Wolman, M. G., and L. B. Leopold. 1957. River flood plains: Some observations on their formation. U.S. Geological Survey Professional Paper 282–C.

———, and J. P. Miller. 1960. Magnitude and frequency of forces in geomorphic processes. Journal of Geology 68:54–74.

Yeager, T. D. 1996. Critical groundwater hydroperiods for maintaining riparian plant species. Thesis, University of Wyoming, Laramie, Wyoming, USA.

Yin, Y. 1998. Flooding and forest succession in a modified stretch along the Upper Mississippi River. Regulated Rivers: Research and Management 14:217–225.

Zimmerman, R. C. 1969. Plant ecology of an arid basin: Tres Alamos–Reddington area, southeastern Arizona. Pages 1–51 in U.S. Geological Survey Professional Paper 485D.

CHAPTER 4

Wildlife Use of Riverine Wetland Habitats

KIRK LOHMAN

Introduction

The importance of riparian habitats to wildlife is well documented, particularly in the Intermountain West (Thomas et al. 1979, Mosconi and Hutto 1982, Knopf 1985, Ohmart and Anderson 1986, Bock et al. 1993). Most terrestrial vertebrates are either dependent on or make substantial seasonal use of riparian habitats (Johnson 1989). In addition, riparian areas in the Intermountain West provide habitat for a disproportionately high number of threatened and endangered species (Niering 1988, Feierabend 1992, Carrier and Czech 1996). Streams, ponds, wetlands, and their associated riparian areas are essential breeding habitats for large numbers of amphibians and reptiles, and many species are restricted to such habitats throughout their life cycles (Brinson et al. 1981). A number of studies have documented greater abundance and greater species richness of small mammals in riparian areas than in adjacent uplands (Cross 1988, Doyle 1990). Although few large mammals are wholly dependent on riparian habitats, seasonal use of such areas may be critical for many ungulate species (Coady 1982, Peek 1984, Raedeke et al. 1988). The importance of riparian areas to some mammalian species, including beaver and moose, cannot be overemphasized, nor can the impacts that these species commonly have on riverine habitats (Naiman et al. 1988, Raedeke et al. 1988, Butler 1995, McKinstry et al. 2001). Throughout western North America, numerous studies have emphasized the importance of riparian habitats for breeding birds (Mosconi and Hutto 1982, Knopf 1985, Bock et al. 1993).

Valuable Riparian Attributes for Wildlife

Many factors explain the disproportionate abundance of wildlife in riparian areas. Brinson et al. (1981) stated that the importance of riparian areas could be attributed to 4 features: (1) the predominance of woody plant communities, (2) the presence of surface water and abundant soil moisture, (3) structural diversity, and (4) the linear nature of riparian habitats, which create migration corridors for many species. Similarly, Ohmart and Anderson (1986) emphasized 4 riparian attributes: (1) plant community size, (2) continuity, (3) edge, and (4) water. Although all of these factors are likely to influence wildlife populations, there are considerable regional differences in their importance. In much of the Intermountain West, riparian areas are narrow and well-defined zones of vegetation that sharply contrast with drier and less productive uplands. The presence of water, as well as greater plant productivity and diversity, compared to adjacent uplands, make riparian areas especially valuable for wildlife. This is also characteristic of palustrine wetlands in the region, which like riparian areas are relatively scarce but are extremely important to a diverse group of fauna (see Chapter 7 of this volume).

The presence of surface water and greater soil moisture is certainly of overriding importance to most wildlife using riparian areas. For species with aquatic life histories (e.g., fish and some amphibians, reptiles, birds, and mammals) the value is obvious, but surface water associated with riparian areas may also be critical to many species that are generally considered upland species. Many riparian-obligate species depend on running water as feeding habitat (e.g., American dippers and mergansers). In addition, many animals, such as amphibians, require surface water for breeding habitat.

Greater plant productivity in riparian areas is largely a function of water availability and higher soil moisture (Brinson 1990; see Chapter 3 of this volume). Nutrient levels are higher in floodplain soils as a result of recurring sediment deposition (Mitsch et al. 1979, Brinson et al. 1981). Western riparian areas generally have greater structural diversity as well as greater biomass than adjacent uplands. This may account for higher animal species diversity, particularly among avian communities (Anderson and Ohmart 1977, Brinson et al. 1981). Higher avian densities and a greater number of nesting species were reported in cottonwood communities along Catherine Creek, Oregon, compared to hawthorn and bluegrass riparian communities, which Kauffman et al. (1985) and Kauffman (1988) attributed to a greater number of vegetation layers in cottonwood communities. Rotenberry (1985) and Knopf and Samson (1994), however, cautioned that foliage structure is highly correlated with plant species composition, and birds may respond to the presence of particular plant species rather than to vegetation structure. Plant species diversity is commonly high in riparian areas compared to adjacent uplands (Nilsson 1992). Insect abundance and diversity may also contribute to greater wildlife diversity in riparian areas. Among tree taxa, Southwood (1961) has reported that willows harbor among the richest and most diverse insect faunas.

Riparian ecosystems may also play an important role as migration corridors. Thomas et al. (1979) emphasized that riparian areas served as migration routes for big game moving between summer and winter range. Riparian corridors may also enable dispersal by birds (Boyce and Payne 1997). Knopf and Samson (1994) described how creation of riparian woodlands along the Platte River has permitted eastern woodland birds to invade western regions. Riparian corridors also provide critical habitat for migrating waterfowl and shorebirds.

Longitudinal Patterns

The importance of riparian habitat varies with stream size among different wildlife taxa. Smaller streams often support a greater diversity of amphibians, whereas reptiles are scarce in headwaters but increase in abundance in more open habitats of intermediate-sized streams (Bury 1988). Small streams generally do not provide habitat patches of sufficient size for most large mammals, but larger riparian floodplains at lower elevations can include the entire seasonal home ranges for species such as elk, moose, and white-tailed deer (Schoen 1977, Raedeke et al. 1988). The distribution of riparian birds also varies with stream size. For example, Knopf (1985) investigated avian species richness along an elevational gradient in the Colorado Front Range and found that riparian avifauna were most diverse at lower elevations.

Characteristic Riparian Species
Birds

Birds are often the most common and conspicuous wildlife in riparian areas, and the importance of riparian areas in providing habitat for birds is well documented. Brinson et al. (1981) categorized avian use of riparian areas based on seasonal occurrence: (1) summer residents (breeding birds), (2) winter residents, (3) transients, and (4) permanent residents. Most research has focused on the use of riparian areas by breeding birds. The highest densities of breeding birds are often associated with riparian habitats (Carothers and Johnson 1975, Knopf 1985, Ohmart and Anderson 1986). For example, Johnson et al. (1977) reported that 77% of the 166 nesting species of birds in the Southwest are at least partially dependent on riparian habitat, and more than half use riparian areas exclusively. Similarly, Mosconi and Hutto (1982) found that 59% of land birds breed in riparian habitat in western Montana and that 36% of those do so exclusively. Throughout western North America, most migratory land birds are associated with riparian habitats during the breeding season (Saab et al. 1995). Brinson et al. (1981) noted that across the

United States, most riparian woodlands have densities of breeding birds that generally range from 4 to 14 breeding pairs/ha.

Winter use of riparian habitats has drawn less attention, but in many areas, species richness and abundance of winter residents are often similar to those of breeding birds (Brinson et al. 1981, Rocklage and Ratti 2000). Bird densities and species richness generally increase during spring and fall migrations, when both transient and resident species are present. Many species are dependent on feeding areas provided by riparian habitats to complete successful migrations. Stevens et al. (1977) found that densities of migrating birds were up to 10 times higher in riparian plots than in adjacent nonriparian plots.

Riparian bird communities generally include numerous passerine species, several birds of prey, many upland game and waterfowl species, and a wide variety of birds with aquatic feeding habits. Among avian groups with obligate riparian species are loons, grebes, cormorants, ducks, geese, hawks, falcons, herons, cranes, rails, coots, kingfishers, and passerines (Kelsey and West 1998). Brinson et al. (1981) listed more than 250 bird species in the United States that use riparian vegetation for cover or feeding during some part of the year.

A number of studies have found higher avian densities and diversity in riparian habitats than in adjacent uplands (Dickson 1978, Stauffer and Best 1980, Tubbs 1980, Emmerich and Vohs 1982, Finch 1989). For example, Knopf (1985) investigated the use of riparian and adjacent uplands by breeding birds along an elevational gradient within the Platte River drainage of northern Colorado. Of 124 species, 82% were observed in riparian areas, compared to 54% in upland habitats. Species richness was greater in riparian than adjacent upland areas regardless of elevation with the exception of sites surveyed at the highest elevation (2,747 m). He also found that the greatest numbers of species unique to a site (38) were seen at the lowest-elevation (1,200 m) site, an old-growth cottonwood community. Knopf (1985) stressed that these areas should be the primary focus of management actions to enhance avian communities. Manuwal (1983, 1986) reported about 5 more breeding pairs/ha in 2 riparian strips characterized by dogwood, alder, and scattered cottonwood than in adjacent Douglas fir forest in western Montana. Similarly, Sanders and Edge (1998) compared breeding bird communities in relation to riparian vegetation structure in the Blue Mountains of eastern Oregon. They found that total bird abundance and the abundance of 3 riparian-associated species (willow flycatcher, yellow warbler, song sparrow) were strongly correlated with willow volume. Riparian corridors also serve as important migratory corridors, funneling birds through deserts and grasslands. The loss of such corridors can impact migratory birds throughout large parts of their range.

Mammals

Many mammal species occur in riparian areas of the Intermountain West (Brinson et al. 1981). For example, Oakley et al. (1985) suggested that of 103 mammals found in western Oregon and Washington, 89% make use of riparian or wetland habitats.

BEAVER AND OTHER SEMIAQUATIC MAMMALS

Among mammals, only humans exceed beaver in the extent to which they influence riparian and stream ecosystems. Beaver are found throughout the United States and Canada, and although their overall range has not shrunk significantly, their abundance has. Naiman et al. (1988) estimated the 1988 beaver population in North America at 6–12 million, an order of magnitude less than the estimate of 60–400 million before the arrival of Europeans in North America (Seton 1929). McKinstry et al. (2001) found that beaver had been extirpated from more than 25% of the first- through third-order streams in Wyoming where they had historically been present and argued that they were ecologically absent from a far greater percentage. Beaver are most abundant in first- to fourth-order streams, but they may also be found along larger rivers where they may make use of side channels and backwaters (Naiman et al. 1988).

Beaver alter riparian systems by cutting trees and impounding streams. The number of trees cut by beaver can be substantial (Naiman et al. 1988, Johnston and Naiman 1990). In riparian zones with aspen, beaver may selectively clear-cut this species, creating open conditions for shrubs and nonbrowsed species and a mosaic of successional states (Jenkins 1979). The number of ponds created by beaver can be quite high, with dam densities ranging from 0.14 to 14.3/km (Naiman et al. 1986, McComb et al. 1990, Woo and Waddington 1990). The wetlands created by these dams can increase the wetlands in a watershed by three times (McKinstry et al. 2001).

Beaver alter the structural and functional attributes of stream ecosystems. Ohmart (1996) included among the potential impacts: (1) alteration of channel morphology and hydrology; (2) increases in sediment and organic matter retention; (3) creation and maintenance of wetlands; (4) changes in nutrient cycles and decomposition processes; (5) changes in plant species composition and physiognomy; (6) modification of the timing, rate, and volume of water and sediments moving downstream; and (7) creation of pools and backwaters generating fish and wildlife habitat and increases in species diversity. Beaver can be successfully transplanted to improve riparian habitat, although it is expensive and time-consuming and may conflict with other goals and activities in the watershed (McKinstry and Anderson 2002).

Other semiaquatic mammals in the Intermountain West include river otter, mink, and muskrat. River otter are strictly aquatic and depend on riparian habitat for dens, breeding areas, and prey, primarily fish (Melquist and Hornocker 1983). Mink are less aquatic than river otters but still spend most of their time in and around streams and riparian areas (Raedeke et al. 1988). In addition to fish, mink feed on a variety of small birds, mammals, frogs, and crayfish (Dalquest 1948).

INSECTIVORES AND RODENTS

Riparian areas can be the primary habitat for small insectivorous mammal species and rodents (Cross 1988). Species richness and total numbers are often greater in riparian zones than in adjacent uplands (Doyle 1990, McComb et al. 1993a,b). For example, Olson and Knopf (1988) compared small mammal communities in riparian and upland habitats along an elevational gradient (1,200–2,750 m) in northern Colorado. Species diversity was greater in upland than in riparian sites at the lowest and highest elevations, but similar at 3 of 4 intermediate sites. Riparian areas at low elevations were dominated by deer mice and voles, whereas shrews were most common at high elevations. Riparian habitat is good for small mammals because there is a greater availability of water and plant forage, a greater density of insects, a more stable temperature regime, and coarser and more friable soils that facilitate burrowing (Doyle 1990).

BATS

Twenty-four species of bats (Order Chiroptera) occur in the Intermountain West (Burt and Grossenheider 1980), and many are known to use stream corridors for roosting, foraging, and drinking (Cross 1988, Kelsey and West 1998), but there is a general lack of knowledge on habitat use patterns of most bats in relation to riparian areas (Christy and West 1991). Many bats are known to feed heavily on the adult stages of aquatic insects (Barclay 1991, Verts et al. 1999), which likely accounts for the strong association of bats with riparian areas (Racey 1998).

LARGE MAMMALS

Most large mammals are not obligate riparian species, but many make at least seasonal use of riparian areas (Raedeke et al. 1988). Food abundance has been suggested as the most important attribute of riparian areas for large mammals (Raedeke et al. 1988). Peek (1984) stated that winter ranges along river bottoms were critical to white-tailed deer in

Montana. In contrast, riparian areas seem to be less critical to mule deer during winter but may provide important sources of water and thermal cover during summer (Wallmo 1981). Similarly, riparian habitat may be important for elk during summer as hiding or thermal cover and as a source of succulent vegetation when uplands become drier (Wittmer and de Calesta 1983, Marcum and Scott 1985). Riparian areas may also provide important calving areas for elk (Wittmer and de Calesta 1983).

Moose in North America are commonly associated with riparian habitats, but their use of riparian areas and streams varies both seasonally and geographically (Peek 1997). In the northern Rocky Mountains, moose make extensive use of alluvial floodplains and stream valley habitats, particularly during winter. Houston (1968) reported that 60% of moose observations were in riparian willow communities. Moose seek out aquatic and riparian habitats for water, food, relief from insects, and thermoregulation. Important components of high-quality moose habitat found in riparian zones include: (1) an abundance of winter browse, (2) shelter areas that allow access to food, (3) isolated sites for calving, (4) aquatic feeding areas, and (5) young forest stands with deciduous shrubs and forbs for summer feeding (Thompson and Stewart 1997).

Herbivores such as snowshoe hare and eastern cottontail use both upland and riparian habitats, but they may be more abundant in riparian areas, particularly during spring when riparian plants green up earlier (Raedeke et al. 1988). High densities of hares and other small mammals may also attract bobcat, lynx, ermine, and fisher to riparian area s (Fitzgerald 1977, Simms 1979, Raedeke et al. 1988). Raedeke et al. (1988) also suggested that carrion is abundant in riparian areas because deer, elk, and moose are more abundant in these areas during winter. Animals dying from malnutrition or disease attract a variety of scavengers, including black bear, grizzly bear, striped skunk, western spotted skunk, and raccoon.

Amphibians and reptiles

The importance of riparian habitats to the distribution, abundance, and diversity of amphibians and reptiles has received limited attention in the Intermountain West. However, considerable work on amphibians in mountain streams of the Pacific Northwest has identified the importance of riparian habitat for some species (Bury 1988, Kelsey and West 1998). Some of the same or similar species occur in the northern Rocky Mountains. For example, the Rocky Mountain tailed frog is restricted to small streams in forested watersheds (Daugherty and Sheldon 1982, Nielson et al. 2001). The Idaho giant salamander is also an obligate riparian species found in cold, high-gradient streams and is often the most important vertebrate predator in streams where it occurs (Murphy and Hall 1981, Nussbaum et al. 1983).

Most reptiles are less confined to riparian habitat and generally occur in larger stream systems than amphibians (Bury 1988). Taxa that are dependent on riparian habitat include painted turtle, snapping turtle, spiny softshell turtle (Nussbaum et al. 1983, Brown et al. 1995) and garter snake, rubber boa, and ringneck snake (Nussbaum et al. 1983, Kelsey and West 1998).

In a survey of herpetofauna in Arizona, Jones (1988a,b) related species distributions and abundance to habitat types, and riparian habitats were among the most species-rich and harbored the highest densities of amphibians and reptiles. The presence of downed trees and dead surface litter, which enhanced moisture retention and moderated temperature, is considered a key riparian attribute for herpetofauna.

Conclusions

Riverine riparian areas are used by a wide variety of species across North America. The dramatic contrast between riparian and upland habitats in the Intermountain West accentuates the value of riparian areas to wildlife and makes them the single most important habitat type for wildlife in the region. The limited occurrence of riparian systems and the drastic reduction in both the quality and quantity of these habitats in the Intermountain West highlight the need for wise management and restoration.

Literature Cited

Anderson, B. W., and R. D. Ohmart. 1977. Vegetation structure and bird use in the lower Colorado River Valley. Pages 23–34 in R. R. Johnson and D. A. Jones, editors. Importance, preservation, and management of riparian habitat: a symposium. U.S. Forest Service General Technical Report RM-43.

Barclay, R. M. R. 1991. Population structure of temperate zone insectivorous bats in relation to foraging behaviour and energy demand. Journal of Animal Ecology 60: 165–178.

Bock, C. E., V. A. Saab, T. D. Rich, and D. S. Dobkin. 1993. Effects of livestock grazing on neotropical migratory landbirds in western North America. Pages 296–309 in D. M. Finch and P. W. Stangel, editors. Status and management of neotropical migratory birds. U.S. Forest Service General Technical Report RM-229.

Boyce, M. S., and N. F. Payne. 1997. Applied disequilibriums: riparian habitat management for wildlife. Pages 133–146 in M. S. Boyce and A. Haney, editors. Ecosystem management: applications for sustainable forest and wildlife resources. Yale University Press, New Haven, Connecticut, USA.

Brinson, M. M. 1990. Riverine forests. Pages 87–141 in A. E. Lugo, M. M. Brinson, and S. Brown, editors. Forested wetlands. Elsevier Scientific Publishers, Amsterdam, Netherlands.

———, B. L. Swift, R. C. Plantico, and J. S. Barclay. 1981. Riparian ecosystems: their ecology and status. U.S. Fish and Wildlife Service, Office of Biological Services, FWS/OBS-81/17, Washington, D.C., USA.

Brown, H. A., R. B. Bury, D. M. Darda, L. V. Diller, C. R. Peterson, and R. M. Storm. 1995. Reptiles of Washington and Oregon. Seattle Audubon Society, Seattle, Washington, USA.

Burt, W. H., and R. P. Grossenheider. 1980. A field guide to the mammals. Houghton Mifflin, New York, New York, USA.

Bury, R. B. 1988. Habitat relationships and ecological importance of amphibians and reptiles. Pages 61–76 in K. J. Raedeke, editor. Streamside management: riparian wildlife and forestry interactions. Contribution Number 59. University of Washington Institute of Forest Resources, Seattle, Washington, USA.

Butler, D. R. 1995. Zoogeomorphology: animals as geomorphic agents. Cambridge University Press, Cambridge, England.

Carothers, S. W., and R. R. Johnson. 1975. Water management practices and their effects on nongame birds in range habitats. Pages 210–222 in D. R. Smith, technical coordinator. Proceedings of the symposium on management of forest and range habitats for nongame birds. U.S. Forest Service General Technical Report WO-1.

Carrier, W. D., and B. Czech. 1996. Threatened and endangered wildlife and livestock interactions. Pages 39–47 in P. R. Krausman, editor. Rangeland wildlife. Society of Rangeland Management, Denver, Colorado, USA.

Christy, R. E., and S. D. West. 1991. Biology of bats in Douglas-fir forests. U.S. Forest Service General Technical Report PNW-308.

Coady, J. W. 1982. Moose. Pages 902–922 in J. Chapman and G. Feldhamer, editors. Wild mammals of North America. Johns Hopkins University Press, Baltimore, Maryland, USA.

Cross, S. P. 1988. Riparian systems and small mammals and bats. Pages 93–112 in K. J. Raedeke, editor. Streamside management: riparian wildlife and forestry interactions. Contribution Number 59. University of Washington Institute of Forest Resources, Seattle, Washington, USA.

Dalquest, W. W. 1948. Mammals of Washington. Volume 2. Museum of Natural History. University of Kansas Publications, Lawrence, Kansas, USA.

Daugherty, C. H., and A. L. Sheldon. 1982. Age-determination, growth, and life history of a Montana population of the tailed frog (Ascaphus truei). Herpetologia 38: 461–468.

Dickson, J. G. 1978. Forest bird communities of the bottomland hardwoods. Pages 66–73 in R. M. DeGraaf, technical coordinator. Proceedings of the workshop on management of southern forests for nongame birds. U.S. Forest Service General Technical Report SE-14.

Doyle, A. T. 1990. Use of riparian and upland habitats by small mammals. Journal of Mammalogy 71:14–23.

Emmerich, J. M., and P. A. Vohs. 1982. Comparative use of four woodland habitats by birds. Journal of Wildlife Management 46:43–49.

Feierabend, S. J. 1992. Endangered species, endangered wetlands: life on the edge. National Wildlife Federation, Washington, D. C.

Finch, D. M. 1989. Habitat use and habitat overlap of riparian birds in three elevational zones. Ecology 70:866–880.

Fitzgerald, B. M. 1977. Weasel production on a cyclic population of montane vole, Microtus montanus in California. Journal of Animal Ecology 46:367–397.

Houston, D. B. 1968. The Shiras moose in Jackson Hole, Wyoming. Technical Bulletin 1. Grand Teton Natural History Association, Jackson, Wyoming, USA.

Jenkins, S. H. 1979. Seasonal and year-to-year differences in food selection by beavers. Oecologia 44:112–116.

Johnson, A. S. 1989. The thin, green line: riparian corridors and endangered species in Arizona and New Mexico. Pages 35–46 in G. Mackintosh, editor. In defense of wildlife: preserving communities and corridors. Defenders of Wildlife, Washington, D.C., USA.

Johnson, R. R., L. T. Haight, and J. M. Simpson. 1977. Endangered species vs. endangered habitats: a concept. Pages 68–79 in R. R. Johnson and D. A. Jones, editors. Importance, preservation, and management of riparian habitat: a symposium. U.S. Forest Service General Technical Report RM-43.

Johnston, C. A., and R. J. Naiman. 1990. Browse selection by beaver: effects on riparian forest composition. Canadian Journal of Forest Research 20:1036–1043.

Jones, K. B. 1988a. Comparison of herpetofaunas of a natural and altered riparian ecosystem. Pages 222–227 in R. C. Szaro, K. E. Severson, and D. R. Patton, technical coordinators. Management of amphibians, reptiles, and small mammals in North America. U.S. Forest Service General Technical Report RM-166.

———. 1988b. Distribution and habitat associations of herpetofauna in Arizona: comparison by habitat type. Pages 109–129 in R. C. Szaro, K. E. Severson, and D. R. Patton, technical coordinators. Management of amphibians, reptiles, and small mammals in North America. U.S. Forest Service General Technical Report RM-166.

Kauffman, J. B. 1988. The status of riparian habitats in Pacific Northwest forests. Pages 45–55 in K. J. Raedeke, editor. Streamside management: riparian wildlife and forestry interactions. Contribution Number 59. University of Washington Institute of Forest Resources, Seattle, Washington, USA.

———, W. C. Krueger, and M. Vavra. 1985. Ecology and plant communities of the riparian area associated with Catherine Creek in northwestern Oregon. Technical Bulletin 147, Agricultural Experiment Station, Oregon State University, Corvallis, Oregon, USA.

Kelsey, K. A., and S. D. West. 1998. Riparian wildlife. Pages 235–258 in R. J. Naiman and R. E. Bilby, editors. River ecology and management: lessons from the Pacific coastal ecoregion. Springer-Verlag, New York, New York, USA.

Knopf, F. L. 1985. Significance of riparian vegetation to breeding birds across an altitudinal cline. Pages 105–111 in R. R. Johnson, C. D. Ziebel, D. R. Patton, P. F. Ffolliott, and R. H. Hamre, editors. Riparian ecosystems and their management: reconciling conflicting uses. U.S. Forest Service General Technical Report RM-120.

———, and F. B. Samson. 1994. Scale perspectives on avian diversity in western riparian ecosystems. Conservation Biology 8:669–676.

Manuwal, D. A. 1983. Avian abundance and guild structure in two Montana coniferous forests. Murrelet 64:1–11.

———. 1986. Characteristics of bird assemblages along linear riparian zones in western Montana. Murrelet 67:10–18.

Marcum, C. L., and M. D. Scott. 1985. Influences of weather on elk use of spring-summer habitat. Journal of Wildlife Management 49:73–76.

McComb, W. C., C. L. Chambers, and M. Newton. 1993a. Small mammal and amphibian communities and habitat associations in red alder stands, central Oregon Coast Range. Northwest Science 67:181–188.

―――, K. McGarigal, and R. G. Anthony. 1993b. Small mammal and amphibian abundance in streamside and upslope habitats of mature Douglas-fir stands, western Oregon. Northwest Science 67:7–14.

―――, J. R. Sedell, and T. D. Buchholz. 1990. Dam-site selection by beavers in an eastern Oregon basin. Great Basin Naturalist 50:273–281.

McKinstry, M. C., and S. H. Anderson. 2002. Survival, fates, and success of transplanted beavers, *Castor canadensis*, in Wyoming. Canadian Field-Naturalist 116: 60–68.

―――, P. Caffrey, and S. H. Anderson. 2001. The importance of beaver to wetland habitats and waterfowl in Wyoming. Journal of American Water Resources Association 37:1517–1577.

Melquist, W. E., and M. G. Hornocker. 1983. Ecology of river otters in west central Idaho. Wildlife Monographs 83:1–60.

Mitsch, W. J., C. L. Dorge, and J. R. Weimhoff. 1979. Ecosystem dynamics and a phosphorus budget of an alluvial cypress swamp in southern Illinois. Ecology 60: 1116–1124.

Mosconi, S. L., and R. L. Hutto. 1982. The effect of grazing on the land birds of a western Montana riparian habitat. Proceedings of the Wildlife-Livestock Relationships Symposium 10:221–233.

Murphy, M. L., and J. D. Hall. 1981. Varied effects of clear-cut logging on predators and their habitat in small streams of the Cascade Mountains, Oregon. Canadian Journal of Fisheries and Aquatic Sciences 38:137–145.

Naiman, R. J., C. A. Johnston, and J. C. Kelley. 1988. Alteration of North American streams by beaver. BioScience 38:753–762.

―――, J. M. Melillo, and J. E. Hobbie. 1986. Ecosystem alteration of boreal forest streams by beaver (*Castor canadensis*). Ecology 67:1254–1269.

Nielson, M., K. Lohman, and J. Sullivan. 2001. Phylogeography of the tailed frog (*Ascaphus truei*): implications for the biogeography of the Pacific Northwest. Evolution 55:147–160.

Niering, W. A. 1988. Endangered, threatened, and rare wetland plants and animals of the continental United States. Pages 227–238 in D. D. Hook, W. H. McKee Jr., H. K. Smith, J. Gregory, V. G. Burrell Jr., M. R. DeVoe, R. E. Sojka, S. Gilbert, R. Banks, L. H. Stölzy, C. Brooks, T. D. Matthews, and T. H. Shear, editors. Ecology of wetlands. Volume 1 of The ecology and management of wetlands. Timber Press, Portland, Oregon, USA.

Nilsson, C. 1992. Conservation management of riparian communities. Pages 353–372 in L. Hansson, editor. Ecological principles of nature conservation. Elsevier Applied Science, London, England.

Nussbaum, R. A., E. D. Brodie, and R. M. Storm. 1983. Amphibians and reptiles of the Pacific Northwest. University Press of Idaho, Moscow, Idaho, USA.

Oakley, A. L., J. A. Collins, L. B. Everson, D. A. Heller, J. C. Howerton, and R. E. Vincent. 1985. Riparian zones and freshwater uplands. Pages 57–80 in E. R. Brown, editor. Management of wildlife and fish habitats in forests of western Oregon and Washington. U.S. Forest Service, Publication Number R6–F&WL-192–1985.

Ohmart, R. D. 1996. Historical and present impacts of livestock grazing on fish and wildlife resources in western riparian habitats. Pages 245–279 in P. R. Krausman, editor. Rangeland wildlife. Society of Rangeland Management, Denver, Colorado, USA.

————, and B. W. Anderson. 1986. Riparian habitat. Pages 169–199 *in* A. Y. Cooperrider, R. J. Boyd, and H. R. Stuart, editors. Inventory and monitoring of wildlife habitat. U.S. Department of Interior, Bureau of Land Management, BLM/YA/PT-87/001+6600, Denver, Colorado, USA.

Olson, T. E., and F. L. Knopf. 1988. Patterns of relative diversity within riparian small mammal communities, Platte River watershed, Colorado. Pages 379–386 *in* R. C. Szaro, K. E. Severson, and D. R. Patton. Management of amphibians, reptiles, and small mammals in North America. U.S. Forest Service General Technical Report RM-166.

Peek, J. M. 1984. Northern Rocky Mountains. Pages 497–504 *in* L. Hall, editor. White-tailed deer, ecology and management. Stackpole Books, Harrison, Pennsylvania, USA.

————. 1997. Habitat relationships. Pages 351–375 *in* A. W. Franzmann, and C. C. Schwartz, editors. Ecology and management of the North American moose. Smithsonian Institution Press, Washington, D.C., USA.

Racey, P. A. 1998. The importance of the riparian environment as a habitat for British bats. Pages 69–91 *in* N. Dunstone and M. L. Gorman, editors. Behaviour and ecology of riparian mammals. Cambridge University Press, Cambridge, England.

Raedeke, K. J., R. D. Taber, and D. K. Paige. 1988. Ecology of large mammals in riparian systems of Pacific Northwest forests. Pages 113–132 *in* K. J. Raedeke, editor. Streamside management: riparian wildlife and forestry interactions. Contribution Number 59. University of Washington Institute of Forest Resources, Seattle, Washington, USA.

Rocklage, A. M., and J. T. Ratti. 2000. Avian use of recently evolved riparian habitat on the lower Snake River, Washington. Northwest Science 74:286–293.

Rotenberry, J. T. 1985. The role of vegetation in avian habitat selection: physiognomy or floristics? Oecologia 67:213–217.

Saab, V. A., C. E. Bock, T. D. Rich, and D. S. Dobkin. 1995. Livestock grazing effects in western North America. Pages 311–353 *in* T. E. Martin and D. M. Finch, editors. Ecology and management of neotropical migratory birds. Oxford University Press, Oxford, England.

Sanders, T. A., and W. D. Edge. 1998. Breeding bird community composition in relation to riparian vegetation structure in the western United States. Journal of Wildlife Management 62:461–473.

Schoen, J. 1977. The ecological distribution and biology of wapiti (*Cervus elaphus nelsoni*) in the Cedar River watershed, Washington. Dissertation, University of Washington, Seattle, Washington, USA.

Seton, E. T. 1929. Rodents. Volume 4, Part 2 of Lives of game animals. Doubleday, New York, New York, USA.

Simms, D. A. 1979. North American weasels: resource utilization and distribution. Canadian Journal of Zoology 57:504–520.

Southwood, T. R. E. 1961. The numbers of species of insects associated with various trees. Journal of Animal Ecology 30:1–8.

Stauffer, D. F., and L. B. Best. 1980. Habitat selection by birds of riparian communities: evaluating effects of habitat alterations. Journal of Wildlife Management 44:1–15.

Stevens, L. E., B. T. Brown, J. M. Simpson, and R. R. Johnson. 1977. The importance of riparian habitat to migrating birds. Pages 156–164 *in* R. R. Johnson and D. A.

Jones, technical coordinators. Importance, preservation, and management of riparian habitat: a symposium. U.S. Forest Service General Technical Report RM-43.

Thomas, J. W., C. Maser, and J. E. Rodiek. 1979. Riparian zones. Pages 40–47 *in* J. W. Thomas, editor. Wildlife habitats in managed forests: the Blue Mountains of Oregon and Washington. U.S. Forest Service Agricultural Handbook No. 553.

Thompson, I. D., and R. W. Stewart. 1997. Management of moose habitat. Pages 377–401 *in* A. W. Franzmann and C. C. Schwartz, editors. Ecology and management of the North American moose. Smithsonian Institution Press, Washington, D.C., USA.

Tubbs, A. A. 1980. Riparian bird communities of the Great Plains. Pages 419–433 *in* R. M DeGraaf, technical coordinator. Proceedings of a workshop for management of western forest and grasslands for nongame birds. U.S. Forest Service General Technical Report INT-86.

Verts, B. J., L. N. Carraway, and J. O. Whitaker Jr. 1999. Temporal variation in prey consumed by big brown bats (*Eptesicus fuscus*) in a maternity colony. Northwest Science 73:114–120.

Wallmo, O. C. 1981. Mule and black-tailed deer of North America. University of Nebraska Press, Lincoln, Nebraska, USA.

Wittmer, G. W., and D. S. de Calesta. 1983. Habitat use by female Roosevelt elk in the Oregon Coast Range. Journal of Wildlife Management 47:933–939.

Woo, M.-K., and J. M. Waddington. 1990. Effects of beaver dams on subarctic wetland hydrology. Arctic 43:223–230.

CHAPTER 5

Management of Riverine Wetland Habitats

ROBERT C. EHRHART AND PAUL L. HANSEN

Introduction

Riverine habitats are among the most impacted ecosystems in the Inter-mountain West (Swift 1984, Kauffman 1988, Noss et al. 1995). European settlers focused activities in or near riverine areas, including transportation, resource extraction, agricultural production, livestock grazing, flood control and hydroelectric power development, urban development, and recreation. Human activities along rivers have been detrimental to riparian ecosystems (Johnson 1979). Riverine habitats have been altered throughout this region, and riparian habitat losses have been estimated at more than 95% in most western states (Krueper 1993).

Understanding the importance of riverine ecosystems and how they function has been slow in coming. As late as the 1970s, Johnson (1979) referred to them as "among the most neglected and poorly understood entities within the vast array of North American ecosystems." We address the major human activities that have impacted riverine habitats in the Intermountain West and identify ways in which management can reduce the impacts.

Water Development
Impacts

Humans have altered riverine habitats throughout the Intermountain West through dam building (Hirsch et al. 1990, Merigliano 1996), channelization, pumping of groundwater (Groeneveld and Griepentrog 1985, Stromberg et al. 1996), road building (Dobyns 1981, Reeder 1994), irrigation diversions (Schmidly and Ditton 1979, Ohmart and Anderson 1982), and urban floodplain development (Johnson 1979, Johnson and Haight 1984). Dams affect the timing, magnitude, duration, and periodicity of flows (Klimas 1988) that in turn affect riparian plant communities (Bradley and Smith 1986, Rood and Mahoney 1990, Auble et al. 1994, Busch and Scott 1995, Scott et al. 1996) and contribute to the expansion of exotic plant species (Rea 1983, Howe and Knopf 1991). Dams affect the geomorphology of riverine habitats (Williams and Wolman 1984, Ligon et al. 1995, Chavez 1996) and aquatic biota (Stanford and Ward 1979, Williams et al. 1985, Rinne 1994). Loss of native riparian vegetation affects terrestrial animals, especially passerine birds (Johnson and Jones 1977, Cohan et al. 1979, Stauffer and Best 1980, Ohmart 1984).

In an effort to increase water yields in southwestern rivers, massive projects to eliminate phreatophytic (water-loving) plants, both exotic and native, were undertaken in the 1950s and 1960s. However, the loss of riparian vegetation severely disrupted ecosystem functions and resulted in degraded watersheds, with little increase in available water (Johnson and Haight 1984).

Management

Dismantling dams in parts of the Intermountain West may be an option for river and riparian restoration in some watersheds, but this is likely to be a rare event. Many dams are in need of rehabilitation, but costs are excessive for private entities or municipalities to absorb. More likely there will be efforts to modify dam operations to more closely mimic natural processes, as was done at Glen Canyon Dam on the Colorado in 1996 (Collier et al. 1996). Management of instream flows to maintain or enhance groundwater levels and associated riparian and wetland vegetation is one option. Stromberg (1993) developed instream flow models for a semiarid river to enhance water table recharge and floodplain soil wetting in order to maintain riparian forests. However, instream flows do not consider long-term needs of plant communities for flooding, channel meandering, and floodplain building. The pressures of an increasing human population continue to impose added demands on available water and to alter riverine habitat. Unless society adopts new priorities, as Cooper (1994:32) notes, "There is not enough water in any river basin for both the West's growing urban and agricultural populations and the native ecosystems that depend upon large amounts of water."

Timber Harvesting
Impacts

The fundamental relationships among the riparian zone and the aquatic and upland ecosystems that adjoin it are demonstrated by the impacts of timber harvesting on riverine habitats (Likens and Bormann 1974, Bilby 1988, Bisson et al. 1992). The most widespread impact is increased sedimentation (Binkley and Brown 1993a), which affects riparian vegetation, channel morphology, and habitat for aquatic life (Hartman et al. 1996). The primary causes of erosion and subsequent sedimentation are improper construction, use, and maintenance of logging roads (Burroughs and King 1989, Satterlund and Adams 1992), clear-cut logging, and loss of binding roots after harvesting. Clear-cutting can increase the total amount of streamflow as well as alter the volume and timing of peak flows. By compacting and disturbing soils, timber harvesting in riparian areas can reduce infiltration, increase erosion, and alter surface and groundwater flows.

Riparian vegetation contributes to the healthy functioning of a riverine ecosystem (Mitsch and Gosselink 2000, Beschta 1991), and disturbance or removal of this vegetation can have serious consequences. Removal of the forest canopy increases stream temperatures (Beschta et al. 1987) and affects aquatic organisms (Everest et al. 1985, Binkley and Brown 1993a). Loss of streamside vegetation affects aquatic food chains, especially in lower-order streams, where most of the detritus and nutrients enter the stream from riparian plants (Cummins and Spengler 1978). Removal of trees reduces or eliminates recruitment of large woody debris into streams, which alters both physical and biological components of the system (Bilby and Likens 1980, Heede 1985, Harmon et al. 1986, Sedell et al. 1988, Sidle and Sharma 1996, Smith 1996). Forest practices also affect biochemical components of the aquatic environment (Binkley and Brown 1993b).

The impacts of timber harvesting on aquatic organisms have been documented, especially in the Pacific Northwest (Brown 1985, Gregory and Bisson 1997, Sedell et al. 1997). Impacts on other animal species that use forested riverine habitats have also been addressed (Thomas et al. 1979, Raedeke 1988, Hagar et al. 1995) and are generally detrimental.

Management

Most adverse impacts of timber harvesting can be mitigated by management. Avoidance of sensitive sites (Garland 1987, Rice 1992) and proper design, construction, and maintenance of roads (Windsor 1989, Furniss et al. 1991, LaFayette et al. 1996) are 2 practices with wide applicability. Major emphasis has been on activities in the riparian area because of direct impacts on the aquatic zone and because of the riparian zone's importance as a buffer (Nutter and Gaskin 1989, Belt et al. 1992). Much emphasis has been placed on delineation of buffer zones along streams within which timber and road construction actions are restricted or prohibited. Buffer zones, referred to as "riparian management zones" and "streamside management zones" can preserve physical and biological linkages among streams, riparian zones, and upland areas (Bisson et al. 1992).

There is no consensus on the appropriate width of buffer zones or on which activities should be limited and to what extent (Oliver and Hinckley 1987, Lynch and Corbett 1990, Belt et al. 1992, Binkley and McDonald 1994, Blinn and Dahlman 1996). Prohibiting or limiting the number of roads in a buffer zone and delineating strict parameters on their construction and maintenance can reduce soil disturbance, compaction, and erosion. Of particular importance is the need to limit the number of stream crossings and to properly design and locate them because they can contribute as much as 50% of the sediment that enters streams as a result of logging operations (Burroughs and King 1989). Roads should not be built in wet areas, crossings should be perpendicular to stream direction and at the same grade, and culverts should be aligned with stream direction and gradient. Temporary crossings, including reinforced fords and portable bridges, should be used where feasible. Landings as well as fueling and maintenance areas should be outside the buffer zone.

Restrictions on operations may include the exclusion of mechanized harvesting and skidding machines, the use of equipment with low ground pressure, and soft-impact felling and skidding techniques. Leaving a proportion of merchantable as well as nonmerchantable trees in the buffer zone provides shade, wildlife habitat, and a source of large woody debris and enhances the filtering functions of the riparian zone. Requirements for the types and number of "leave trees" as well as for the width of the buffer zone vary with stream type, size of the clear-cut, slope angle, parent material and soil types, and other biological and physical considerations.

Many of these practices have been adopted as best management practices (BMPs) required by state laws. For example, the 1991 Montana Streamside Management Act requires a streamside management zone (SMZ) of at least 15 m (and wider where necessary to include adjoining wetlands or areas with steep slopes) and prohibits the following activities in this buffer zone: (1) clear-cutting; (2) use of wheeled or tracked equipment except on established roads; (3) construction of roads except when necessary to cross a stream or wetland; (4) burning; (5) the handling of hazardous or toxic materials in a manner that would result in pollution or harm to humans and animals; (6) side-casting of road material into streams or wetlands; and (7) deposit of slash in streams. It also specifies the number, types, and locations of leave trees (Montana State University Extension Service 1991).

Although blanket rules are easier to enforce, BMPs are more effective when they provide the flexibility to allow for variation in equipment options and site conditions, accessibility, soil conditions, special habitat concerns, and planned activities in adjoining areas (Blinn and Dahlman 1996). There is evidence that BMPs can be effective (Lynch and Corbett 1990, Rice 1992, Binkley and Brown 1993b). Equally important is the need to manage timber activities within a watershed context and clearly recognize and adapt to the inherent relationships among streams, riparian areas, and uplands.

Livestock Grazing
Impacts

Like many others, Knopf and Cannon (1982:198) have observed that "overgrazing by livestock is considered the most widespread cause of deterioration of riparian systems." There is little doubt that livestock have adversely affected riverine wetland habitats throughout the Intermountain West (Platts and Raleigh 1984, Skovlin 1984). Excessive livestock grazing, primarily of cattle since World War II, affects vegetation by defoliation, mechanical damage, and alteration of plant communities, affects soil by compaction, disturbance of the soil surface, and streambank sloughing, and affects water by increasing sedimentation, water temperature, and bacteria and algae (Meehan and Platts 1978, Kauffman and Krueger 1984, Platts 1991; also see Chapters 8 and 11 of this volume). Overgrazed riparian areas are less able to perform critical ecosystem functions such as water storage, flow energy dissipation, sediment trapping, streambank stabilization, and protection of soil and water. In addition, degraded riparian zones provide less habitat for terrestrial and aquatic organisms (Skovlin 1984; Medin and Clary 1989, 1990; Schultz and Leininger 1991, Saab et al. 1995).

Management

While there is consensus that excessive grazing damages riverine habitats, what constitutes "excessive" differs widely depending on such factors as topography, soil type, climate, vegetation (present and potential), type of animal, and season of use. According to some, any livestock grazing in riparian areas is too much (Platts 1979, Fleischner 1994). Until the mid-1980s, grazing in riparian areas for the most part had been integrated into conventional upland grazing systems such as season-long grazing, rest rotation, and deferred rotation (Clary and Webster 1989, Buckhouse and Elmore 1991, Platts 1991, Elmore 1992).

It has become apparent that traditional grazing systems do not influence livestock behavior sufficiently to reduce impacts on riparian areas. Management has shifted from general grazing systems to specific techniques to reduce the intensity in riparian areas (Ehrhart and Hansen 1997, Leonard et al. 1997, Mosley et al. 1997, George 1998). In addition, because of limitations inherent in many early studies on grazing impacts and management options, emphasis is being placed on development of rigorous, long-term studies (Rinne 1988, Larsen et al. 1998).

The dominant theme running through contemporary literature on riparian grazing is that every situation is in some way unique and must be managed accordingly. Common to this theme is a greater emphasis on active management and efforts to respond to problems as they arise. Because it is frequently addressed in both scientific and popular literature, the issue of "season of use" merits special attention. Despite frequent assertions that riparian areas can only be grazed in a certain season or should never be grazed during some seasons, there is no universally applicable "best time" in which to graze riparian zones. Not surprisingly, there are advantages and disadvantages to grazing during each season (Ehrhart and Hansen 1997).

Managers may implement numerous practices to reduce the amount of time cattle spend in riparian areas: (1) development of alternate (off-stream) water sources; (2) use of stable access points to limit streambank use; (3) placement of salt and mineral blocks; (4) improvements in upland forage; (5) use of riders and herders; (6) use of smaller pastures or reconfiguration of pastures; (7) use of temporary or permanent fencing; (8) location of gates and turn-in points; (9) determination of appropriate carrying capacity; and (10) selection of kind, class, and age of animal. None of these techniques is likely to work everywhere, and they are more likely to be successful when used in combination.

Mining
Impacts

Although not as pervasive as other land uses affecting riverine habitats in the Intermountain West, mining may have "degraded the quality of American surface waters more than any other component of the environment" (Nelson et al. 1991). Perhaps the most severe impacts of mining operations on riverine habitat have been introductions of toxic metals and acid mine drainage from mine spoils. Surface mining, both strip and open pit, exposes large areas of land to erosion, accelerates the movement of sediment into streams, and disrupts groundwater and streamflow by blocking or redirecting aquifer and surface flows.

Alluvial mining has had dramatic impacts on riverine habitat. Although rarely conducted any more, hydraulic mining with high-pressure hoses radically altered the geomorphology of streams and contributed massive quantities of sediment to adjacent and downstream channels. For example, hydraulic mining in the Yuba River Basin in California in the 19th century resulted in a debris plain of more than 100 km^2 where the Yuba River enters the Sacramento River Valley (Kondolf 1994). So massive were the alterations of landscapes by this process that in many places huge debris piles remain obvious more than 100 years after operations ceased. Dredging is still being done in many places, and it changes the channel morphology by placing the material along the channel or on the floodplain, where it covers vegetation, reduces biotic productivity, and contributes sediment back to the stream. Dredging may cause incisement both upstream and downstream, lateral channel instability through streambank erosion, turbidity due to suspended sediment, and replacement of streambed materials useful to aquatic organisms with coarser, less useful materials (Kondolf 1994).

Demands for water for ore processing, milling, and refining have also altered hydraulic regimes in many streams. Moreover, the demand for wood for fuel and mine construction has altered riparian plant communities, especially in the southwest, where many plant communities have not recovered from degradation imposed in the late 19th and early 20th centuries (Dobyns 1981). Adverse impacts from mining on aquatic organisms have resulted from the increased sedimentation and turbidity as well as from the introduction of toxic substances into the channel (Martin and Platts 1981).

Management

Because of the localized nature of mining operations, ecologic impacts are more easily influenced by management actions than are some other human activities that affect riverine habitat. Success of new management techniques depends on political will and economic considerations more than technical feasibility. Measures identified to diminish mining impacts include topsoil removal and reuse, revegetation of sites, and prevention of toxic waste intrusion (Anderson and Ohmart 1985, Brooks 1990). Even with restrictions and improved practices on current mining operations, thousands of abandoned mines remain throughout the Intermountain West that continue to introduce acid mine drainage, toxic metals, and sediment into streams. Methods for mine reclamation and riverine restoration include reconstruction of channels and restoration of damaged plant communities, including introduction of plant species tolerant of severely altered conditions (Gore 1985, Manci 1989, Clary et al. 1992, Williams et al. 1997).

Recreation

Impacts

Riverine ecosystems are among the most popular recreation sites in the Intermountain West, with recreation activities occurring in urban to wilderness settings. Recreation along a river can affect several elements of riverine habitats: soil, vegetation, water, and wildlife (Settergren 1977, Gosz 1982, Johnson and Carothers 1982, Cole 1987, Hammitt and Cole 1987).

Recreation sites, particularly campsites and picnic areas, are often characterized by compacted soil, reduced vegetative cover, large areas of bare ground, damaged trees and shrubs, an absence of young plants, and a prevalence of disturbance-tolerant plant communities (Manning 1979). Other ways in which recreationists impact the riverine area include off-road vehicle use, fire, spread of litter and waste, degradation of water quality, and reduction of wildlife habitat (Brickler and Utter 1975, Aitchison et al. 1977, Ditton et al. 1977). The impacts of recreational use are not necessarily correlated with the amount of use an area receives. Many impacts can occur at a relatively light level of recreational use (Cole and Marion 1988).

Management

The objective of management must be to limit the degree of such impact to acceptable levels (Clark and Gibbons 1991), but determination of what constitutes "acceptable" must encompass not only ecological but also social, political, and economic factors. Management must be site-specific and based on environmental characteristics as well as temporal variation, spatial distribution, and intensity of use (Rasmussen and Padgett 1994). Management actions include: (1) design of facilities and access, (2) efforts to educate users, and (3) time and space limitations on the number of users (Craig 1977). Nevertheless, the possibility of eliminating recreational impacts on riverine habitats has become increasingly difficult as a result of the combination of the increasing numbers of recreational users and reduced funding for agencies responsible for resources management.

Conclusion

Human activities have adversely affected riverine riparian and wetland habitats throughout the Intermountain West. The long-term effect has been a simplification of naturally complex environments, with a concomitant degradation of ecologic functions (Johnson and Haight 1984, Bisson et al. 1992). Just as obvious is the fact that humans will continue to affect these vital components of the landscape. However, increased concern about these ecological effects and an expanding understanding of how these systems work are leading to identification of new methods to attain the objectives society wants from riverine ecosystems. Use of best management practices (BMPs) for timber harvesting, livestock grazing, road construction and maintenance, and mining can significantly reduce adverse impacts.

Beyond such specific techniques are several other approaches that are increasingly recognized as essential to maintaining or improving riverine ecosystems. The first is a greater effort to understand the cumulative, long-term effects of our actions (Sidle and Hornbeck 1991). Because cumulative effects may not become apparent for many years and may take many forms, this will necessitate long-term, multidisciplinary studies (Scrivener 1988, Rinne 1990, Ziemer et al. 1991). In addition, activities within riverine systems must be managed from a broader perspective than in the past. The more we understand the relationships within riverine ecosystems and between them and the surrounding landscape, the more obvious becomes the need for a larger perspective of the potential effects of human activities at a watershed or multiple-watershed level and not in terms of an individual stream reach or stream (DeBano and Schmidt 1989, Swanson et al. 1990, Bisson et al. 1997). Finally, effective riverine management must include consideration of social factors (Lee 1992, Ice 1996, Karr 1996). Given the range of interests, the various levels of knowledge, and the diversity of values within society, the greatest challenge for management of riverine ecosystems will continue to be the human component.

Literature Cited

Aitchison, S. W., S. W. Carothers, and R. R. Johnson. 1977. Some ecological considerations associated with river recreation management. Pages 222–225 *in* River recreation management and research symposium. U.S. Forest Service General Technical Report NC-28.

Anderson, B. W., and R. D. Ohmart. 1985. Riparian revegetation as a mitigating process in stream and river restoration. Pages 41–80 *in* J. A. Gore, editor. The restoration of rivers and streams: theories and experience. Butterworth, Boston, Massachusetts, USA.

Auble, G. T., J. M. Friedman, and M. L. Scott. 1994. Relating riparian vegetation to present and future streamflows. Ecological Applications 4:544–554.

Belt, G., J. O'Laughlin, and T. Merrill. 1992. Design of forest buffer strips for the protection of water quality: analysis of scientific literature. Idaho Forest, Wildlife, and Range Policy Analysis Group. Report 8. University of Idaho, Moscow, Idaho, USA.

Beschta, R. L. 1991. Stream habitat management for fish in the northwestern United States: the role of riparian vegetation. American Fisheries Society Symposium 10: 53–58.

———, R. E. Bilby, G. W. Brown, L. B. Holtby, and T. D. Hofstra. 1987. Stream temperature and aquatic habitat: fisheries and forestry interactions. Pages 191–232 in E. O. Salo and T. W. Cundy, editors. Streamside management: forestry and fishery interactions. Institute of Forest Resources Contributions 57. University of Washington, Seattle, Washington, USA.

Bilby, R. E. 1988. Interactions between aquatic and terrestrial systems. Pages 13–30 in K. J. Raedeke, editor. Streamside management: riparian wildlife and forestry interactions. Institute of Forest Resources Contribution 59. University of Washington, Seattle, USA.

———, and G. E. Likens. 1980. Importance of organic debris dams in the structure and function of stream ecosystems. Ecology 61:1107–1113.

Binkley, D., and T. C. Brown. 1993a. Management impacts on water quality of forests and rangelands. U.S. Forest Service General Technical Report RM-39.

———, and———. 1993b. Forest practices as nonpoint sources of pollution in North America. Water Resources Bulletin 29:729–740.

———, and L. McDonald. 1994. Forests as nonpoint sources of pollution and effectiveness of best management practices. National Council for Air and Stream Improvement Technical Bulletin 672. Research Triangle Park, North Carolina, USA.

Bisson, P. A., T. P. Quinn, G. H. Reeves, and S. V. Gregory. 1992. Best management practices, cumulative effects, and long-term trends in fish abundance in Pacific Northwest river systems. Pages 189–225 in R. J. Naiman, editor. Watershed management: balancing sustainability and environmental change. Springer-Verlag, New York, New York, USA.

———, G. H. Reeves, R. E. Bilby, and R. J. Naiman. 1997. Watershed management and Pacific salmon desired future conditions. Pages 447–474 in D. J. Stouder, P. A. Bisson, and R. J. Naiman, editors. Pacific salmon and their ecosystems: status and trends. Chapman and Hall, New York, New York, USA.

Blinn, C. R., and R. A. Dahlman. 1996. Riparian harvesting with a soft footprint. Pages 76–81 in S. B. Laursen, editor. At the water's edge: the science of riparian forestry. Proceedings of the science of riparian forestry conference, June 19–20, 1995, Duluth, Minnesota, USA. University of Minnesota, Saint Paul, Minnesota, USA.

Bradley, C. E., and D. G. Smith. 1986. Plains cottonwood recruitment and survival on a prairie meandering river floodplain, Milk River, southern Alberta and northern Montana. Canadian Journal of Botany 64:1433–1442.

Brickler, S. K., and J. G. Utter. 1975. Impact of recreation use and development on water quality in Arizona: an overview. Pages 195–201 in J. D. Mertes, editor. Man, leisure, and wildlands: a complex interaction. Eisenhower Consortium Bulletin Number 1. Springfield, Virginia, USA.

Brooks, R. P. 1990. Wetland and waterbody restoration and creation associated with mining. Pages 529–548 in J. A. Kusler and M. E. Kentula, editors. Wetland creation and restoration: the status of the science. Island Press, Covelo, California, USA.

Brown, E. R., technical editor. 1985. Management of wildlife and fish habitats in western Oregon and Washington. U.S. Forest Service, Pacific Northwest Region, Portland, Oregon, USA.

Buckhouse, J. C., and W. Elmore. 1991. Grazing practice relationships: predicting riparian vegetation response from stream systems. Pages 47–52 in T. Bedell, editor.

Watershed management guide for the interior Northwest. Oregon State University Extension Service, Corvallis, Oregon, USA.

Burroughs, E. R. Jr., and J. G. King. 1989. Reduction of soil erosion on forest roads. U.S. Forest Service General Technical Report INT-264.

Busch, D. E., and M. L. Scott. 1995. Western riparian ecosystems. Pages 286–290 *in* E. T. LaRoe, G. S. Farris, C. E. Puckett, P. D. Doran, and M. J. Mac, editors. Our living resources: a report to the nation on the distribution, abundance, and health of U.S. plants, animals, and ecosystems. U.S. National Biological Service, Washington, D.C., USA.

Chavez, L. 1996. Above-below diversion study. Pages 145–150 *in* D. Neary, K. C. Ross, and S. C. Coleman, editors. Proceedings of the National Hydrology Workshop. U.S. Forest Service General Technical Report RM-279.

Clark, R. N., and D. R. Gibbons. 1991. Recreation. Pages 459–481 *in* W. R. Meehan, editor. Influences of forest and rangeland management on salmonid fishes and their habitats. American Fisheries Society Special Publication 19, Bethesda, Maryland, USA.

Clary, W. P., E. D. McArthur, D. Bedunah, and C. L. Wambolt, compilers. 1992. Proceedings of symposium on ecology and management of riparian shrub communities. U.S. Forest Service General Technical Report INT-289.

———, and B. F. Webster. 1989. Managing grazing of riparian areas in the Intermountain region. U.S. Forest Service General Technical Report INT-263.

Cohan, D. R., B. W. Anderson, and R. D. Ohmart. 1979. Avian population responses to salt cedar along the lower Colorado River. Pages 371–381 *in* R. R. Johnson and J. F. McCormick, technical coordinators. Strategies for protection and management of floodplain wetlands and other riparian ecosystems. U.S. Forest Service General Technical Report WO-12.

Cole, D. N. 1987. Research on soil and vegetation in wilderness: a state-of-knowledge review. Pages 135–177 *in* R. C. Lucas, compiler. National wilderness research conference: perspectives, state of knowledge, and future directions. U.S. Forest Service General Technical Report INT-220.

———, and J. L. Marion. 1988. Recreational impacts in some riparian forests of the eastern United States. Environmental Management 12:99–107.

Collier, M., R. H. Webb, and J. C. Schmidt. 1996. Dams and rivers: a primer on the downstream effects of dams. U.S. Geological Survey Circular 1126. Tucson, Arizona, USA.

Cooper, D. J. 1994. Sustaining and restoring western wetland and riparian ecosystems threatened by or affected by water development projects. Pages 27–33 *in* W. W. Covington and L. F. DeBano, technical coordinators. Sustainable ecological systems: implementing an ecological approach to land management. U.S. Forest Service General Technical Report RM-247.

Craig, W. S. 1977. Reducing impacts from river recreation use. River recreation management and research symposium. U.S. Forest Service General Technical Report NC-28.

Cummins, K. W., and G. L. Spengler. 1978. Stream ecosystems. Water Spectrum 10(4):1–9.

DeBano, L. F., and L. J. Schmidt. 1989. Improving southwestern riparian areas through watershed management. U.S. Forest Service General Technical Report RM-182.

Ditton, R. B., D. J. Schmidly, W. J. Boeer, and A. R. Graefe. 1977. A survey and analysis of recreational and livestock impacts on the riparian zone of the Rio Grande in

Big Bend National Park. Pages 256–265 *in* River recreation management and research symposium. U.S. Forest Service General Technical Report NC-28.

Dobyns, H. F. 1981. From fire to flood: historic human destruction of Sonoran Desert riverine oases. Ballena Press, Socorro, New Mexico, USA.

Ehrhart, R. C., and P. L. Hansen. 1997. Effective cattle management in riparian zones: a field survey and literature review. Montana Bureau of Land Management Riparian Technical Bulletin 3. Montana Forest and Conservation Experiment Station, University of Montana, Missoula, Montana, USA.

Elmore, W. 1992. Riparian responses to grazing practices. Pages 442–457 *in* R. J. Naiman, editor. Watershed management: balancing sustainability and environmental change. Springer-Verlag, New York, New York, USA.

Everest, F. H., N. B. Armantrout, S. M. Keller, J. D. Sedell, T. E. Nickelson, J. M. Johnston, and G. N. Haugen. 1985. Salmonids. Pages 199–230 *in* E. R. Brown, technical editor. Management of wildlife and fish habitats in western Oregon and Washington. U.S. Forest Service Pacific Northwest Region, Portland, Oregon, USA.

Fleischner, T. L. 1994. Ecological costs of livestock grazing in western North America. Conservation Biology 8:629–644.

Furniss, M. J., T. D. Roelofs, and C. S. Yee. 1991. Road construction and maintenance. Pages 297–323 *in* W. R. Meehan, editor. Influences of forest and rangeland management on salmonid fishes and their habitats. American Fisheries Society Special Publication 19, Bethesda, Maryland, USA.

Garland, J. J. 1987. Aspects of practical management in the streamside zone. Pages 277–288 *in* E. O. Salo and T. W. Cundy, editors. Streamside management: forestry and fishery interactions. Institute of Forest Resources, Contribution 57. University of Washington, Seattle, Washington, USA.

George, M. 1998. Management practices to change livestock behavior in grazed watersheds. Pages 37–46 *in* S. Swanson, M. R. George, J. C. Buckhouse, and R. E. Larson, editors. Evaluation of effectiveness of livestock and range management practices in grazed watersheds. U.S. Environmental Protection Agency, Washington, D.C., USA.

Gore, J. A., editor. 1985. The restoration of rivers and streams. Butterworth, Stoneham, Massachusetts, USA.

Gosz, J. R. 1982. Non-point source pollution of water by recreation: research assessment and research needs. Eisenhower Consortium Bulletin 13. Springfield, Virginia, USA.

Gregory, S. V., and P. A. Bisson. 1997. Degradation and loss of anadromous salmonid habitat in the Pacific Northwest. Pages 277–305 *in* D. J. Stouder, P. A. Bisson, and R. J. Naiman, editors. Pacific salmon and their ecosystems: status and trends. Chapman and Hall, New York, New York, USA.

Groeneveld, D. P., and T. E. Griepentrog. 1985. Interdependence of groundwater, riparian vegetation, and streambank stability: a case study. Pages 44–48 *in* R. R. Johnson, C. D. Ziebell, D. R. Patton, P. F. Ffolliott, and R. H. Hamre, technical coordinators. Riparian ecosystems and their management: reconciling conflicting uses. U.S. Forest Service General Technical Report RM-120.

Hagar, J. C., W. C. McComb, and C. C. Chambers. 1995. Effects of forest practices on wildlife. Chapter 9 *in* R. L. Beschta. Cumulative effects of forest practices in Oregon: literature and synthesis. Oregon Department of Forestry, Salem, Oregon, USA.

Hammitt, W. E., and D. N. Cole. 1987. Wildland recreation: ecology and management. John Wiley and Sons, New York, New York, USA.

Harmon, M. E., J. F. Franklin, F. J. Swanson, P. Sollins, S. V. Gregory, J. D. Lattin, N. H. Anderson, S. P. Cline, N. G. Aumen, J. R. Sedell, G. W. Lienkaemper, K. Cromack Jr., and K. W. Cummins. 1986. Ecology of coarse woody debris in temperate ecosystems. Pages 133–302 in A. Macfadyen and E. D. Ford. Advances in ecological research. Academic Press, New York, New York, USA.

Hartman, G. F., J. C. Scrivener, and M. J. Miles. 1996. Impacts of logging in Carnation Creek, a high-energy coastal stream in British Columbia, and their implications for restoring fish habitat. Canadian Journal of Fisheries and Aquatic Science 53 (Supplement 1): 237–251.

Heede, B. H. 1985. Interactions between streamside vegetation and stream dynamics. Pages 54–58 in R. R. Johnson, C. D. Ziebell, D. R. Patton, P. F. Ffolliott, and R. H. Hamre, technical coordinators. Riparian ecosystems and their management: reconciling conflicting uses. U.S. Forest Service General Technical Report RM-120.

Hirsch, R. M., J. F. Walker, J. C. Day, and B. R. Kallio. 1990. The influence of man on hydrologic systems. Pages 329–349 in M. G. Wolman and H. C. Riggs. The geology of North America. Volume 0-1. Surface water hydrology. The Geological Society of America, Boulder, Colorado, USA.

Howe, W. H., and F. L. Knopf. 1991. On the imminent decline of Rio Grande cottonwoods in central New Mexico. The Southwest Naturalist 36:218–224.

Ice, G. G. 1996. Approaches to solving nonpoint source issues. Pages 74–80 in D. Neary, K. C. Ross, and S. C. Coleman, editors. National Hydrology Workshop Proceedings. U.S. Forest Service General Technical Report RM-279.

Johnson, R. R. 1979. The lower Colorado River: a western system. Pages 41–55 in R. R. Johnson and J. F. McCormick, technical coordinators. Strategies for protection and management of floodplain wetlands and other riparian ecosystems. U.S. Forest Service General Technical Report WO-12.

———, and S. W. Carothers. 1982. Riparian habitats and recreation: interrelationships and impacts in the southwest and Rocky Mountain region. Eisenhower Consortium for Western Environmental Forestry Bulletin 12, Springfield, Virginia, USA.

———, and L. T. Haight. 1984. Riparian problems and initiatives in the American southwest: a regional perspective. Pages 401–412 in R. E. Warner and K. M. Hendrix, editors. California Riparian Systems. University of California, Berkeley, California, USA.

———, and D. A. Jones, editors. 1977. Importance, preservation and management of riparian habitat: a symposium. July 9, 1977, Tucson, Arizona. U.S. Forest Service General Technical Report RM-43.

Karr, J. R. 1996. Making meaning of all the science. Pages 149–152 in S. B. Laursen, editor. At the water's edge: the science of riparian forestry. University of Minnesota, Saint Paul, Minnesota, USA.

Kauffman, J. B. 1988. The status of riparian habitats in Pacific Northwest forests. Pages 45–56 in K. J. Raedeke, editor. Streamside management: riparian wildlife and forestry interactions. Institute of Forest Resources Contribution 59. University of Washington, Seattle, Washington, USA.

———, and W. C. Krueger. 1984. Livestock impacts on riparian ecosystems and streamside management implications—a review. Journal of Range Management 37:430–438.

Klimas, C. V. 1988. River regulation effects on floodplain hydrology and ecology. Pages 40–49 in D. D. Hook, W. H. McKee Jr., H. K. Smith, J. Gregory, V. G. Burrell Jr., M. R. DeVoe, R. E. Sojka, S. Gilbert, R. Banks, L. H. Stolzy, C. Brooks, T. D. Matthews, and T. H. Shear, editors. Ecology of wetlands. Volume 1 of The ecology and management of wetlands. Timber Press, Portland, Oregon, USA.

Knopf, F. L., and R. W. Cannon. 1982. Structural resilience of a willow riparian community to changes in livestock grazing practices. Pages 198–207 in Wildlife-livestock relationships symposium: proceedings 10. University of Idaho Forest, Wildlife, and Range Experiment Station, Moscow, Idaho, USA.

Kondolf, G. M. 1994. Geomorphic and environmental effects of instream gravel mining. Landscape and Urban Planning 28:225–243.

Krueper, D. J. 1993. Effects of land use practices on western riparian ecosystems. Pages 321–220 in D. M. Finch and P. W. Stangel, editors. Status and management of neotropical migratory birds. U.S. Forest Service General Technical Report RM-229.

LaFayette, R. A., J. R. Pruitt, and W. D. Zeedyk. 1996. Riparian area enhancement through road design and maintenance. Pages 85–95 in D. Neary, K. C. Ross, and S. C. Coleman, editors. National Hydrology Workshop Proceedings. U.S. Forest Service General Technical Report RM-279.

Larsen, R. E., W. C. Krueger, M. R. George, M. R. Barrington, J. C. Buckhouse, and D. E. Johnson. 1998. Viewpoint: livestock influences on riparian zones and fish habitat: literature classification. Journal of Range Management 51:661–664.

Lee, R. G. 1992. Ecologically effective social organization as a requirement for sustaining watershed ecosystems. Pages 73–90 in R. J. Naiman, editor. Watershed management: balancing sustainability and environmental change. Springer-Verlag, New York, New York, USA.

Leonard, S., G. Kinch, V. Elsbernd, M. Borman, S. Swanson. 1997. Riparian area management: grazing management for wetland areas. Technical Bulletin 1737-14. U.S. Bureau of Land Management. Washington, D.C., USA.

Ligon, F. K., W. E. Dietrich, and W. J. Trush. 1995. Downstream ecological effects of dams: a geomorphic perspective. BioScience 45:183–192.

Likens, G. E., and F. H. Bormann. 1974. Linkages between terrestrial and aquatic ecosystems. BioScience 24:447–456.

Lynch, J. A., and E. S. Corbett. 1990. Evaluation of best management practices for controlling nonpoint pollution from silvicultural operations. Water Resources Bulletin 26:41–52.

Manci, K. M. 1989. Riparian ecosystem creation and restoration: a literature summary. U.S. Fish and Wildlife Service. Biological Report 89(20). Washington, D.C., USA.

Manning, R. E. 1979. Impacts of recreation on riparian soils and vegetation. Water Resources Bulletin 15:30–43.

Martin, S. B., and W. S. Platts. 1981. Influence of forest and rangeland management on anadromous fish habitat in western North America: effects of mining. U.S. Forest Service General Technical Report PNW-119.

Medin, D. E., and W. P. Clary. 1989. Small mammal populations in a grazed and ungrazed riparian habitat in Nevada. U.S. Forest Service Research Paper INT-413.

———, and———. 1990. Bird and small mammal populations in a grazed and ungrazed riparian habitat in Idaho. U.S. Forest Service Research Paper INT-425.

Meehan, W. R., and W. S. Platts. 1978. Livestock grazing and the aquatic environment. Journal of Soil and Water Conservation, November/December:274–278.

Merigliano, M. F. Jr. 1996. Flood-plain and vegetation dynamics along a gravel bed, braided river in the Northern Rocky Mountains. Dissertation, University of Montana, Missoula, Montana, USA.

Mitsch, W. J and J. G. Gosselink. 2000. Wetlands. Third Edition. John Wiley and Sons, New York, New York, USA.

Montana State University Extension Service (MSU). 1991. Montana forestry BMPs (best management practices). Montana State University, Bozeman, Montana, USA.

Mosley, J. C., P. S. Cook, A. J. Griffis, and J. O'Laughlin. 1997. Guidelines for managing cattle grazing in riparian areas to protect water quality: review of research and best management practices policy. Idaho Forest, Wildlife, and Range Policy Analysis Group. Report 15. University of Idaho, Moscow, Idaho, USA.

Nelson, R. L., M. L. McHenry, and W. S. Platts. 1991. Mining. Pages 425–457 in W. R. Meehan, editor. Influences of forest and rangeland management on salmonid fishes and their habitats. American Fisheries Society Special Publication 19, Bethesda, Maryland, USA.

Noss, R. F., E. T. LaRoe III, and J. M. Scott. 1995. Endangered ecosystems of the United States: a preliminary assessment of loss and degradation. Microform. U.S. Department of the Interior, National Biological Service. Washington, D.C., USA.

Nutter, W. L., and J. W. Gaskin. 1989. Role of streamside management zones in controlling discharges to wetlands. Pages 81–84 in D. D. Hook and R. Lea, editors. The forested wetlands of the United States. U.S. Forest Service General Technical Report SE-50.

Ohmart, R. D. 1984. The effects of human-induced changes in the avifauna of western riparian habitats. Studies in Avian Biology 15:273–285.

———, and B. W. Anderson. 1982. North American desert riparian ecosystems. Pages 433–480 in G. L. Bender, editor. Reference handbook on the deserts of North America. Greenwood Press, Westport, Connecticut, USA.

Oliver, C. D., and T. M. Hinckley. 1987. Species, stand structure, and silvicultural manipulation patterns for the streamside zone. Pages 259–276 in E. O. Salo and T. W. Cundy, editors. Streamside management: forestry and fishery interactions. Institute of Forest Resources, Contribution 57. University of Washington, Seattle, Washington, USA.

Platts, W. S. 1979. Livestock grazing and riparian/stream ecosystems—an overview. Proceedings of the forum on grazing and riparian/stream ecosystems. Trout Unlimited, Vienna, Virginia, USA.

———. 1991. Livestock grazing. Pages 389–423 in W. R. Meehan, editor. Influences of forest and rangeland management on salmonid fishes and their habitats. American Fisheries Society Special Publication 19. Bethesda, Maryland, USA.

———, and R. F. Raleigh. 1984. Pages 1105–1118 in Developing strategies for rangeland management. National Research Council/National Academy of Sciences. Westview Press, Boulder, Colorado, USA.

Raedeke, K. J., editor. 1988. Streamside management: riparian wildlife and forestry interactions. Institute of Forest Resources Contribution 59. University of Washington, Seattle, Washington, USA.

Rasmussen, G. A., and W. Padgett. 1994. Recreational effects on riparian areas. Pages 45–48 in G. A. Rasmussen and J. P. Dobrowolski, editors. Riparian resources: a symposium on the disturbances, management, economics, and conflicts associated with riparian ecosystems. College of Natural Resources, Utah State University, Logan, Utah, USA.

Rea, A. M. 1983. Once a river: bird life and habitat changes on the Middle Gila. University of Arizona Press, Tucson, Arizona, USA.

Reeder, R., editor. 1994. Riparian road guide: managing roads to enhance riparian areas. Terrene Institute in cooperation with EPA, Region 6 (water quality management branch), U.S. Forest Service Pacific Southwest Region. Albany, California, USA.

Rice, R. M. 1992. The science and politics of best management practices in forestry: California experiences. Pages 385–400 in R. J. Naiman, editor. Watershed management: balancing sustainability and environmental change. Springer-Verlag, New York, New York, USA.

Rinne, J. N. 1988. Grazing effects on stream habitat and fishes: research design considerations. North American Journal of Fisheries Management 8:240–247.

———. 1990. Minimizing livestock grazing effects on riparian stream habitats: recommendations for research and management. Pages 15–28 in Proceedings of a national conference on enhancing the states' lake and wetland management programs, May 18–19, 1989, Chicago, Illinois. Northeastern Illinois Planning Commission, Chicago, USA.

———. 1994. Declining southwestern aquatic habitat and fishes: are they sustainable? Pages 256–265 in W. W. Covington and L. F. DeBano, technical coordinators. Sustainable ecological systems: implementing an ecological approach to land management. U.S. Forest Service General Technical Report RM-247.

Rood, S. B., and J. M. Mahoney. 1990. Collapse of riparian forests downstream from dams in western prairies: probable causes and prospects for mitigation. Environmental Management 14:451–64.

Saab, V. A., C. E. Bock, T. D. Rich, and D. S. Dobkin. 1995. Pages 311–353 in T. E. Martin and D. M. Finch, editors. Ecology and management of neotropical migratory birds: a synthesis and review of critical issues. Oxford University Press, New York, New York, USA.

Satterlund, D. R., and P. W. Adams. 1992. Wildland watershed management. John Wiley and Sons, New York, New York, USA.

Schmidly, D. J., and R. B. Ditton. 1979. Relating human activities and biological resources in riparian habitats of western Texas. Pages 107–115 in R. R. Johnson and J. F. McCormick, technical coordinators. Strategies for protection and management of floodplain wetlands and other riparian ecosystems. U.S. Forest Service General Technical Report WO-12.

Schultz, T. T., and W. C. Leininger. 1991. Nongame wildlife communities in grazed and ungrazed montane riparian sites. Great Basin Naturalist 51(3):286–292.

Scott, M. L., J. M. Friedman, and G. T. Auble. 1996. Fluvial process and the establishment of riparian trees. Geomorphology 14:327–339.

Scrivener, J. C. 1988. Changes in composition of the streambed between 1973 and 1985 and the impacts on salmonids in Carnation Creek. Pages 59–65 in T. W. Chamberlin, editor. Proceedings of the workshop: applying 15 years of Carnation Creek results. Pacific Biological Station, Carnation Creek Steering Committee, Nanaimo, British Columbia, Canada.

Sedell, J. R., G. H. Reeves, and P. A. Bisson. 1997. Habitat policy for salmon in the Pacific Northwest. Pages 375–388 in D. J. Stouder, P. A. Bisson, and R. J. Naiman, editors. Pacific salmon and their ecosystems: status and trends. Chapman and Hall, New York, New York, USA.

———, P. A. Bisson, F. J. Swanson, and S. V. Gregory. 1988. What we know about large trees that fall into streams and rivers. Pages 47–81 in C. Maser, R. F. Tarrant, J. M. Thorpe, and J. F. Franklin, technical editors. From the forest to the seas: a story of fallen trees. U.S. Forest Service General Technical Report PNW-229.

Settergren, C. D. 1977. Impacts of river recreation on streambank soils and vegetation—state-of-the-knowledge. Pages 55–59 in River recreation management and research symposium. U.S. Forest Service General Technical Report NC-28.

Sidle, R. C., and J. W. Hornbeck. 1991. Cumulative effects: a broader approach to water quality research. Journal of Soil and Water Conservation 46:268–271.

———, and A. Sharma. 1996. Stream channel changes associated with mining and grazing in the Great Basin. Journal of Environmental Quality 25:1111–1121.

Skovlin, J. M. 1984. Impacts of grazing on wetlands and riparian habitat: a review of our knowledge. Pages 1001–1103 in Developing strategies for rangeland management. National Research Council/National Academy of Sciences. Westview Press, Boulder, Colorado, USA.

Smith, R. D. 1996. Geomorphic effects of large woody debris in streams. Pages 113–127 in D. Neary, K. C. Ross, and S. C. Coleman, editors. National Hydrology Workshop proceedings. U.S. Forest Service General Technical Report RM-279.

Stanford, J. A., and J. V. Ward. 1979. Stream regulation in North America. Pages 215–236 in J. V. Ward and J. A. Stanford, editors. The ecology of regulated streams. Plenum Press, New York, New York, USA.

Stauffer, D. F., and L. B. Best. 1980. Habitat selection by birds of riparian communities: evaluating effects of habitat alterations. Journal of Wildlife Management 44:1–15.

Stromberg, J.C. 1993. Instream flow models for mixed deciduous riparian vegetation within a semiarid region. Regulated Rivers: Research and Management 8:225–235.

———, R. Tiller, and B. Richter. 1996. Effects of groundwater decline on riparian vegetation of semiarid regions: the San Pedro River, Arizona. Ecological Applications 6:113–131.

Swanson, F. J., J. F. Franklin, and J. R. Sedell. 1990. Landscape patterns, disturbance, and management in the Pacific Northwest, USA. Pages 191–213 in I. S. Zonneveld and R. T. T. Forman, editors. Changing landscapes: an ecological perspective. Springer-Verlag, New York, New York, USA.

Swift, B. L. 1984. Status of riparian ecosystems in the United States. Water Resources Bulletin 20: 223–228.

Thomas, J. W., C. Maser, and J. E. Rodiek. 1979. Wildlife habitats in managed rangelands—the Great Basin of southeastern Oregon. Riparian Zones. U.S. Forest Service General Technical Report PNW-80.

Williams, G. P., and M. G. Wolman. 1984. Downstream effects of dams on alluvial rivers. U.S. Geological Survey Professional Paper 1286. Government Printing Office, Washington, D.C., USA.

Williams, J. E., D. B. Bowman, J. E. Brooks, A. A. Echelle, R. J. Edwards, D. A. Hendrickson, and J. J. Landye. 1985. Endangered aquatic ecosystems in North American deserts with a list of vanishing fishes of the region. Journal of the Arizona-Nevada Academy of Science 20:1–62.

————, C. A. Wood, and M. P. Dombeck, editors. 1997. Watershed restoration: principles and practices. American Fisheries Society, Bethesda, Maryland, USA.

Windsor, C. L. 1989. Recommended management practices for forested wetlands road construction. Pages 51–53 *in* D. D. Hook and R. Lea, editors. The forested wetlands of the United States. U.S. Forest Service General Technical Report SE-50.

Ziemer, R. R., J. Lewis, R. M. Rice, and T. E. Lisle. 1991. Modeling the cumulative watershed effects of forest management strategies. Journal of Environmental Quality 20:36–42.

CHAPTER 6

Irrigation, Salinity, and Landscape Patterns of Natural Palustrine Wetlands

JAMES R. LOVVORN AND
E. ANDREW HART

Introduction

In large intermountain basins of the western United States, water for wetlands comes mostly from snowmelt in adjacent mountains (Lemly et al. 1993, Engilis and Reid 1997, Lovvorn et al. 1999). In many cases this water reaches wetlands via irrigation systems, either through ditches, as groundwater (interflow) derived from leaky ditches or flood irrigation, or by sprinklers drawing from confined aquifers that are recharged by mountain snowmelt at basin peripheries (Powell 1958, Burritt 1962, Hamilton et al. 1986, Harmon 1989, Lico 1992, Peck and Lovvorn 2001). Owing to high evaporation and salt deposition, the wetland community at a given site and time generally results from short- and long-term interactions between hydroperiod and salinity (Christiansen and Low 1970, Kadlec and Smith 1989, Hallock and Hallock 1993, Lovvorn et al. 1999, Hart 2001). Thus, annual mountain snowmelt and irrigation deliveries alter the size, spatial arrangement, and foodweb functions of wetlands of different salinities across the landscape.

Allocation of irrigation flows varies substantially with water supplies in current and preceding years and with varying annual and monthly demands of users with different water rights. Wetlands are seldom considered in water distribution schemes, as they are not a "beneficial use" in western water law (Jacobs et al. 1990; also see Chapter 1 of this volume). However, when potential exists to create or enhance wetlands, or when proposed changes in water management threaten existing wetlands, criteria are needed to predict or evaluate their ecosystem functions. The most useful criteria are indicator variables that subsume habitat structure, community composition, and trophic function and that can be used in various wetlands across the landscape to assess cumulative values (Klopatek 1988, Schaeffer et al. 1988, Keddy et al. 1993).

If effects of altered inflow can be predicted in terms of indicator variables, and if inflow changes can be predicted from models of irrigation systems, it should be possible to optimize water management for wetland, agricultural, and domestic functions (Salazar et al. 1989, Sojda et al. 1994). For example, required inflows have been modeled with salinity as an indicator variable in various coastal estuaries (Hutchison and Midgley 1978, Bradley et al. 1990, Tung et al. 1990, Powell and Matsumoto 1994, Jassby et al. 1995). However, with the exception of plant communities in wetlands around Great Salt Lake (Christiansen and Low 1970), this approach has rarely been taken in analogous inland situations of irrigation-fed saline wetlands.

Thus, in wetlands of large intermountain basins, efforts to maximize ecosystem integrity, biodiversity, and resilience to disturbance would be aided by (1) identifying indicators of ecosystem state and foodweb function, as a basis for regulating inflow to specific wetlands; (2) determining how the spatial arrangement of wetland types affects consumers that move among wetlands, as a basis for distributing water into appropriate wetland complexes; and (3) incorporating these elements into models of water allocation for irrigation and domestic use to predict cumulative effects of different water management schemes.

Although the importance of irrigation to regional wetlands is widely recognized, no studies have been completed that integrate these goals. Effects of salinity, a direct indicator of freshwater inflow, have been examined for wetland plant communities in the Laramie Basin of Wyoming (Lovvorn et al. 1999, Hart and Lovvorn 2000), the Great Salt Lake area (Christiansen and Low 1970, Kadlec and Smith 1989), and the Lahontan Basin of Nevada (Hamilton and Auble 1993). Effects of vegetation and salinity on invertebrate communities have been studied in the Laramie Basin (Wollheim and Lovvorn 1995, 1996; Lovvorn et al. 1999; Hart 2001), the Great Salt Lake area (Cox and Kadlec 1995), and the San Luis Valley of Colorado (Severn 1992, Cooper and Durfee 1996). We know of no studies on the foodweb function of palustrine or lacustrine wetlands of intermountain basins in western Montana, Idaho, eastern Washington (see Harris 1954), eastern Oregon, or Arizona.

To our knowledge, the only research in this region seeking to integrate studies of geochemistry, detritus, algae, macrophytes, invertebrates, and foodweb structure, and of irrigation effects on the dispersion of wetland types and mobile vertebrates, has been done in the Laramie Basin (Lovvorn et al. 1999; Hart and Lovvorn 2000; Hart 2001; Peck and Lovvorn 2001; Hart and Lovvorn 2002). Consequently, in this chapter we focus on the Laramie Basin, which resembles a number of other large basins of the Intermountain West (Szymczak 1986, Windell et al. 1986; see Figure 6.1).

FIGURE 6.1. Location of large intermountain basins of the central Rocky Mountains: LB = Laramie Basin, NP = North Park, MP = Middle Park, SP = South Park, SLV = San Luis Valley

Hydrology and Vegetation

Typical of other large intermountain basins of the Intermountain West, the Laramie Basin is about 95 km long and 40 km wide and lies at an elevation of about 2,200 m between the Laramie Range to the east and Medicine Bow Range to the west (Reheis et al. 1991; also see Figure 6.2). The short, cool growing season (mean frost-free period of 93 days; Mart-

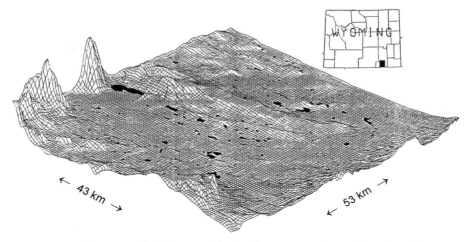

FIGURE 6.2. Exaggerated relief map of the southern Laramie Basin, Wyoming, showing the dispersion of shallow lakes (blackened areas) throughout the landscape

ner 1986) restricts crop production, and the main land uses are cattle grazing and hay production through flood irrigation. Average evaporation from lakes of 127 cm/y is 5 times the total precipitation of 26 cm/y (Martner 1986), so essentially all wetlands are saline (conductivity of >0.8 mS/cm or total dissolved solids [TDS] of >0.5 g/L, Cowardin et al. 1979). The many scattered wetlands within the area (Figure 6.2) are mostly wind-eroded playas, often enhanced by dikes, ditches, and water control structures. As in many basins of the Intermountain West (e.g., Powell 1958, Szymczak 1986, Lico 1992), local surface runoff is negligible, and snowmelt from surrounding mountains reaches wetlands via irrigation ditches and associated groundwater. Occurrence and amount of inflow to wetlands from hyporheic groundwater (about 0.75 g/L TDS) depend on the wind-scoured depth of a particular wetland's basin and its location relative to alluvial deposits recharged by leaking ditches and return flows (Burritt 1962, Reheis et al. 1991, Stanford and Ward 1993). The salinity of most area wetlands varies appreciably with frequency and amount of inflow from irrigation ditches and associated near-surface groundwater, mainly in May and June.

In climate, hydrology, and native vegetation, the Laramie Basin resembles other high-altitude intermountain basins in the Intermountain West, such as Colorado's North Park, South Park, and San Luis Valley (Figure 6.1; Ramaley 1942; Szymczak 1986; Doesken and McKee 1989; also see Chapter 2 of this volume). Unlike the other areas, the more extensive confined aquifer of the San Luis Valley has led to replacement of flood irrigation by center-pivot sprinklers as the main form of irrigation.

Despite high evaporative loss and power costs of pumping from confined aquifers, sprinkler irrigation requires less water than flood or subsurface irrigation (McFadden 1989). The resulting decrease in diversion of water onto irrigated meadows has lowered the local water table and reduced the number and seasonal permanence of wetlands (Szymczak 1986). In general, wetlands in the San Luis Valley tend to be seasonal and palustrine (dominated by emergent plants), whereas wetlands in the Laramie Basin are mainly permanent and lacustrine (dominated by submersed plants), often with little or no area of emergent vegetation, depending on salinity. In all these intermountain basins, upland vegetation near wetlands includes mostly black greasewood, rabbitbrush, and saltgrass, whose relative dominance depends largely on depth of the water table (Szymczak 1986, Dixon 1989).

A number of important wetlands in the Intermountain West occur as large, relatively contiguous wetlands in terminal basins and often are associated with large lakes. Although small saline wetlands occur in local terminal basins throughout the region, including scattered sites in the Laramie Basin and San Luis Valley, a number of those in the Great Basin are quite large, e.g., those in the Lahontan and Ruby Basins of Nevada, the Malheur-Harney Basin of Oregon, and around Great Salt Lake (Hamilton et al. 1986, Kadlec and Smith 1989, Engilis and Reid 1997). Water reaching these terminal basins also varies with mountain snowmelt and the amount of water diverted for irrigation (Riley 1972, Horton et al. 1983, Smith and Kadlec 1986, Lico 1992, Kruse et al. 2003). These large, closed-basin wetlands include mosaics of emergent and submersed plants whose species composition depends on variations in hydroperiod and resulting salinity (Christiansen and Low 1970, Kadlec and Smith 1989). Despite their lower elevation than the high basins of Wyoming and Colorado, these wetlands have similar plant taxa.

Attributes of Indicator Variables

Ecological indicators have been proposed for assessing and monitoring the state of ecosystems, before and after both perturbations and restoration efforts (Schaeffer et al. 1988, Keddy et al. 1993). Good indicators should (1) integrate information on ecosystem state, species composition, diversity of trophic function, and resilience to natural or human disturbance; (2) be responsive to natural and anthropogenic changes; (3) respond predictably to changes, so that planning models accurately predict changes in the indicator; (4) be usable in assessing cumulative functions; and (5) require minimal training for measurement and no long-term laboratory work to delay results, so the indicator can be easily monitored and promptly regulated.

Single indicators, especially water quality variables that supposedly subsume biotic characteristics, have been criticized as too simplistic (Karr 1987). However, societal demand for metrics that yield rapid results inexpensively by minimally trained personnel has sustained the search for such indicators. In snow-driven irrigation systems, allocation decisions are made as quickly as changing temperature can influence snowmelt, sometimes daily. Time and resources are insufficient for monitoring short-term responses of biota or for placing water-level gauges in all wetlands. Thus, a simple indicator such as salinity, which can be measured with conductivity meters or inexpensive refractometers, is desirable. Salinity and its correlates have fundamental and often dominant effects on habitat structure, species composition, primary production, and trophic function of both inland and coastal wetlands (Hammer 1986, Kadlec and Smith 1989, Longley 1994, McIvor et al. 1994, Cox and Kadlec 1995, Glenn et al. 1996, Schumann and Pearce 1997, Lovvorn et al. 1999). Consequently, salinity has often been selected as an indicator for modeling needed freshwater inflows (Christiansen and Low 1970, Hutchison and Midgley 1978, Bradley et al. 1990, Tung et al. 1990, Powell and Matsumoto 1994, Jassby et al. 1995).

Evaluation of Salinity as an Indicator Variable

In the Laramie Basin, oligosaline wetlands (0.8–8 mS/cm, 0.5–5 g/L TDS) have much more stable salinities than do mesosaline wetlands (8–30 mS/cm, 5–18 g/L; definitions from Cowardin et al. 1979). The oligosaline wetlands generally receive inflow from ditches or shallow groundwater recharged by irrigation every year. The mesosaline wetlands do not receive such flow every year and can vary between oligosaline and mesosaline, depending on water supply. For wetlands classified as mesosaline, the biota are probably affected not only by the higher mean salinity but also by the much wider variation in hydroperiod and salinity (Beadle 1969, Brock and Lane 1983, Smith and Kadlec 1986, Montague and Ley 1993, Hart 2001, Herbst 2001, Noe 2002).

Salinity effects on plants

Salinity or its correlates strongly influence plant community structure in wetlands of intermountain basins. In the Laramie Basin (Figure 6.3), oligosaline lakes have a fringe of hardstem bulrush, whereas mesosaline lakes are surrounded by unvegetated mudflat apparently due to the salt intolerance of hardstem bulrush (Christiansen and Low 1970, Hammer 1986). Oligosaline lakes are dominated by the low-growing macroalgae muskgrass (e.g., *Chara globularis, C. aspera*), although in some years

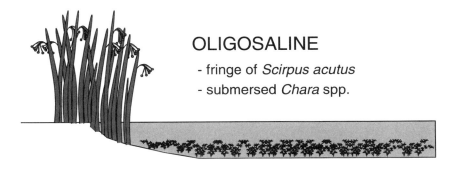

OLIGOSALINE
- fringe of *Scirpus acutus*
- submersed *Chara* spp.

MESOSALINE
- fringe of unvegetated mudflat
- submersed *Potamogeton pectinatus*

FIGURE 6.3. Vegetative characteristics of oligosaline and mesosaline wetlands in the Laramie Basin, Wyoming

they also support patches of fennelleaf pondweed and watermilfoil (Wollheim and Lovvorn 1995, 1996). After consistently high water levels for several years, muskgrass can completely replace the other submersed macrophytes. In contrast, mesosaline lakes are dominated by the erect submersed angiosperm fennelleaf pondweed, with widgeongrass occurring in the upper mesosaline range. *Chara globularis* and *C. aspera* found in oligosaline lakes apparently cannot tolerate mesosaline waters (Hammer 1986). However, if mesosaline lakes (which do not receive inflow every year) are flooded to high levels and maintained in the lower mesosaline to upper oligosaline range for a few years, *Chara longifolia* can become abundant offshore in deeper areas. Extended high water in formerly mesosaline lakes can also eliminate all macrophytes, leaving a state dominated by unattached *Enteromorpha* and other metaphyton (see also Scheffer et al. 1993, Goldsborough and Robinson 1996).

The more variable hydroperiods and more variable and higher salinities in mesosaline wetlands also have important impacts on production of algae (Hart and Lovvorn 2000), which in these wetlands are a more significant food source for most invertebrates than are macrophytes (Hart 2001; see also Campeau et al. 1994). Muskgrass habitats support a much higher biomass of epiphyton than do fennelleaf pondweed habitats. However, the more erect growth form and lower canopy density of fennelleaf pondweed, by providing better light conditions for phytoplankton, epiphyton, and epipelon (benthic algae), can lead to similar total algal production (Hart and Lovvorn 2000). These changes in the form of algal production may have important consequences for invertebrate community structure.

In Great Salt Lake wetlands, plant community structure was also a function of soil profiles of salinity as affected by hydroperiod (Kadlec and Smith 1989). However, in impoundments that were drained and reflooded, *Chara* (species not given) colonized early and was later replaced by fennelleaf pondweed and widgeongrass, as opposed to *C. globularis*, *C. aspera*, and *C. longifolia* gradually replacing fennelleaf pondweed in more permanent wetlands in the Laramie Basin. Fennelleaf pondweed appears to dominate intermittently drained habitats such as impoundments in Utah or the periphery of shallow lakes in the Laramie Basin, whereas at least some muskgrass species gradually replace fennelleaf pondweed in oligosaline habitats with more stable water levels and lower salinities (see also Blindow 1992).

Salinity effects on invertebrates

Effects of vegetation structure on invertebrate taxa and biomass in wetlands of different salinity have been examined only in the Laramie Basin (Wollheim and Lovvorn 1995, 1996; Lovvorn et al. 1999; see also Cox and Kadlec 1995). Plant growth forms examined included thin-stemmed emergents (hardstem bulrush), erect aquatics (fennelleaf pondweed, watermilfoil), and low macroalgae (muskgrass or filamentous algae) (Figure 6.3). Results revealed that in oligosaline lakes, invertebrate biomass differed among plant growth forms, but invertebrate taxa did not, and within the same growth forms and for all submersed habitats combined, oligosaline and mesosaline lakes did not differ in total invertebrate biomass, but taxa differed substantially. Snails and amphipods dominated both epiphytic and total biomass of invertebrates in oligosaline lakes (Figure 6.4). Snails were almost absent and amphipods much less abundant in mesosaline lakes. Chironomid larvae and crustacean zooplankton (Order Cladocera and Class Copepoda) and their insect predators (Orders Odonata and Hemiptera) were much more abundant in mesosaline lakes. These differences might result partly from elimination of snails and reduction of amphipods by salt toxicity or associated low oxygen levels during winter, with subsequent competitive release of other grazers and their invertebrate predators.

Effects of different growth forms of macrophytes on algal production

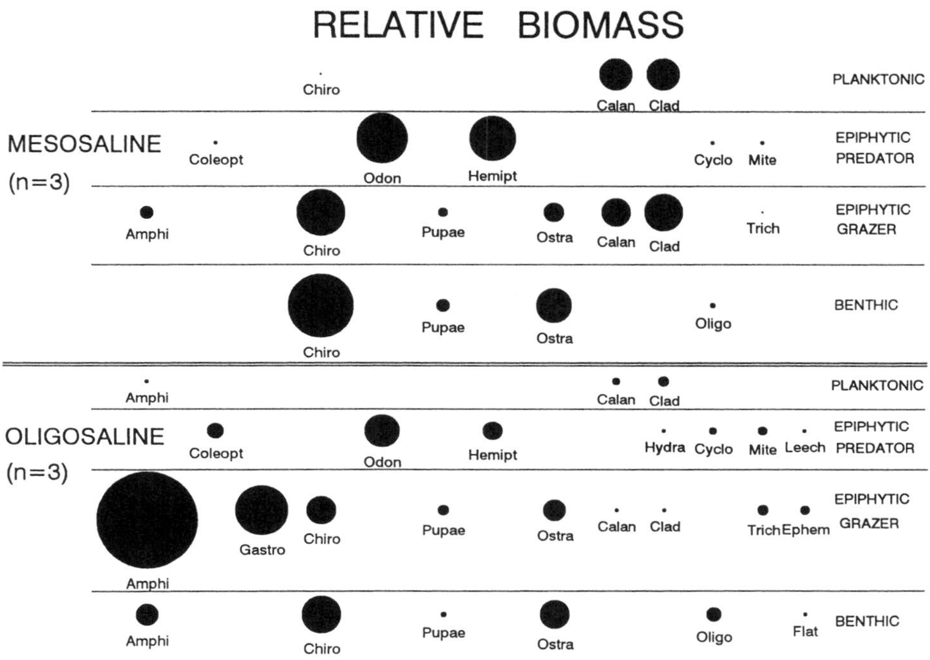

RELATIVE BIOMASS

FIGURE 6.4. Relative dry mass of major macroinvertebrate taxa (>500 μ) in oligo-saline and mesosaline wetlands of the Laramie Basin, Wyoming, June–August 1992. Planktonic, epiphytic predator, epiphytic grazer (all g/m³), and benthic (g/m²) com-munities are shown. Amphi = Amphipoda, Coleopt = Coleoptera, Gastro = Gas-tropoda, Chiro = Chironomidae, Odon = Odonata, Pupae = insect pupae (mainly Chironomidae), Hemipt = Hemiptera, Ostra = Ostracoda, Calan = Calanoid Copepoda, Clad = Cladocera, Cyclo = Cyclopoid Copepoda, Oligo = Oligochaeta, Trich = Trichoptera, Ephem = Ephemeroptera, Flat = flatworms. (Reproduced, with kind permission from Kluwer Academic Publishers, Figure 4 from W. M. Wollheim and J. R. Lovvorn, Salinity effects on macroinvertebrate assemblages and waterbird food webs in shallow lakes of the Wyoming High Plains, *Hydrobiologia* 310:207–223, 1995 © 1995 Kluwer Academic Publishers.)

in different microhabitats might also be important to invertebrates (Hart and Lovvorn 2000). In muskgrass habitats where most algal production is epiphytic, macroinvertebrate consumers were mostly scrapers and epiphytic deposit-feeders (snails and amphipods). In fennelleaf pond-weed habitats where phytoplankton and epipelon were more abundant, consumers were mostly filter-feeders and often benthic deposit-feeders (cladocerans, copepods, and chironomid larvae).

In Great Salt Lake wetlands (Cox and Kadlec 1995), a number of taxa found at lower salinities (about 3 mS/cm), such as amphipods, snails, chironomids, dragonflies, beetles, cladocerans, and copepods, were rare or absent at higher salinities (about 28 mS/cm). At the higher salinities, more salt-tolerant brine flies, water-boatmen, and brine shrimp were dominant. Relations between invertebrate taxa and changes in macrophyte or algal assemblages were not investigated, and no mechanisms for these differences were proposed.

In the San Luis Valley, Cooper and Durfee (1996) found little effect of salinity on invertebrate communities, but almost all samples were at salinities of only 0 to 5 mS/cm (fresh to mid-oligosaline). Statistical ordinations indicated that invertebrate taxa were similar among emergent plant communities dominated by creeping spikerush, juncus, and saltgrass. However, the researchers felt that these plant communities were residual and had not yet responded to recent flooding that had imposed similar hydroperiods and salinities across all plant types. Thus, the wider range of salinities normally associated with these different plants, and corresponding variation in invertebrate communities, were not apparent (D. J. Cooper, pers. comm.). The investigators did find different invertebrate assemblages among submersed habitats and suggested that these variations were influenced by different species of submersed plants; however, these relations were not investigated. In the same area, Severn (1992) studied aquatic insect communities along a gradient of water depth and permanence ranging from submersed habitats (common marestail, baby pondweed, and horned pondweed) to hardstem bulrush to woolly and Nebraska sedges. However, conductivities ranged only from 0.20 to 0.35 mS/cm, so this study revealed little about effects of wider ranges of salinity commonly found in the Intermountain Region.

Salinity effects on bird habitat

Regarding bird habitat in lacustrine wetlands, the main structural differences are the lack of emergent cover around mesosaline lakes and the height of submersed plants relative to the water surface in lakes that are oligosaline (muskgrass-dominated) versus mesosaline (dominated by fennelleaf pondweed) (Figure 6.3). Around mesosaline lakes, the soil is either unvegetated alkali flat or only sparsely vegetated by pickleweed. Low-growing saltgrass and at higher elevations foxtail barley often grow farther back from shorelines. In general, these vegetation types do not provide adequate cover for nesting dabbling ducks, although hayfields and even dense stands of greasewood in some cases provide nearby nesting cover. In contrast, shorebirds such as American avocets and killdeer nest and feed on this bare or sparsely vegetated substrate (Colwell and Oring 1988, 1990).

In oligosaline lakes (Figure 6.3), the emergent fringe of hardstem bulrush is used by a variety of overwater nesters such as diving ducks, grebes, and coots. Night-herons, egrets, and ibises nest on mounded hardstem bulrush in the interior of stands, and blackbirds and wrens nest on erect stems. Recent studies at the Russell Lakes State Wildlife Area in the San Luis Valley revealed that many mallards and cinnamon teal nested on lodged softstem bulrush or cattail at the marsh periphery, especially when mixed with dense baltic rush (Gammonley 1996 and pers. comm.; Arnold et al. 1993). It appears that lack of adequate upland cover in many areas of this dry region makes emergent plants a critical habitat for typically upland nesters. The endangered Wyoming toad also appears to require dense emergent or nearshore vegetation (Parker 2000). A bulrush fringe is present only around oligosaline and not mesosaline lakes, because of high salt concentrations in the shoreline sediments of mesosaline lakes (Lieffers and Shay 1983).

In the Laramie Basin, areas of other emergent plants such as spikerush and baltic rush are quite limited, but these habitats are common nesting or feeding sites for ducks and shorebirds in the San Luis Valley (Gilbert et al. 1996, Laubhan and Gammonley 2000). In that area, these habitats are flooded in spring and early summer but usually dry up later in summer. At the Monte Vista National Wildlife Refuge, which has the highest nesting densities and production of ducks reported for North America, by far the most important nesting habitat for ducks was residual cover of baltic rush (Gilbert et al. 1996). All duck species selected baltic rush and avoided greasewood and saltgrass relative to availability. Flood irrigation in late March favored stands of baltic rush (Gilbert et al. 1996) and was shown to greatly increase invertebrate numbers for spring migrant and prebreeding resident ducks (Schroeder 1972). Baltic rush is replaced by saltgrass and pickleweed at higher soil salinities. Because the latter habitats are avoided by nesting ducks but are important to nesting by various shorebirds, salinity has a key influence on the suitability of emergent plant communities for different birds.

Another important difference in habitat structure between oligosaline and mesosaline wetlands (Figure 6.3) is the height of the dominant submersed macrophytes, muskgrass versus fennelleaf pondweed (Wollheim and Lovvorn 1996, Hart and Lovvorn 2000). The canopy of muskgrass is usually well below the water surface, whereas that of fennelleaf pondweed often forms a surface mat. We expect that seedheads, foliage, and epiphytic invertebrates are much more available to surface-feeding birds and especially chicks in erect fennelleaf pondweed than in low-growing muskgrass (availability of emerging insects like chironomids might not be so affected). Although this factor might help explain poor correspondence between total invertebrate densities and bird use (Crome 1986, Murkin and Kadlec 1986), to our knowledge the influence of submersed canopy structure on food availability to surface-feeding birds has not been investigated.

Salinity effects on foodweb structure

In the Laramie Basin, taxonomic composition of invertebrates differed dramatically between oligosaline and mesosaline lakes (Figure 6.4), and such changes with salinity have also been observed in wetlands around Great Salt Lake (Cox and Kadlec 1995). From a foodweb perspective, why might these differences occur?

Much of the primary production in these wetlands is by algae (Hart and Lovvorn 2000). In oligosaline lakes, primary production averaged 39% by muskgrass, 44% by epiphyton on muskgrass, 15% by phytoplankton, and only 1% by epipelon (benthic algae). In fennelleaf pondweed habitats of mesosaline lakes, production averaged 54% by fennelleaf pondweed, 14% by epiphyton on fennelleaf pondweed, 14% by phytoplankton, and 18% by epipelon. In mesosaline lakes, dense low-growing carpets of muskgrass were replaced by erect, more open stands of fennelleaf pondweed, apparently because of muskgrass' intolerance to salt (Lovvorn et al. 1999). This change in vegetation structure decreased macrophyte surface area for epiphyton but increased light penetration for all forms of algae (Hart and Lovvorn 2000).

The main epiphyton grazers in oligosaline wetlands are snails and amphipods, which disappear or decline at higher salinities (Figure 6.4) presumably from salt toxicity or low oxygen levels during winter (Hart 2001). Chironomid larvae, which are mainly epiphyton grazers, increase in mesosaline wetlands perhaps due to loss or reduction of competing snails and amphipods (Lovvorn et al. 1999). Benthic chironomids (detritus and epipelon grazers) also increase, perhaps because of loss of muskgrass, increased light to sediments, and resulting increase of epipelon production.

In mesosaline wetlands, there are more crustacean zooplankton (cladocerans and copepods, Figure 6.4). These zooplankton might have more food in mesosaline wetlands, as suggested by 172% higher particulate phosphorus and 67% higher chlorophyll a in the water column than in oligosaline wetlands (Hart and Lovvorn 2000). Insect predators (hemipterans, odonates) also increase at higher salinities. Our simulation models indicate these predators are food-limited at both salinities and increase at higher salinities due to greater availability of their main prey, chironomids and crustacean zooplankton (Hart 2001, Hart and Lovvorn

2002). Abundant amphipods and snails at lower salinities are largely unavailable as prey for corixids and damselfly larvae.

By this construct, the pronounced differences in foodweb structure between oligosaline and mesosaline lakes result mainly from direct effects of salinity or its correlates on muskgrass, snails, and amphipods, with resulting indirect effects on other community components. Muskgrass controls zooplankton and benthos through its effects on algae by lowering nutrient availability and resuspension of microalgae to the water column and by reducing light to sediments. Snails and amphipods suppress chironomid biomass and production and thus insect predators that eat mainly chironomids. Together, these 3 "foundation taxa" (Thorp and Bergey 1981) control the total amount and diversity of foods available to top vertebrate consumers. Thus, these communities may be structured by suppression of 3 competitive dominants by conditions of high salinity, which are in turn a function of annual hydrologic inputs (Lovvorn et al. 1999).

Use of different wetlands by top consumers such as birds can also be strongly influenced by salinity, through both direct salt toxicity to birds and indirect effects on their preferred foods (Serie and Swanson 1976, Swanson et al. 1988, Kingsford and Porter 1994, Wollheim and Lovvorn 1995, Rubega and Robinson 1997). Chicks are especially sensitive to salinity, and adults feeding altricial young often fly long distances to obtain prey from freshwater (Swanson et al. 1984, 1988; Johnston and Bildstein 1990; Dosch 1997). Even if adults can tolerate high salinities where food abundance is often greater (Swanson et al. 1988, Kingsford and Porter 1994), they often prefer or need access to fresher wetlands for drinking (Adair et al. 1996). In addition to shifts in invertebrate prey described above, plant foods available to birds also change with salinity. The foliage, seeds, and below-ground tubers of fennelleaf pondweed (Kantrud 1990) are generally considered more important foods than the less frequently consumed oogonia, tubercles, and vegetative parts of muskgrass. However, muskgrass is consumed heavily by some species in some areas (Bailey and Titman 1984, Swiderek et al. 1988), and further studies in the Intermountain West are needed.

Salinity and stable states

It is widely believed that shallow lakes are characterized by alternative states dominated by different primary producers, where these states are stable in the sense of being self-perpetuating. The best-known paradigm (Scheffer et al. 1993) entails 2 stable states, 1 with turbid water dominated by phytoplankton, and the other with clear water dominated by macrophytes. Once established, the existing state is perpetuated by factors such as competition for nutrients, shading of the competing plant guild, buffering of sediment resuspension by macrophytes, and interactions with primary and secondary consumers. Major perturbations, such as dramatic change in nutrient inputs, or biomanipulation of top predators in trophic cascades, are needed to change one stable state to another.

Goldsborough and Robinson (1996) extended this concept to suggest 4 stable states for wetlands, depending on relative dominance of algal guilds: phytoplankton, epiphyton, epipelon, and metaphyton. By this construct, macrophytes are important mainly as substrate for epiphyton and metaphyton (McDougal et al. 1997). These different states are not considered stable (self-perpetuating) but rather as successional stages in the wet-dry cycles of prairie wetlands (van der Valk and Davis 1978). These cyclic algal states are correlated with abundance of microcrustacean grazers (Hann and Goldsborough 1997), but effects on other invertebrate guilds have not been investigated.

In intermountain basins—in addition to effects of nutrients, predators, and water levels—salinity is a key influence on the system state of wetlands (Christiansen and Low 1970, Kadlec and Smith 1989, Hamilton and Auble 1993, Cox and Kadlec 1995, Rubega and Robinson 1997, Lovvorn et al. 1999). Community structure differs dramatically and rather discontinuously between oligosaline and mesosaline wetlands (Figure 6.3), perhaps through direct salt toxicity or associated low-oxygen winterkill of a few competitive dominants (see above). Although nutrient levels can alter the total biomass of invertebrates, taxonomic structure in the Laramie Basin varied mainly with salinity regardless of nutrient levels (Wollheim and Lovvorn 1995, 1996). In lacustrine wetlands, the shift in system state appeared to be not between macrophytes versus phytoplankton but rather between muskgrass versus fennelleaf pondweed as dominant submersed plants with associated algal guilds (Hart and Lovvorn 2000). This vegetation shift has also been observed in freshening shallow lakes created by damming estuaries in the Netherlands, with associated changes in invertebrate communities (Coops and Doef 1996, van den Berg et al. 1997).

Salinity as an indicator variable

The above discussion shows that salinity is strongly correlated with shifts in ecosystem state due to variations in hydroperiod, and meets several important criteria for indicator variables. Although relevant studies are lacking for much of the region, it appears that salinity is a promising indicator for predicting and evaluating effects of varying freshwater inflow in the Intermountain West. Similar conclusions have been reached in arid areas subject to water diversions for irrigation and other purposes, both within and outside the region (Hutchison and Midgley 1978, Bradley et al. 1990, Tung et al. 1990). For example, Christiansen and Low (1970) developed equations to estimate water requirements of marsh vegetation around Great Salt Lake based on salinity tolerances of plants. In California and Texas, minimum flows (after irrigation diversions) needed to maintain the integrity of estuarine wetlands are based on the response of community structure to salinity as an indicator variable (Longley 1994, Powell and Matsumoto 1994, Jassby et al. 1995).

Cumulative Values on a Landscape Scale

Annually changing mountain snowpack results in highly variable wetland hydroperiods, so a variety of wetland types in appropriate complexes is needed to ensure habitat diversity in all years. Although changes in water distribution affect individual wetlands, the overall result of many small changes is cumulative on a landscape scale (Klopatek 1988). Cumulative effects are especially important to mobile animals such as birds that may use different types of wetlands for different functions. How to assess cumulative effects of many small impacts on entire landscapes has been a problem for regulatory agencies. Both permitting under Section 404 of the Clean Water Act and impact statements required by the National Environmental Policy Act call for consideration of cumulative impacts (Hirsch 1988). Nevertheless, although values of individual wetlands in the context of wetland mosaics at larger scales are widely recognized as important, these values generally are not considered because of a lack of methodology. Thus, impact evaluation and mitigation typically proceed on a case-by-case basis at the level of individual wetlands (Preston and Bedford 1988).

Birds are good integrators of cumulative wetland functions. Different feeding and nesting guilds depend on different wetland types with different habitat and foodweb structures (Poysa 1983). Also, individuals of the same species often move among wetlands of different types, thereby depending on complexes of wetlands with different habitat functions (Patterson 1976, Rotella and Ratti 1992) and the size and spatial arrangement of individual wetlands and complexes (Brown and Dinsmore 1986, Gibbs 1991, Fairbairn and Dinsmore 2001).

Spatial configurations of wetlands are perhaps even more important for flightless taxa such as amphibians and small mammals (Gibbs 1993, Lehtinen et al. 1999). Distance and connectivity between wetlands is especially critical in arid western environments, where habitats separating wetlands are notably hostile. Field data on optimal wetland configurations are scarce. However, theoretical analyses suggest that because of poor dispersal capabilities of some animals, a variety of wetland types in a few large, contiguous complexes are better than disjunct wetlands scattered throughout the landscape (Gibbs 1993). Hyporheic corridors along irrigation channels, in which interacting surface water and groundwater can yield a series of interconnected habitats (Stanford and Ward 1993), provide excellent templates for wetland habitat corridors.

Simulation Models of Irrigation Systems

"Irrigation scheduling" refers to the amounts and timing of water allocated among users. Because irrigation systems are complex and allocation must often be altered on a daily basis, computer models are used in some areas to guide control of flows (Salazar et al. 1989, Leib et al. 2002). In areas lacking models for daily regulation, long-term models of irrigation systems have often been written to help plan water development projects. For example, in the Laramie Basin, the program Wyoming Integrated River System Operation Study (WIRSOS) was developed by Western Water Consultants (Laramie, Wyoming) to estimate monthly amounts of water delivered to each headgate based on gauged flow rates of the 3 main streams entering the basin, allocation of those flows by water rights, and estimated return flows. Wetlands generally are not integrated into such models. However, these models may be excellent tools for identifying opportunities for wetland enhancement and for incorporating wetlands into plans for agricultural and domestic water use.

Geographic information systems (GIS) have been combined with hydrologic models to estimate runoff from watersheds with different land uses in prairie regions and thus to model the condition and fate of wetlands under different climate regimes (MacMillan et al. 1993, Poiani and Johnson 1993, Poiani et al. 1996). Simulation models have also been developed to evaluate effects of weather and regional water management on wetlands in coastal areas, with salinity as the main ecological indicator to be predicted (Littlejohn 1977, Hutchison and Midgley 1978, Fennema et al. 1994). Although irrigation is often a major determinant of freshwater inflow into estuarine bays and minimum inflows to maintain ecosystems are modeled based on salinity (Starfield et al. 1989, Tung et al. 1990, Powell and Matsumoto 1994, Jassby et al. 1995), we are aware of no published attempts to model salinities in wetlands associated with irrigation systems (cf. Saysel and Barlas 2001).

An important advantage of modeling is the ability to simulate changes in water allocation over long periods that span climatic extremes (Hamilton et al. 1986). Simulations can indicate flows needed to maintain an adequate mix of wetland types of suitable sizes and spatial configurations in all years. Such analyses could help prioritize preservation and creation efforts based on large scales of space and time and provide insight into long-term effects of different water management options on a cumulative, landscape basis.

Relating long-term patterns of water delivery to the resulting type of wetland at a given site (oligosaline versus mesosaline) requires knowing how salinity in a given wetland responds to different inflows. This inflow-salinity relation could be estimated from a water budget for each wetland, accounting for direct precipitation, groundwater exchange, transpiration from emergent plants, and evaporation from the water surface (Christiansen and Low 1970, Kadlec 1983, Poiani and Johnson 1993). In many cases, a more achievable approach might be to observe conditions in different wetlands over a series of years of varying water supplies and then to relate those observations to modeled inflows in those years. The state of a wetland is also greatly affected by conditions in preceding years (Starfield et al. 1989), so running averages or some other time-integrative function of salinity probably must be used.

In this approach, the condition of specific wetlands is placed in the context of long-term frequencies of occurrence of different wetland types in the landscape. This method avoids the tendency in mitigation agreements to expect a certain wetland to function optimally and in a similar way in all years. Fluctuating water levels are essential to maintaining wetland functions (cf. Richter et al. 1997). Thus, in a highly variable climate it is more reasonable to expect a mosaic of different wetland types with fluctuating water regimes to sustain ecosystem functions consistently in the long term.

Issues and Applications in Intermountain Basins

In the above discussion we have focused on mechanisms of foodweb function in wetlands of intermountain landscapes and have identified gaps in knowledge and capabilities needed to manage these ecosystems. Growing demands on water in the Intermountain West have intensified the need to justify current amounts consumed and have encouraged efforts to increase irrigation efficiency (area irrigated per unit of water applied). Many wetlands in the region were in fact created entirely by irrigation (Peck and Lovvorn 2001), and incorporating the water needs of wetlands into irrigation schemes will become increasingly important if wetlands are to be conserved.

One way to increase water-use efficiency of irrigation is to line irrigation canals with concrete or impermeable fabrics to reduce seepage.

Seepage losses can be substantial (20% or more) but may also supply re-turn flows for downstream irrigators. Moreover, seepage losses recharge hyporheic groundwater that is often critical to wetlands. This important function of seepage should be considered before ditches are lined or flows rediverted.

A major trend throughout the Intermountain West is to replace tradi-tional flood irrigation with center-pivot sprinklers. Sprinklers lower net evaporation rates and the salinity of return flows. For example, a study in the Eden-Farson Valley of Wyoming attributed 85% of salt entering the Big Sandy River to return flows from flood irrigation. This salt could be reduced by about 50,000 tons/yr if 80% of the land were converted to sprinkler irrigation, which would also decrease water use by nearly 50% (Wyoming Hydrogram 1994). However, reduced diversion of water onto fields also decreases recharge of the unconfined aquifer, resulting in loss of groundwater-fed wetlands (Szymczak 1986). In the Star Valley of Wyo-ming, proliferation of more efficient center-pivot systems resulted in higher channel flows in early summer and lower flows in late summer than with previous flood irrigation. Flood irrigation was essential to bank storage that attenuated flood peaks, maintained riparian vegetation that reduced erosion during high flows, and contributed to instream flows in late summer (Sando et al. 1988). These examples emphasize that effects on wetlands from increased water-use efficiency should be quantified and accounted for when implementing new irrigation practices.

Increasing withdrawals of water for domestic purposes can also lessen water available for flood irrigation. For example, South Park, Colorado, historically had extensive flood irrigation, but much of that water is now piped to Denver for domestic use, with resulting loss of wetlands (Szymczak 1986).

Benefits of flood irrigation for lacustrine and palustrine wetlands must be weighed against instream flow considerations for river and stream ecosystems. For example, an average 30% of the Laramie River's peak flows have been diverted for irrigation over the past 100 years (Thor-burn 1993). This diversion provides water for many lentic wetlands that would not otherwise exist but greatly reduces flows needed to maintain instream habitat for fish (Copes 1970). Finally, increased demand for water has sparked litigation among states based on claims that water is unused or used inefficiently. In such cases, quantification of important water uses becomes essential. Water needs of irrigation-fed wetlands, es-pecially those supplied by hyporheic groundwater recharged by seepage and return flows, are poorly understood and unquantified. If such wet-lands are to be protected or enhanced, adequate knowledge and method-ology must be developed.

Literature Cited

Adair, S. E., J. L. Moore, and W. H. Kiel. 1996. Wintering diving duck use of coastal ponds: an analysis of alternative hypotheses. Journal of Wildlife Management 60: 83–93.

Arnold, T. W., M. D. Sorenson, and J. J. Rotella. 1993. Relative success of overwater and upland nests in southwestern Manitoba. Journal of Wildlife Management 57: 578–581.

Bailey, R. O., and R. D. Titman. 1984. Habitat use and feeding ecology of postbreeding redheads. Journal of Wildlife Management 48:1144–1155.

Beadle, L. C. 1969. Osmotic regulation and the adaptation of freshwater animals to inland saline waters. Verhandlungen der Internationalen Vereinigung fur Limnologie 17:421–429.

Blindow, I. 1992. Long- and short-term dynamics of submerged macrophytes in two shallow eutrophic lakes. Freshwater Biology 28:15–27

Bradley, P. M., B. Kjerfve, and J. T. Morris. 1990. Rediversion salinity change in the Cooper River, South Carolina: ecological implications. Estuaries 13:373–379.

Brock, M. A., and J. A. K. Lane. 1983. The aquatic macrophyte flora of saline wetlands in western Australia in relation to salinity and permanence. Hydrobiologia 105: 63–76.

Brown, M., and J. J. Dinsmore. 1986. Implications of marsh size and isolation for marsh bird management. Journal of Wildlife Management 50:392–397.

Burritt, E. C. 1962. A ground water study of part of the southern Laramie Basin, Albany County, Wyoming. Thesis, University of Wyoming, Laramie, Wyoming, USA.

Campeau, S., H. R. Murkin, and R. D. Titman. 1994. Relative importance of algae and emergent plant litter to freshwater marsh invertebrates. Canadian Journal of Fisheries and Aquatic Sciences 51:681–692.

Christiansen, J. E., and J. B. Low. 1970. Water requirements of waterfowl marshlands in northern Utah. Utah Division of Fish and Game Publication 69–12.

Colwell, M. A., and L. W. Oring. 1988. Habitat use by breeding and migrating shorebirds in southcentral Saskatchewan. Wilson Bulletin 100:554–566.

———, and L. W. Oring. 1990. Nest-site characteristics of prairie shorebirds. Canadian Journal of Zoology 68:297–302.

Cooper, D. J., and R. Durfee. 1996. Aquatic macroinvertebrate communities in wetlands of the Russell Lakes Region, San Luis Valley, Colorado. Unpublished report to Colorado Division of Wildlife, Fort Collins, Colorado, USA.

Coops, H., and R. W. Doef. 1996. Submerged vegetation development in two shallow, eutrophic lakes. Hydrobiologia 340:115–120.

Copes, F. A. 1970. A study of the ecology of the native fishes of Sand Creek, Albany County, Wyoming. Dissertation, University of Wyoming, Laramie, Wyoming, USA.

Cowardin, L. M., V. Carter, F. C. Golet, and E. T. LaRoe. 1979. Classification of wetlands and deepwater habitats of the United States. U.S. Fish and Wildlife Service, FWS/OBS-79/31.

Cox, R. R., and J. A. Kadlec. 1995. Dynamics of potential waterfowl foods in Great Salt Lake marshes during summer. Wetlands 15:1–8.

Crome, F. H. J. 1986. Australian waterfowl do not necessarily breed on a rising water level. Australian Wildlife Research 13:461–480.

Dixon, H. N. 1989. Relationships of the greasewood community to groundwater in the San Luis Valley. Pages 169–176 *in* E. J. Harmon, editor. Water in the valley. Colorado Ground-water Association, Lakewood, Colorado, USA.

Doesken, N. J., and T. B. McKee. 1989. The incredible climate of the San Luis Valley. Pages 79–98 *in* E. J. Harmon, editor. Water in the Valley. Colorado Ground-water Association, Lakewood, Colorado, USA.

Dosch, J. J. 1997. Salt tolerance of nestling laughing gulls: an experimental field investigation. Colonial Waterbirds 20:449–457.

Engilis, A., and F. A. Reid. 1997. Challenges in wetland restoration of the western Great Basin. Pages 71–79 *in* J. M. Reed, N. Warnock, and L. W. Oring, editors. Conservation and management of shorebirds in the western Great Basin of North America. International Wader Studies 9.

Fairbairn, S. E., and J. J. Dinsmore. 2001. Local and landscape-level influences on wetland bird communities of the prairie pothole region of Iowa, USA. Wetlands 21: 41–47.

Fennema, R. J., C. J. Neidrauer, R. A. Johnson, T. K. MacVicar, and W. A. Perkins. 1994. A computer model to simulate natural Everglades hydrology. Pages 249–289 *in* S. M. Davis and J. C. Ogden, editors. Everglades: the ecosystem and its restoration. St. Lucie Press, Delray Beach, Florida, USA.

Gammonley, J. H. 1996. Cinnamon teal (*Anas cyanoptera*). *In* A. Poole and F. Gill, editors. Birds of North America, Number 209. Academy of Natural Sciences, Philadelphia, Pennsylvania, and American Ornithologists' Union, Washington, D.C., USA.

Gibbs, J. P. 1991. Spatial relationships between nesting colonies and foraging areas of great blue herons. Auk 108:764–770.

———. 1993. Importance of small wetlands for the persistence of local populations of wetland-associated animals. Wetlands 13:25–31.

Gilbert, D. W., D. R. Anderson, J. K. Ringelman, and M. R. Szymczak. 1996. Response of nesting ducks to habitat and management on the Monte Vista National Wildlife Refuge, Colorado. Wildlife Monographs 131:1–44.

Glenn, E. P., C. Lee, R. Felger, and S. Zengel. 1996. Effects of water management on the wetlands of the Colorado River Delta, Mexico. Conservation Biology 10: 1175–1186.

Goldsborough, L. G., and G. G. C. Robinson. 1996. Pattern in wetlands. Pages 77–117 *in* R. J. Stevenson, M. L. Bothwell, and R. L. Lowe, editors. Algal ecology. Academic Press, New York, New York, USA.

Hallock, R. J., and L. L. Hallock, editors. 1993. Detailed study of irrigation drainage in and near wildlife management areas, west-central Nevada, 1987–90. Part B. Effect on biota in Stillwater and Fernley Wildlife Management Areas and other nearby wetlands. U.S. Geological Survey Water-Resources Investigations Report 92–4024B.

Hamilton, D. B., and G. T. Auble. 1993. Wetland modeling and information needs at Stillwater National Wildlife Refuge. Unpublished workshop proceedings, Division of Refuges and Wildlife, Region 1, U.S. Fish and Wildlife Service.

———, G. T. Auble, R. A. Ellison, and J. E. Roelle. 1986. Effects of flood control alternatives on the hydrology, vegetation, and wildlife resources of the Malheur-Harney Lakes basin. National Ecology Center, U.S. Fish and Wildlife Service, Washington, D.C., USA. NEC-86/20.

Hammer, U. T. 1986. Saline lake ecosystems of the world. Dr. W. Junk Publishers, Dordrecht, Netherlands.

Hann, B. J., and L. G. Goldsborough. 1997. Responses of a prairie wetland to press and pulse additions of inorganic nitrogen and phosphorus: invertebrate community structure and interactions. Archiv fur Hydrobiologie 140:169–194.

Harmon, E. J., editor. 1989. Water in the valley. Colorado Ground-water Association, Lakewood, Colorado, USA.

Harris, S. W. 1954. An ecological study of the waterfowl of the potholes area, Grant County, Washington. American Midland Naturalist 52:403–432.

Hart, E. A. 2001. Macroinvertebrate foodwebs in saline wetlands of the Laramie Basin. Dissertation, University of Wyoming, Laramie, Wyoming, USA.

———, and J. R. Lovvorn. 2000. Vegetation dynamics and primary production in saline, lacustrine wetlands of a Rocky Mountain basin. Aquatic Botany 66: 21–39.

———, and J. R. Lovvorn. 2002. Interpreting stable isotopes from macroinvertebrate foodwebs in saline wetlands. Limnology and Oceanography 47:580–584.

Herbst, D. B. 2001. Gradients of salinity stress, environmental stability and water chemistry as a templet for defining habitat types and physiological strategies in inland salt waters. Hydrobiologia 466:209–219.

Hirsch, A. 1988. Regulatory context for cumulative impact research. Environmental Management 12:715–723.

Horton, S. K., C. D. Littlefield, D. G. Paullin, and R. E. Vorderstrasse. 1983. Migratory bird populations and habitat relationships in Malheur-Harney Lakes Basin, Oregon. Final Report. U.S. Fish and Wildlife Service, Portland, Oregon, USA.

Hutchison, I. P. G., and D. C. Midgley. 1978. Modelling the water and salt balance in a shallow lake. Ecological Modelling 4:211–235.

Jacobs, J. J., and G. Fassett, and D. J. Brosz. 1990. Wyoming water law: a summary. Publication B-849R. Cooperative Extension Service, University of Wyoming, Laramie, Wyoming, USA.

Jassby, A. D., W. J. Kimmerer, S. G. Monismith, C. Armor, J. E. Cloern, T. M. Powell, J. R. Schubel, and T. J. Vendlinski. 1995. Isohaline position as a habitat indicator for estuarine populations. Ecological Applications 5:272–289.

Johnston, J. W., and K. L. Bildstein. 1990. Dietary salt as a physiological constraint in white ibis breeding in an estuary. Physiological Zoology 63:190–207.

Kadlec, J. A. 1983. Water budgets for small diked marshes. Water Resources Bulletin 19:223–229.

———, and L. M. Smith. 1989. The Great Basin marshes. Pages 451–474 in L. M. Smith, R. L. Pederson, and R. M. Kaminski, editors. Habitat management for migrating and wintering waterfowl in North America. Texas Tech University Press, Lubbock, Texas, USA.

Kantrud, H. A. 1990. Sago pondweed (*Potamogeton pectinatus* L.): a literature review. U.S. Fish and Wildlife Service Resource Publication 176.

Karr, J. R. 1987. Biological monitoring and environmental assessment: a conceptual framework. Environmental Management 11:249–256.

Keddy, P. A., H. T. Lee, and I. C. Wisheu. 1993. Choosing indicators of ecosystem integrity: wetlands as a model system. Pages 61–79 in S. Woodley, J. Kay, and G. Francis, editors. Ecological integrity and the management of ecosystems. Saint Lucie Press, Ottawa, Canada.

Kingsford, R. T., and J. L. Porter. 1994. Waterbirds on an adjacent freshwater lake and salt lake in arid Australia. Biological Conservation 69:219–228.

Klopatek, J. M. 1988. Some thoughts on using a landscape framework to address cumulative impacts on wetland food chain support. Environmental Management 12:703–711.

Kruse, K. L., J. R. Lovvorn, J. Y. Takekawa, and J. Mackay. 2003. Long-term productivity of canvasbacks in a snowpack-driven desert marsh. Auk 120: in press.

Laubhan, M. K., and J. H. Gammonley. 2000. Density and foraging habitat selection of waterbirds breeding in the San Luis Valley of Colorado. Journal of Wildlife Management 64:808–819.

Lehtinen, R. M., S. M. Galatowisch, and J. R. Tester. 1999. Consequences of habitat loss and fragmentation for wetland amphibian assemblages. Wetlands 19:1–12.

Leib, B. G., M. Hattendorf, T. Elliott, and G. Matthews. 2002. Adoption and adaptation of scientific irrigation scheduling: trends from Washington, USA, as of 1998. Agricultural Water Management 55:105–120.

Lemly, A. D., S. E. Finger, and M. K. Nelson. 1993. Sources and impacts of irrigation drainwater contaminants in arid wetlands. Environmental Toxicology and Chemistry 12:2265–2279.

Lico, M. S. 1992. Detailed study of irrigation drainage in and near wildlife management areas, west-central Nevada, 1987–90. Part A. Water quality, sediment composition, and hydrogeochemical processes in Stillwater and Fernley Wildlife Management Areas. U.S. Geological Survey Water-Resources Investigations Report 92–4024A.

Lieffers, V. J., and J. M. Shay. 1983. Ephemeral saline lakes on the Canadian prairies: their classification and management for emergent macrophyte growth. Hydrobiologia 105:85–94.

Littlejohn, C. 1977. An analysis of the role of natural wetlands in regional water management. Pages 451–476 in C. A. S. Hall and J. W. Day, editors. Ecosystem modeling in theory and practice. Wiley, New York, New York, USA.

Longley, W. L., editor. 1994. Freshwater inflows to Texas bays and estuaries: ecological relationships and methods for determination of needs. Texas Water Development Board and Texas Parks and Wildlife Department, Austin, Texas, USA.

Lovvorn, J. R., W. M. Wollheim, and E. A. Hart. 1999. High Plains wetlands of southeast Wyoming: salinity, vegetation, and invertebrate communities. Pages 603–633 in D. Batzer, R. B. Rader, and S. A. Wissinger, editors. Invertebrates in freshwater wetlands of North America: ecology and management. Van Nostrand Reinhold, New York, New York, USA.

MacMillan, R. A., P. A. Furley, and R. G. Healey. 1993. Using hydrological models and geographic information systems to assist with the management of surface water in agricultural landscapes. Pages 181–209 in R. Haines-Young, D. R. Green, and S. Cousins, editors. Landscape ecology and geographic information systems. Taylor and Francis, New York, New York, USA.

Martner, B. E. 1986. Wyoming climate atlas. University of Nebraska Press, Lincoln, Nebraska, USA.

McDougal, R. L., L. G. Goldsborough, and B. J. Hann. 1997. Responses of a prairie wetland to press and pulse additions of inorganic nitrogen and phosphorus: production by planktonic and benthic algae. Archiv fur Hydrobiologie 140:145–167.

McFadden, D. H. 1989. Aspects of San Luis Valley water in 1989: administrative, investigative, and litigative. Pages 109–123 *in* E. J. Harmon, editor. Water in the valley. Colorado Ground-water Association, Lakewood, Colorado, USA.

McIvor, C. C., J. A. Ley, and R. D. Bjork. 1994. Changes in freshwater inflow from the Everglades to Florida Bay including effects on biota and biotic processes: a review. Pages 117–146 *in* S. M. Davis and J. C. Ogden, editors. Everglades: the ecosystem and its restoration. Saint Lucie Press, Delray Beach, Florida, USA.

Montague, C. L., and J. A. Ley. 1993. A possible effect of salinity fluctuation on abundance of benthic vegetation and associated fauna in northeastern Florida Bay. Estuaries 16:703–717.

Murkin, H. R., and J. A. Kadlec. 1986. Relationships between waterfowl and macroinvertebrate densities in a northern prairie marsh. Journal of Wildlife Management 50:212–217.

Noe, G. B. 2002. Temporal variability matters: effects of constant vs. varying moisture and salinity on germination. Ecological Monographs 72:427–443.

Parker, J. M. 2000. Habitat use and movements of the Wyoming toad, *Bufo baxteri:* a study of wild juvenile, adult, and released captive-raised toads. Thesis, University of Wyoming, Laramie, Wyoming, USA.

Patterson, J. H. 1976. The role of environmental heterogeneity in the regulation of duck populations. Journal of Wildlife Management 40:22–32.

Peck, D. E., and J. R. Lovvorn. 2001. The importance of flood irrigation in water supply to wetlands in the Laramie Basin, Wyoming. Wetlands 21:370–378.

Poiani, K. A., and W. C. Johnson. 1993. A spatial simulation model of hydrology and vegetation dynamics in semi-permanent prairie wetlands. Ecological Applications 3:279–293.

——, ——, G. A. Swanson, and T. C. Winter. 1996. Climate change and northern prairie wetlands: simulations of long-term dynamics. Limnology and Oceanography 41:871–881.

Powell, G. L., and J. Matsumoto. 1994. Texas Estuarine Mathematical Programming Model: a tool for freshwater inflow management. Pages 401–406 *in* K. R. Dyer and R. J. Orth, editors. Changes in fluxes in estuaries: implications from science to management. Olsen and Olsen, Fredensborg, Denmark.

Powell, W. J. 1958. Ground-water resources of the San Luis Valley, Colorado. U.S. Geological Survey Water-Supply Paper 1379.

Poysa, H. 1983. Resource utilization pattern and guild structure in a waterfowl community. Oikos 40:295–307.

Preston, E. M., and B. L. Bedford. 1988. Evaluating cumulative effects on wetland functions: a conceptual overview and generic framework. Environmental Management 12:565–583.

Ramaley, F. 1942. Vegetation of the San Luis Valley in southern Colorado. University of Colorado Studies D 1(4):231–276.

Reheis, M. C., R. C. Palmquist, S. S. Agard, C. Jaworowski, B. Mears, R. F. Madole, A. R. Nelson, and G. D. Osborn. 1991. Quaternary history of some southern and central Rocky Mountain basins. Pages 407–440 *in* R. B. Morrison, editor. Quaternary nonglacial geology: coterminous U.S. The Geology of North America. Volume K-2. Geological Society of North America, Boulder, Colorado, USA.

Richter, B. D., J. V. Baumgartner, R. Wigington, and D. P. Braun. 1997. How much water does a river need? Freshwater Biology 37:231–249.

Riley, J. P., editor. 1972. The Great Salt Lake and Utah's water resources. Utah Water

Research Laboratory of Utah State University and Utah Division of Water Resources, Salt Lake City, Utah, USA.

Rotella, J. J., and J. T. Ratti. 1992. Mallard brood movements and wetland selection in southwestern Manitoba. Journal of Wildlife Management 36:508–515.

Rubega, M. A., and J. A. Robinson. 1997. Water salinization and shorebirds: emerging issues. Pages 45–54 in J. M. Reed, N. Warnock, and L. W. Oring, editors. Conservation and management of shorebirds in the western Great Basin of North America. International Wader Studies 9.

Salazar, L. J., J. T. Helgren, and L. A. Wheeler. 1989. Computer-assisted irrigation scheduling for the San Luis Valley. Pages 99–108 in E. J. Harmon, editor. Water in the Valley. Colorado Ground-water Association, Lakewood, Colorado, USA.

Sando, S. K., J. Borrelli, and D. J. Brosz. 1988. Hydrologic impacts of improved irrigation efficiencies. Journal of Irrigation Drainage and Engineering 114:334–342.

Saysel, A. K., and Y. Barlas. 2001. A dynamic model of salinization on irrigated lands. Ecological Modelling 139:177–199.

Schaeffer, D. J., E. E. Herricks, and H. W. Kerster. 1988. Ecosystem health: I. Measuring ecosystem health. Environmental Management 12:445–455.

Scheffer, M., S. H. Hosper, M.-L. Meijer, B. Moss, and E. Jeppesen. 1993. Alternative equilibria in shallow lakes. Trends in Ecology and Evolution 8:275–279.

Schroeder, L. 1972. Effects of invertebrate utilization on waterfowl production. Thesis, Colorado State University, Fort Collins, Colorado, USA.

Schumann, E. H., and M. W. Pearce. 1997. Freshwater inflow and estuarine variability in the Gamtoos Estuary, South Africa. Estuaries 20:124–133.

Serie, J. R., and G. A. Swanson. 1976. Feeding ecology of breeding gadwalls on saline wetlands. Journal of Wildlife Management 40:69–81.

Severn, C. 1992. Distribution of aquatic insects along a hydrologic gradient in the Russell Lakes area, San Luis Valley, Colorado. Thesis, Colorado School of Mines, Golden, Colorado, USA.

Smith, L. M., and J. A. Kadlec. 1986. Habitat management for wildlife in marshes of Great Salt Lake. Transactions of the North American Wildlife and Natural Resources Conference 51:222–231.

Sojda, R. S., D. J. Dean, and A. E. Howe. 1994. A decision support system for wetland management on National Wildlife Refuges. AI Applications 8(2):44–50.

Stanford, J. A., and J. V. Ward. 1993. An ecosystem perspective of alluvial rivers: connectivity and the hyporheic corridor. Journal of the North American Benthological Society 12:48–60.

Starfield, A. M., B. P. Farm, and R. H. Taylor. 1989. A rule-based ecological model for the management of an estuarine lake. Ecological Modeling 46:107–119.

Swanson, G. A., V. A. Adomaitis, F. B. Lee, J. R. Serie, and J. A. Shoesmith. 1984. Limnological conditions influencing duckling use of saline lakes in south-central North Dakota. Journal of Wildlife Management 48:340–349.

———, T. C. Winter, V. A. Adomaitis, and J. W. LaBaugh. 1988. Chemical characteristics of prairie lakes in south-central North Dakota—their potential for influencing use by fish and wildlife. U.S. Fish and Wildlife Service, Fish and Wildlife Technical Report 18.

Swiderek, P. K., A. S. Johnson, P. E. Hale, and R. L. Joyner. 1988. Production, management, and waterfowl use of sea purslane, Gulf Coast muskgrass, and widgeongrass in brackish impoundments. Pages 441–457 in M. W. Weller, editor. Waterfowl in winter. University of Minnesota Press, Minneapolis, Minnesota, USA.

Szymczak, M. R. 1986. Characteristics of duck populations in the intermountain parks of Colorado. Colorado Division of Wildlife Technical Publication 35.

Thorburn, J. L. 1993. Irrigation diversions on the Laramie River, Wyoming: their effects on stream channel morphology and sinuosity. Thesis, University of Wyoming, Laramie, Wyoming, USA.

Thorp, J. H., and E. A. Bergey. 1981. Field experiments on responses of a freshwater, benthic macroinvertebrate community to vertebrate predators. Ecology 62: 365–375.

Tung, Y.-K., Y. Bao, L. W. Mays, and G. Ward. 1990. Optimization of freshwater inflow to estuaries. Journal of Water Resources Planning and Management 116:567–584.

van den Berg, M. S., H. Coops, R. Noordhuis, J. van Schie, and J. Simons. 1997. Macroinvertebrate communities in relation to submerged vegetation in two Chara-dominated lakes. Hydrobiologia 342/343:143–150.

van der Valk, A. G., and C. B. Davis. 1978. The role of seed banks in the vegetation dynamics of prairie glacial marshes. Ecology 59:322–335.

Windell, J. T., B. E. Willard, D. J. Cooper, S. Q. Foster, C. F. Knud-Hansen, L. P. Rink, and G. N. Kiladis. 1986. An ecological characterization of Rocky Mountain montane and subalpine wetlands. U.S. Fish and Wildlife Service Biological Report 86(11).

Wollheim, W. M., and J. R. Lovvorn. 1995. Salinity effects on macroinvertebrate assemblages and waterbird food webs in shallow lakes of the Wyoming High Plains. Hydrobiologia 310:207–223.

———, and———. 1996. Effects of macrophyte growth forms on invertebrate communities in saline lakes of the Wyoming High Plains. Hydrobiologia 323:83–96.

Wyoming Hydrogram. 1994. Eden-Farson salinity project proves effective. 6(4):6.

CHAPTER 7
Wildlife of Natural Palustrine Wetlands
JAMES H. GAMMONLEY

Introduction

Among the many ecological functions performed by palustrine wetlands, their role in providing wildlife habitat is particularly valued by
society. Numerous vertebrate species are wetland-dependent; that is,
they require wetland habitats during some or all life history events.
Many other species are wetland-associated; they do not require wetlands
to meet life requisites, but populations benefit from and regularly use
resources provided by wetland habitats (Niering 1988, Boylan and Mac-
Lean 1997). Although naturally formed palustrine wetlands (Cowardin
et al. 1979) comprise a relatively small proportion of the total land area
in the Intermountain West, they provide essential or suitable resources
for a tremendous diversity of vertebrate species. This chapter provides a
broad overview of (1) patterns of use of palustrine wetlands by birds,
mammals, amphibians, reptiles, and fishes; (2) some important features
of palustrine wetlands that influence their use by wildlife; and (3) some
implications for wetland conservation and management in the Intermountain West. Many natural palustrine habitats are associated with
floodplains along river and stream corridors, and readers are referred to
Chapter 4 for additional discussion of characteristics of these habitats
which influence wildlife use. In addition, Chapter 10 provides information on wildlife responses to created wetlands, with an emphasis on
waterfowl.

The Intermountain West region includes portions of 4 geologic provinces: the Columbia Plateau, Basin and Range, Colorado Plateau, and
Rocky Mountains (Shimer 1972; also see Chapter 2 of this volume). Because of the large land area and the considerable variation in climate,
geomorphology, hydrological processes, and plant associations within
and among these geologic provinces (Bailey 1995), the species composition and timing of use by wetland-associated wildlife varies across
the Intermountain West. Aridity is a unifying feature throughout the
Intermountain West (Bailey 1995), however, and the relative scarcity of

wetlands heightens their influence on local and regional wildlife species assemblages.

Patterns of Use by Taxonomic Groups
Birds

Palustrine wetlands in the Intermountain West are used by more than 140 species of wetland-dependent and wetland-associated birds from 25 families. Birds exploit most classes, subclasses, and water regimes in palustrine systems and use palustrine wetlands in the Intermountain West during some or all annual cycle events, including spring and fall migration, courtship and pairing, nesting, brood rearing, molting, and wintering. Greatest avian abundance and diversity occurs during migration, because populations of many species breed and winter outside the region.

Waterfowl comprise a diverse group of birds that require wetlands throughout the annual cycle, and 23 of 45 North American species regularly use palustrine wetlands in the Intermountain West region (Bellrose 1980, Ducks Unlimited Inc. 1994). Waterfowl occur throughout the region, but highest concentrations occur in the extensive marsh complexes of the northern Great Basin (Great Salt Lake, Carson Sink, Klamath Basin) and the southwestern Columbia Basin (Malheur Basin, Summer Lake). Areas of relatively high use in other geologic provinces include the Mogollon Rim of the Colorado Plateau (Brown 1985, Gammonley 1996) and the mountain parks of the southern Rocky Mountains (Szymczak 1986).

An estimated 12 to 18 million ducks, 1 to 2 million geese, and 60,000 swans use palustrine wetlands in the Intermountain West for roosting and feeding during fall migration, with similar numbers during spring migration (U.S. Fish and Wildlife Service 1995). Annual breeding populations in the Intermountain West include 1.6 to 2.1 million ducks, as well as tens of thousands of Canada geese and the Rocky Mountain population (peak numbers >2,000) of trumpeter swans (U.S. Fish and Wildlife Service 1995). Dabbling ducks are the most widespread and abundant breeding waterfowl; about 5% of breeding dabbling ducks in North America occupy the Intermountain West (Bellrose 1979). Breeding duck densities are <2 pairs/km^2 over most areas (Frary 1954, Harris 1954, Gates 1962, Rutherford and Hayes 1976, Peterson and Low 1977, Szymczak 1986, Gammonley and Fredrickson 1998, Laubhan and Gammonley 2000), but in some areas they can equal or exceed densities observed in the Prairie Pothole region of the northern Great Plains (Jensen and Chattin 1964, Michot et al. 1979, Gilbert et al. 1996, Sanders 1997). Midwinter (January) indices of waterfowl populations in the Intermountain

West total about 2.3 million ducks, 900,000 geese, and 60,000 swans (U.S. Fish and Wildlife Service 1995). Although some waterfowl winter throughout the Intermountain West, most occur at lower elevations in the Great Basin and to a lesser extent the Columbia Plateau (Ball et al. 1989, Kadlec and Smith 1989). Many shallow, smaller palustrine basins are dry or freeze during winter, so waterfowl concentrate on perennial rivers and large, deep lakes and reservoirs, and wetlands fed by warm groundwater sources.

The Intermountain West is regularly used by 32 of the 51 species of shorebirds that commonly occur in North America (Gill et al. 1995). The region is important (populations are common or abundant compared to other regions) for 19 species during migration, 9 species during breeding, and 16 species during winter (Oring and Reed 1997, Brown and Hickey 1999). Breeding species are large- or medium-sized (except for the snowy plover) and except for the Wilson's phalarope are short-distance migrants (Morrison and Ross 1989, Skagen and Knopf 1993). Key sites with extensive wetland habitats support high concentrations of shorebirds during migration; these include Benton Lake, Montana; the Carson Sink, Nevada; Mono Lake, California; and the Great Salt Lake, Utah (Skagen and Knopf 1993).

Grebes, herons, and egrets, as well as white-faced ibises, rails, coots, and cranes, also rely on palustrine wetlands for breeding and foraging habitats. Most of these birds use more permanently flooded wetlands with robust emergent perennial vegetation, trees, and shrubs. Northern harriers and short-eared owls commonly use herbaceous emergent wetlands for foraging or nesting. Forested, scrub-shrub, and emergent palustrine wetlands are used by numerous passerines, including flycatchers, swallows, wrens, vireos, warblers, sparrows, and blackbirds. Specific activities and habitat associations in wetlands are poorly documented for most of these taxa, but yellow-headed blackbirds and marsh wrens use wetland habitats throughout their annual cycles (Twedt and Crawford 1995, Kroodsma and Verner 1997).

Mammals

Few mammals in North America are wetland-dependent (Fritzell 1988), but several species occur in palustrine wetlands of the Intermountain West. Beaver usually occupy perennial stream systems in wooded habitats (Slough and Sadlier 1977, Novak 1987). They regularly occupy forested or scrub-shrub palustrine wetlands, and their water diversion activities are responsible for the creation of many palustrine wetlands that are used by other wildlife (Grasse 1951, Lawrence 1952, McComb et al. 1990, Brown et al. 1996, McKinstry et al. 2001). Moose occupy boreal forests in the Rocky Mountains (Fitzgerald et al. 1994). Moose require abundant browse provided by early successional tree species, such as willow and aspen, but they include many aquatic plants in their diet, and emergent and aquatic bed palustrine wetlands are consistently an important component of the home range (Coady 1982). Muskrats are ubiquitous in the Intermountain West in wetlands with more permanent flooding periods where robust emergent vegetation grows (Willner et al. 1980). Muskrats often experience local population cycles and during peak densities can have dramatic impacts on marsh vegetation (Smith and Kadlec 1985). Mink often occupy wetlands inhabited by muskrats and are top carnivores (Mitchell 1961, Mason and MacDonald 1983). Relatively little is known about the ecology of the water shrew and water vole, but these species inhabit palustrine wetlands throughout the Intermountain West (Conaway 1952, Ludwig 1984, Beneski and Stinson 1987).

At least 25 other species of mammals are regularly associated with palustrine wetlands in the Intermountain West. Numerous species of shrews and small rodents prefer or commonly occupy palustrine wetlands (Spencer and Pettus 1966; Long 1972; Armstrong 1977a, 1979; Feldhamer 1979; Hoffman and Owen 1980; Tomasi and Hoffman 1984; Raphael 1988; Zeveloff and Collett 1988; Belk et al. 1990). Soil conditions and composition and structure of plant communities in seasonally flooded palustrine wetlands create favorable sites for small mammals during foraging and reproduction. These attributes and the abundance of prey items also make wetlands attractive foraging sites for predators, including weasels, skunks, raccoons, ringtails, opossums, bats, foxes, wolves, and bobcats (Quick 1951, Trapp 1978, Key 1979, Hart 1982, Kantrud et al. 1989, Fitzgerald et al. 1994). Bears feed on plants and insects in floodplain meadows and wet basins (Singer 1978, Windell et al. 1986), and elk and deer browse and graze in willow carrs, sedge-dominated seasonal wetlands, and wet meadows (Kufeld 1973, Windell et al. 1986). In addition, many mammals usually associated with drier upland habitats may seek food and shelter in palustrine wetlands (Armstrong 1977b, 1979; Bernard and Brown 1977; Zeveloff and Collett 1988; Hayward et al. 1997). Except for wetland-dependent species, the effects of changes in wetland habitat quantity and quality on local or regional populations of mammals are largely unknown (Fritzell 1988).

Amphibians and reptiles

Of the 38 amphibian species in the Intermountain West, 36 require flooded habitats during reproduction or larval development and often use wetlands to meet other life history requirements (Stebbins 1985).

Several species have restricted or disjunct ranges, 5 species were introduced into the Intermountain West, and 10 species occupy the Intermountain West only in the southern deserts of the Basin and Range province (Stebbins 1985, Jones 1988).

Tiger salamanders are ubiquitous in the Intermountain West, occupying a broad range of wetland habitats (Worthylake and Hovingh 1989, Stebbins and Cohen 1995). Spadefoot toads and red-spotted toads are primarily terrestrial but breed in temporarily flooded pools and playas (Dimmitt and Ruibal 1980, Hovingh et al. 1985). Other toad and frog species are more closely associated with saturated or flooded habitats throughout their life cycles. For example, boreal toads, a subspecies of the western toad, must rehydrate daily in standing water and hibernate in contact with water in winter burrows (Campbell 1970). The introduced bullfrog is highly aquatic and inhabits permanent water bodies. Toads often exploit seasonally flooded environments and frequently are the first amphibians to exploit new habitats (Johnson 1992).

Of the 116 reptile species in the Intermountain West, 30 species regularly use palustrine wetlands. The snapping turtle, northwestern pond turtle, Sonoran mud turtle, yellow mud turtle, painted turtle, slider, and Texas spiny softshell require aquatic environments (Stebbins 1985, Jones 1988). The western box turtle is primarily terrestrial but may enter water to feed or hibernate (Grzimek 1974, Hammerson 1986). At least 16 species of snakes and 6 species of lizards forage in palustrine wetlands, particularly in floodplains and basins associated with intermittent and perennial streams, but most of these species are capable of foraging in terrestrial habitats if wetlands are not available (Stebbins 1985). Garter snakes comprise a complex of 7 species that often inhabit wetland habitats in the Intermountain West. (Fleherty 1967, Rossman et al. 1996).

Fishes

Many natural palustrine wetlands in the Intermountain West are marked by shallow water depths, fluctuating water levels (including dry periods), seasonally high water temperatures or winter freeze, low dissolved oxygen content, and high salinities (see Chapter 2). These conditions are hostile for most fishes (Peterka 1989). Thus, unless they are permanently flooded or have surface connections to permanent lacustrine, riverine, or deepwater habitats, palustrine wetlands generally do not support fish species.

Most native river fishes evolved under conditions of dramatic fluctuations in streamflows, and some species exploit seasonally flooded areas for spawning, nursery areas, feeding, and resting (Crance 1988). These are generally long-lived species that successfully recruit new year classes only periodically when habitat conditions are favorable. For example, Colorado pikeminnow larvae move from channel spawning sites to shallow floodplain habitat, where they remain and develop as water levels recede during summer, and subsequently re-enter river channels during the following spring when floodplains are reconnected (Tyus 1991).

Some palustrine habitats in springs, seeps, and shallow marshes associated with rivers and lakes are occupied by species of small, short-lived native fishes in the Cyprinidae and Cyprinodontidae families (Woodling 1985, Sigler and Sigler 1987). Numerous species inhabit dense emergent or submersed vegetation in desert springs, where waters are characterized by relatively stable depths, low pH, low dissolved oxygen, high temperatures, and high salt concentrations (Williams and Bond 1980, Minckley et al. 1991, Rinne and Minckley 1991). Many of these species have extremely limited distributions in isolated waters.

Nonnative fishes have been introduced to waters throughout the Intermountain West (Courtney and Stauffer 1984, Woodling 1985, Hardy 1986), and numerous species use palustrine habitats in association with the riverine or lacustrine waters they occupy. Many of these species were introduced from the Mississippi River drainage and are well adapted to warm, vegetated aquatic habitats. Species such as common carp and fathead minnow can tolerate high water temperatures, high nutrient concentrations, low dissolved oxygen levels, and high turbidity (Woodling 1985).

Wetland Attributes that Influence Wildlife Use

Ecologists and wildlife managers are interested in understanding (i.e., being able to reliably predict) the important factors that determine and sustain the composition of vertebrate communities in wetlands. Figure 7.1 roughly corresponds to the pools (top portion), filters (middle portion), and traits (bottom portion) described by Keddy (1999) to examine how ecological communities are assembled on wetlands at a local level. The unique climatic features, geologic processes, and evolutionary—speciation and extinction (see Wiens 1983)—and biogeographic patterns of plants and animals in the Intermountain West have resulted in a regional pool of native vertebrate species, any of which is potentially available to occupy local palustrine wetland habitats. Variation in dispersal capabilities further influences which species are available at a particular wetland. Given the available species pool, local and landscape-level features of the wetland act as filters on the resulting vertebrate community. Species persist only if they possess adaptive traits enabling them to tolerate (or exploit) the ecological filters (Figure 7.1; Keddy 1999). Thus, much effort has been devoted to understanding the dominant

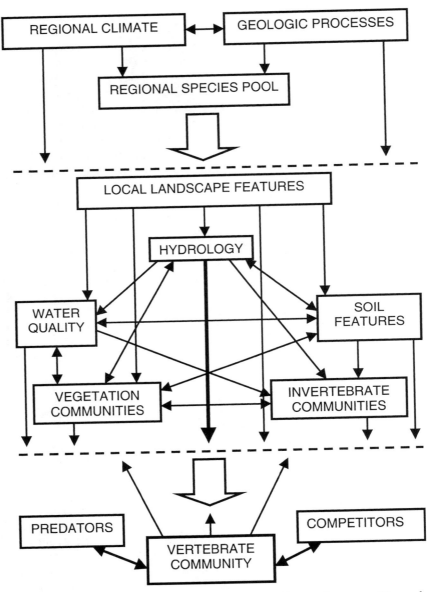

FIGURE 7.1. Important abiotic and biotic factors that influence the composition and structure of vertebrate communities in palustrine wetlands. Large-scale climatic, geologic, and evolutionary processes result in a regional species pool (top portion); local abiotic and biotic features of a wetland (with hydrology as a dominant force) act as environmental filters on this species pool (middle portion); and species with life history traits that allow them to adapt to these filters persist, forming the local vertebrate community (Keddy 1999). Important interactions occur among many of the environmental features, and the vertebrate community itself can produce important system feedbacks that influence the environmental filters (e.g., beaver alteration of hydrology).

environmental filters in wetlands and the life history traits that allow wildlife to adjust to these filters.

Hydrology

Hydrology is the dominant environmental filter in wetlands (Keddy 1999). Hydrologic patterns influence wildlife use of palustrine wetlands in 2 important ways. First, the water regime is a primary force driving the ecological processes and structure of wetlands, including nutrient exchange, soil conditions, primary production, decomposition rates, and plant community development (Mitsch and Gosselink 1993). Second, the frequency, timing, duration, and depth of flooding directly determine the availability of wetland habitats for wildlife. Water must be present (or absent) at appropriate times and depths to meet species needs.

Except at higher elevations, evaporation greatly exceeds precipitation in the Intermountain West (Bailey 1995). Consequently, many natural palustrine basins at lower elevations are flooded only for short periods. Palustrine habitats with longer hydroperiods usually are associated with riverine and lacustrine wetlands. Plants and invertebrates in habitats with dynamic flooding regimes often have extremely high reproductive or emergence rates (van der Valk and Davis 1978, Wiggins et al. 1981, Williams 1987). Vertebrate species exploit this food abundance on temporary and seasonal wetlands. Water depth has an important influence on wildlife use of palustrine wetlands. Many wetland-dependent birds forage primarily in water <20 cm deep (Laubhan and Fredrickson 1997).

Temporarily flooded wetlands provide high-quality breeding sites for amphibians because they are often free from fish and large aquatic insects that prey on larvae, but these habitats also may dry before metamorphosis of larvae is completed. Consequently, considerable intra- and interspecific variation in use of temporary wetlands can occur, depending on annual conditions (Dodd and Charest 1988). Amphibians have developed a range of adaptations for breeding and larval development that allow them to exploit the full range of hydrologic patterns observed in Intermountain West wetlands (Wassersug 1975, Wells 1977, Newman 1989, Denver et al. 1998).

Water quality and soil features

High evaporation to precipitation ratios, soil salinity, sediment loads from surface water inputs, and mineral contents and temperature of water from deep groundwater sources, as well as other factors, often result in high seasonal fluctuations and extremes of water quality in natural palustrine wetlands. Water quality and soil features largely influence salinity and fertility (via nutrient import and export processes) in wetlands, which in turn can act as important controls on the composition of plant and animal communities (Keddy 1999; also see Chapter 7 of this volume). Many wetland-dependent bird species in the Intermountain West forage in highly saline wetlands (Mahoney and Jehl 1985, Boula 1986, Osmundson 1990) but require relatively fresh waters to meet physiological constraints (Rubega and Robinson 1996). Adult life forms of some amphibians are able to occupy waters with broad temperature ranges, low dissolved oxygen content, high salinity or alkalinity, and high amounts of dissolved solids (Turner 1960, Licht 1975, Sexton and Bizer 1978, Hovingh et al. 1985, Hovingh 1993). Other species have more specific water quality requirements, and larval amphibians generally have narrower tolerances for environmental conditions (Wassersug 1975, Seale 1980, Gascon and Planas 1986, Stebbins and Cohen 1995).

Shallow water, declining or receding water levels, and high water temperature, along with high salinities and vegetation biomass, are common features during summer and fall in palustrine wetlands and can lead to epizootics of avian (type C) botulism (Friend 1987). This disease occurs commonly throughout much of the Intermountain West region and results in substantial avian mortality.

Vegetation and invertebrate communities

The distribution, coverage, structure, and species composition of vegetation affects the suitability of a wetland for different wildlife taxa (Figure 7.1). Primary plant production provides the substrates and detrital food base that support aquatic and semi-aquatic invertebrate communities, which in turn are important food resources for many vertebrate species (Mitsch and Gosselink 1993). Within wetlands, abundance and species richness of breeding waterbirds are often highest when emergent vegetation and open water occur in about equal proportions and are well interspersed (Weller and Spatcher 1965, Gammonley 1996). Unvegetated wetlands or basins with sparse, short vegetation are preferred foraging habitats for most shorebirds and are preferred breeding habitats for some amphibians.

Landscape setting

Many wetland-dependent and wetland-associated species also require terrestrial or deepwater habitats in order to complete specific life history events. For example, many ducks and shorebirds nest in upland habitats, and some small mammals and amphibians forage and overwinter in specialized terrestrial environments. Furthermore, because wetlands are transitional habitats between terrestrial and aquatic environments, features of these adjacent habitats directly influence the ecological processes and structure of wetlands. Consequently, habitat features of the landscape in which a wetland is located influence its use by wildlife and should be considered part of the wetland ecosystem (see, for example, Burke and Gibbons 1995).

Wetland basin size (area) can influence avian species composition (Brown and Dinsmore 1986), but larger wetlands may receive greater use because they often provide a diversity of habitats in close proximity (Gammonley 1996). Small wetland basins of different types can also allow less mobile species to meet life history requisites when they are spatially distributed to be accessible (Gibbs 1993).

As with features of surrounding terrestrial and aquatic habitats, the distribution of wetlands within the surrounding landscape influences patterns of wildlife use of an individual wetland. Many species require numerous wetland types during different annual-cycle events. Thus, complexes of different wetland habitats must be available at appropriate spatial and temporal distributions for species to satisfy their resource needs (Fredrickson and Reid 1988, Fredrickson and Laubhan 1994, McKinstry and Anderson 2002).

Highly mobile species have evolved life history strategies that allow them to exploit patterns of wetland availability at regional scales (Robinson and Warnock 1997, Haig et al. 1998). For example, duck species that are adapted to nesting in environments with less predictable wetland conditions tend to settle in suitable areas as they encounter them during spring migration, whereas species breeding in more stable permanently flooded wetlands tend to home to past breeding sites and then seek new locations if conditions are not suitable (Johnson and Grier 1988). Once waterfowl have settled on breeding areas, however, their mobility decreases substantially, and suitable habitats for foraging, nest sites, brood rearing (Monda and Ratti 1988), and postbreeding molt (Oring 1964, Cox 1993) must be available within relatively close proximity.

Because palustrine wetlands are widely scattered through the Intermountain West, less mobile wildlife species often occur in isolated, disjunct populations. The highly variable terrain in the Intermountain West provides a mechanism for the evolution of small, isolated populations of less mobile species. Changes in wetland distribution and attributes of surrounding landscapes since the last glacial period have led to population fragmentation of many less mobile species, and genetic isolation has resulted in the development of new species, often with extremely limited distributions (Tanner 1978, Zeveloff and Collett 1988, Echelle 1991, Green et al. 1996). Local complexes of wetland habitats that provide for all life history requisites are vital for sustaining these populations.

Human impacts

Human activity can have substantial effects on wetland wildlife communities (Figure 7.1). Humans can directly alter the regional species pool by introducing exotic species and by causing species extinction. Similar anthropomorphic effects can occur at a local scale on individual wetlands. However, the greatest effects may result from indirect human impacts on the landscape-level or local features and processes that filter the pool of available species according to their ecological traits (Keddy 1983).

Human-induced landscape changes have significant impacts on patterns of wildlife use of palustrine wetlands, including the distribution, species composition, and suitability of areas for wetland wildlife to complete annual-cycle events. For example, replacement of seasonally flooded shallow wetlands with large reservoirs or agricultural development in river floodplains can change the migration and winter distribution patterns of waterfowl (Ball et al. 1989). Irrigation of semidesert areas has allowed range expansion by amphibians (McCoy et al. 1967) but has also allowed invasions and expansion of nonindigenous plant and animal species (Galatowitsch et al. 1999). Grazing can reduce duck nest densities and nesting success (Gilbert et al. 1996), and shrews and other small mammals are adversely affected by soil compaction and trampling of raceways by livestock (Quigley et al. 1996).

Conservation Issues for Wetland Wildlife

As in other parts of North America, wetlands have been destroyed (Dahl 1990, Dahl and Johnson 1991) and degraded (Darnell 1979) throughout the Intermountain West (see Chapter 2). Increasingly high demands and limited supply make competition among uses of water a key feature of the region. Decreases in total wetland area, changes in the proportions of different wetland types, and changes in wetland distribution have occurred. Shallow wetlands that are flooded less frequently and for shorter periods are more prone to destruction or alteration than deeper, more permanently flooded wetlands (Fredrickson and Laubhan 1994). Water tends to be recycled for multiple uses, and water quality often decreases with each use (Lemly 1994). Other land use practices, such as grazing and agricultural crop production, have altered wetlands and their surrounding landscapes. Human disturbance from recreational activities (e.g., boating, fishing, bird watching) can reduce the value of wetlands to wildlife by interrupting life history events and increasing energy demands (Bouffard 1982, Ryder and Manry 1994). Human activities have brought invasions of nonnative plants in the Intermountain West that have changed the composition and structure of wetland plant communities (Galatowitsch et al. 1999) and introduced nonnative species into waters and wetland types that have been detrimental to native species. For example, common carp and fathead minnows feed on aquatic plants and invertebrates used by other wildlife (Robel 1961, Gasaway and Drada 1977, Crivelli 1983, Hanson and Riggs 1995, McKnight and Hepp 1995, Bouffard and Hanson 1997).

As a consequence of these changes, more than 70% of federally listed threatened and endangered vertebrates in the Intermountain West are wetland-dependent or wetland-associated species (Niering 1988, Feierabend 1992). Population declines and distributional changes have occurred for many species that use palustrine wetlands in the Intermountain West.

Concerns over the status of waterfowl populations during the 1980s prompted the development of the North American Waterfowl Management Plan (NAWMP), which established numeric objectives for many waterfowl populations in North America and acreage objectives for habitat conservation efforts designed to help achieve the population objectives. In 1994 the Intermountain West Joint Venture (IWJV) of the NAWMP was established with geographic boundaries that roughly correspond to the area considered in this chapter (Ratti and Kadlec 1992, U.S. Fish and Wildlife Service 1994). From 1994 to 1997, $11 million was spent to protect 2,000 ha, restore 11,000 ha, and enhance 17,000 ha of wetlands in the IWJV (Williams et al. 1999).

Several shorebird species appear to be declining in western North America (Page and Gill 1994, Gill et al. 1995). The population status of many other shorebird species using Intermountain West wetlands is poorly documented. The Western Hemisphere Shorebird Reserve Network (WHSRN) has designated wetlands in the Lahontan Valley of Nevada and the Great Salt Lake in Utah as Hemisphere Reserves, which are sites that support at least 500,000 shorebirds or 30% of a flyway population (WHSRN 1992). A United States Shorebird Conservation Plan is being developed to direct efforts toward conservation of shorebird populations and their habitats in the Intermountain West (Brown and Hickey 1999).

Recent declines in many amphibian populations have been noted globally (Vial and Saylor 1993, Blaustein et al. 1994), and within the Intermountain West significant population declines have been identified for the Wyoming toad (Lewis et al. 1985, Johnson 1992), Armagosa toad (Altig and Dodd 1987), boreal toad (Corn et al. 1989), and northern leopard frog (Corn and Fogleman 1984, Clarkson and Rorabaugh 1989). Many amphibian populations are small and isolated, and population size and recruitment can exhibit considerable annual fluctuations (Harte and

Hoffman 1989, Wissinger and Whiteman 1992, Weitzel and Panik 1993, Pechman and Wilbur 1994, Hecnar and M'Closkey 1996), increasing their vulnerability to local extirpations. Fragmentation of suitable habitats, relatively low mobility, and strong site fidelity in some species (Sinsch 1990) decrease the potential to recolonize areas where local extinctions have occurred (Blaustein et al. 1994). Habitat destruction, introduced predators (Hayes and Jennings 1986, Kupferberg 1997), acid precipitation (Corn et al. 1989, Dunson et al. 1992), changes in climate, atmospheric conditions (Ovaska et al. 1997, Rogers et al. 2001), and disease (Carey 1993) are among the postulated causes of declines. However, common species have declined over large, relatively pristine areas, and some population declines have occurred where sympatric populations have remained stable (Corn 1994), indicating multiple and complex causes for declines.

In the past century, numerous native freshwater fish species that occupied waters in the Intermountain West have gone extinct (Miller et al. 1989), and many species are currently declining (Deacon 1979, Minckley et al. 1991). Most declines have resulted from the cumulative effects of habitat alteration (e.g., stream channelization, groundwater mining, construction of dams and reservoirs) and the introduction of nonnative fish species that are better adapted to altered environmental conditions and that outcompete or prey on native species (Courtney and Stauffer 1984, Moyle et al. 1986, Meffe 1989). Extirpations of local populations lead to important genetic losses, because many native populations have been isolated over geologic time (Bisson and Bond 1971, Echelle 1991). Conservation efforts have focused on protecting remaining waters where natives occur or creating new habitats for the introduction of populations at risk (Minckley et al. 1991, Winemiller and Anderson 1997).

Conclusions

Despite their scarcity, palustrine wetlands are key to the diversity and abundance of wildlife in the Intermountain West. Numerous species are specifically adapted to and require wetlands or regularly use palustrine wetlands because they provide suitable resources. Species differ in their resource requirements for completion of life cycle events as well as in their spatial and temporal patterns of wetland use. One important implication for wildlife conservation efforts is that a single wetland basin or category rarely provides all resources required by a species but may provide some resources for a variety of species (Fredrickson and Reid 1988, Laubhan and Fredrickson 1993). A second implication is that enhancements of existing wetlands to better suit the needs of some species may be detrimental to other species. Further, the historically rich variation in local abiotic and biotic features of different wetland types and the often isolated or linear distribution of wetlands across landscapes suggest that the cumulative effects (Bedford 1999) on vertebrate populations of wetland loss, degradation, and conversion are relatively high in the Intermountain West.

Given the dramatic loss and alteration of palustrine wetlands that has occurred throughout the Intermountain West, wetland wildlife may benefit most from protection of remaining wetlands that retain historic processes and functions and from restoration of degraded wetlands. While the protection of declining or economically valuable species is important, conservation efforts that attempt to integrate the resource needs of a variety of locally and regionally representative native species are likely to be most effective and efficient (Laubhan and Fredrickson 1993, Fredrickson and Laubhan 1994). Such landscape-level efforts should focus on protecting and restoring all historically representative wetland types in complexes that account for the spatial requirements of less mobile taxa (Laubhan and Fredrickson 1997) and with linkages to suitable adjacent terrestrial and aquatic habitats.

Literature Cited

Altig, R., and C. K. Dodd Jr. 1987. The status of the Armagosa toad (*Bufo nelsoni*) in the Armagosa River drainage of Nevada. Southwestern Naturalist 32:276–278.

Armstrong, D. M. 1977a. Ecological distribution of small mammals in the upper Williams Fork Basin, Grand County, Colorado. Southwestern Naturalist 22: 289–304.

———. 1977b. Distributional patterns of mammals in Utah. Great Basin Naturalist 37:457–474.

———. 1979. Ecological distribution of rodents in Canyonlands National Park, Utah. Great Basin Naturalist 39:199–205.

Bailey, R. G. 1995. Description of the ecoregions of the United States. Second edition. U.S. Forest Service Miscellaneous Publication Number 1391 (revised).

Ball, I. J., R. D. Bauer, K. Vermeer, and M. J. Rabenberg. 1989. Northwest riverine and Pacific coast. Pages 429–449 in L. M. Smith, R. L. Pederson, and R. M. Kaminski, editors. Habitat management for migrating and wintering waterfowl in North America. Texas Tech University Press, Lubbock, Texas, USA.

Bedford, B. L. 1999. Cumulative effects on wetlands: links to wetland restoration in the United States and southern Canada. Wetlands 19:775–788.

Belk, M. C., C. L. Pritchett, and H. D. Smith. 1990. Patterns of microhabitat use by *Sorex monticolus* in summer. Great Basin Naturalist 50:387–389.

Bellrose, F. C. 1979. Species distribution, habitats, and characteristics of breeding dabbling ducks in North America. Pages 1–15 in T. A. Bookhout, editor. Waterfowl and wetlands—an integrated review. North Central Section of the Wildlife Society, Madison, Wisconsin USA.

———. 1980. Ducks, geese, and swans of North America. Third edition. Stackpole Books, Harrisburg, Pennsylvania, USA.

Beneski, J. T., Jr., and D. W. Stinson. 1987. *Sorex palustris.* Mammalian Species 296: 1–6. American Society of Mammalogists.

Bernard, S. R., and K. F. Brown. 1977. Distribution of mammals, reptiles, and amphibians by BLM physiographic regions and A. W. Kuchler's associations for the eleven western states. U.S. Bureau of Land Management Technical Note 301.

Bisson, P. A., and C. E. Bond. 1971. Origin and distribution of the fishes of the Harney Basin, Oregon. Copeia 1971:268–281.

Blaustein, A. R., D. B. Wake, and W. B. Sousa. 1994. Amphibian declines: judging stability, persistence, and susceptibility of populations to local and global extinctions. Conservation Biology 8:60–71.

Bouffard, S. H. 1982. Wildlife values versus human recreation: Ruby Lake National Wildlife Refuge. Transactions of the North American Wildlife and Natural Resources Conference 47:553–558.

———, and M. A. Hanson. 1997. Fish in waterfowl marshes: waterfowl managers' perspectives. Wildlife Society Bulletin 25:146–157.

Boula, K. M. 1986. Foraging ecology of migrant landbirds, Lake Albert, Oregon. Thesis, Oregon State University, Corvallis, Oregon, USA.

Boylan, K. D., and D. R. MacLean. 1997. Linking species loss with wetland loss. National Wetlands Newsletter 19:1–17.

Brown, D. E. 1985. Arizona wetlands and waterfowl. University of Arizona Press, Tucson, Arizona, USA.

Brown, D. J., W. A. Hubert, and S. H. Anderson. 1996. Beaver ponds create wetland habitat for birds in mountains of southeastern Wyoming. Wetlands 16:127–133.

Brown, M., and J. J. Dinsmore. 1986. Implications of marsh size and isolation for marsh bird management. Journal of Wildlife Management 50:392–397.

Brown, S., and C. Hickey. 1999. United States Shorebird Conservation Plan. Internet URL http://www.manomet.org/USSCP.htm.

Burke, V. J., and J. W. Gibbons. 1995. Terrestrial buffer zones and wetland conservation: a case study of freshwater turtles in a Carolina bay. Conservation Biology 9: 1365–1369.

Campbell, J. 1970. Life history of *Bufo boreas boreas* in the Colorado Front Range. Dissertation, University of Colorado, Boulder, Colorado, USA.

Carey, C. 1993. Hypothesis concerning the causes of the disappearance of boreal toads from the mountains of Colorado. Conservation Biology 7:355–362.

Clarkson, R. W., and J. C. Rorabaugh. 1989. Status of leopard frogs (*Rana pipiens* complex: Ranidae) in Arizona and southwestern California. Southwestern Naturalist 34:531–538.

Coady, J. W. 1982. Moose. Pages 902–922 *in* J. A. Chapman and G. A. Feldhamer, editors. Wild mammals of North America, biology, management, and economics. Johns Hopkins University Press, Baltimore, Maryland, USA.

Conaway, C. H. 1952. Life history of the water shrew *Sorex palustris navigator.* American Midland Naturalist 48:219–248.

Corn, P. S. 1994. What we know and don't know about amphibian declines in the West. Pages 59–67 *in* W. W. Covington and L. F. DeBano, editors. Sustainable ecological systems: implementing an ecological approach to land management. U.S. Forest Service General Technical Report RM-247.

———, and J. C. Fogleman. 1984. Extinction of montane populations of the northern leopard frog (*Rana pipiens*) in Colorado. Journal of Herpetology 18:147–152.

————, W. Stolzenburg, and R. B. Bury. 1989. Acid precipitation studies in Colorado and Wyoming: interim report on surveys of montane amphibians and water chemistry. U.S. Fish and Wildlife Service, Biological Report 80 (40.26), Report Number 26.

Courtney, W. R. Jr., and J. R. Stauffer Jr., editors. 1984. Distribution, biology, and management of exotic fishes. John Hopkins University Press, Baltimore, Maryland, USA.

Cowardin, L. M., V. Carter, F. C. Golet, and E. T. LaRoe. 1979. Classification of wetlands and deepwater habitats of the United States. U.S. Fish and Wildlife Service FWS/OBS-79/31.

Cox, R. R. Jr. 1993. Postbreeding ecology of adult male northern pintails and cinnamon teal near Great Salt Lake, Utah. Thesis, Utah State University, Logan, Utah, USA.

Crance, J. H. 1988. Relationships between palustrine wetlands of forested riparian floodplains and fishery resources: a review. U.S. Fish and Wildlife Service Biological Report 88(32).

Crivelli, A. J. 1983. The destruction of aquatic vegetation by carp. Hydrobiologia 106: 37–41.

Dahl, T. E. 1990. Wetland losses in the United States 1780s to 1980s. U.S. Fish and Wildlife Service, Washington, D.C., USA.

————, and C. E. Johnson. 1991. Status and trends of wetlands in the coterminous United States, mid-1970s to mid-1980s. U.S. Fish and Wildlife Service, Washington, D.C., USA.

Darnell, R. M. 1979. Impact of human modification on the dynamics of wetland systems. Pages 200–209 in P. E. Greeson, J. R. Clark, and J. E. Clark, editors. Wetland functions and values: the state of our understanding. American Water Resources Association, Minneapolis, Minnesota, USA.

Deacon, J. E. 1979. Endangered and threatened fishes of the West. Great Basin Naturalist Memoirs 3:41–64.

Denver, R. J., N. Mirhadi, and M. Phillips. 1998. Adaptive plasticity in amphibian metamorphosis: response of Scaphiopus hammondii tadpoles to habitat desiccation. Ecology 79:1859–1872.

Dimmitt, M. A., and R. Ruibal. 1980. Environmental correlates of emergence in spadefoot toads (Scaphiopus). Journal of Herpetology 14:21–29.

Dodd, C. K. Jr., and B. G. Charest. 1988. The herpetofaunal community of temporary ponds in north Florida sandhills: species composition, temporal use, and management implications. Pages 87–96 in R. C. Szaro, K. E. Severson, and D. R. Patton, editors. Management of amphibians, reptiles, and small mammals in North America. U.S. Forest Service General Technical Report RM-166.

Ducks Unlimited Inc. 1994. Continental conservation plan; an analysis of North American waterfowl populations and a plan to guide the conservation programs of Ducks Unlimited through the year 2000. Prepared for the Board of Directors of Ducks Unlimited Canada, Ducks Unlimited Inc., and Ducks Unlimited de Mexico.

Dunson, W. A., R. L. Wyman, and E. S. Corbett. 1992. A symposium on amphibian declines and habitat acidification. Journal of Herpetology 26:349–442.

Echelle, A. A. 1991. Conservation genetics and genetic diversity in freshwater fishes of western North America. Pages 141–153 in W. L. Minckley and J. E. Deacon, editors. Battle against extinction; native fish management in the American West. University of Arizona Press, Tucson, Arizona, USA.

Feierabend, J. S. 1992. Endangered species, endangered wetlands: life on the edge. National Wildlife Federation, Washington, D.C., USA.

Feldhamer, G. A. 1979. Vegetative and edaphic factors affecting abundance and distribution of small mammals in southeastern Oregon. Great Basin Naturalist 39: 207–218.

Fitzgerald, J. P., C. A. Meaney, and D. M. Armstrong. 1994. Mammals of Colorado. Denver Museum of Natural History and University of Colorado Press, Boulder, Colorado, USA.

Fleherty, E. D. 1967. Comparative ecology of *Thamnophis elegans, T. cyrtopsis,* and *T. rufipuncatus* in New Mexico. Southwestern Naturalist 12:207–230.

Frary, L. G. 1954. Waterfowl production on the White River Plateau, Colorado. Thesis, Colorado State University, Fort Collins, Colorado, USA.

Fredrickson, L. H., and M. K. Laubhan. 1994. Intensive wetland management: a key to biodiversity. Transactions of the North American Wildlife and Natural Resources Conference 59:555–565.

———, and F. A. Reid. 1988. Waterfowl use of wetland complexes. U.S. Fish and Wildlife Service leaflet 13.2.1, Waterfowl management handbook.

Friend, M. 1987. Field guide to wildlife diseases. U.S. Fish and Wildlife Service Resource Publication 167.

Fritzell, E. K. 1988. Mammals and wetlands. Pages 213–226 in D. D. Hook, W. H. McKee Jr., H. K. Smith, J. Gregory, V. G. Burrell Jr., M. R. DeVoe, R. E. Sojka, S. Gilbert, R. Banks, L. H. Stolzy, C. Brooks, T. D. Matthews, and T. H. Shear et al., editors. The ecology of wetlands. Volume 1 of The ecology and management of wetlands. Timber Press, Portland, Oregon, USA.

Galatowitsch, S. M., N. O. Anderson, and P. D. Ascher. 1999. Invasiveness in wetland plants in temperate North America. Wetlands 19:733–755.

Gammonley, J. H. 1996. Seasonal use of montane wetlands by waterbirds on the rim of the Colorado Plateau. Dissertation, University of Missouri, Columbia, Missouri, USA.

———, and L. H. Fredrickson. 1998. Breeding duck populations and productivity on montane wetlands in Arizona. Southwestern Naturalist 43:219–227.

Gasaway, R. D., and T. F. Drada. 1977. Effects of grass carp introduction on waterfowl habitat. Transactions of the North American Wildlife and Natural Resources Conference 44:73–85.

Gascon, C., and D. Planas. 1986. Spring pond water chemistry and the reproduction of the wood frog, *Rana sylvatica.* Canadian Journal of Zoology 64:543–550.

Gates, J. M. 1962. Breeding biology of the gadwall in northern Utah. Wilson Bulletin 74:43–67.

Gibbs, J. P. 1993. Importance of small wetlands for the persistence of local populations of wetland-associated animals. Wetlands 13:25–31.

Gilbert, D. W., D. R. Anderson, J. K. Ringelman, and M. R. Szymczak. 1996. Response of nesting ducks to habitat and management on the Monte Vista National Wildlife Refuge, Colorado. Wildlife Monograph 131:1–44.

Gill, R. E. Jr., C. M. Handel, and G. W. Page. 1995. Western North America shorebirds. Pages 60–65 in E. T. LaRoe, G. S. Farris, C. E. Puckett, P. D. Doran, and M. J. Mac, editors. Our living resources: a report to the nation on the distribution, abundance, and health of United States plants, animals, and ecosystems. U.S. National Biological Service, Washington, D.C., USA.

Grasse, J. E. 1951. Beaver ecology and management in the Rockies. Journal of Forestry 49:3–6.

Green, D. M., T. F. Sharbel, J. Kearsley, and H. Kraiser. 1996. Post glacial range fluctuation, genetic subdivision and speciation in the western North America spotted frog complex, *Rana pretiosa*. Evolution 50:374–390.

Grzimek, B., editor. 1974. Reptiles. Volume 6 of Grzimek's animal life encyclopedia. Von Nostrand Reinhold, New York, New York, USA.

Haig, S. M., D. W. Mehlman, and L. W. Oring. 1998. Avian movements and wetland connectivity in landscape conservation. Conservation Biology 12:748–758.

Hammerson, G. A. 1986. Amphibians and reptiles in Colorado. Colorado Division of Wildlife, Denver, Colorado, USA.

Hanson, M. A., and M. R. Riggs. 1995. Potential effects of fish predation: a comparison of wetlands with and without fathead minnows. Wetlands 15:167–175.

Hardy, T. B. 1986. Introduced fishes of the southwest. Southwestern Naturalist 31: 23–38.

Harris, S. W. 1954. An ecological study of the waterfowl of the potholes area, Grant County, Washington. American Midland Naturalist 52:403–432.

Hart, E. B. 1982. The raccoon, *Procyon lotor*, in Wyoming. Great Basin Naturalist 42:599–600.

Harte, J., and E. Hoffman. 1989. Possible effects of acidic deposition on a Rocky Mountain population of the tiger salamander *Ambystoma tigrinum*. Conservation Biology 3:149–158.

Hayes, M. P., and M. R. Jennings. 1986. Decline of ranid frog species in western North America: are bullfrogs (*Rana catesbeiana*) responsible? Journal of Herpetology 20: 490–509.

Hayward, B., E. J. Heske, and C. W. Painter. 1997. Effects of livestock grazing on small mammals at a desert cienega. Journal of Wildlife Management 61:123–129.

Hecnar, S. J., and R. T. M'Closkey. 1996. Regional dynamics and the status of amphibians. Ecology 77:2091–2097.

Hoffman, R. S., and J. G. Owen. 1980. *Sorex tenellus* and *Sorex nanus*. Mammalian Species 131:1–4. American Society of Mammalogists.

Hovingh, P. 1993. Aquatic habitats, life history observations, and zoogeographic considerations of the spotted frog (*Rana pretiosa*) in the Tule Valley, Utah. Great Basin Naturalist 53:168–179.

———, B. Benton, and D. Bornholdt. 1985. Aquatic parameters and life history observations of the Great Basin spadefoot toad in Utah. Great Basin Naturalist 45: 22–30.

Jensen, G. H., and J. E. Chattin. 1964. Western production areas. Pages 79–88 *in* J. P. Linduska, editor. Waterfowl tomorrow. U.S. Government Printing Office, Washington, D.C., USA.

Johnson, B. 1992. Habitat loss and declining amphibian populations. Pages 71–75 *in* C. A. Bishop and K. E. Pettit, editors. Declines in Canadian amphibian populations: designing a national monitoring strategy. Canadian Wildlife Service Occasional Paper Number 76.

Johnson, D. H., and J. W. Grier. 1988. Determinants of breeding distributions of ducks. Wildlife Monograph 100:1–37.

Jones, K. B. Jr. 1988. Distribution and habitat associations of herpetofauna in Arizona: comparisons by habitat type. Pages 109–128 *in* R. C. Szaro, K. E. Severson, and D. R. Patton, editors. Management of amphibians, reptiles, and small mammals in North America. U.S. Forest Service General Technical Report RM-166.

Kadlec, J. A., and L. M. Smith. 1989. The Great Basin marshes. Pages 451–474 *in* L. M. Smith, R. L. Pederson, and R. M. Kaminski, editors. Habitat management for migrating and wintering waterfowl in North America. Texas Tech University Press, Lubbock, Texas, USA.

Kantrud, H. A., G. L. Krapu, and G. A. Swanson. 1989. Prairie basin wetlands of the Dakotas: a community profile. U.S. Fish and Wildlife Service Biological Report 85(7.28).

Keddy, P. A. 1983. Freshwater wetland human-induced changes: indirect effects must also be considered. Environmental Management 7:299–302.

———. 1999. Wetland restoration: the potential for assembly rules in the service of conservation. Wetlands 19:716–732.

Key, C. H. 1979. Mammalian utilization of floodplain habitats along the North Fork of the Flathead River in Glacier National Park. Thesis, University of Montana, Missoula, Montana, USA.

Kroodsma, D. E., and J. Verner. 1997. Marsh wren (*Cistothorus palustris*). *In* A. Poole and F. Gill, editors. The birds of North America, Number 308. Academy of Naturalist Sciences, Philadelphia, and American Ornithologists' Union, Washington, D.C., USA.

Kufeld, R. C. 1973. Foods eaten by the Rocky Mountain elk. Journal of Range Management 26:106–113.

Kupferberg, S. D. 1997. Bullfrog (*Rana catesbeiana*) invasion of a California river: the role of larval competition. Ecology 78:1736–1757.

Laubhan, M. K., and L. H. Fredrickson. 1993. Integrated wetland management: concepts and opportunities. Transactions of the North American Wildlife and Natural Resources Conference 58:323–334.

———, and———. 1997. Wetlands of the Great Plains: habitat characteristics and vertebrate associations. Pages 20–48 *in* F. L. Knopf and F. B. Samson, editors. Ecology and conservation of Great Plains vertebrates. Ecological Studies 125. Springer-Verlag, New York, New York, USA.

———, and J. H. Gammonley. 2000. Density and foraging habitat selection of waterbirds breeding in the San Luis Valley of Colorado. Journal of Wildlife Management 64:808–819.

Lawrence, W. H. 1952. Evidence of the age of beaver ponds. Journal of Wildlife Management 16:69–79.

Lemly, A. D. 1994. Irrigated agriculture and freshwater wetlands: a struggle for coexistence in the western United States. Wetlands Ecology and Management 3:3–15.

Lewis, D. T., G. T. Baxter, K. M. Johnson, and M. D. Stone. 1985. Possible extinction of the Wyoming toad, *Bufo hemiophrys baxteri*. Journal of Herpetology 19:166–168.

Licht, L. E. 1975. Comparative life history features of the western spotted frog, *Rana pretiosa*, from low- and high-elevation populations. Canadian Journal of Zoology 53:1254–1257.

Long, C. A. 1972. Notes on habitat preference and reproduction in pygmy shrews, *Microsorex*. Canadian Field-Naturalist 86:155–160.

Ludwig, D. R. 1984. *Microtus richardsonii* microhabitats and life history. Pages 319–331 *in* J. F. Merritt, editor. Winter ecology of small mammals. Carnegie Museum of Natural History Special Publication Number 10, Pittsburgh, Pennsylvania, USA.

Mahoney, S. A., and J. R. Jehl Jr. 1985. Adaptations of migratory shorebirds to highly saline and alkaline lakes: Wilson's phalarope and American avocet. Condor 87: 520–527.

Mason, C. F., and S. M. MacDonald. 1983. Some factors influencing the distribution of mink (*Mustella vison*). Journal of Applied Ecology 20:281–283.

McComb, W. C., J. R. Sedell, and T. D. Buchholz. 1990. Dam-site selection by beavers in an eastern Oregon basin. Great Basin Naturalist 50:273–281.

McCoy, C. J., H. M. Smith, and J. A. Tinen. 1967. Natural hybrid toads, *Bufo punctatus* x *Bufo woodhousei*, from Colorado. Southwestern Naturalist 12:45–54.

McKinstry, M. C., and S. H. Anderson. 2002. Creating wetlands for waterfowl in Wyoming. Ecological Engineering 18:293–304.

————, P. Caffrey, and S. H. Anderson. 2001. The importance of beaver to wetland habitats and waterfowl in Wyoming. Journal American Water Resources Association 37:1571–1577.

McKnight, S. K., and G. R. Hepp. 1995. Potential effect of grass carp herbivory on waterfowl foods. Journal of Wildlife Management 59:720–727.

Meffe, G. K. 1989. Fish utilization of cienegas and springs in the arid Southwest. Pages 475–485 *in* R. R. Sharitz and J. W. Gibbons, editors. Freshwater wetlands and wildlife: perspectives on natural, managed, and degraded ecosystems. U.S. Department of Energy, Office of Scientific and Technical Information, Oak Ridge, Tennessee, USA.

Michot, T. C., J. B. Low, and D. R. Anderson. 1979. Decline of redhead duck nesting on Knudson Marsh, Utah. Journal of Wildlife Management 43:224–229.

Miller, R. R., J. D. Williams, and J. E. Williams. 1989. Extinction in North American fishes during the past century. Fisheries 14:22–29, 31–38.

Minckley, W. L., G. K. Meffe, and D. L. Soltz. 1991. Conservation and management of short-lived fishes: the cyprinodontoids. Pages 247–282 *in* W. L. Minckley and J. E. Deacon, editors. Battle against extinction: native fish management in the American West. University of Arizona Press, Tucson, Arizona, USA.

Mitchell, J. L. 1961. Mink movements and populations on a Montana river. Journal of Wildlife Management 25:48–54.

Mitsch, W. J., and J. G. Gosselink. 1993. Wetlands. Second edition. Van Nostrand Reinhold, New York, New York, USA.

Monda, M. J., and J. T. Ratti. 1988. Niche overlap and habitat use by sympatric duck broods in eastern Washington. Journal of Wildlife Management 52:95–103.

Morrison, R. I. G., and R. K. Ross. 1989. Atlas of Nearctic shorebirds on the coast of South America. Canadian Wildlife Service Special Publication, Ottawa, Ontario, Canada.

Moyle, P. B., H. W. Li, and B. A. Barton. 1986. The Frankenstein effect: impact of introduced fishes on native fishes in North America. Pages 415–426 *in* R. H. Stroud, editor. Fish culture in fisheries management. American Fisheries Society, Bethesda, Maryland, USA.

Niering, W. A. 1988. Endangered, threatened, and rare wetland plants and animals of the continental United States. Pages 227–238 *in* D. W. Hook, W. H. McKee Jr., H. K. Smith, J. Gregory, V. G. Burrell Jr., M. R. DeVoe, R. E. Sojka, S. Gilbert, R. Banks, L. H. Stolzy, C. Brooks, T. D. Matthews, and T. H. Shear, editors. Ecology of wetlands. Volume 1 of The ecology and management of wetlands. Timber Press, Portland, Oregon, USA.

Newman, R. A. 1989. Developmental plasticity of *Scaphiopus couchii* tadpoles in an unpredictable environment. Ecology 70:1775–1787.

Novak, M. 1987. Beaver. Pages 283–312 *in* M. Novak, J. A. Baker, M. E. Obbard, and B. Malloch, editors. Wild furbearer management and conservation in North America. Ontario Trappers Association, Toronto, Canada.

Oring, L. W. 1964. Behavior and ecology of certain ducks during the postbreeding period. Journal of Wildlife Management 28:223–233.

———, and J. M. Reed. 1997. Shorebirds of the western Great Basin of North America: overview and importance to continental populations. International Wader Studies 9:6–12.

Osmundson, B. C. 1990. Feeding of American avocets (*Recurvirostra americana*) during the breeding season. Thesis, Utah State University, Logan, Utah, USA.

Ovaska, K., T. M. Davis, and I. N. Flamarique. 1997. Hatching success and larval survival of the frogs *Hyla regilla* and *Rana aurora* under ambient and artificially enhanced solar ultraviolet radiation. Canadian Journal of Zoology 75:1081–1088.

Page, G. W., and R. E. Gill Jr. 1994. Shorebirds in western North America: late 1800s to late 1900s. Studies in Avian Biology 15:147–160.

Pechman, J. H. K., and H. M. Wilbur. 1994. Putting declining amphibian populations in perspective: natural fluctuations and human impacts. Herpetologica 50:65–84.

Peterka, J. J. 1989. Fishes in northern prairie wetlands. Pages 302–315 *in* A. G. van der Valk, editor. Northern prairie marshes. Iowa State University Press, Ames, Iowa, USA.

Peterson, S. R., and J. B. Low. 1977. Waterfowl use of Uintah Mountain wetlands in Utah. Journal of Wildlife Management 41:112–117.

Quick, H. F. 1951. Notes on the ecology of weasels in Gunnison County, Colorado. Journal of Mammalogy 32:281–290.

Quigley, T. M., R. W. Haynes, and R. T. Graham, technical editors. 1996. Integrated scientific assessment for ecosystem management in the interior Columbia Basin. U.S. Forest Service and U.S. Bureau of Land Management General Technical Report PNW-GTR-382.

Raphael, M. G. 1988. Habitat associations of small mammals in a subalpine forest, southeastern Wyoming. Pages 359–367 *in* R. C. Szaro, K. E. Severson, and D. R. Patton, editors. Management of amphibians, reptiles, and small mammals in North America. U.S. Forest Service General Technical Report RM-166.

Ratti, J. T., and J. A. Kadlec. 1992. Concept plan for the preservation of wetland habitat of the Intermountain West. U.S. Fish and Wildlife Service, Region 1, Portland, Oregon, USA.

Rinne, J. N., and W. L. Minckley. 1991. Native fishes of arid lands: a dwindling resource in the arid Southwest. U.S. Forest Service General Technical Report RM-206.

Robel, R. J. 1961. The effects of carp populations on the production of waterfowl food plants on a western waterfowl marsh. Transactions of the North American Wildlife and Natural Resources Conference 26:147–159.

Robinson, J. A., and S. E. Warnock. 1997. The staging paradigm and wetland conservation in arid environments: shorebirds and wetlands of the North American Great Basin. International Wader Studies 9:37–44.

Rogers, K., A. Schmidt, J. Wilkonson, and T. Merz. 2001. Effects of incident UV-B radiation on periphyton in four alpine freshwater ecosystems in central Colorado: impacts on boreal toads (*Bufo boreas*). Journal of Freshwater Ecology 16:283–301.

Rossman, D. A., N. B. Ford, and R. A. Seigel. 1996. The garter snakes: evolution and ecology. University of Oklahoma Press, Norman, Oklahoma, USA.

Rubega, M. A., and J. A. Robinson. 1996. Water salinization and shorebirds: emerging issues. International Wader Studies 9:45–54.

Rutherford, W. H., and C. R. Hayes. 1976. Stratification as a means for improving waterfowl surveys. Wildlife Society Bulletin 4:74–78.

Ryder, R. A., and D. E. Manry. 1994. White-faced ibis (*Plegadis chihi*). *In* A. Poole and F. Gill, editors. The birds of North America, Number 130. Academy of Naturalist Sciences, Philadelphia, and American Ornithologists' Union, Washington, D.C., USA.

Sanders, R. L. 1997. Montane wetland characteristics and waterfowl use on the Routt National Forest, Colorado. Thesis, University of Missouri, Columbia, Missouri, USA.

Seale, D. B. 1980. Influence of amphibian larvae on primary production, nutrient flux, and competition in a pond ecosystem. Ecology 61:1531–1550.

Sexton, O. J., and J. R. Bizer. 1978. Life history patterns of *Ambystoma tigrinum* in montane Colorado. American Midland Naturalist 99:101–118.

Shimer, J. A. 1972. A field guide to landforms in the United States. MacMillan, New York, New York, USA.

Sigler, W. F., and J. W. Sigler. 1987. Fishes of the Great Basin: a natural history. University of Nevada, Reno, Nevada, USA.

Singer, F. J. 1978. Seasonal concentrations of grizzly bears, North Fork of Flathead River, Montana. Canadian Field Naturalist 82:283–286.

Sinsch, U. 1990. Migration and orientation in anuran amphibians. Ethology, Ecology, and Evolution 2:65–79.

Skagen, S. K., and F. L. Knopf. 1993. Towards conservation of mid-continent shorebird migrations. Conservation Biology 7:533–541.

Slough, B. G., and R. M. F. S. Sadlier. 1977. A land capability classification system for beaver (*Castor canadensis* Kuhl.). Canadian Journal of Zoology 55:1324–1335.

Smith, L. M., and J. A. Kadlec. 1985. Fire and herbivory in a Great Salt Lake marsh. Ecology 66:259–265.

Spencer, A. W., and D. Pettus. 1966. Habitat preferences of five species of long-tailed shrews. Ecology 47:677–683.

Stebbins, R. C. 1985. A field guide to western reptiles and amphibians. Houghton Mifflin, Boston, Massachusetts, USA.

———, and N. W. Cohen. 1995. A natural history of amphibians. Princeton University Press, Princeton, New Jersey, USA.

Szymczak, M. R. 1986. Characteristics of duck populations in the intermountain parks of Colorado. Colorado Division of Wildlife Technical Publication Number 35, Denver, Colorado, USA.

Tanner, W. W. 1978. Zoogeography of reptiles and amphibians in the Intermountain Region. Great Basin Naturalist Memoirs 2:43–54.

Tomasi, T. E., and R. S. Hoffmann. 1984. *Sorex preblei* in Utah and Wyoming. Journal of Mammalogy 65:708.

Trapp, G. R. 1978. Comparative behavioral ecology of the ringtail (*Bassariscus astutus*) and gray fox (*Urocyon cinereoargentatus*) in southwestern Utah. Carnivore 1: 3–32.

Turner, F. B. 1960. Population structure and dynamics of the western spotted frog, *Rana p. pretiosa* Baird and Girard, in Yellowstone Park, Wyoming. Ecological Monographs 30:251–278.

Twedt, D. J., and R. D. Crawford. 1995. Yellow-headed blackbird (*Xanthocephalus xanthocephalus*). *In* A. Poole and F. Gill, editors. The birds of North America, Number 192. Academy of Naturalist Sciences, Philadelphia, and American Ornithologists' Union, Washington, D.C., USA.

Tyus, H. M. 1991. Ecology and management of Colorado squawfish. Pages 379–402 *in* W. L. Minckley and J. E. Deacon, editors. Battle against extinction: native fish management in the American West. University of Arizona Press, Tucson, Arizona, USA.

U.S. Fish and Wildlife Service. 1994. Update to the North American waterfowl management plan. U.S. Fish and Wildlife Service and Canadian Wildlife Service, Washington, D.C.

———. 1995. Intermountain West Joint Venture implementation plan. Unpublished report. U.S. Fish and Wildlife Service and Canadian Wildlife Service, Washington, D.C.

van der Valk, A. G., and C. B. Davis. 1978. The role of seed banks in the vegetation dynamics of prairie glacial marshes. Ecology 59:322–335.

Vial, J. L., and L. Saylor. 1993. The status of amphibian populations, a compilation and analysis. International Union for Conservation of Nature and Natural Resources (IUCN), Declining Amphibian Populations Task Force Working Document Number 1.

Wassersug, R. J. 1975. The adaptive significance of the tadpole stage with comments on the maintenance of complex life cycles in anurans. American Zoologist 15:405–417.

Wiens, J. A. 1983. Avian community ecology: an iconoclastic view. Pages 355–403 *in* A. H. Brush and G. A. Clark Jr., editors. Perspectives in ornithology. Essays presented for the centennial of the American Ornithologists' Union. Cambridge University Press, Cambridge, England.

Weitzel, N. H., and H. R. Panik. 1993. Long-term fluctuations of an isolated population of the Pacific chorus frog (*Pseudacris regilla*) in northwestern Nevada. Great Basin Naturalist 53:379–384.

Weller, M. W., and C. S. Spatcher. 1965. Role of habitat in the distribution and abundance of marsh birds. Iowa State University Agriculture and Home Economics Experiment Station Special Report 43, Ames, Iowa, USA.

Wells, K. D. 1977. The social behavior of anuran amphibians. Animal Behavior 25:666–693.

Western Hemisphere Shorebird Reserve Network (WHSRN). 1992. Western Hemisphere Shorebird Reserve Network site profiles. Publication Number 4. Wetlands for the Americas, Manomet, Massachusetts, USA.

Wiggins, G. B., R. J. MacKay, and I. M. Smith. 1981. Evolutionary and ecological strategies of animals in annual temporary pools. Archives Hydrobiologia (supplement) 58:97–206.

Williams, B. K., M. D. Koneff, and D. A. Smith. 1999. Evaluation of waterfowl conservation under the North American Waterfowl Management Plan. Journal of Wildlife Management 63:417–440.

Williams, D. D. 1987. The ecology of temporary waters. Timber Press, Portland, Oregon, USA.

Williams, J. E., and C. E. Bond. 1980. Status and life history notes on the native fishes of the Alvord Basin, Oregon and Nevada. Great Basin Naturalist 43:409–420.

Willner, G. R., G. A. Feldhamer, E. E. Zucker, and J. A. Chapman. 1980. *Ondatra zibethicus.* Mammalian Species 141:1–8. American Society of Mammalogists.

Windell, J. T., B. E. Willard, D. J. Cooper, S. Q. Foster, C. F. Knud-Hansen, L. P. Rink, and G. N. Kiladis. 1986. An ecological characterization of Rocky Mountain montane and subalpine wetlands. U.S. Fish and Wildlife Service Biological Report 86(11).

Winemiller, K. O., and A. A. Anderson. 1997. Response of endangered desert fish populations to a constructed refuge. Restoration Ecology 5:204–213.

Wissinger, S. A., and H. Whiteman. 1992. Fluctuation in a Rocky Mountain population of salamanders: anthropogenic acidification or natural variation? Journal of Herpetology 26:377–391.

Woodling, J. 1985. Colorado's little fish, a guide to the minnows and other lesser known fishes in the state of Colorado. Colorado Division of Wildlife, Denver, Colorado, USA.

Worthylake, K. M., and P. Hovingh. 1989. Mass mortality of salamanders (*Ambystoma tigrinum*) by bacteria (Acinetobacter) in an oligotrophic seepage mountain lake. Great Basin Naturalist 49:364–372.

Zeveloff, S. I., and F. R. Collett. 1988. Mammals of the Intermountain West. University of Utah Press, Salt Lake City, Utah, USA.

CHAPTER 8

Management of Natural Palustrine Wetlands

NEAL D. NIEMUTH, MICHAEL A. BOZEK, AND NEIL F. PAYNE

Introduction

Palustrine wetlands, like all aquatic ecosystems, are inextricably linked to the upland habitats that surround them. Attempts to understand these systems become even more complex when issues of scale (e.g., spatial and temporal scales) are applied to ecosystem processes (Gelwick and Matthews 1990, Schramm and Hubert 1996). Aquatic systems act as integrators of terrestrial ecosystem characteristics (e.g., catchment size, slope, soil) and activities (e.g., land use) and thus can be indicators of changes in environmental quality. In this chapter we adopt a landscape-level approach that addresses causes, in addition to symptoms, of problems in management of palustrine wetlands. Because of the general aridity of the environment, wetland management is particularly important and problematic in the Intermountain West. However, the Intermountain West also offers unique opportunities for landscape-level management of wetlands because large-block land ownership patterns are conducive to manipulating landscape and regional inputs as well as local inputs to wetlands.

Timber Harvesting and Road Building
Impacts of timber harvesting and road building on palustrine systems

Timber-harvesting and road-building activities can have a substantial impact on aquatic systems, although research specifically focused on the Intermountain West lags behind that occurring in either coastal region of North America. Differences in watershed responses to timber harvesting among regions can be attributed to differences in climate, topography, soil and geology, and vegetation (Burns 1972, Bormann et al. 1974, Scrivener 1982, Swank and Crossley 1988). However, while there are region-specific differences in effects (i.e., specific organisms, degree of perturbation), the fundamental physical processes that regulate environmental effects are manifested in similar ways among regions (i.e., operative physical processes are universal) and thus can be generalized at a coarse scale.

Timber harvesting involves the interaction of a complex set of anthropogenic activities and ecological and hydrological processes. The physical activities involved in timber harvesting include the felling, skidding, and transporting of logs; road construction; slash removal; site preparation (scarification, herbicide application, burning, etc.); and site rehabilitation including seeding or planting (Haupt and Kidd 1965, Miller 1984, Holopainen et al. 1991). The effects of timber harvesting actually result from many of the activities associated with logging beyond actual cutting and removal of trees. For instance, skidding logs can destroy other vegetation that helps prevent soil erosion, while heavy equipment compacts soil, increasing runoff rates and exacerbating erosion (Johnson and Beschta 1980, Clayton 1990). However, the effects of timber harvesting on aquatic systems often are discussed synonymously with other activities such as road building because the activities often occur together. Yet their operative processes differ in how they elicit effects in upland areas and how these effects are transferred to and manifest themselves in aquatic systems. In many cases, disturbances from these additional activities are the source of many environmental effects in watersheds and receiving waters.

Timber harvesting and road building are major influences on hydrology of catchments (Rothacher 1970, Likens et al. 1977, Swank and Crossley 1988); effects to aquatic systems cascade from these hydrologic responses. Increased runoff results in increased sediment, nutrient, and organic transport (Patric and Reinhart 1971, Hartman and Holtby 1982, Hall et al. 1987), which affects water chemistry (Bormann et al. 1974, Nicholson et al. 1982), productivity (Webster et al. 1988), fish habitat (Hall et al. 1987), and abundance and community composition of various taxa (Burns 1972, Murphy and Hall 1981, Hall et al. 1987). Other consequences of timber harvesting unrelated to hydrological processes include thermal changes, resource access, and habitat fragmentation (Franklin and Forman 1987) and changes in land use of large blocks of land near wetland complexes.

Timber-harvesting activities universally increase water yield in catchments, which is the most predictable response (Hibbert 1967, Harr et al. 1975, Likens et al. 1977, Hornbeck et al. 1986, Hetherington 1987, Bonell 1993). However, the actual water yield within a catchment differs locally based on differences in climate, topography, and native vegetation. Increased runoff after timber harvesting results from decreased interception of precipitation onto vegetation and into soil (Harr 1977), reduced evapotranspiration, and reduced landscape roughness. Timber harvesting exposes forest soils directly to erosive forces of precipitation and overland flow. Increased water yield increases the transport energy of moving water, which leads to increased erosion. Moreover, reduced vegetative cover increases the erosional power of water at the point of impact of water on bare soil where mobilization can occur. The link between water yield and erosion is clear: exposed or unvegetated soil in upland areas is a source of sediment during rainfall or spring runoff. Heavy rainfall saturates the soil, making it transportable via overland flow, while erosive forces increase considerably once flow becomes channelized in rills, ditches, and even streams. The riparian-wetland ecotone is critical in evaluating how specific sites will be affected, as it is the transfer point between upland and aquatic environments. Upland and riparian areas that have steeper slopes or more channelized drainage patterns increase transport potential of sites. The amount and location of natural areas positioned between these sites and wetlands reduces transport potential. As such, riparian zones buffer transport of terrestrial material (e.g., soil, leaves, needles, woody structure) to wetlands (see Chapter 5).

Harvesting in watersheds can directly alter soil structure through disturbance and compaction by heavy machinery. Moreover, tree cutting eliminates root structure that binds and stabilizes soils, while the rate at which precipitation is intercepted by the forest canopy decreases, thus increasing runoff. As runoff increases, the amount of sediment being transported also increases. Effects of increased suspended sediment include increased turbidity, reduced dissolved oxygen—particularly where high amounts of organic material are transported—and abrasion to gills and even suffocation of fish (Newcombe and MacDonald 1991, Bozek and Young 1994). Increased levels of sedimentation increase rates of eutrophication, increase turbidity, decrease oxygen levels, and increase nutrient loadings of aquatic systems that alter ecological, biological, and physiological processes. Organic soils can reduce oxygen by increasing the biological oxygen demand (BOD) and decreasing photosynthetic production of oxygen if transported sediment remains in suspension for prolonged periods.

Depending upon soil characteristics and chemistry, mobilized soils can transfer a variety of nutrients and contaminants (Bormann et al. 1974, Norris et al. 1991). While granitic soils of some intermountain drainages are nutrient-poor, thin topsoil layers and duff contain nutrients and organic matter that can be transported to wetland complexes. Increased nutrients can increase primary productivity and lead to nuisance blooms of noxious blue-green algae and macrophytes. In general, however, nutrient loadings in runoff can increase after timber harvesting, but effects are usually ameliorated in fewer than 8 years (Scrivener 1982).

Changes in hydrographs associated with increased water delivery also affect depth, storage, and quality of water in wetland complexes. More overland flow results in quicker and more pronounced peaks in hydrographs and lower water levels during drier periods. Moreover, increased runoff decreases infiltration and recharge of aquifers that can result in lower discharge rates from springs that feed wetlands (Freeze and Cherry 1979).

The principal source of thermal inputs to most aquatic systems is direct solar radiation (Hynes 1970, Barton et al. 1985), although reduced groundwater discharge caused by declines in aquifer recharge rates (Freeze and Cherry 1979) also can influence temperatures. Temperature changes, particularly on smaller systems, can be dramatic as a result of timber harvest, while larger systems, with less initial shading by riparian vegetation and greater thermal mass, are affected less.

Impacts of road building on palustrine habitats

Road building can have both direct and indirect effects on palustrine habitats. Roads are the largest source of sediment transported to aquatic systems (Swanston and Swanson 1976, Beschta 1978). In fact, erosion from roads contributes more sediment per unit area than all other forest activities (see Gibbons and Salo 1973). Sediment associated with road development and maintenance comes from road surfaces, drainage ditches along roads, and culverts or drainage crossings. Soil on roads is exposed continuously to hydrologic forces, making them highly susceptible to erosion. Moreover, road grading makes additional sediment available for transport, and drainage ditches along roads are among the most hydrologically active areas in forested environments. Where drainage patterns require culverts, proper design and regular maintenance are essential (McCashion and Rice 1983, Ontario Ministry of Natural Resources 1990). Improper drainage also can disrupt hydrological processes important to wetland functions, resulting in direct loss or impaired use of habitat. Other important effects of road building are the filling of wetland habitats during road construction, causing direct loss of wetlands, disruption of drainage patterns, and habitat fragmentation.

A road crossing is often the point where effects from upland land use activities are transferred to aquatic systems. Construction of roads accelerates erosional processes in watersheds by exposing soil on roads and adjacent ditches to direct erosion and by altering the natural drainage networks in watersheds (Beschta 1978, Reid and Dunne 1984). In particular, hydrologic runoff patterns are altered (i.e., from sheet to channel flow) and hydraulic forces are concentrated, both of which increase rates of erosion.

General best management practices for timber harvesting and road building

In assessing effects of timber harvesting, attention needs to be paid to both scale issues and techniques to minimize impacts to aquatic systems (Heede and King 1990). In selecting best management practices (BMPs) that ameliorate the effects of timber harvesting on palustrine habitats, several principles apply. First, the best practices are those that are preventive (designed to reduce the incidence of a problem at its source) rather than remedial (intended to mitigate the effects after they occur). Second, techniques need to be based on site-specific conditions such as soil type, disturbance level, topography and specific slope, proximity to wetland complex, and overall management objectives. Third, several alternatives may produce the same result, and combinations of practices often are better than single approaches. Fourth, excluding timber harvesting or road building may be the best management practice for some areas.

Best management practices should be planned with resource managers. Careful attention should be paid to the design of any project at landscape and local scales. During planning, roads should be diverted away from sensitive environmental habitat or positioned to minimize environmental consequences. Often, less damaging alternatives can be found before plans are set, projects bid out, and activities begun. Changes to plans after activities start are costly and might be viewed as obstructionist in extreme cases. Sound evidence presented to resource managers in advance can reduce cost and protect resources without compromising the integrity of the aquatic environment.

Use of buffer reserves in riparian areas next to aquatic systems is the most widely recognized BMP (Ontario Ministry of Natural Resources 1988). This approach tends to be remedial by reducing sediment transport after it has begun rather than stopping transport before it starts. Many states and provinces have guidelines for design of riparian buffer widths, but in general, recommended reserve widths are a function of soil particle size, land slope, and vegetation. These guidelines stipulate that riparian buffer corridors along or around aquatic areas be extended to a distance (width) whereby transported sediment gets filtered by natural vegetation. These distances vary among governmental agencies because research has been equivocal in designating a "catch-all" buffer width. Climatological, geographical, and vegetational differences play a key role in observed differences in research results.

Some of the earliest and most convincing research on sediment transport (Trimble and Sartz 1957) showed that steeper slopes of undisturbed forest transported sediment farther and thus required greater buffer widths. Minimizing site disturbance, avoiding highly erodible sites, and revegetating sites also help reduce the amount of sediment moving from harvested areas. In general, increased slope and decreased vegetation cover and soil particle sizes increase transport risk. Generalized buffer reserve widths are as follows: 30 m for slopes 0–15%; 50 m for slopes 16–30%; 70 m for slopes 31–45%; and 90 m for slopes 46–60%. The best guidelines to apply are those developed for local conditions. Of critical importance in protecting wetlands is determining what should be protected and where the buffer reserve should be placed so that all transported material is stopped before reaching the area of concern.

Thermal effects to wetlands resulting from timber harvesting are not well quantified. Most work has been conducted in small streams where the ratio of surface water to riparian interface is highest, and significant thermal buffering has been demonstrated (Barton et al. 1985, Campbell and Doeg 1989). But buffer reserves set up to minimize transport of sediment, nutrients, and organic matter to wetlands generally will provide adequate thermal buffering.

Constructing roads that have no effects on the environment is difficult. Rather, effort should be placed on designing roads that minimize their exposure to sensitive aquatic areas, using proper design and best management practices, and maintaining currently used roads or removing and rehabilitating discontinued roads. Most publications available from resource management agencies on implementing BMPs have not been researched or peer-reviewed (Ontario Ministry of Natural Resources 1990). Many prescriptions proposed in these documents have not been demonstrated to be effective and in some instances might cause more harm than good. This underscores the need to work directly with hydrologists or engineers who specialize in this type of work when undertaking these projects.

Best management practices for forest road construction include techniques that minimize proximity of roads to wetlands, route the increased runoff away from drainage ditches to reduce transport energy, and directly minimize sediment losses from erosion from roads (Rothwell 1978, Ontario Ministry of Natural Resources 1990). The following guidelines can be applied in most cases:

- Minimize proximity of roads, road crossings, and road drainages to wetlands, particularly higher-quality wetlands or sensitive areas
- Avoid road construction routes that occur in areas having high topographic relief or areas having highly erodible soils. Gentle grades <4% are most desirable, and shorter grades are better than longer grades
- Use large particle sizes for rip-rap in drainage ditches and along road crossings to minimize erosion
- Minimize the number of roads

• Design enough culverts and road crossings to handle runoff without causing erosion; the design should be adequate for runoff to pass without damming flows
• Include buffer reserve areas downslope of road construction and drainage
• Disperse runoff drainage rather than concentrate it, thereby minimizing soil transport power
• Encourage vegetative stabilization
• Conduct construction during times that minimize effects to soil movement and to organisms near the road

Grazing
Impact of grazing on palustrine systems

Grazing is the dominant land use in the Intermountain West, with about 70% of the 11 westernmost states grazed by livestock (see Fleischner 1994). Even though the effects of grazing have been extensively studied (see Vallentine 1990, Armour et al. 1994, Kie et al. 1994, Fleischner 1994, Payne 1998, Payne and Bryant 1998), its impacts are hard to generalize, as they vary with location, stocking rate, season, duration of grazing, topography, management practices, precipitation, and species of grazer. Grazing *per se* is not necessarily harmful, particularly in plant communities that evolved with herbivory, and the disturbance associated with limited grazing can increase diversity (Archer and Smeins 1991, Hobbs and Huenneke 1992). In addition, stock tanks and windmills built for cattle provide water and habitat for a vast array of wildlife (Crawford and Bolen 1976, Evans and Krebs 1977, Menasco 1986, Payne and Bryant 1998; also see Chapters 9, 10, and 11).

However, cattle spend a disproportionate amount of time in riparian areas (Ames 1977, Goodman et al. 1989), and the impact of grazing on wetlands can be devastating. These impacts can be direct (e.g., herbivory of wetland vegetation) or indirect (e.g., altered hydrologic regimes caused by reduced vegetative cover and soil permeability of grazed lands).

Grazing reduces emergent and wetland margin vegetation, as well as shrubs and trees associated with wetlands (Glinski 1977, Thomas et al. 1979, Kauffman and Krueger 1984). This reduces fawn-rearing and thermal cover for mule deer (Leckenby et al. 1982). Similarly, decreased nesting success of sandhill cranes in grazed wetlands in southeastern Oregon was attributed to reduced vegetative cover, easy predator access, altered predator communities, and altered prey base associated with high cattle stocking rates (Littlefield and Paullin 1990).

Wet meadows are preferred brood-rearing areas for sage grouse, as these meadows contain succulent forbs required by chicks (Klebenow 1982).

Excessive grazing reduces available vegetation in wet meadows (Call and Maser 1985), which are subsequently avoided by sage grouse (Klebenow 1982). In addition, wet meadows can also dry up from development of cattle-watering tanks at springs that feed the meadows (Thomas et al. 1979).

Management of surrounding uplands for cattle production can impact both water quality and quantity. Ethyl parathion, an organophosphorus insecticide often used to control grasshoppers on rangelands and croplands, can enter wetlands via runoff or spray drift. Ethyl parathion is toxic to waterfowl (Smith 1987) and aquatic invertebrates (Mayer and Ellersieck 1986, Tome et al. 1991). Water quantity is altered as grazing of uplands reduces ground cover and compacts soil, which decreases infiltration and increases surface runoff (Packer 1953, Sharp et al. 1964, Lusby 1970). Consequently, summer flow of water into wetlands is decreased, drying up wet meadows and gully seeps (Call and Maser 1985).

Best management practices for grazing

Total removal of cattle is often recommended as the best, or even only, solution to habitat degradation caused by grazing (Fleischner 1994). But this solution often is not viable for political, social, and economic reasons. Several alternatives will reduce the impact of grazing (see Chapters 5 and 11), but BMPs will vary greatly among wetland types. For all cases, grazing fees that vary with wetland management and intensity of use could serve as incentives for improving range and wetland quality (Elmore and Beschta 1987).

The ecological health of the range and its accompanying wetlands will be influenced greatly by the stocking rate and type of grazing system. These topics are beyond the scope of this chapter but are covered by Holechek et al. (1989), Kinch (1989), Payne (1998), and Payne and Bryant (1998). For example, temporary high stocking rates implemented under short-duration grazing to benefit watershed ecology or vegetation can increase trampling of ground nests (Jensen et al. 1990). And even though grazing is typically considered harmful to wetlands, light to moderate cattle grazing can be used to open dense stands of tall emergent vegetation. This can be especially useful for creating an interspersion of vegetation and water suitable as brood habitat, and possibly increasing the density of invertebrates (see Kantrud 1986; see also Chapters 5 and 11).

Fencing wetlands to exclude cattle can prevent direct damage to wetlands but does not treat deteriorated watershed conditions (i.e., it may treat symptoms rather than problems [Davis 1986]). In addition, fencing is expensive to build and maintain and can impede movement of ungulates, particularly pronghorns. If fences are erected, the bottom strand should be smooth wire 46 cm above ground to permit movement of pronghorns (see Payne and Bryant 1998). When fencing, including a non-grazed buffer strip around the wetland will provide wildlife cover (Brown et al. 1990, Burke and Gibbons 1995) as well as reduce inflow of sediment and contaminants.

Cattle use of wetlands can be reduced by placing shade structures, water tanks, mineral blocks, feed supplements, and oilers at least 400 m and preferably 800 m away from riparian areas (Davis 1986, Kinch 1989). If stock tanks make use of natural springs or seeps, piping and fencing can be used to shift stock use away from wetland areas.

Proper timing can reduce the impact of grazing on wetlands. Because cattle prefer wetland areas through much of the year, continuous grazing usually results in overuse (Kinch 1989). In spring, upland vegetation is similar in succulence to wetland vegetation, and disproportionate use of wetlands is reduced (Clary and Webster 1989). Stocking rate and location of animals must be monitored and adjusted as necessary, as bank damage and soil compaction might be greatest in spring when soils are moist. Removal of cattle following spring grazing allows vegetation regrowth before fall dormancy. Winter grazing reduces soil compaction if soil is frozen, although excessive removal of vegetation before spring runoff can be detrimental to water infiltration (Kinch 1989) and remove nesting cover for birds. Grazing in summer should be avoided, as cattle concentration around wetlands is usually greatest then (Clary and Webster 1989).

Animal type also can affect the impact of grazing on wetlands. For example, yearling steers tend to be wider ranging and use wetlands less than cow-calf pairs (Kinch 1989). Herded sheep offer advantages over cattle in some areas, as herders can control timing, frequency, and duration of grazing (Kinch 1989).

The impact of grazing will vary greatly among sites and even among years for a given site. Therefore, grazing recommendations must be flexible, incorporating local and regional land use, wetland type, precipitation, landscape patterns, stocking rate, type of animal stocked, and timing of grazing. In all situations, wetlands and surrounding range conditions should be monitored and appropriate changes made if water quality or quantity is altered by grazing practices (see also Chapters 5 and 11).

Development and Recreation
Impacts of development and recreation on palustrine habitats

Development of palustrine habitats in the Intermountain West is exacerbated by the predominantly private ownership of riparian areas and wetlands. For example, even though 86% of Nevada's land area is publicly owned, at least 85% of Nevada's lowland meadow habitat is in private ownership (McAdoo et al. 1986). Also, roads often are developed along drainages because of the relatively gentle topography (Thomas et al. 1979). Because of private ownership and good access, wetlands and adjacent uplands are susceptible to development and, in areas with high human densities, urbanization.

Development has dramatic impacts on palustrine wetlands. Habitat is lost as vegetation is destroyed (Liddle 1975) and wetlands are filled. Habitat can be altered as wetlands are converted to pastures or hay meadows through removal of woody vegetation (often willow) and exotic plant species are introduced (Forman 1995). Wildlife travel corridors are fragmented, and increased human presence can disrupt animal activity patterns (see Boyle and Samson 1985), which can be particularly important in winter when wetlands are heavily used by ungulates. Urbanization is also characterized by 4 "standard pollutants" in runoff: (1) sediment and other solid particles, caused mainly by erosion associated with construction; (2) oxygen-demanding components; (3) nitrogen and phosphorous; and (4) traces of heavy metals (U.S. Environmental Protection Agency 1983).

Best management practices for development and recreation

Ideally, zoning should be enacted to prohibit development in and adjacent to wetlands. Unfortunately, zoning is often ineffective due to social and economic pressures and even due to the difficulty of clearly defining and delineating wetlands. But the impact of development can be lessened by clustering impacts, where development (housing, for instance) is aggregated rather than dispersed across the landscape. This concentrates human impacts in one area, reducing impacts on the rest of the landscape.

Buffer zones can also be required around development. Vegetated buffer strips function as horizontal runoff filters, reducing or stabilizing sediment, nutrient, and pollutant loads entering water bodies (Nieswand et al. 1990, Osborne and Kovacic 1993). Characteristics of vegetative buffer strips necessary to protect wetland qualities will vary depending on local conditions. Buffer zones also are used to reduce the impact of human disturbance and development on wildlife. In Florida, a 100 m buffer minimized the flushing of 16 species of waterbirds and shorebirds from walking or vehicular disturbance (Rodgers and Smith 1997). A buffer zone of 275 m was recommended to protect 100% of turtle nest and hibernation sites in uplands surrounding a wetland in South Carolina; 90% of sites would have been protected with a 73 m buffer zone (Burke and Gibbons 1995).

Quality of runoff flowing into wetlands from urban areas can be improved by constructing retention ponds, which are highly effective at trapping and biologically incorporating pollutants (U.S. Environmental Pollution Agency 1983). Similarly, filter fabric placed along the perimeter of construction sites and vegetative buffer strips next to roads can reduce flow of sediment into wetlands. Wetlands themselves also are effective at removing suspended solids, heavy metals, and biological oxygen demand, but at the cost of increased sedimentation of the wetland.

Agriculture
Impacts of agriculture on palustrine habitats

Agriculture has many direct and indirect impacts on palustrine habitats, the most conspicuous of which are habitat conversion (see Mitsch and Gosselink 1993) and altered hydrology. Irrigation projects require that vast amounts of water be retained, stored, moved, and distributed, draining some wetlands and altering the hydrology of others. Typically, water regimes are stabilized by irrigation projects, changing the wetland hydroperiod. These changes can (1) influence composition and species richness of wetland vegetation; (2) reduce primary productivity as water flow and pulsing hydroperiod are reduced; (3) alter accumulation, decomposition, and export of organic material; and (4) influence nutrient cycling and nutrient availability (see Mitsch and Gosselink 1993; see also Chapter 6 of this volume).

Altered hydrology can have local and regional impacts on wildlife. Water impoundments in Colorado and Wyoming have stabilized water regimes and reduced spring flooding along the Platte River in Nebraska, allowing encroachment of woody vegetation onto sandbars that formerly served as roosts for whooping cranes and sandhill cranes (Aronson and Ellis 1979). Wet meadows along the Platte River, which serve as foraging areas for cranes, also have been reduced because of upstream water regulation (Aronson and Ellis 1979). But irrigation drains, ditches, and accompanying seeps also create wetland habitat used by wildlife (Mustard and Rector 1979; Ball et al. 1989; see also Chapter 6).

Irrigation does not completely remove water from local aquatic systems. Excess irrigation water, sometimes called drainwater, might return to local wetlands, often carrying a burden of salts and contaminants leached from agricultural soils. Closed aquatic systems (those with no outlet) are particularly susceptible to degradation, since contaminants become concentrated as water evaporates (see Lemly et al. 1993).

The most famous case of drainwater contamination occurred in the Central Valley of California at Kesterson Reservoir, which suffered extensive inflow of selenium from subsurface drainwater in the late 1970s and early 1980s (Zahm 1986). Selenium bioaccumulates in plants and animals and at high concentrations can cause teratogenesis, reduced hatching success, and mortality of birds (Ohlendorf 1989). Although typically associated with Kesterson Reservoir, symptoms of selenium toxicity and high concentrations of selenium in wetlands are widespread throughout the West (Lemly et al. 1993). Similarly, salts can occur naturally or can enter wetlands from irrigation drainwater. Excessive levels of sodium and magnesium sulfate in drinking water can alter growth and development and even cause death of mallard ducklings (Mitcham and Wobeser 1988a,b).

Agrichemicals (pesticides and fertilizers) can enter wetlands directly through overspray, drift, cultivation, and treatment of dry wetland basins or indirectly through volatilization and runoff (Grue et al. 1986). Herbicides and fertilizers can cause mortality or increased growth, respectively, of wetland vegetation (Solberg and Higgins 1993, Mitsch and Gosselink 1993); other pesticides can cause direct (Grue et al. 1986, Tome et al. 1991, Dieter et al. 1995) and indirect (Hunter et al. 1984, Grue et al. 1986) mortality of wildlife.

Erosion of agricultural lands is a primary cause of sediment loading of wetlands. In some areas of the Pacific Northwest where conventional tillage is used, up to 12 bushels of topsoil are eroded annually for each bushel of wheat produced (Michalson and Papendick 1991). Loss of nutrients accompanies soil erosion; combined erosion losses of nitrogen, phosphorus, and potassium in the United States exceeds 69 million metric tons annually (Larson et al. 1983). Ultimately, high levels of erosion entering wetlands can cause increased biological oxygen demand, altered hydrologic regimes, sedimentation, eutrophication, and loss of open water habitat (Mitsch and Gosselink 1993).

Fragmentation and degradation of uplands next to wetlands can impact wetland wildlife negatively. Increased edge can lead to increased predation of bird nests (see Paton 1994) and turtle nests (Temple 1987). In addition to loss and degradation of habitat, tillage of uplands causes substantial nest loss for waterfowl and other species requiring uplands for nesting (Higgins 1977, Cowan 1982, Rodgers 1983).

Best management practices for agricultural development

Many wetland problems associated with agriculture can be avoided or reduced by using alternative management techniques in adjacent uplands. Foremost among these is the use of conservation tillage techniques. These techniques, which vary in purpose and effectiveness, are also known as no-till, minimum-till, reduced-till, mulch-till, and stubble-mulching. The main purpose of conservation tillage is to reduce erosion by leaving protective crop residue on the soil surface rather than turning residue under the soil as with a moldboard plow. In addition to reducing soil erosion and downstream pollution, conservation tillage can increase soil organic matter, reduce fuel use, reduce soil compaction, and increase storage of soil moisture (Ritchie and Follett 1983). Conservation tillage is not a panacea, however, as weed control and insects might require increased use of chemical pesticides. Conservation tillage can reduce soil and nutrient losses dramatically (Langdale et al. 1983), although implementing conservation tillage widely might require integrating new crop management practices, plant types, pest control methods, and socioeconomic principles (Michalson and Papendick 1991).

Conservation-tillage fields typically have higher nesting densities of upland-nesting birds relative to conventionally tilled fields (Cowan 1982, Basore et al. 1986), although numbers of birds are low relative to undisturbed natural grasslands. Nest losses can be high from machinery disturbance and high rates of predation, however, and conservation-tillage fields can become ecological traps if nesting success is inadequate to sustain populations without immigration from other sources (Basore et al. 1986, Best 1986). Nest loss in conservation-tillage grain fields can be reduced by using undercutters with mulch treaders removed rather than disks, plows, or treaders for the first spring tillage (Rodgers 1983). Where practicable, delaying cultivation and haying until after fledging also will reduce nest loss. If fieldwork is necessary, avoidance of known nests can reduce nest losses, and cutting hay from the center of the field outward will allow some wildlife to escape.

Vegetative buffer strips surrounding wetlands can be extremely effective at reducing sediment, nutrient, and pollutant loads entering wetlands (see Nieswand et al. 1990, Osborne and Kovacic 1993) in addition to providing cover for wildlife (see Payne 1998, Payne and Bryant 1998). Because the effectiveness of vegetative buffer strips varies with slope, topography, vegetation density, vegetation type, soil characteristics, subsurface drainage, upslope land use, and overland flow (see Nieswand et al. 1990, Osborne and Kovacic 1993), universal guidelines for buffer width are inappropriate. In addition, buffer zones of any width are not a remedy for poor land-management practices, and special restrictions might have to be placed on some lands upslope of the buffer zone (Nieswand et al. 1990). Slopes $>15\%$ and impervious surfaces such as roads should not be considered part of a buffer zone, and width of buffer zones should increase with time of travel of overland flow and steepness of slope (Nieswand et al. 1990). The effectiveness of vegetative buffer strips will be maximized if they are placed along smaller headwater streams, the lengths of which dominate drainage networks (Osborne and Wiley 1988).

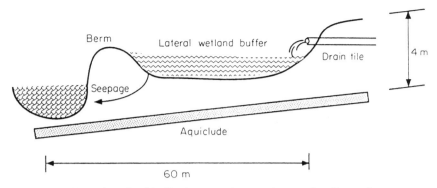

FIGURE 8.1. Lateral wetland buffer for removing nutrients and sediment from water carried by drain tiles or runoff ditches (after Kovacic et al. 1990).

Little information is available on the effectiveness of buffer strips in the Intermountain West, but studies from across North America have shown reduced nitrogen and phosphorous inputs with grass strips as narrow as 5 m and forest strips as narrow as 30 m (see Osborne and Kovacic 1993). Recommended minimum buffer widths to protect water quality in the eastern United States are 91 m for terminal reservoirs with water supply intakes and 15 m for perennial streams (Nieswand et al. 1990). Widths of up to 223 m are recommended to preserve wildlife habitat (Brown et al. 1990). Local conditions must always be considered when determining appropriate width of vegetative buffer strips (see also Chapters 5 and 11).

Vegetative buffer strips are much less effective in areas that have drain tiles, where subsurface flow directly enters water bodies. This can be remedied by having tiles (or runoff ditches) enter small artificial wetlands separated from natural wetlands or water bodies (Figure 8.1). These small artificial wetlands are separated from the natural water body by a vegetative buffer strip that can filter sediment and nutrients (Osborne and Kovacic 1993). Similarly, sediment ponds can be excavated and seeded in the terminus of small gullies in cultivated fields. These impound runoff, which loses much of its silt load because of reduced velocity and the surrounding vegetative buffer strip.

Salt loading of streams from irrigation water can be reduced by closing open drains, reducing the amount of irrigation water used on croplands, and lining canals and laterals with concrete or running them through pipes (Mustard and Rector 1979). However, these control methods also can reduce artificial wetland habitats by eliminating seepage of irrigation water (Mustard and Rector 1979; also see Chapters 5 and 6).

Integrated pest management, IPM (Huffaker 1980), on crop fields adjacent to wetlands can reduce the amount of pesticides entering wet-lands, as well as reduce pesticide costs to farmers. IPM reduces insect populations using crop rotation, biological controls, physical barriers, and precise application of chemical pesticides in conjunction with close monitoring of insect populations. If chemical pesticides are used, appli-cators should (1) use the smallest necessary amount of the least toxic and persistent pesticides; (2) avoid using chemicals during the nesting season; (3) avoid treatments near riparian zones; (4) avoid using pesti-cides in irrigation systems because of drift potential and lack of control over application rate; and (5) avoid chemical use in nontilled areas, which serve as buffer strips and wildlife habitat (Payne 1998, Payne and Bryant 1998).

Mining

Mining provides products such as coal, sand, gravel, crushed stone, quartzite, limestone, granite, gypsum, bentonite, phosphate, oil shale, uranium, and precious and semiprecious minerals including gold, silver, iron, tin, copper, nickel, lead, and cadmium. All mining disturbs habitat directly with alteration of landscape and vegetation (Moore and Mills 1977, Matter and Mannan 1988, Hart 1992). Such alterations can change the water table and groundwater flow (Parizek 1985). Surface-water di-versions and aquifer dewatering can reduce water inflows. In addition, during and following mining operations, runoff and leachate from aban-doned tunnels and shafts and front tailings dissolve trace metals, thus contaminating nearby surface and even downstream water, especially from mining coal and metals. During coal mining, iron pyrite and other metal-bearing minerals are exposed to percolating water, leading to release of acidic leachates (acid mine drainage), producing acid water conditions that can kill invertebrates in wetlands. Mine leachates espe-cially have variable and high concentrations of dissolved iron, sulfate, calcium, magnesium, aluminum, copper, manganese, zinc, cadmium, lead, and arsenic, which can lead to toxic concentrations in fish and wildlife (Parizek 1985). And, of course, turbidity from siltation reduces photosynthesis and dissolved oxygen content.

Impacts of mining on palustrine habitats

Mining can impact wetlands on site or off site by extending to wetlands downstream or upstream by changing water levels due to channeliza-tion or blockage (Cardamone et al. 1984; also see Table 8.1). Impacts can be acute from removing vegetation or chronic from alteration of sea-sonal flows of surface water and groundwater and from chemical factors

Table 8.1. On-site and off-site impacts of mining on wetlands (Cardamone et al. 1984)

Impacted Resource	Impact On-site	Off-site
Water		
Quality degradation	X	X
Aquifer disruption	X	X
Flood control disruption and storage loss	X	X
Alteration of seasonal flow	X	X
Land		
Erosion	X	X
Alteration of land use	X	X
Soil redistribution	X	
Alteration of soil productivity	X	
Alteration of soil stability	X	
Vegetation		
Vegetation removal	X	
Alteration of species composition	X	X
Reduction of diversity	X	X
Wildlife		
Habitat destruction	X	X
Wildlife displacement	X	X
Creation of wildlife barriers	X	
Other		
Alteration of recreational use	X	X
Alteration of esthetic value	X	X
Alteration of scientific/educational/ historical/archeological value	X	X

such as mine drainage. Impacts may take place during any stage of mining, including exploration, dewatering and diversion, topsoil removal, blasting, overburden removal, spoil placement, hauling, soil storage, maintenance, reclamation, and post-operation (Cardamone et al. 1984). Detrimental impacts of mining on wetlands can be chemical and physical (Table 8.2).

Wetlands vary in ability to adapt and recover from disturbance (Payne 1998). Wetland characteristics are measurable (Evans and Krebs 1977, Beule 1979, U.S. Fish and Wildlife Service 1981, Verry 1985, Adamus

Table 8.2. Chemical and physical impacts of mining on wetlands
(Cardamone et al. 1984)

Impact

Chemical
Addition of large amounts of chemicals
Addition of large amounts of chemically reduced materials, especially
    sulfides
Addition of metallic oxides and hydroxides
Addition of large quantities of sulfuric acid
Drastic lowering of pH
Reduction and elimination of carbonates
Placing of heavy metals into solution
Reduction of free oxygen
Contamination of groundwaters that feed wetland areas

Physical
Drainage of wetlands
Filling of wetlands with spoil and tailings
Alteration of stream courses by channelization, diversion, and impoundment
Widening of stream beds
Covering of wetland bottoms with spoil and tailings
Increased silt loads
Increased turbidity
Decreased light penetration
Reduced habitat diversity
Removal of natural cover
Removal and burial of topsoil
Exposure of vast bare rock surfaces
Creation of long highwalls that might seep
Creation of open pits, quarries, and spoil depressions that might fill up
    with seepage
Creation of large areas of spoil piles that seep, erode, and are unstable
Acceleration of surface runoff
Increased erosion
Watercourse modification from spoil and tailing impoundments
Lowering of groundwater
Inadequate buffer zones or refugia

et al. 1987, Bartoldus 1992, McKinstry and Anderson 1994). Sensitivity of vegetation, or ability to resist structural and functional perturbances, is called inertia and can be used to indicate wetland health (Cardamone et al. 1984). Inertia is determined by redundancy in landforms and functional factors, existence of vegetation accustomed to variable conditions, chemical characteristics of water, mixing or flushing capacity, amount of previous disturbance, and management potential of the region. Elasticity (i.e., adaptability of a wetland) is determined by habitat condition or toxin levels at disturbed areas, existence of seed banks to repropagate the disturbed wetland, dispersal ability of seed types, and management capability to control damaged sites (Cardamone et al. 1984). Resilience, or recovery capacity of a wetland, is not well understood, but a wetland system can recover from disturbance a limited number of times before being critically damaged. Extent of reclamation is influenced by natural means of reducing toxins in topsoil through leaching and dilution to allow volunteer seeding. Impact of mining is influenced by methods, timing, and quality control of mining, as well as site conditions, wetland sensitivity, and extent of reclamation (Cardamone et al. 1984).

Mitigation

To alter wetlands, a permit is needed from the U.S. Army Corps of Engineers (Corps) under Section 404 (b)(1) of the Clean Water Act, following guidelines established by the U.S. Environmental Protection Agency (Bean 1983, Salvesen 1990, Cylinder et al. 1995, Studt and Sokolove 1996; also see Chapter 1). The U.S. National Environmental Policy Act (NEPA) of 1970 established the Council on Environmental Quality, which promulgates rules that govern compliance with NEPA. Among those is the definition for mitigation: ". . . (1) avoiding the impact altogether by not taking a certain action; (2) minimizing impacts by limiting the degree of the action; (3) rectifying the impact by repairing, rehabilitating, or restoring the affected environment; (4) reducing or eliminating the impact over time by preservation and maintenance operations; and (5) compensating for the impact by replacing or providing substitute resources . . ." (Marsh et al. 1996).

The Corps generally will grant a permit to alter wetlands if the applicant first takes all practicable steps to avoid adverse impacts to the wetlands, then minimizes unavoidable damage to the wetlands, and then compensates for permanent destruction of wetlands. With compensation, the Corps and EPA prefer that the applicant create the same kind of wetland on the same site as the one being altered, preferably connected to the same water source, and as close to the altered wetland as possible. (See Chapter 1 of this volume for more detail on CWA requirements.)

TYPES OF MITIGATION

Five basic types of compensatory mitigation are available as options for wetlands damaged or destroyed by draining or filling activities: (1) restoration, (2) creation, (3) enhancement, (4) exchange, and (5) preservation (Kruczynski 1990). But preservation of existing wetlands through acquisition is not good compensatory mitigation unless the acquired wetlands have substantially higher quality, because a net loss of wetland area and functions has occurred, and the new area already is regulated through the Section 404 program. Any preservation agreement should be in perpetuity via title transfer to a responsible conservation organization. Preservation is a last mitigation option. Enhancement means increasing or improving at least one of the functions of an existing wetland. Unlike restoration sites, enhancement sites already provide some wetland functions. Extreme enhancement is called *exchange* because it merely exchanges wetland types, such as placing fill material in open water of a deepwater marsh to replace a submerged habitat type with an emergent one. Exchange can improve ecological diversity, but it is generally considered inferior to preservation as a mitigation option.

Restoration of degraded wetlands should be the first option, because it reestablishes what had evolved as a natural part of the landscape and because it often is easiest to do. Sometimes restoration merely involves plugging a drainage ditch or breaking drainage tile (Payne 1998). Other times it might mean using heavy equipment to grade an area to or just below the water table and reestablishing wetland soils and vegetation. Creation and enhancement are intermediate mitigation options. Creation is preferred to enhancement because creation adds to the total wetland area of a site, assuming created wetlands function as natural wetlands being lost.

TIMING AND LOCATION

The best timing for mitigation projects is "up front" (i.e., before the impact occurs), for then success can be ascertained in advance and adjustments made (Kruczynski 1990). Mitigation up front should be required for all projects with substantial risks due to size and complexity. Otherwise, mitigation should proceed concurrently with project construction. It should be discouraged after project completion, when little incentive remains to complete the mitigation phase timely and satisfactorily. On-site and off-site mitigation should occur in the same ecosystem, best defined as the same watershed. If no adequate mitigation sites exist in the same watershed, the construction permit should be denied (Kruczynski 1990).

RATIOS

For each 90% reduction in area, a habitat will lose, on average, 30–50% of its species (Diamond 1975). Species richness is greater in large habitat patches than small patches in terrestrial (Whitcomb et al. 1981) and aquatic systems (Brown and Dinsmore 1986, Gibbs et al. 1991), although density of breeding ducks is higher on small wetlands than large (Cowardin et al. 1995). General ratios exist for the amount of area to be mitigated relative to the amount of area damaged or destroyed, especially for on-site, in-kind (type for type) mitigation (Kruczynski 1990, King and Adler 1992).

Success in restoring most damaged or destroyed herbaceous wetlands is good because a wetland existed at the site and herbaceous vegetation grows fast (Kruczynski 1990). But because success is uncertain and the restored wetland needs time to become fully functional, a 1.5 : 1 ratio is recommended, that is, an area is restored that is 1.5 times larger than the area lost. If natural colonization of desirable plants is unlikely, planting is necessary. If successful restoration occurs up front (in this case, before initiating a filling or draining activity) or if the restored wetland will be an improvement ecologically, the ratio can be 1 : 1. Creating wetlands from uplands is risky. Thus a ratio of 1.5 : 1 or 2 : 1 is recommended. If success is demonstrated up front, the ratio can be 1 : 1. Enhancing wetlands also is risky because although some functions will be improved, other existing functions could be degraded. Thus, a 3 : 1 ratio should be required unless enhancement is performed up front, when a 2 : 1 ratio will suffice.

Exchanging wetland types is undesirable, because one wetland type is merely replaced with another. Still, an exchange could be an improvement if it is an abundant wetland for a rare one. Areal size is determined case by case.

Acquiring wetlands for preservation through donations, conservation easements, restrictive covenants, etc., generally should not be considered as mitigation because of the net loss in overall area and function.

COMMUNITY TYPE

In-kind mitigation, that is, replacement with the same community type, is best (Kruczynski 1990). Out-of-kind mitigation is used only when an improvement is clear, such as when a mining company is granted a 404 permit to mine ore under a wetland dominated by a monotypic stand of cattail, and mitigation calls for out-of-kind replacement to create a more diverse herbaceous community at the same site. Maintaining wetland complexes is also important in providing wildlife habitat and ensuring wetland function (Fairbairn and Dinsmore 2001).

MITIGATION BANKING

Wetland mitigation banking is a form of off-site compensatory mitigation (Kruczynski 1990, Cylinder et al. 1995, Marsh et al. 1996). It has evolved as an alternative to traditional approaches of compensating for "unavoidable" wetland losses under Section 10 of the Rivers and Harbors Act and Section 404 of the Clean Water Act (Short 1988, Kelly 1992). McElfish and Nicholas (1996) described 6 functions of a mitigation banking program: (1) existence of a client (use of credits), (2) permitting the project to proceed, (3) credit production, (4) long-term property ownership, (5) credit evaluation, and (6) bank management. As of mid-1992, the Environmental Law Institute (1993) identified 46 existing mitigation banks in 17 states; almost 75% of all banks provided mitigation solely for public works projects. Brumbaugh and Reppert (1992) listed existing and planned wetland mitigation banks.

Mitigation banking is generally used to aggregate small impacts on wetlands. Variations occur, but generally, someone such as a government agency or an investor buys and restores a degraded wetland, which becomes the bank. Values of this wetland are quantified and used as "credits" that can be withdrawn at a price paid in compensation by a developer who unavoidably damages wetlands elsewhere. The bank should occur in the same watershed and consist of wetland types similar to wetlands where impacts eventually will occur. Much legal, scientific, and administrative complexity is involved, with potential for misuse. Hammer et al. (1994) listed positive and negative effects that mitigation banking has on wildlife, wetlands, and society. Positive effects include: (1) opportunities for restoring degraded wetlands, (2) potential for a net gain in wetlands, (3) improving involvement and cash flow for owners of lands that have little market value, and (4) facilitating conflict resolution. Negative effects include: (1) loss of terrestrial habitats to wetlands conversion, (2) altering the natural distribution of wetlands, (3) altering types and functions of wetlands, and (4) increasing regulatory requirements. Hammer (1994) also listed considerations for a wetland mitigation banking policy, such as including national guidelines in a national wetland policy, state or regional decision making, ecological equivalency as a specific goal of compensatory mitigation, and a monitoring and evaluation plan and funding.

VALUES, EVALUATION, MONITORING

Wetlands are tremendously valuable to society and the environment for a variety of reasons, including hydrology, water quality, food-chain support and nutrient cycling, habitat, and socioeconomic considerations

(Sather and Smith 1984). Foster (1986) recognized intrinsic wetland values and 4 categories of socioeconomic wetland values: (1) economic, (2) scientific and educational, (3) experiential (ethical, spiritual, physical, aesthetic, recreational, inspirational), and (4) ecological (groundwater recharge or discharge, flood control, erosion control, water purification, primary production, secondary production, threatened and endangered species, wildlife refuge).

Wetlands must be evaluated before and monitored during and after mitigation. Acceptable procedures include the Habitat Evaluation Procedure, HEP (U.S. Fish and Wildlife Service 1981) and the Wetland Evaluation Technique, WET (Adamus et al. 1987). Bartoldus (1992) described the Wetland Replacement Evaluation Procedure (WREP) as a better alternative to HEP; other wetland evaluation techniques were listed by Verry (1985) and Dobie (1986). Photographic documentation also is helpful, with permanent photographic stations located to provide a visual record of the mitigation site before, during, and after construction and during monitoring (Cylinder et al. 1995). The system must be given time, about 15 to 20 years for freshwater marshes (Mitsch and Wilson 1996), and monitoring can be one of the conditions of a 404 permit (Hart 1992). Moore and Mills (1977) provided details for mitigation and monitoring its success from impacts of western surface mining.

Conclusion

Management of palustrine habitats must consider large-scale influences. Palustrine wetlands are affected by a wide range of inputs from uplands, and management of surrounding uplands will dramatically affect palustrine wetlands. The hydrology and quality of palustrine wetlands can be directly affected by off-site conditions and uses (e.g., irrigation, drainage projects, water diversion, mine drainage), some of which may be hundreds of kilometers away. The effects of altered habitat can also be far-reaching on wildlife that uses palustrine wetlands for part of the year but migrates to other areas for breeding or wintering. Finally, temporal scale must be included in management decisions. Annual variation in precipitation is particularly important in the arid Intermountain West, and management prescriptions should be appropriate for the worst conditions that might be encountered, not the best. Similarly, timber harvest, mining, and grazing pressures will vary depending on social and economic pressures, and again, management prescriptions should consider all possible conditions.

Management must also consider local variation. No management prescriptions are universal, as they will vary with soil types, precipitation, land use, cattle stocking rates, slope, and economic conditions. In all cases, BMPs should be adapted for local and regional conditions. Human impacts and the quality of palustrine habitats should be monitored and management prescriptions changed as necessary. In some cases, the BMP will be to reduce or eliminate human uses that adversely affect wetlands.

Literature Cited

Adamus, P. R., E. J. Clairain Jr., R. D. Smith, and R. E. Young. 1987. Methodology. Volume 2 of Wetland evaluation technique (WET). U.S. Army Corps of Engineers, Waterways Experiment Station, Vicksburg, Mississippi, USA.

Ames, C. R. 1977. Wildlife conflicts in riparian management: grazing. Pages 49–51 in R. R. Johnson and D. A. Jones, technical coordinators. Importance, preservation, and management of riparian habitat: a symposium. U.S. Forest Service General Technical Report RM-43.

Archer, S., and F. A. Smeins. 1991. Ecosystem-level processes. Pages 109–139 in R. K. Keitschmidt and J. W. Stuth, editors. Grazing management: an ecological perspective. Timber Press, Portland, Oregon, USA.

Armour, C., D. Duff, and W. Elmore. 1994. The effects of livestock grazing on western riparian and stream ecosystem. Fisheries 19(9):9–12.

Aronson, J. G., and S. L. Ellis. 1979. Monitoring, maintenance, rehabilitation and enhancement of critical whooping crane habitat, Platte River, Nebraska. Pages 168–180 in G. A. Swanson, technical coordinator. The mitigation symposium: a national workshop on mitigating losses of fish and wildlife habitats. U.S. Forest Service General Technical Report RM-65.

Ball, I. J., R. D. Bauer, K. Vermeer, and M. J. Rabenberg. 1989. Northwest riverine and Pacific coast. Pages 429–449 in L. M. Smith, R. L. Pederson, and R. M. Kaminski, editors. Habitat management for migrating and wintering waterfowl in North America. Texas Tech University Press, Lubbock, Texas, USA.

Bartoldus, C. C. 1992. A wetland evaluation procedure for the mitigation process. Pages 144–149 in J. A. Kusler and C. Lassonde, editors. Effective mitigation: mitigation banks and joint projects in the context of wetland management plans. Proceedings of the National Wetland Symposium, Association of State Wetland Managers, Berne, New York, USA.

Barton, D. R., W. D. Taylor, and R. M. Biette. 1985. Dimensions of riparian buffer strips to maintain trout habitat in southern Ontario streams. North American Journal of Fisheries Management 5:364–378.

Basore, N. S., L. B. Best, and J. B. Wooley. 1986. Bird nesting in Iowa no-tillage and tilled cropland. Journal of Wildlife Management 50:19–28.

Bean, M. J. 1983. The evolution of national wildlife law. Praeger, New York, New York, USA.

Beschta, R. L. 1978. Long-term patterns of sediment production following road construction and logging in the Oregon Coast Range. Water Resources Research 14:1011–1016.

Best, L. B. 1986. Conservation tillage: ecological traps for nesting birds? Wildlife Society Bulletin 11:343–347.

Beule, J. D. 1979. Control and management of cattails in southeastern Wisconsin wetlands. Wisconsin Department of Natural Resources Technical Bulletin 112.

Bonell, M. 1993. Progress in understanding of runoff generation dynamics in forests. Journal of Hydrology 150:217–275.

Bormann, F. H., G. E. Likens, T. G. Siccama, R. S. Pierce, and J. S. Eaton. 1974. The export of nutrients and recovery of stable conditions following deforestation at Hubbard Brook. Ecological Monographs 44:255–277.

Boyle, S. A., and F. B. Samson. 1985. Effects of nonconsumptive recreation on wildlife: a review. Wildlife Society Bulletin 13:110–116.

Bozek, M. A. and M. K. Young. 1994. Fish mortality resulting from delayed effects of fire in the greater Yellowstone ecosystem. Great Basin Naturalist 54:91–95.

Brown, M., and J. J. Dinsmore. 1986. Implications of marsh size and isolation for marsh bird management. Journal of Wildlife Management 50:392–397.

Brown, M. T., J. M. Schaefer, and K. H. Brandt. 1990. Buffer zones for water, wetlands, and wildlife in east central Florida. Publication 89–07. Center for Wetlands, University of Florida, Gainesville, Florida, USA.

Brumbaugh, R., and R. Reppert. 1992. Wetlands mitigation banking demonstration study—status and summary. Pages 12–17 in J. A. Kusler and C. Lassonde, editors. Effective mitigation: mitigation banks and joint projects in the context of wetland management plans. Proceedings of the National Wetland Symposium, Association of State Wetland Managers, Berne, New York, USA.

Burke, V. J., and J. W. Gibbons. 1995. Terrestrial buffer zones and wetland conservation: a case study of freshwater turtles in a Carolina bay. Conservation Biology 9:1365–1369.

Burns, J. W. 1972. Some effects of logging and associated road construction on northern California streams. Transactions of the American Fisheries Society 101:1–17.

Call, M. W., and C. Maser. 1985. Wildlife habitats in managed rangelands—the Great Basin of southeastern Oregon: sage grouse. U.S. Forest Service General Technical Report PNW-187.

Campbell, I. C., and T. J. Doeg. 1989. Impact of timber harvesting production on streams: a review. Australian Journal of Marine and Freshwater Research 40: 519–539.

Cardamone, M. A., J. R. Taylor, and W. J. Mitsch. 1984. Wetlands and coal surface mining: a management handbook. Research Report 154. Water Resources Research Institute, Lexington, Kentucky, USA.

Clary, W. P., and B. F. Webster. 1989. Managing grazing of riparian areas in the intermountain region. U.S. Forest Service General Technical Report INT-263.

Clayton, J. L. 1990. Soil disturbance resulting from skidding logs on granitic soils in central Idaho. U.S. Forest Service Research Paper INT-436.

Cowan, W. F. 1982. Waterfowl production on zero tillage farms. Wildlife Society Bulletin 10:305–308.

Cowardin, L. M., T. L. Shaffer, and P. M. Arnold. 1995. Evaluation of duck habitat and estimation of duck population sizes with a remote-sensing based system. U.S. Department of the Interior National Biological Service Biological Science Report 2.

Crawford, J. A., and E. G. Bolen. 1976. Effects of land use on lesser prairie chicken populations in west Texas. Journal of Wildlife Management 40:96–104.

Cylinder, P. D., K. M. Bogdan, E. M. Davis, and A. I. Herson. 1995. Wetlands regulation: a complete guide to federal and California programs. Solano Press, Point Arena, California, USA.

Davis, J. W. 1986. Options for managing livestock in riparian habitats. Transactions of the North American Wildlife and Natural Resources Conference 51:290–297.

Diamond, J. M. 1975. The island dilemma: lessons of modern biogeographic studies for the design of nature preserves. Biological Conservation 7:129–145.

Dieter, C. D., L. D. Flake, and W. G. Duffy. 1995. Effects of phorate on ducklings in northern prairie wetlands. Journal of Wildlife Management 59:498–505.

Dobie, B. 1986. Private financing for wetland restoration. Pages 14–28 in J. L. Piehl, editor. Wetland restoration: a techniques workshop. Minnesota Chapter of the Wildlife Society, Fergus Falls, Minnesota, USA.

Elmore, W., and R. L. Beschta. 1987. Riparian areas: perceptions in management. Rangelands 9:260–265.

Environmental Law Institute. 1993. Wetland mitigation banking. Environmental Law Institute, Washington, D.C., USA.

Evans, K. E., and R. R. Krebs. 1977. Avian use of livestock watering ponds in western South Dakota. U.S. Forest Service General Technical Report RM-35.

Fairbairn, S. E., and J. J. Dinsmore. 2001. Local and landscape-level influences on wetland bird communities of the prairie pothole region of Iowa, USA. Wetlands 21: 41–47.

Fleischner, T. L. 1994. Ecological costs of livestock grazing in western North America. Conservation Biology 8:629–644.

Forman, R. T. T. 1995. Land mosaics: the ecology of landscapes and regions. Cambridge University Press, Cambridge, England.

Foster, S. A. 1986. Wetland values. Pages 177–214 in J. T. Windell, B. E. Willard, D. J. Cooper, S. Q. Foster, C. F. Kund-Hansen, L. P. Rink, and G. N. Kiladis, editors. An ecological characterization of Rocky Mountain montane and subalpine wetlands. U.S. Fish and Wildlife Service Biological Report 86(11).

Franklin, J. F. and R. T. T. Forman. 1987. Creating landscape patterns by logging: ecological consequences and principles. Landscape Ecology 1:5–18.

Freeze, R. A. and J. A. Cherry. 1979. Groundwater. Prentice-Hall, Englewood Cliffs, New Jersey, USA.

Gelwick, F. P., and W. J. Matthews. 1990. Temporal and spatial patterns in littoral-zone fish assemblages in a reservoir. Environmental Biology of Fishes 27:107–120.

Gibbons, D. R. and E. O. Salo. 1973. An annotated bibliography of the effects of logging on fish of the western United States and Canada. U.S. Forest Service General Technical Report PNW-10.

Gibbs, J. P., J. R. Longcore, D. G. McAuley, and J. K. Ringelman. 1991. Use of wetland habitats by selected nongame water birds in Maine. U.S. Fish and Wildlife Service Fish and Wildlife Research Paper 9.

Glinski, R. L. 1977. Regeneration and distribution of sycamores and cottonwood trees along Sonoita Creek, Santa Cruz County, Arizona. Pages 166–174 in R. R. Johnson and D. A. Jones, technical coordinators. Importance, preservation, and management of riparian habitat: a symposium. U.S. Forest Service General Technical Report RM-43.

Goodman, T., G. B. Donart, H. E. Kiesling, J. L. Holchek, J. P. Neel, D. Manzanares, and K. E. Severson. 1989. Cattle behavior with emphasis on time and activity allocations between upland and riparian habitats. Pages 95–102 in R. E. Gresswell, B. A. Barton, and J. L. Kershner, editors. Practical approaches to riparian resource management: an educational workshop. U.S. Bureau of Land Management, Publication BLM-MT-PT-89-001-4351.

Grue, C. E., L. R. DeWeese, P. Mineau, G. A. Swanson, J. R. Foster, P. M. Arnold, J. N.

Huckins, P. J. Sheehan, W. K. Marshall, and A. P. Ludden. 1986. Potential impacts of agricultural chemicals on waterfowl and other wildlife inhabiting prairie wetlands: an evaluation of research needs and approaches. Transactions of the North American Wildlife and Natural Resources Conference 51:357–383.

Hall, D. J., G. W. Brown, and R. L. Lantz. 1987. The Alsea watershed study: a retrospective. Pages 399–416 in E. O. Salo and T. W. Cundy, editors. Streamside management: forestry and fishery interactions. Contribution Number 57. Institute of Forest Resources, University of Washington, Seattle, Washington, USA.

Hammer, D. A. 1994. Mitigation banking and wetland categorization: the need for a national policy on wetlands. Wildlife Society Technical Review 94–1.

Harr, R. D. 1977. Water flux in soil and subsoil on a steep forested slope. Journal of Hydrology 33:37–58.

———, W. C. Harper, J. T. Krygier, and F. S. Hseih. 1975. Changes in storm hydrographs after road building and clear-cutting in the Oregon Coast Range. Water Resources Research 11:436–444.

Hart, M. 1992. Aggregate mining and wetlands: an overview. Great Lakes Wetlands 3(3):1–4, 8.

Hartman, G. F., and L. B. Holtby. 1982. Fish population responses to logging in Carnation Creek, British Columbia. Pages 348–372 in G. F. Hartman, editor. Proceedings of the Carnation Creek workshop: a ten-year review. February 24–26, 1982, Malaspina College, Nanaimo, British Columbia, Canada.

Haupt, H. F., and W. J. Kidd Jr. 1965. Good logging practices reduce sedimentation in central Idaho. Journal of Forestry 63:644–670.

Heede, B. H. and R. M. King. 1990. State-of-the-art timber harvest in an Arizona mixed conifer forest has minimal effect on overland flow and erosion. Hydrological Sciences 35:623–635.

Hetherington, E. D. 1987. The importance of forests in the hydrological regime. Pages 179–211 in M. C. Healey and R. R. Wallace, editors. Canadian Aquatic Resources. Canadian Bulletin of Fisheries and Aquatic Sciences 215.

Hibbert, A. R. 1967. Forest treatment effects on water yield. Pages 527–543 in W. E. Sopper and H. W. Hull, editors. Forest Hydrology. Pergamon Press, Terrytown, New York, USA.

Higgins, K. F. 1977. Duck nesting in intensively farmed areas of North Dakota. Journal of Wildlife Management 41:232–242.

Hobbs, R. J., and L. F. Huenneke. 1992. Disturbance, diversity, and invasion: implications for conservation. Conservation Biology 6:324–337.

Holchek, J. L., R. D. Pieper, and C. H. Herbel. 1989. Range management principles and practices. Prentice-Hall, Englewood Cliffs, New Jersey, USA.

Holopainen, A. L., P. Huttunen, and M. Ahtianen. 1991. Effects of forestry practices on water quality and primary productivity in small forest brooks. Verhandlungen der Internationalen Vereinigung fur Limnologie 24:1760–1766.

Hornbeck, J. W., C. W. Martin, R. S. Pierce, F. H. Bormann, G. E. Likens, and J. S. Eaton. 1986. Clearcutting northern hardwoods: effects on hydrologic and nutrient ion budgets. Forest Science 32:667–686.

Huffaker, C. B., editor. 1980. New technology of pest control. John Wiley and Sons, New York, New York, USA.

Hunter, M. L. Jr., J. W. Witham, and H. Dow. 1984. Effects of a carbaryl-induced depression in invertebrate abundance on the growth and behavior of American black duck and mallard ducklings. Canadian Journal of Zoology 62:452–456.

Hynes, H. B. N. 1970. The ecology of running waters. University of Toronto Press, Toronto, Canada.

Jensen, H. P., D. Rollins, and R. L. Gillen. 1990. Effects of cattle stock density on trampling loss of simulated ground nests. Wildlife Society Bulletin 18:71–74.

Johnson, M. G., and R. L. Beschta. 1980. Logging, infiltration capacity, and surface erodibility in western Oregon. Journal of Forestry 78:334–337.

Kantrud, H. A. 1986. Effects of vegetation manipulation on breeding waterfowl in prairie wetlands—a literature review. U.S. Fish and Wildlife Service Technical Report 3.

Kauffman, J. B., and W. C. Krueger. 1984. Livestock impacts on riparian ecosystems and streamside management implications: a review. Journal of Range Management 37:430–437.

Kelly, L. 1992. A review of mitigation banking. Pages 24–29 in J. A. Kusler and C. Lassonde, editors. Effective mitigation: mitigation banks and joint projects in the context of wetland management plans. Proceedings of the National Wetland Symposium, Association of State Wetland Managers, Berne, New York, USA.

Kie, J. G., V. C. Bleich, A. L. Medina, J. D. Yoakum, and J. W. Thomas. 1994. Managing rangelands for wildlife. Pages 633–688 in T. A. Bookhout, editor. Research and management techniques for wildlife and habitats. Wildlife Society, Bethesda, Maryland, USA.

Kinch, G. 1989. Riparian area management: grazing management in riparian areas. U.S. Bureau of Land Management Technical Reference 1737–4.

King, D. M., and K. J. Adler. 1992. Scientifically defensible compensation ratios for wetland mitigation. Pages 64–73 in J. A. Kusler and C. Lassonde, editors. Effective mitigation: mitigation banks and joint projects in the context of wetland management plans. Proceedings of the National Wetland Symposium, Association of State Wetland Managers, Berne, New York, USA.

Klebenow, D. A. 1982. Livestock grazing interactions with sage grouse. Pages 113–123 in J. M. Peek and P. D. Dalke, editors. Symposium on wildlife-livestock relationships. Forest, Wildlife, and Range Experimental Station, University of Idaho, Moscow, Idaho, USA.

Kruczynski, W. L. 1990. Options to be considered in preparation and evaluation of mitigation plans. Pages 555–570 in J. A. Kusler and M. E. Kentula, editors. Wetland creation and restoration: the status of the science. Island Press, Washington, D.C., USA.

Langdale, G. W., H. F. Perkins, A. P. Barnett, J. C. Reardon, and R. L. Wilson Jr. 1983. Soil and nutrient losses with in-row, chisel-planted soybeans. Journal of Soil and Water Conservation 38:297–301.

Larson, W. E., F. J. Pierce, and R. H. Dowdy. 1983. The threat of soil erosion to long-term crop production. Science 219:458–465.

Leckenby, D. A., D. P. Sheehy, C. H. Nellis, R. J. Scherzinger, I. D. Luman, W. Elmore, J. C. Lemos, L. Doughty, and C. E. Trainer. 1982. Wildlife habitats in managed rangelands—the Great Basin of southeastern Oregon: mule deer. U.S. Forest Service General Technical Report PNW-139.

Lemly, A. D., S. E. Finger, and M. K. Nelson. 1993. Sources and impacts of irrigation drainwater contaminants in arid wetlands. Environmental Toxicology and Chemistry 12:2265–2279.

Liddle, M. J. 1975. A selective review of the ecological effects of human trampling on natural ecosystems. Biological Conservation 17:17–36.

Likens, F. H. Bormann, R. S. Pierce, J. S. Eaton and N. M. Johnson. 1977. Biogeochemistry of a forested ecosystem. Springer-Verlag, New York, New York, USA.

Littlefield, C. D., and D. G. Paullin. 1990. Effects of land management on nesting success of sandhill cranes in Oregon. Wildlife Society Bulletin 18:63–65.

Lusby, G. C. 1970. Hydrologic and biotic effects of grazing vs. non-grazing near Grand Junction, Colorado. Journal of Range Management 23:256–260.

Marsh, L. L., D. R. Porter, and D. A. Salvesen. 1996. Mitigation banking: theory and practice. Island Press, Covelo, California, USA.

Matter, W. J., and R. W. Mannan. 1988. Sand and gravel pits as fish and wildlife habitat in the southwest. U.S. Fish and Wildlife Service Resource Publication 171.

Mayer, F. L. Jr., and M. R. Ellersieck. 1986. Manual of acute toxicity: interpretation and data base for 410 chemical and 66 species of freshwater animals. U.S. Fish and Wildlife Service Resource Publication 160.

McAdoo, J. K., G. N. Back, M. R. Barrington, and D. A. Klebenow. 1986. Wildlife use of lowland meadows in the Great Basin. Transactions of the North American Wildlife and Natural Resources Conference 51:310–319.

McCashion, J. D., and R. M. Rice. 1983. Erosion on logging roads in northwestern California: how much is avoidable? Journal of Forestry 81:23–26.

McElfish, J. M. Jr., and S. Nicholas. 1996. Structure and experience of wetland mitigation banks. Pages 15–36 in L. L. Marsh, D. R. Porter, and D. A. Salvesen, editors. Mitigation banking: theory and practice. Island Press, Covelo, California, USA.

McKinstry, M. C., and S. H. Anderson. 1994. Evaluation of wetland creation and waterfowl use in conjunction with abandoned mine lands in northeast Wyoming. Wetlands 14:284–292.

Meehan, W. R., and W. S. Platts. 1978. Livestock grazing and the aquatic environment. Journal of Soil and Water Conservation 33:274–278.

Menasco, K. A. 1986. Stocktanks: an underutilized resource. Transactions of the North American Wildlife and Natural Resources Conference 51:304–309.

Michalson, E. L., and R. I. Papendick. 1991. STEEP: A regional model for environmental research and education. Journal of Soil and Water Conservation 46:245–250.

Miller, E. L. 1984. Sediment yield and storm flow response to clear-cut harvest and site preparation in the Ouachita mountains. Water Resources Research 20:471–475.

Mitcham, S. A., and G. Wobeser. 1988a. Effects of sodium and magnesium sulfate in drinking water on mallard ducklings. Journal of Wildlife Diseases 24:30–44.

———, and———. 1988b. Toxic effects of natural saline waters on mallard ducklings. Journal of Wildlife Diseases 24:45–50.

Mitsch, W. J., and J. G. Gosselink. 1993. Wetlands. Second edition. Van Nostrand Reinhold, New York, New York, USA.

———, and R. F. Wilson. 1996. Improving the success of wetland creation and restoration with know-how, time, and self-design. Ecological Applications 6:77–83.

Moore, R., and T. Mills. 1977. Impacts, mitigation, and monitoring. Part 2 of An environmental guide to western surface mining. U.S. Fish and Wildlife Service FWS/OBS-78/04.

Murphy, M. L., and J. D. Hall. 1981. Varied effects of clear-cut logging on predators and their habitat in small streams of the Cascade Mountains, Oregon. Canadian Journal of Fisheries and Aquatic Sciences 38:137–145.

Mustard, E. W., and C. D. Rector. 1979. Wetlands, irrigation, and salinity control: lower Gunnison Basin, Colorado. Pages 310–317 in G. A. Swanson, technical coordinator. The mitigation symposium: a national workshop on mitigating losses of fish and wildlife habitats. U.S. Forest Service, General Technical Report RM-65.

Newcombe, C. P. and D. D. MacDonald. 1991. Effects of suspended sediments on aquatic ecosystems. North American Journal of Fisheries Management 11:72–82.

Nicholson, J. A., N. W. Foster, and I. K. Morrison. 1982. Forest harvesting effects on water quality and nutrient status in the boreal forest. Proceedings of the Canadian Hydrology Symposium 82:71–89.

Nieswand, G. H., R. M. Hordon, T. B. Shelton, B. B. Chavooshian, and S. Blarr. 1990. Buffer strips to protect water supply reservoirs: a model and recommendations. Water Resources Bulletin 26:959–966.

Norris, L. A., H. W. Lorz, and S. V. Gregory. 1991. Forest chemicals. Pages 207–296 in W. R. Meehan, editor. Influences of forest and rangeland management on salmonid fishes and their habitats. American Fisheries Society Special Publication 19. American Fisheries Society, Bethesda, Maryland, USA.

Ohlendorf, H. M. 1989. Bioaccumulation and effects of selenium in wildlife. Pages 133–177 in L. W. Jacobs, editor. Selenium in agriculture and the environment. Special Publication Number 23. Soil Science Society of America, Madison, Wisconsin, USA.

Ontario Ministry of Natural Resources. 1988. Timber management guidelines for the protection of moose habitat. Ontario Ministry of Natural Resources, Toronto, Canada.

———. 1990. Environmental guidelines for access roads and water crossings. Ontario Ministry of Natural Resources, Toronto, Canada.

Osborne, L. L., and M. J. Wiley. 1988. Empirical relationships between land use/cover and stream water quality in an agricultural watershed. Journal of Environmental Management 26:9–27.

———, and D. A. Kovacic. 1993. Riparian vegetated buffer strips in water-quality restoration and stream management. Freshwater Biology 29:243–258.

Packer, P. E. 1953. Effects of trampling disturbance on watershed condition, runoff, and erosion. Journal of Forestry 51:28–31.

Parizek, R. R. 1985. Exploitation of hydrogeologic systems for abatement of acidic drainages and wetland protection. Pages 19–53 in R. P. Brooks, D. E. Samuel, and J. B. Hill, editors. Wetlands and water management on mined lands. Proceedings of the Conference School of Forest Resources, College of Agriculture, Pennsylvania State University, University Park, Pennsylvania, USA.

Paton, P. W. C. 1994. The effect of edge on avian nest predation: how strong is the evidence? Conservation Biology 8:17–26.

Patric, J. H., and K. G. Reinhart. 1971. Hydrologic effects of deforesting two mountain watersheds in West Virginia. Water Resources Research 7:1182–1188.

Payne, N. F. 1998. Wildlife habitat management of wetlands, Second printing. Krieger, Melbourne, Florida, USA.

———, and F. C. Bryant. 1998. Techniques for wildlife habitat management of forestlands, rangelands, and farmlands. Second printing. Krieger, Melbourne, Florida, USA.

Reid, L. M., and T. Dunne. 1984. Sediment production from forest road surfaces. Water Resources Research 20:1753–1761.

Ritchie, J. C., and R. F. Follett. 1983. Conservation tillage: where to from here? Journal of Soil and Water Conservation 38:267–269.

Rodgers, J. A. Jr., and H. T. Smith. 1997. Buffer zone distances to protect foraging and loafing waterbirds from human disturbance in Florida. Wildlife Society Bulletin 25:139–145.

Rodgers, R. D. 1983. Reducing wildlife losses to tillage in fallow wheat fields. Wildlife Society Bulletin 11:31–38.

Rothacher, J. 1970. Increases in water yield following clear-cut logging in the Pacific Northwest. Water Resources Research 6:653–658.

Rothwell, R. L. 1978. Watershed management guidelines for logging and road construction in Alberta. Northern Forest Research Centre Information Report NOR-X-208.

Salvesen, D. 1990. Wetlands: mitigating and regulating development impacts. Urban Land Institute, Washington, D.C., USA.

Sather, J. H., and R. D. Smith. 1984. An overview of major wetland functions and values. U.S. Fish and Wildlife Service FWS/OBS-84/18.

Schramm, H. L., and W. A. Hubert. 1996. Ecosystem management: implications for fisheries management. Fisheries 21:6–11.

Scrivener, J. C. 1982. Logging impacts on the concentration patterns of dissolved ions in Carnation Creek, British Columbia. Pages 64–80 in G. F. Hartman, editor. Proceedings of the Carnation Creek workshop: a ten-year review. Pacific Biological Station, Nanaimo, British Columbia, Canada.

Sharp, A. L., J. J. Bond, J. W. Neuberger, A. R. Kuhlman, and J. K. Lewis. 1964. Runoff as affected by intensity of grazing on rangeland. Journal of Soil and Water Conservation 19:103–106.

Short, C. 1988. Mitigation banking. U.S. Fish and Wildlife Service Biological Report 88(41).

Smith, G. J. 1987. Pesticide use and toxicity in relation to wildlife: organophosphorous and carbamate compounds. U.S. Fish and Wildlife Service Resource Publication 170.

Solberg, K. L., and K. F. Higgins. 1993. Effects of glyphosate herbicide on cattails, invertebrates, and waterfowl in South Dakota wetlands. Wildlife Society Bulletin 21:299–307.

Studt, J., and R. D. Sokolove. 1996. Federal wetland mitigation policies. Pages 37–53 in L. L. Marsh, D. R. Porter, and D. A. Salvesen, editors. Mitigation banking: theory and practice. Island Press, Covelo, California, USA.

Swank, W. T., and D. A. Crossley, editors. 1988. Forest hydrology and ecology at Coweeta. Springer-Verlag, New York, New York, USA.

Swanston, D. N., and F. J. Swanson. 1976. Timber harvesting, mass erosion, and steepland forest geomorphology in the Pacific northwest. Pages 199–221 in D. R. Coates, editor. Geomorphology and Engineering. Dowden, Hutchinson, and Ross, Stroudsburg, Pennsylvania, USA.

Temple, S. A. 1987. Predation on turtle nests increases near ecological edges. Copeia 1987:250–252.

Thomas, J. W., C. Maser, and J. E. Rodiek. 1979. Wildlife habitats in managed rangelands—the Great Basin of southeastern Oregon: riparian zones. U.S. Forest Service, General Technical Report PNW-80.

Tome, M. W., C. E. Grue, and L. R. De Weese. 1991. Ethyl parathion in wetlands following aerial application to sunflowers in North Dakota. Wildlife Society Bulletin 19:450–457.

Trimble, G. R., and R. S. Sartz. 1957. How far from a stream should a logging road be located? Journal of Forestry 55:339–341.

U.S. Environmental Protection Agency. 1983. Results of the nationwide urban runoff program. Volume 1, final report. National Technical Information Service Accession Number PB84–185552. U.S. Environmental Protection Agency, Washington, D.C., USA.

U.S. Fish and Wildlife Service. 1981. Habitat evaluation procedures. U.S. Fish and Wildlife Service Ecological Service Manual 102–ESM1.

Vallentine, J. F. 1990. Grazing management. Academic Press, New York, New York, USA.

Verry, E. S. 1985. Selection of water impoundment sites in the lake states. Pages 31–38 in M. D. Knighton, compiler. Water impoundments for wildlife: a habitat management workshop. U.S. Forest Service General Technical Report NC-100.

Webster, J. R., E. F. Benfield, S. W. Golladay, R. F. Kazmierczak Jr., W. B. Perry, and G. T. Peters. 1988. Effects of watershed disturbance on stream seston characteristics. Pages 279–294 in W. T. Swank and D. A. Crossley, editors. Forest hydrology and ecology at Coweeta. Springer-Verlag, New York, New York, USA.

Whitcomb, R. F., C. S. Robbins, J. F. Lynch, B. L. Whitcomb, M. K. Klimkiewicz, and D. Bystrak. 1981. Effects of forest fragmentation on avifauna of the eastern deciduous forest. Pages 123–205 in R. L. Burgess and D. M. Sharpe, editors. Forest island dynamics in man-dominated landscapes. Springer-Verlag, New York, New York, USA.

Zahm, G. R. 1986. Kesterson Reservoir and Kesterson National Wildlife Refuge: History, current problems, and management alternatives. Transactions of the North American Wildlife and Natural Resources Conference 51:324–329.

CHAPTER 9

Components, Processes, and Design of Created Palustrine Wetlands

RICHARD A. OLSON

Introduction

Many types of created palustrine wetlands exist throughout the Intermountain West. Some examples include state and federal refuge wetlands; irrigation-created wetlands; livestock ponds; nutrient and sediment control (including wastewater treatment) wetlands; floodwater-retarding basins; ponds created from surface coal, bentonite, phosphate, and gravel extraction; potholes created with explosives or mechanical excavation; and ditches. Although each type of created wetland is designed for a specific purpose, all are widely recognized for wetland-wildlife habitat value (Bue et al. 1964, Rumble 1989, Payne 1992, Adamus 1993, Hoag and Sellers 1994). Impoundments have numerous wetland values, but they are not as numerous in the Intermountain West as the western portions of the Great Plains. Montana and Colorado have 25,000 to 50,000 impoundments, and Idaho, Nevada, Utah, and Wyoming each has fewer than 25,000 impoundments (Modde 1980). Comparatively, the western portions of North Dakota and Nebraska have 50,000 to 100,000 impoundments, whereas South Dakota has 100,000 to 150,000 impoundments (Modde 1980). In regions where natural wetlands are scarce, impoundments may constitute more than 67% of the wetlands (Ruwaldt et al. 1979).

Wetlands developed on state and federal wildlife management areas commonly are created by diverting water from adjacent rivers and streams or by excavating basins where water tables are close to the ground surface. The purpose of these created wetlands is to provide wetland wildlife habitat, and in most cases they are managed for specific wetland plant communities.

Wetlands created from irrigated cropland arise from groundwater and surface runoff accumulations. These wetlands generally lack permanent water, may be small in area, usually are located near ditches and canals, and are dominated by a few emergent (herbaceous) plant species (Adamus

1993). As a by-product of agricultural production, however, irrigated wetlands support a variety of wetland wildlife (see Chapter 6).

Wetlands created for livestock watering are classified as retention reservoirs, dugouts or pit reservoirs, or diked dugouts or pit retention reservoirs (Lokemoen 1973, Eng et al. 1979). Retention reservoirs have short dams across intermittent streams or large gullies to intercept spring runoff or rainwater from upland slopes. Dugouts or pit reservoirs have steep sides and fill from groundwater or surface runoff (Bue et al. 1964). Diked dugouts or pit retention reservoirs are built like regular dugouts, but spoil material is placed on the downstream side as a dam to flood the shallow area around the dugout (Payne 1992). Both retention reservoirs and dugouts are constructed for livestock watering, although wildlife habitat benefits accrue (Bue et al. 1964).

Nutrient and sediment control (including wastewater treatment) wetlands are biological and physiochemical treatment systems that utilize wetland vegetation and microbes to reduce and assimilate excess nutrients and agricultural chemicals in surface runoff from dry and irrigated croplands, pastures, feedlots, or animal-waste facilities (DuPoldt et al. 1993). A properly designed system removes nitrogen, phosphorus, and sediment from wastewater. These systems also improve water quality by reducing total suspended solids, total dissolved solids, turbidity, some heavy metals, bacteria, and several trace elements (Dortch 1992). They function like natural wetlands to remove nutrients, sediment, and contaminants from surface water or groundwater, but they also improve wildlife habitat quality (Hoag and Sellers 1994).

Floodwater-retarding basins are reservoirs 10–20 ha in size that can include drain valves to manipulate water levels. Although primarily designed for flood control, they also provide waterfowl habitat (Payne 1992).

The mining of coal, bentonite, phosphate, and gravel often results in open pits that fill with runoff and groundwater. Wetlands created after surface coal mining are distinguished as sediment basins, shallow wet depressions and emergent marshes, moss-dominated springs and seeps, final-cut deep wetland basins, intermittent streams, slurry ponds, or other coal-refuse disposal areas (Brooks 1990). Sediment basins and final-cut deep wetland basins offer the greatest potential for multiple-use management opportunities. Sediment basins are designed for erosion and sedimentation control (Brooks and Gardner 1995), whereas final-cut deep wetland basins fill with water to form deep ponds surrounded by steep, high banks. Both provide wetland wildlife habitat value (Riley 1954, Rumble 1989). All of these wetlands can be modified during or after the mining process to enhance wetland wildlife value (Payne 1992, McKinstry and Anderson 2002).

Potholes are shallow depressions, usually less than 1.5 ha, created by explosives or mechanical excavation. Potholes are developed to provide breeding territories, brood-rearing areas, and feeding habitat for ducks (Payne 1992).

Level ditches are ungraded trenches dug at right angles to existing natural water channels where the water table is 40 cm or less below the ground surface. They are constructed to improve water distribution in adjacent wetlands with dense stands of emergent vegetation, increase wetland plant production, provide open-water habitat for waterfowl courtship and brood rearing, and enhance production of other wetland wildlife (Payne 1992).

A variety of ecological functions, consumptive and nonconsumptive resource uses, and economic benefits occur with these created wetlands, including mitigation for natural wetland losses, enhanced landscape diversity, wildlife and fisheries habitat, water for agricultural operations, recreational activities, sediment retention, treatment of mined-land drainage, and filtration of pollutants (Samuel et al. 1978, Leedy 1981, Leedy and Franklin 1981, Olson 1981). Additional values include community open spaces and water supplies for homes, fire protection, and industrial uses (Glazier et al. 1981).

Although created palustrine wetlands in the Intermountain West serve various purposes, all possess common ecosystem components of water, hydric soils, and distinct wetland plant species. Presence of these components does not guarantee a functioning ecosystem, especially in the early years following creation. However, as created wetlands mature, these components become ecologically interrelated, gradually evolving into a functioning wetland.

Creating successfully functioning wetlands requires careful planning, design, and construction that optimizes water availability and quality, hydric-soil formation, and establishment of wetland vegetation. Once the wetlands are created, resource managers must fully understand the ecological interaction of biological, chemical, and physical factors prior to developing management plans to maintain or enhance ecosystem function. A carefully designed, constructed, and managed created wetland should provide maximum wetland-wildlife values.

Ecosystem Components and Processes

Ecosystem functioning in created wetlands is governed by the complex interaction of hydrologic processes and water quality, properties of the submerged substrate, and influences of wetland vegetation. Development of specific wetland plant communities reflects the abiotic and biotic conditions of the ecosystem, which are a product of ecosystem component interactions. Subsequent plant community development and hydrologic processes influence wetland wildlife habitat value. These primary components are continually interacting and evolving over time into a fully functioning ecosystem that provides a host of consumptive and nonconsumptive values (McKinstry et al. 2001).

Water properties

Of the ecosystem components, water quantity and quality are the critical components driving development and perpetuation of ecosystem function in created wetlands. Knowledge of wetland hydrology is basic for understanding all wetland functions (Hollands 1990).

HYDROLOGY

Variations in water depth, period and frequency of occurrence, and duration of inundation among different created wetlands result in site-specific hydrologic regimes. These hydrologic regimes determine abiotic factors such as water and nutrient availability, aerobic or anaerobic soil conditions, soil particle size and composition, water chemistry features, and water velocity (Mitsch and Gosselink 1993). Hydrologic regimes are influenced by wetland vegetation through interception of precipitation and evapotranspiration rates. Wetland plants, in turn, influence water depth, velocity, and circulation patterns within a system (Hammer 1997).

Hydrologic regimes also influence biological productivity by controlling nutrient cycling and availability, import and export of nutrients, and fixed energy supplies in the form of organic particulates and decomposition rates. Nutrients in submersed substrate are unavailable to plants under reducing conditions, but periodic drying results in oxidizing processes of these substances that can trigger explosive growth of wetland vegetation (Hammer 1997). Surface runoff and groundwater flowing into wetland basins carry varied quantities of minerals, macro- and micronutrients, and organic matter that enhance productivity. Likewise, surface outflows and groundwater seepage export organic material, minerals, and nutrients, reducing wetland productivity potential (Hammer 1997).

Water quality in created wetlands is strongly influenced by hydrologic regimes and therefore partially determines the composition of wetland vegetation, especially submersed aquatic plant species. Hydrologic regimes partially control the concentration of dissolved solids, which can restrict submerged plant growth by limiting light penetration or creating toxic conditions. Evaporation from the water surface, evapotranspiration from marginal wetland vegetation, runoff, and groundwater seepage inflow all increase the concentration of dissolved solids, while direct precipitation, groundwater seepage outflow, and overflow reduce dissolved solid concentrations (Eisenlohr 1969, Rozkowska and Rozkowski 1969). Eisenlohr (1969) found wetlands with low dissolved solids concentrations at higher elevations due to the flushing effect from seepage outflow, whereas wetlands at lower elevations generally have higher concentrations of dissolved solids from seepage inflow.

The hydrologic regime of a created wetland affects water quantity and quality, substrate (soil) properties, and vegetation production. Hydrologic regimes are established by the balance between water inflows and outflows, or the water budget.

WATER BUDGETS

A wetland water budget is the balance between water gains from inflow and water losses from outflow. Hollands (1990) described a simplified water budget as

$$PPt + SWi + GWi + IF + RO \text{ (Inputs)} = Et + SWo + GWo + S \text{ (Outputs)}$$

where

PPt = precipitation as rainfall or snowfall directly on the wetland surface;
SWi = streamflow in;
SWo = streamflow out;
GWi = groundwater discharge into the wetland;
GWo = groundwater recharge out of the wetland;
IF = interflow or horizontal shallow groundwater flow above the water table;
RO = surface water runoff;
Et = evaporation and evapotranspiration; and
S = water storage within the wetland as surface water or soil water.

However, the components of water budgets vary widely among wetlands due to site-specific conditions, and the water budget is modified as vegetation and organic soils develop in created wetlands (Hollands 1990).

The amount of water entering a wetland in spring is determined by snow accumulation on the watershed, intensity of snowmelt, rainfall, level of soil moisture at freeze-up, and depth of frost penetration the preceding fall (Millar 1969a, Daborn 1976). Surface runoff is usually the greatest source of water inflow. However, during a precipitation event the structure and coverage of vegetation surrounding a wetland affects the amount of water intercepted and thus the amount of surface runoff (Hammer 1997).

Water outflow occurs primarily by evapotranspiration from marginal vegetation, seepage outflow from the pond bottom, evaporation from the water surface, and overflow around pond margins (Olson 1981). Evapotranspiration increases with increased leaf surface-area exposure, solar radiation, air and surface temperatures, and wind speed (Hammer 1997).

Extensive emergent vegetation complicates the water budget by reducing evaporative water loss by sheltering the water surface from wind and radiation and increasing water loss through transpiration (Eisenlohr 1965, 1969). Eisenlohr (1965) found that plant transpiration rates at the beginning and end of a growing season were less than evaporative loss from the water surface. However, total evapotranspiration loss for the entire growing season on a vegetated wetland may be greater than the evaporation rate if no vegetation were present.

In dry years when evapotranspiration is higher, water loss from a wetland filled with vegetation may deplete moisture required by wet-meadow plant communities located on the outer fringes of a wetland. To decrease water loss from evapotranspiration, vegetation can be thinned by blasting or mechanical means. On sparsely vegetated wetlands, contouring basin slopes and water level manipulation may enhance wetland plant development along basin margins, thereby reducing water loss by evaporation. Likewise, removal of peripheral vegetation through cultivation or grazing may reduce spring runoff by reducing the amount of trapped snow (Millar 1969b).

Working in small wetlands, Millar (1971) found that the rate of water loss per unit area varied directly with the length of shoreline and inversely with wetland area. Water loss occurred principally by lateral seepage to transpiring marginal vegetation, evaporation from shoreline soil surfaces, and seepage to groundwater. Millar (1971) stated that during the growing season 60–80% of the water loss is attributed to transpiration by phreatophytic vegetation and evaporation from the soil surface. Shoreline-related water loss accounted for =60% of total water loss in wetlands =0.04 ha in area and 30–35% in wetlands >1 ha.

Adamus (1993), working on created wetlands in the Colorado Plateau (Colorado, eastern Utah, and western Wyoming), described the hydrologic roles of wetlands as either a sink (removing water from local surface-flow systems) or a source (conserving water and providing moisture in local areas). Sink wetlands occur where surface water runoff is retained or converted to water vapor through evaporation or evapotranspiration by wetland vegetation. Source wetlands act as conduits for discharging groundwater and occur where water inputs are increased or conserved from intercepting precipitation, detaining drifted snow, or reducing open-water evaporation (Adamus 1993).

Evidence of created wetlands serving as sinks or sources within a watershed is limited. Studying the effects of stock ponds within an Arizona watershed, Milne and Young (1989) reported no measurable effect on streamflow from stock ponds in a river basin at a density of 0.2 ponds/km^2. Other western restoration studies suggest that some headwater riparian wetlands conserve water (Winegar 1977, Stabler 1985, Van Haveren 1986, Debano and Schmidt 1990, Ponce and Lindquist 1990). These wetlands conserve water by reducing evaporation losses from wind and maintain cooler water temperatures by vegetative shading, and they contribute water by reducing downstream velocity, thereby increasing infiltration rates of runoff (Adamus 1993).

NATURAL WATER LEVEL FLUCTUATIONS

Seasonal water levels fluctuate to some degree in all wetlands through inflow and outflow pathways. These fluctuations enhance wetland plant establishment. Moderate fluctuations periodically expose mudflats, resulting in aerobic decomposition of substrate organic material. The subsequent availability of nutrients following aerobic decomposition of organic matter and optimum moisture conditions stimulate wetland vegetation establishment and production. Natural seasonal water level fluctuations are needed to remobilize nutrients chemically bound to the substrate and stimulate germination of wetland plant seeds (Welling et al. 1988). Seasonal water level fluctuations in natural wetlands and their effects on wetland vegetation, substrate properties, and associated wetland wildlife are well documented. However, little is known about seasonal water level fluctuations in created wetlands.

In coal strip-mine ponds, water levels fluctuate less markedly because underground springs buffer the loss of water from evaporation and evapotranspiration. This stability in water level fluctuations reduces exposed shoreline areas, limiting wetland plant establishment and development. However, water level fluctuations in stock ponds produce more exposed mudflat areas, resulting in a mosaic community of wetland plants in these gradually sloped basins (Olson 1981).

Adamus (1993) reported that overbank flooding in created wetlands of the Colorado Plateau can increase plant and animal production by diluting high salinity and accumulated toxicants, resuspending excessive accumulations of sediment, scouring and rejuvenating dense stands of emergent vegetation, and facilitating recolonization by crayfish, other noninsect invertebrates, and waterborne seeds of wetland plants. Stock ponds in New Mexico created by damming washes (therefore receiving outside water) support more waterfowl than isolated, pit-type stock ponds (Tolle 1977). A hydrologic regime, which includes seasonal water level fluctuations, is critical for creating a functioning ecosystem in created wetlands.

WATER QUALITY

A properly designed and constructed wetland can improve water quality by removing nitrogen, soluble and insoluble phosphorus, and sediment from surface runoff (Hoag and Sellers 1994). Created wetlands also reduce total suspended and dissolved solids, turbidity, some heavy metals, and several trace elements (Dortch 1992).

Adamus (1993) described processes that improve water quality in created wetlands of the Colorado Plateau:

(1) Water deceleration and storage. Created wetlands that lack outlets (e.g., livestock ponds) or those having flat gradients with dense perennial vegetation and low hydraulic loading (e.g., large wetland area with low amount of incoming runoff) delay downslope movement of water, permitting increased pollutant processing time.

(2) Filtration, settling, burial, and stabilization. Wetlands that physically confine suspended sediments or chemicals promote settling by physical processes (e.g., gravity) or possible burial by erosion-resistant, accumulating layers of sediment or precipitate. This process occurs where sediments are coarse-textured, the wetland is sheltered from wind turbulence (e.g., from surrounding vegetation cover), and warm, hypersaline conditions (which otherwise keep fine sediments buoyant and inhibit plant growth) do not exist.

(3) Deoxygenation. Wetlands that are highly saline, are sheltered from wind turbulence, are subject to warmer temperatures, or have fine sediments and high primary productivity generally have higher oxygen deficits. Oxygen deficiency facilitates retention of some substances that affect water quality but mobilizes others.

(4) Adsorption and physicochemical precipitation. Increased amounts of fine-particle sediments and organic detritus cause greater chemical bonding of many incoming contaminants, thus improving water quality. Created wetlands most capable of this process are those having soils with high clay content, organic carbon, iron or aluminum, and salinity levels of approximately 5 ppt, which promotes deposition through chemical flocculation (Akhurst and Breen 1988).

(5) Uptake and accumulation. Wetland organisms directly accumulate or transform chemicals and sediment through normal metabolic

Table 9.1. Water quality parameters required to support aquatic organisms (Payne 1992)

Parameter	Range of Values
pH	6.5–9.0
Alkalinity	20 mg/L
Hardness	20–150 mg/L
Dissolved oxygen	5 mg/L
Total dissolved solids	Productivity generally positively correlated with TDS
Temperature	20–30°C, depending on species and acclimation

and only emergent wetland plants were present at pH values <6.4. Generally, water pH of =7.0 are required for good wetland vegetation establishment (Crawford 1942, Coe and Schmelz 1972).

Salinity Salinity levels in substrate and water limit production of wetland plants (Kauskik 1963, McKnight and Low 1969, Christiansen and Low 1970, Cooper and Severn 1992), which reduces aquatic invertebrate abundance. High salinity directly reduces invertebrate abundance, amphibians, and some fish. As a result, most isolated, saline, created wetlands in the Colorado Plateau are not used heavily by piscivorous birds such as kingfishers, loons, grebes, herons, or egrets (Adamus 1993).

Hammer (1981) concluded that most biologically productive saline lakes have high alkalinity, moderate salinity (<30mS/cm^2), and rich soluble-phosphorus levels. Salinity >1.5 dS/m causes digestive stress in some birds, and salinity >5.0 dS/m is considered unsatisfactory for livestock (National Academy of Sciences 1974).

Studies in Utah suggest that a specific conductance <1 mS/cm^2 is excellent for waterfowl and >8 mS/cm^2 is restrictive (Christiansen and Low 1970). In the San Luis Valley of south-central Colorado, wetlands having the greatest diversity of herbaceous plants were seasonally flooded areas with low salinity and high water tables (Cooper and Severn 1992). Generally, freshwater impoundments have >1 ppt salinity (Payne 1992).

Limited data exist on salinity in western strip mining wetlands. McWhorter (1975), Hinkley and Taylor (1977), and Ringen et al. (1979) reported that sodium and magnesium sulfate salts, the by-products of oxidative reactions on spoil material, were the major water quality problems of western mining. Likewise, Rockett (1976) and Wangsness (1977), both studying coal strip-mine ponds in Wyoming, concluded that sulfate was the predominate anion. High salinity from sodium and magnesium sulfate salts can dictate specific associations of wetland plant species (Stewart and Kantrud 1972).

Organic macronutrients Nitrogen and phosphorus are primary metabolic nutrients, and their abundance often regulates biological productivity in wetlands (Wetzel 1975). Excessive loading of nitrogen and phosphorus can cause eutrophication, leading to algae blooms and dissolved oxygen deficits (Adamus 1993). Uptake and release rates of nitrogen and phosphorus depend on sediment characteristics, water chemistry, and vegetation composition (Levine and Willard 1990).

Sediments, particularly inorganic clays, influence the amount of phosphorus retained in a wetland. The amount of adsorbed phosphorus depends on clay type (e.g., illite, montmorillonite, and kaolinite), amount, and pH. Potential adsorption also is a function of water nutrient concentration and redox potential at the sediment-water interface (Levine and Willard 1990).

Uptake and release of nitrogen and phosphorus within a wetland vary seasonally. During the growing season, emergent and submerged plants utilize phosphorus from sediment and water. As plants senesce in fall, phosphorus is released into the water from decomposing tissue. Where anaerobic decomposition is slow and water phosphorus concentration is high, decomposing tissue becomes a significant phosphorus source with increased tissue accumulation over time (Kadlec 1979, Levine and Willard 1990). Likewise, emergent and submerged plants act as a nitrogen sink during the growing season. However, nitrogen release from dead plant litter is much slower, taking months or years (Levine and Willard 1990).

Mere presence or absence of water and fluctuations in water level influence organic macronutrient cycling. Klopatek (1978) reported that draining a wetland resulted in large releases of organic nitrogen and nitrate (NO_3) from the substrate due to increased aerobic decomposition rates. Reflooding resulted in a net input of nitrogen into the wetland, with soil nitrogen significantly increasing within a year.

Water level fluctuations affect plant species composition, which influences nutrient cycling. During high water, more nitrogen and phosphorus are released into the water by living plants. During drawdowns, nitrogen and phosphorus are released through decomposition (Levine and Willard 1990).

Adamus (1993) reported that created wetlands in the Colorado Plateau play a greater role in removing nitrogen than in retaining phosphorus because of their high soil organic content and associated denitrify-

pacity is important in chemical transformation processes that supply minerals and nutrients for aquatic plants (Hammer 1997).

Redox potential (Eh) is the soil or water's capacity to oxidize or reduce chemical substances. The range of Eh in wetland soils is -300 to $+300$ millivolts (mV). The interaction of Eh and pH (which ranges from $3-11$ in wetland soils) influences CEC, which in turn affects the solubility and availability of minerals and nutrients for aquatic plant uptake. Typical wetland soils have a pH of 7.0 and an Eh of -200 mV where common substances occur in reduced forms, such as nitrogen as N_2O, N_2, or NH_4^+, iron as Fe^{2+}, manganese as Mn^{2+}, carbon as CH_4, and sulfur as S^- (Hammer 1997). Little data exist on substrate characteristics of created wetlands or of comparisons between created and natural wetlands. However, several researchers reported that nitrogen, phosphorus, and organic matter increase with age of created wetlands (Reimold et al. 1978, Lindau and Hossner 1981, Craft et al. 1988).

Nitrogen, an essential element in plant growth, is generally found as the ammonium ion in flooded soil (converted by anaerobic bacteria) because conversion to nitrite and nitrate by aerobic bacteria is minimal. However, when water levels periodically fluctuate, regular microbial nitrification processes proceed under aerobic conditions and increase availability of nitrogen for plant utilization (Emerson 1961, Kadlec 1962).

Periodic water level drawdowns are desirable to promote a greater rate of organic matter decomposition under aerobic conditions in substrates, with a subsequent release of available nutrients required for plant growth. Complex anaerobic and aerobic processes of substrates, associated with periodic flooding and receding water levels, influence nutrient cycling and subsequent germination, establishment, and production of wetland vegetation.

More research on substrate properties, chemical transformations of organic and inorganic materials, and nutrient cycling is needed to better understand vegetation production in created wetlands. Until that information is available, resource managers must use data from studies of natural wetlands in designing and constructing wetlands.

Wetland vegetation

Wetland vegetation is the cornerstone for ecological functions, consumptive and nonconsumptive resource values, and the economic benefits of wetlands. Wetland plants assemble organic materials from nonliving substances, providing the foundation for all other wetland life forms (Hammer 1997). Numerous studies have documented the importance of wetland vegetation composition and production to waterfowl and other wetland wildlife. Wetland plant species provide wildlife habitat in the form of nesting sites, food sources, and shelter from weather and predators. The highest diversity of wetland bird species occurs in created wetlands with diverse plant community types and 50–75% open water (Adamus 1993). In the lower Gunnison Valley of Colorado, Rector et al. (1979) reported similar bird densities in forested, shrub, and emergent plant-dominated wetlands, but the greatest diversity in emergent plant-dominated wetlands occurred with open water.

Germination, establishment, and production of wetland vegetation in created wetlands are strongly affected by hydrologic regimes, water quality, substrate properties, and propagation factors. Fluctuating water levels, alkalinity and acidity levels, salinity, substrate properties, dissolved solids, and suspended sediments all influence wetland plant productivity in created wetlands. However, wetland vegetation also modifies hydrologic regimes, water quality, and substrate properties over time. Wetland vegetation influences hydrologic regimes by intercepting precipitation and runoff, trapping snow, and regulating water loss through evapotranspiration processes and evaporative losses from open-water surfaces. Water depth is modified by trapping sediment from runoff and contributing to the accumulation of organic matter by shedding dead plant tissue. As wetland plant communities mature and spread, the associated plant biomass modifies hydrologic regimes by influencing inflow and outflow pathways, improves water quality by filtering out pollutants from runoff, enhances soil fertility by depositing more organic matter, and reduces shoreline slopes by increasing sediment deposition from slowed surface runoff (Olson 1981, Mitsch and Gosselink 1993).

Early plant invaders of newly created wetlands are cattails and pondweeds, especially where moderate water acidity occurs, such as in strip-mine ponds. In these cases, as acidity decreases, the diversity of colonizing plant species increases, eventually modifying conditions for further colonization and establishment by other species.

A major factor governing the development of wetland vegetation in created wetlands is basin slope. Interacting with fluctuating water levels, basin slope influences wetland plant development by regulating water depth and permanence within zones of wetland vegetation. Since aquatic plant development is closely linked with moisture conditions, extreme basin slope limits the amount of shoreline area having favorable moisture conditions under fluctuating water levels. This results in narrower emergent communities, restricted submersed plant community zones, and lack of wet meadow communities (Olson and Barker 1979). Steep basin slope limits the amount of light penetration reaching submersed plants. Photosynthesis is severely restricted with increasing water depths, limiting community development to narrow bands near

maximizing the potential development of primary ecosystem components: hydrology and water quality, substrate properties, and wetland vegetation development.

Areas that once supported a wetland that was lost to sedimentation, deliberate filling, or long-term degradation of water quality should be the first priority for site selection. These sites have the capability to support a functioning wetland and already contain seed banks, substrate nutrients, and potential hydrology. Second-choice locations are sites adjacent to existing permanent water sources such as lakes, rivers, and water channels where establishing hydrologic regimes is convenient. Finally, third-choice locations are upland areas situated over a water table close to the ground surface (Levine and Willard 1990).

Another consideration for selecting created wetland locations is wetland density within the larger regional area. To optimize waterfowl breeding habitat, many researchers emphasize locating wetlands within "complexes" of ephemeral, semipermanent, and permanent wetland types (Kantrud and Stewart 1977, Dwyer et al. 1979, Ruwaldt et al. 1979, Brown and Dinsmore 1986, Fredrickson and Reid 1987, McKinstry and Anderson 2002). This arrangement allows maximum dispersal of territorial breeding pairs and provides high-protein food sources (invertebrates) for breeding hens and broods in ephemeral wetlands but still offers permanent, open-water wetlands for brood security when ephemeral wetlands are dry.

Once a project location is selected, potential water hydrology, expected water quality characteristics, and substrate properties must be evaluated. The most important hydrologic factors to determine include the extent and periodicity of water level fluctuations; other considerations include water depth potential, expected wave action, and degree of sheltering from wind and waves. Among the important water quality factors to consider are potential turbidity, alkalinity/acidity, pH, nutrient levels, heavy metal concentration, and organic contaminant sources. Substrate characteristics to consider are texture, nutrient levels, contamination potential by heavy metals or organic toxicants, and presence of a viable seed bank (Levine and Willard 1990, Hammer 1992).

Basin morphometry

Basin size (area) is generally governed by limitations of the construction site and specific project objectives. If waterfowl production is the primary objective, then basins should be ≥ 0.5 ha to attract waterfowl (Hudson 1983, McKinstry and Anderson 2002). However, Williams (1985) reported that bird species richness increases with wetland areas up to 4 ha, with subsequent stability of species richness in larger wetlands. However, habitat diversity at both the plant community and landscape scales, including presence of small wetlands, is also necessary to attract waterfowl and other wetland wildlife (Gibbs 1993). Basins should include a variety of bottom and side topography to attract a diversity of wetland plants and wildlife.

Water depths should be varied throughout the basin to attract a wide diversity of flora and fauna. Deep wetlands are more likely to be mesotrophic or oligotrophic, while shallow wetlands tend to be more eutrophic with greater amounts of wetland vegetation and higher primary productivity (Brooks 1990). Again, specific project objectives will dictate final water depths. Dikes or dams should be constructed with slopes of 3:1 or 5:1, and rip-rap should be placed on the top and pondward toe of the dike to resist wave erosion (Farmes 1985, Payne 1992).

Shorelines should consist primarily of gently sloping gradients ($<5°$) if the primary objective is to maximize wetland vegetation production and waterfowl use. However, some shoreline with slopes up to 90° may also be desirable to provide benefits to other wildlife and fish species (Brooks 1990). The shoreline should be contoured so shallow shelves comprise 25–30% of the basin area, and deep, open-water areas comprise 70–75%. This construction design will result in ratios of emergent vegetation to open water of about 1:3 or 1:4, which have been shown to attract high waterfowl numbers (Levine and Willard 1990).

Kaminski and Prince (1981) documented maximum bird diversity in wetlands with a 50:50 ratio of open water to emergent vegetation. The Wyoming Game and Fish Department (1976) recommends a maximum of 30% emergent cover on strip-mine ponds reclaimed for waterfowl habitat. To discourage emergent growth, water depth must exceed 1 m. Consequently, not more than 30% of a wetland basin should be shallower than 1 m.

Another design feature to include is convoluted shorelines to produce irregular basin shape. A high shoreline development index (length of shoreline divided by the circumference of a circle of equal area) provides more edge habitat for wildlife, reduces wind and wave impacts to emergent and submerged vegetation (Brooks 1984), and provides more visual isolation for waterfowl, thus reducing territorial conflicts. Irregular basin shape also disperses water flows, which helps to maximize retention time and thus benefits flood control objectives and water quality treatment time (Brooks 1990).

Earthen islands should be developed during construction phases to enhance waterfowl nesting and wetland use. Draglines, dozers, scrapers, or dredgers can be used to mound basin material during construction.

full vegetation establishment and little control over initial plant species composition.

Artificial establishment is expensive and time-consuming, but species composition can be controlled. Considerations in selecting the species and propagule type for artificially revegetating a created wetland include plant species that are best suited for the environmental conditions, availability of planting stock (seeds, rhizomes, tubers, whole plants), the size of the planting area, and the planting method, density, and timing for planting (Levine and Willard 1990, Marburger 1992, Reinartz and Warne 1993).

Postconstruction monitoring

Monitoring the progress of a created wetland after completion is essential for determining project success and identifying any need for midcourse corrections. The monitoring plan should describe what factors will be monitored, methods for gathering the information, required intervals and overall time periods for monitoring, and how collected data will be interpreted (Levine and Willard 1990, Hammer 1992).

D'Avanzo (1990) lists 6 criteria used to evaluate success in a wetland creation project: (1) comparison of vegetation growth characteristics (e.g., biomass or density) in artificial and natural wetlands after 2 or more growing seasons; (2) habitat requirements (e.g., upland versus wetland) of plants invading the created site; (3) success of planted species; (4) comparison of animal species composition and biomass in human-made and natural sites; (5) chemical analyses of artificial wetland soils compared to natural wetlands; and (6) evidence of geologic or hydrologic changes with time. These criteria are typically used in wetland ecosystem studies. In addition, plants are emphasized as wetland indicators because they reflect the hydrologic regime and perform numerous important functions (D'Avanzo 1987). Avian species richness and diversity also provide good indicators of wetland function.

Long-term management

Long-term management following successful wetland creation is just as important as initial design and construction for maintaining ecosystem functioning. Popular long-term management practices include manipulating water levels, controlled burning, mechanical treatments to maintain ratios of emergent vegetation to open water, and controlled livestock grazing to enhance upland nesting cover (Levine and Willard 1990, Payne 1992).

Summary

Potential consumptive, nonconsumptive, and economic benefits for created wetlands include enhanced landscape diversity, wildlife and fisheries habitat, agricultural values, recreational activities, sediment retention, water-pollution control, public water supplies, and industrial uses. However, long-term management plans, developed from research-based knowledge of ecosystem processes and functioning, are required before multiple-use values of created wetlands can be realized.

Ecosystem function on created palustrine wetlands, as on natural wetland systems, is governed by a complex, interrelated matrix of environmental factors such as hydrology, water quality factors, substrate properties, basin characteristics, and wetland plant community dynamics. Our current knowledge about ecological processes in constructed impoundments of the Intermountain West is extremely limited, as evidenced by the scarce literature. Herein is the challenge for present and future wetland resource managers. Before comprehensive, long-term management plans can be formulated for these unique wetland ecosystems, we must identify voids in our knowledge about created wetland ecosystem functioning, adopt research programs to obtain this information, and develop subsequent management practices that optimize multiple-use values.

The implications of developing management plans for constructed impoundments are far-reaching, considering the number of created palustrine wetlands already requiring management attention and the potential number of future impoundments. As the demand for energy sources accelerates, public desire for consumptive and nonconsumptive resource use increases, and pressures to enhance economic gains continue, new, potentially valuable constructed impoundments will emerge. Wetland managers must be prepared to intensively manage these new habitat parcels to optimize multiple uses and restore value in previously constructed impoundments.

Literature Cited

Adamus, P. R. 1993. Irrigated wetlands of the Colorado Plateau: information synthesis and habitat evaluation method. U.S. Environmental Protection Agency, Environmental Research Laboratory, Corvallis, Oregon, USA.

Akhurst, E. G. J., and C. M. Breen. 1988. Ionic content as a factor influencing turbidity in two floodplain lakes after a flood. Hydrobiologia 160:19–31.

Anderson, D. R., and F. A. Glover. 1967. Effects of water manipulation on waterfowl production and habitat. Transactions of the North American Wildlife and Natural Resources Conference 32:292–300.

————, and T. S. Taylor. 1982. Management of seasonally flooded impoundments for wildlife. U.S. Fish and Wildlife Service Resource Publication 148.

Gersberg, R. M., B. V. Elkins, and C. R. Goldman. 1983. Nitrogen removal in artificial wetlands. Water Resources Research 17:1009–1014.

Gibbs, J. P. 1993. Importance of small wetlands for the persistence of local populations of wetland-associated animals. Wetlands 13:25–31.

Glazier, R. C., R. W. Nelson, and W. J. Logan. 1981. Planning for mine cut lakes. Pages 533–540 in D. H. Graves, editor. Proceedings of a symposium on surface mining, hydrology, sedimentology, and reclamation. University of Kentucky, Lexington, Kentucky, USA.

Guntenspergen, G. R., and F. Stearns. 1985. Ecological perspectives on wetland systems. Pages 69–97 in P. J. Godfrey, E. R. Kaynor, S. Pelczarski, and J. Benforado, editors. Ecological considerations in wetlands treatment of municipal wastewaters. Van Nostrand Reinhold, New York, USA.

Hammer, D. A. 1992. Creating freshwater wetlands. Lewis Publishers, Chelsea, Michigan, USA.

————. 1997. Creating freshwater wetlands. CRC Press, Boca Raton, Florida, USA.

Hammer, U. T. 1981. Primary production in saline lakes. Hydrobiologia 81:47–57.

Hantzsche, N. N. 1985. Wetland systems for wastewater treatment: engineering applications. Pages 7–25 in Godfrey, E. R. Kaynor, S. Pelczarski, and J. Benforado, editors. Ecological considerations in wetlands treatment of municipal wastewaters. Van Nostrand Reinhold, New York, New York, USA.

Harris, S. W., and W. H. Marshall. 1963. Ecology of water level manipulations on a northern marsh. Ecology 44:331–342.

Hawkes, C. L. 1978. Aquatic habitat of coal and bentonite clay strip mine ponds in the northern Great Plains. Pages 609–614 in M. K. Wali, editor. Ecology and coal resource development. Volume 2. Pergamon Press, New York, New York, USA.

Hinkley, T. K., and H. E. Taylor. 1977. Chemistry of sediment and water in mined and unmined watersheds, Hidden Water Creek area, Wyoming. Pages 6–13 in Geochemical survey of the western energy regions. U.S. Geological Survey, Denver, Colorado, USA.

Hoag, J. C., and M. E. Sellers. 1994. Constructed wetland system for water quality improvement of irrigation wastewater. U.S. Natural Resources Conservation Service, U.S. Bureau of Land Management, U.S. Bureau of Reclamation, U.S. Fish and Wildlife Service, U.S. Forest Service, Idaho Fish and Game Department, Idaho Transportation Department, and Idaho Power Company Riparian/Wetland Project Information Series Number 8.

Hollands, G. G. 1990. Regional analysis of the creation and restoration of kettle and pothole wetlands. Pages 281–298 in J. A. Kusler and M. E. Kentula, editors. Wetland creation and restoration: the status of the science. Island Press, Covelo, California, USA.

Hudson, M. S. 1983. Waterfowl production of three age-classes of stock ponds in Montana. Journal of Wildlife Management 47:112–117.

Johnsgard, P. A. 1956. Effects of water fluctuation and vegetation change on bird populations, particularly waterfowl. Ecology 37:689–701.

Jupp, B. P., and D. H. N. Spence. 1977. Limitations of macrophytes in a eutrophic lake, Loch Leven. II. Wave action, sediments and waterfowl grazing. Journal of Ecology 65:431–446.

Kadlec, J. A. 1962. Effects of a drawdown on a waterfowl impoundment. Ecology 43: 267–281.

———. 1979. Nitrogen and phosphorous dynamics in inland freshwater wetlands. Pages 17–41 in T. A. Bookhout, editor. Waterfowl and wetlands: an integrated review. La Crosse Printing, La Crosse, Wisconsin, USA.

———. 1985. Wetlands, wastewater, and wildlife. Pages 439–443 in P. J. Godfrey, E. R. Kaynor, S. Pelczarski, and J. Benforado, editors. Ecological considerations in wetlands treatment of municipal wastewaters. Van Nostrand Reinhold, New York, New York, USA.

———, and W. A. Wentz. 1974. Report of research. Volume 1 of State-of-the-art survey and evaluation of marsh plant establishment techniques: induced and natural. U.S. Army Corps of Engineers, Fort Belvoir, Virginia, USA.

Kaminski, R. M., and H. H. Prince. 1981. Dabbling duck and aquatic macroinvertebrate responses to manipulated wetland habitat. Journal of Wildlife Management 45:1–15.

Kantrud, H. A., and R. E. Stewart. 1977. Use of natural basin wetlands by breeding waterfowl in North Dakota. Journal of Wildlife Management 41:243–253.

Kauskik, I. K. 1963. The influence of salinity on the growth and rejuvenation of marsh plants. Dissertation, Utah State University, Logan, Utah, USA.

Klopatek, J. M. 1978. Nutrient dynamics of freshwater riverine marshes and the role of emergent macrophytes. Pages 195–216 in R. E. Good, D. F. Whighman, and R. L. Simpson, editors. Freshwater wetlands: ecological processes and management potential. Academic Press, New York, USA.

Kusler, J. A. 1988. Hydrology: an introduction for wetland managers. Pages 4–23 in J. A. Kusler and G. Brooks, editors. Proceedings of the National Wetland Symposium on Wetland Hydrology. Chicago, Illinois, USA.

Lathwell, D. J., H. F. Mulligan, and D. R. Bouldin. 1969. Chemical properties, physical properties, and plant growth in 20 artificial wildlife marshes. New York Fish and Game Journal 16:158–183.

Leedy, D. L. 1981. Coal surface mining reclamation and fish and wildlife relationships in the eastern United States. Volume 1. U.S. Fish and Wildlife Service Technical Report FWS/OBS-80/24.

———, and T. L. Franklin. 1981. Coal surface mining reclamation and fish and wildlife relationships in the eastern United States. Volume 2. U.S. Fish and Wildlife Service Technical Report FWS/OBS-80/25.

Lemme, T. H. 1988. Denitrification and tillage relationships on two eastern South Dakota soils. Dissertation, South Dakota State University, Brookings, South Dakota, USA.

Levine, D. A., and D. E. Willard. 1990. Regional analysis of fringe wetlands in the midwest: creation and restoration. Pages 299–325 in J. A. Kusler and M. E. Kentula, editors. Wetland creation and restoration: the status of the science. Island Press, Covelo, California, USA.

Lindau, C. W., and L. R. Hossner. 1981. Substrate characterization of an experimental marsh and three natural marshes. Journal of Soil Science Society of America 45: 1171–1176.

Linde, A. F. 1969. Techniques for wetland management. Wisconsin Department of Natural Resources, Report 45. Madison, Wisconsin, USA.

Linn, D. M., and J. W. Doran. 1984. Aerobic and anaerobic microbial populations in no-till and plowed soils. Soil Science Society of America Journal 48:794–799.

Rozkowska, A. D., and A. Rozkowski. 1969. Seasonal changes of slough and lake water chemistry in southern Saskatchewan. Journal of Hydrology 7:1–13.

Rumble, M. A. 1989. Surface mine impoundments as wildlife and fish habitat. U.S. Forest Service General Technical Report RM-183.

——, and L. D. Flake. 1983. Management considerations to enhance use of stock ponds by waterfowl broods. Journal of Range Management 36:691–694.

Rumburg, C. B. 1969. Yield and concentration of meadow hay fertilized with three N sources. Agronomy Journal 61:824–825.

Ruwaldt, J. J., L. D. Flake, and J. M. Gates. 1979. Waterfowl pair use of natural and manmade wetlands in South Dakota. Journal of Wildlife Management 43:375–383.

Samuel, D. E., J. R. Stauffer Jr., C. H. Hocutt, and W. T. Mason Jr., editors. 1978. Surface mining and fish/wildlife needs in the eastern United States. U.S. Fish and Wildlife Service Technical Report FWS/OBS-78/81.

Scheffer, M., A. A. Achterberg, and B. Beltman. 1984. Distribution of macroinvertebrates in a ditch in relation to the vegetation. Freshwater Biology 14:367–370.

Schmidt, F. V. 1951. Planned water level control and the resultant effect on vegetation. Mimeo. New Jersey Division of Fish and Game, Trenton, New Jersey, USA.

Sculthorpe, C. D. 1967. The biology of aquatic vascular plants. Edward Arnold Publishing, London, England.

Sloey, W. E., F. L. Spangler, and C. W. Fetter Jr. 1978. Management of freshwater wetlands for nutrient assimilation. Pages 321–340 in R. Good, D. Whigham, and R. Simpson, editors. Freshwater wetlands. Academic Press, New York, New York, USA.

Stabler, D. F. 1985. Increasing summer flow in small streams through management of riparian areas and adjacent vegetation: a synthesis. Pages 206–210 in R. R. Johnson, C. D. Ziebell, D. R. Patton, P. F. Ffolliott, R. H. Hamre, technical coordinators. Riparian ecosystems and their management: reconciling conflicting uses. U.S. Forest Service General Technical Report RM-120.

Stearns, F. 1978. Management potential: summary and recommendations. Pages 357–363 in R. Good, D. Whigham, and R. Simpson, editors. Freshwater wetlands. Academic Press, New York, New York, USA.

Stewart, R. E., and H. A. Kantrud. 1972. Vegetation of prairie potholes, North Dakota, in relation to quality of water and other environmental factors. U.S. Geological Survey Professional Paper 585–D.

Tolle, D. A. 1977. A survey of breeding and migratory birds southwest of Farmington, New Mexico. Great Basin Naturalist 37:489–500.

Uhler, F. M. 1964. Bonus from waste places. Pages 643–654 in J. P. Linduska, editor. Waterfowl tomorrow. U.S. Fish and Wildlife Service, Washington, D.C., USA.

U.S. Department of Agriculture Natural Resource Conservation Service. 1994. Constructed wetlands bibliography. Parts 1–7. National Agricultural Library, Water Quality Information Center. Washington, D.C., USA.

U.S. Environmental Protection Agency. 1993. Constructed wetlands for treating agricultural wastewater. West Lafayette, Indiana, USA.

Van Haveren, B. P. 1986. Management of instream flows through runoff detention and retention. Water Resources Bulletin 22:399–404.

Veatch, J. O. 1932. Some relationships between water plants and water soils in Michigan. Transactions of the Michigan Academy of Science 27:409–413.

Wangsness, D. J. 1977. Physical, chemical, and biological relations of four ponds in the

Hidden Water Creek strip mine area, Powder River Basin, Wyoming. U.S. Geological Survey Water Resources Investigation 77–72.

Weller, M. W. 1981. Freshwater marshes: ecology and wildlife management. Second edition. University of Minnesota Press, Minneapolis, Minnesota, USA.

Welling, C. H., R. L. Pederson, and A. G. van der Valk. 1988. Recruitment from the seed bank and the development of zonation of emergent vegetation during a drawdown in a prairie wetland. Journal of Ecology 76:483–496.

Wetzel, R. C. 1975. Limnology. W. B. Saunders, Philadelphia, Pennsylvania, USA.

Wile, I., G. Miller, and S. Black. 1985. Design and use of artificial wetlands. Pages 26–37 in P. J. Godfrey, E. R. Kaynor, S. Pelczarski, and J. Benforado, editors. Ecological considerations in wetlands treatment of municipal wastewaters. Van Nostrand Reinhold, New York, New York, USA.

Williams, G. L. 1985. Classifying wetlands according to relative wildlife value: application to water impoundments. Pages 110–119 in M. D. Knighton, compiler. Proceedings of water impoundments for wildlife: a habitat management workshop. U.S. Forest Service, St. Paul, Minnesota, USA.

Winegar, H. H. 1977. Camp Creek channel fencing: plant, wildlife, soil, and water response. Rangemen's Journal 4:10–12.

Wyoming Game and Fish Department. 1976. Considerations for wildlife in industrial development and reclamation. Wyoming Game and Fish Department, Cheyenne, Wyoming, USA.

Zutshi, D. P. 1975. Associations of macrophytic vegetation in Kashmir lakes. Vegetatio 30:61–66.

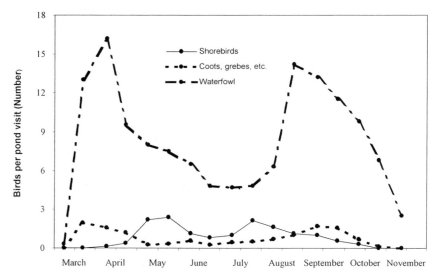

FIGURE 10.1. Greatest use of impoundments occurs by birds during migration periods. Waterfowl, coots, grebes, etc. migrate earlier than shorebirds in the spring and later in the fall (adapted from Evans and Kerbs 1977).

but sufficient habitat quality must exist for successful nesting and survival of broods (Gjersing 1975).

DABBLING DUCKS

Dabbling ducks are the most numerous ducks at created wetlands; these include mallards, pintails, blue-winged teal, green-winged teal, common gadwall, American wigeon, northern shoveler, and wood ducks (Lokemoen et al. 1984). Dabbling duck use and production can be 2 to 4 times greater per surface hectare on impoundments than on natural wetlands (Ruwaldt et al. 1979, Forman et al. 1996). Resource manipulations such as habitat modifications or new impoundments that are designed to increase carrying capacity of breeding dabbling ducks are usually successful (Nudds 1983).

In this chapter we focus on impoundments of <8 ha, but larger wetlands with shallow areas are also important to migrating ducks. Impoundments >0.04 ha are optimum for breeding pairs of dabbling ducks during spring, but the larger the impoundment, the greater the overall use (Lokemoen 1973, Leschisin et al. 1992). In addition to size, impounded wetlands with the greatest proportion of shallow water (<1 m) will attract the greatest numbers of breeding dabbling ducks (Lokemoen et al. 1984; Uresk and Severson 1988; see also Chapter 9 of this volume).

Impoundments with abundant submersed aquatic vegetation and emergent vegetation covering approximately 50% of the surface area will attract more dabbling ducks during the breeding season (Anderson et al. 1994, McKinstry and Anderson 2002). Aquatic vegetation is the most important determinant of use by dabbling ducks that are migrating (Hobaugh and Teer 1981). The density of breeding ducks is directly related to the coverage of shallow marsh vegetation and emergent vegetation to open-water interspersion (Kaminski and Prince 1981a). However, wetlands dominated by emergent vegetation are of little value to breeding ducks (Evans and Black 1956, Smith 1969). Breeding mallards and some other species select wetlands for available foods provided directly or indirectly by vegetation and open water (Ball and Nudds 1989). Pre-laying ducks need food rich in protein and nutrients necessary for egg laying (Sudgen 1973, Krapu 1979). Ultimately breeding dabbling ducks select wetlands for greater availability of aquatic invertebrates (Kaminski and Prince 1981b, Ball and Nudds 1989).

Complexes of impoundments should include some that are shallow and temporary, as they contain an abundance of invertebrates consumed by breeding ducks (Krapu 1974, Swanson et al. 1974, Krapu and Swanson 1975). McKinstry and Anderson (2002) recommended that complexes have a minimum of 5 impoundments/km^2, and Lokemoen et al. (1984) recommended 12–40 impoundments/km^2 for waterfowl.

Mudflats resulting from lowered water levels (drawdown) and bare shorelines are attractive to pairs of breeding waterfowl (McKinstry and Anderson 1995) as resting areas. Retention-type stock ponds often have drawdown areas and are ideal for breeding mallards (Evans and Kerbs 1977). While some drawdown is good, impoundments with excessive bare shorelines and little upland nesting cover attract few breeding ducks (Mundinger 1976). These impoundments can become excessively turbid, which interferes with wetland productivity (Bjugstad et al. 1983, Anderson and Hawkes 1985). Breeding dabbling ducks respond quickly to improved nesting conditions, including herbaceous and shrubby vegetative cover, on lands surrounding impoundments (McEnroe 1976, Mundinger 1976). Because nesting for some species is initiated before the growing season, residual vegetation from the previous year's growth provides necessary cover.

Many of the food and cover features identified for breeding ducks influence use of impoundments by duck broods. Impoundments that attract more breeding ducks also have greater use by broods (Gjersing 1975, Mack and Flake 1980). The extent that broods use impoundments is associated with upland vegetative nesting conditions (Gjersing 1975, Mundinger 1976) and surrounding wetland density (Rumble and Flake 1983). Hens with broods are mobile and will move broods to impound-

Table 10.1. Birds other than waterfowl that occur in palustrine habitats of impoundments of the Intermountain West. The occurrence of these species (listed by common name) will depend upon suitable habitat and nesting conditions that may be specific to each species.

Clark's grebe
Usually nest in colonies; densely spaced attached to edge of emergent vegetation; large lakes with several km^2 of open water bordered by emergent vegetation.

Western grebe
Similar to Clark's grebe, but feed closer to shore in deeper lakes than Clark's grebe.

Horned grebe
Most nesting is north of Intermountain West.

Eared grebe
Usually nest in colonies; floating nests anchored to vegetation or platform; usually on impoundments >7 ha.

Pied-billed grebe
Usually one pair per impoundment; floating nest in emergent vegetation; prefer open water 38–60 cm deep with fish or aquatic animals for food.

American white pelican
Usually nest in colonies on flat islands; use larger bodies of water than impoundments discussed in this chapter.

Double-crested cormorant
Nest in colonies of few to several thousand; nest on ground on rocky islands or cliffs; feed on fish; water 1.5–8 m deep.

American bittern
Solitary nester 10–12 cm above water in dense cattails; food includes any small animal, fish, amphibians, mollusks, or insects.

Black-crowned night heron
Nest with other herons in colonies; nests located in trees, emergent vegetation, or tall grass; food includes fish, small animals, reptiles, mollusks, or insects.

Green-backed heron
A solitary nester on muskrat houses or trees near water; food includes small animals, fish, mollusks, or insects.

Snowy egrets
Nest in colonies on ground or cattail marshes; food includes small fish, amphibians, crustaceans, or insects.

Great blue heron
Nest in colonies in trees; food includes small fish, amphibians, reptiles, crustaceans, or insects.

White-faced ibis
Nest in colonies near other herons or egrets in large patches of bulrushes or cattails > 0.3 m above water; food includes insects, crustaceans, mollusks or amphibians.

Sandhill cranes
6–400 ha territory; nest over water but also land; marshlands above 1,500 m elevation with *Scirpus, Typha,* and *Sparganium* spp. and well-watered river valleys; areas without excessive human intrusion and with adjacent cropland; Intermountain West—3 populations (Rocky Mountains, Lower Colorado River Valley, Central Valley).

Virginia rail
Freshwater marshes with dense emergent vegetation (40–70%), mudflats, and open water; nest 0–15 cm above shallow water (<70 cm) in robust emergent vegetation including *Typha* or *Scirpus* spp.; primarily feeds on invertebrates.

Sora rail
Sympatric with Virginia rails, partition food but not habitat; nest above water in robust emergent vegetation including *Typha, Scirpus,* or *Carex* spp. over 15–20 cm of water; prefer similar interspersion of emergent vegetation to water as Virginia rails; will use wetlands <1 ha; feed on surface for mollusks or insects.

Common moorhen
In Utah; 4 types of nests including sham or false nests possibly for displaying, egg nests, brood nests, and platform nests for roosting; deepwater marshes close to dense emergent vegetation that is evenly interspersed; 1–6 ha of marsh; diet mostly vegetation except during breeding/brooding.

American coot
Persistent emergent freshwater wetlands with interspersion of open water with *Typha* or *Scirpus* spp.; nest is floating platform or on muskrat house; food includes pondweeds, other plants except during breeding season.

American avocet
Colony nester on ground or mudflats with grass tufts, shallow impoundments, and marshes; feed by wading and probing mud.

California gull

Nest in colonies on islands or sandy shorelines, prefer low sparse vegetation; food includes insects, garbage, carrion, bird eggs.

Common tern

Nest in colonies on ground in sparse vegetation; avoid highly turbid water; feed in shallow water for fish, crustaceans, or insects.

Forster's tern

Nest in small colonies in mats of emergent vegetation, muskrat houses, or abandoned nests of grebes in large wetlands near open water; food includes small fish, insects, crustaceans, or frogs found over water.

Black tern

Nest in colonies or sometimes singly; sparse emergent vegetation, floating masses of emergent vegetation, muskrat houses, or abandoned nests of grebes, other terns, or American coots over water <1.0 m deep and near open water with large open-water areas; food includes aquatic and terrestrial insects, small mollusks and crustaceans, or small fish.

Belted kingfisher

Excavate nest burrows in bank up to 1.6 km from water; prefer low-turbidity water with perch sites for foraging; feed mostly on fish 7–10 cm long, crustaceans, or amphibians.

Marsh wren

Nest 1–1.6 m over shallow water in abundant emergent vegetation in tall emergent vegetation such as *Typha* or *Scripus* spp. but prefer narrow-leaf cattail to broad-leaf cattails; insects and spiders gleaned from ground and emergent vegetation.

Yellow-headed blackbird

Nest in colonies of *Typha* or fine grasses or *salix* with robust standing vegetation in standing water <1.0 m deep; food includes vegetation and animal matter gleaned from ground.

Red-winged blackbird

Nest in marsh or vegetation along marshes or fields but do not require marsh vegetation; food includes vegetation, animal matter, or small grains.

Sources: Weller and Spatcher (1965), Sanderson (1977), Rundle and Fredrickson (1981), Sayre and Rundle (1984), Johnson and Dinsmore (1986), DeGraff et al. (1991), Storer and Nuechterlein (1992), and Tacha and Braun (1994)

Mink are semiaquatic and generally require about 8 ha of palustrine habitats with permanent water that is relatively free of grazing (Boggess 1984). Thus, many small impoundments are too small to sustain viable mink populations. Mink frequently prey on birds and nests constructed in vegetation over water (Lokemoen et al. 1984). Predation by mink can reduce populations of birds nesting in limited palustrine habitat (Boggess 1984), and mink can also be major predators on ducklings (Eberhardt 1973).

Reptiles and amphibians

It is known that herpetofaunal abundance and diversity are highest in smaller natural ponds (Semlitsch and Bodie, 1998; Semlitsch 2000a), but the effects of impoundments on herpetofaunal abundance and diversity are poorly documented. Typically, studies of herpetofauna in impoundments provide a list of species. To our knowledge, no studies have specifically addressed the effects of created impoundments on herpetofauna distribution and abundance throughout the Intermountain West. Richter and Azous (1995) studied amphibians in created wetlands of western Washington. Several authors have found tiger salamanders in "cattle tanks" (presumably created impoundments) but have not explicitly studied the characteristics of these impoundments (Gehlbach 1965, Webb 1969, Webb and Roueche 1971, Collins 1981, Degenhardt et al. 1996, Hammerson 1999). In Arizona, Collins (1981) found that an introduced subspecies of tiger salamander used only created impoundments, whereas the native subspecies occurred only in natural ponds.

Reptiles and amphibians are a diverse group, and we would not expect all herpetofauna to benefit equally from impoundments. Species most likely to benefit are those that require pond water to reproduce and survive. All amphibians of the Intermountain West need water for breeding and larval development. Amphibians of the Intermountain West can generally be characterized as: (1) pond breeders, that is, amphibians with larval development periods >6 weeks requiring semipermanent or permanent wetlands for reproduction, (2) temporary pond breeders, or amphibians with larval development periods <6 weeks that usually breed in roadside ditches, bison wallows, or similar impoundments, or (3) stream breeders. The most common amphibians of the Intermountain West are pond or temporary breeders. Larger impoundments (>8 ha) are probably not as important for temporary pond breeders as small intermittent wetlands, but amphibians will use larger ponds to some extent (B. E. Smith, personal observation). Pond breeders and temporary pond breeders are likely to be potential beneficiaries of impoundments. Stream breeders are generally a minor or missing component of Intermountain West herpetofauna, and it is doubtful that they would use impoundments to a great extent.

Reptiles are not as dependent on water as amphibians, and impoundments may not be as important for their survival. However, garter snakes are known to be major predators on amphibians such as northern leopard frogs (Dole 1965, 1968) and tiger salamanders (Petranka 1998) and probably benefit from a substantial prey base in impoundments, especially of small fish and amphibians.

Vegetation complexity may influence population density or use of impoundments by the northern leopard frog, as this species is seldom found in bodies of water lacking emergent vegetation such as cattails, sedges, and rushes. Northern leopard frogs are common in livestock watering impoundments with semipermanent and permanent water if predaceous fish are absent. Many of these impoundments have gentle slopes into the water rather than steep slopes typical of unreclaimed surface mine impoundments in the Plains region (e.g., Rumble et al. 1985). The chorus frog is found in nearly any still-water habitat, from temporary ponds lasting only a few weeks to much larger ponds and even the margins of lakes. Again, predaceous fish must be absent. Chorus frogs are prolific and develop rapidly, so they tend to use more temporary habitat than many other anurans. The Plains spadefoot and Great Plains toad use temporary wetlands of various types, including roadside ditches and natural depressions. They seldom use stock ponds. Aquatic vegetation is minimal or absent in and around temporary ponds used as breeding habitat by these toads. Woodhouse's toad appears to be less dependent on emergent vegetation for suitable habitat. It more commonly breeds in old oxbows of former river beds. Toad eggs and tadpoles can be noxious to predators (Licht 1969, Brodie 1987), and most produce an "alarm substance" when injured (Altig and Christensen 1981, Hews and Blaustein 1985). The lack of use of ponds by Woodhouse's toads may reflect their lower resistance to predation as eggs, tadpoles, and adults.

Proximity of other water sources to restored wetlands influences species richness and colonization rates of amphibians and reptiles at the restored wetlands (e.g., Tilton and Denison 1992, Semlitsch 2000b). This should also be true of created impoundments. Wetlands connected to water have the highest rates of colonization by reptiles and amphibians and the highest species richness (Tilton and Denison 1992). However, colonization by reptiles can be extremely slow, with some wetlands lacking any appreciable colonization after 5 years. Little is known about colonization abilities of the herpetofauna of the Intermountain West, but dispersal could be substantially slower than elsewhere, given the harsh environment in which these species occur and the distance between natural bodies of water. Interconnectedness of aquatic resources is important for management of aquatic-breeding amphibian populations (Semlitsch 2000b).

When predaceous fish are introduced to natural ponds or created impoundments, amphibian populations will be reduced or eliminated (Emery et al. 1972, Brönmark and Edenhamn 1994, Hecnar and M'Closkey 1997). Bullfrogs, which have been introduced to many wetlands and impoundments across the Intermountain West, also eat various frogs and their eggs and tadpoles (Stebbins and Cohen 1995).

The few data we have on herpetofauna and impoundments indicate that complex vegetative structure and shallow water in pond margins are critical to maintaining the biodiversity of frogs within the landscape. Other fauna of impoundments are likely to depend on the density of frogs and other herpetofauna as prey items, so any enhancements that favor frog reproduction in impoundments will probably be beneficial for other species as well. Increasing the area containing emergent vegetation will create oviposition sites and habitat where tadpoles, metamorphs, and adult frogs can successfully evade predation. Warm water in shallow areas should increase developmental rates of the tadpoles. Increasing the number of refuges for frogs and their eggs is critical to sustaining frog populations in impoundments that are stocked with fish. However, it appears that introduced predaceous fish are frequently able to reduce or eliminate amphibian populations in created impoundments regardless of vegetation complexity. This will also affect reptile populations, such as garter snakes, that depend on these amphibians for food (Gibbons et al. 2000), and it will probably affect other fauna as well.

Fishes of Impoundments

Because impoundments are the result of human intervention on the landscape, public or private landowners might include fisheries options in future management. However, maximizing both fish and wildlife is not possible because habitat requirements differ between fish and wildlife. Impoundments managed for waterfowl are shallow with abundant plant growth, while impoundments managed for sport fisheries would have greater depth and fewer shallow areas with extensive vegetation (e.g., <25% of pond surface with vegetation, Scalet and Modde 1984). Extensive shallow areas with submersed macrophytes can interfere with predator-prey relationships among fishes and increase risk of winterkill due to low oxygen levels beneath the ice. Nonetheless, palustrine habitats in impoundments provide invertebrates that are food for prey and sport fishes. The palustrine habitat also provides needed habitat for successful reproduction and recruitment of sport fishes, such as the largemouth bass and bluegill.

Fishes useful for sport fisheries in impoundments of the Intermountain West include native and exotic species (Table 10.2). In some situations, ecologically safe fisheries can be developed in small impoundments with associated wetlands. Impoundments >0.8 ha usually can support a sport fishery. Depending on habitat characteristics, viable sport fisheries might involve a single species, such as a species of trout or largemouth bass, or multiple species such as warmwater predator-

Table 10.2. Fish species (listed by common name) and some constraints that might be included in sport-fish management for small impoundments of the Intermountain West

---

Coldwater fishes
Water temperatures <21°C; do not stock with warmwater fishes, largemouth bass; fathead minnows will compete with trout for zooplankton.

Rainbow trout
Will hybridize with cutthroat trout.

Brown trout
Tolerate water >21°C for short periods; are predacious, and presence requires that larger fingerlings be used for restocking.

Cutthroat trout
Select subspecies native to geographic location.

Brook trout
Do not release in watershed with native trout.

Splake
Brook trout/lake trout hybrid; fertile, can backcross with parental species.

Warmwater fishes
Water temperatures >21°C

Largemouth bass
May be stocked alone or with prey fishes; predator of amphibians.

Smallmouth bass
Predators of insects and amphibians; will not effectively control panfish.

Bluegill
Prolific; potential to overpopulate but good sport fish if sufficient largemouth bass are present.

Black crappie
Prolific; potential to overpopulate if sufficient predators are not present; prefer clear water.

Table 10.2 *continued*

White crappie
Prolific; potential to overpopulate if sufficient predators are not present; tolerate turbid water.

Channel catfish
Not likely to successfully recruit in created wetlands with largemouth bass.

Black bullbead
Overpopulate in turbid water or absence of predator fish.

Fathead minnow
Prey fish; vulnerable to predation from largemouth bass.

Golden shiner
Prey fish; submersed aquatic plants required to maintain populations in presence of predators.

Common carp
Do not release in created wetlands.

Northern pike
Large predator; most useful in large wetlands.

Walleye
Predator; reproduction and recruitment uncommon in small waters.

Yellow perch
Prolific; potential to overpopulate but good sport fish if sufficient predators control perch.

Sources: *Reiger (1963), Marriage et al. (1971), Anderson (1978), Novinger and Legler (1978), Stone and Modde (1982), Gabelhouse (1984), Guy and Willis (1990), Saffel et al. (1990), Willis et al. (1990), Guy and Willis (1991), Behnke (1992), Satterfield and Koupal (1995), Gurtin et al. (1996), Lott et al. (1996).*

---

prey combinations of largemouth bass and bluegill. Managing a sport fishery in a small impoundment cannot be done without considerable planning and continued monitoring. We recommend Marriage et al. (1971), Satterfield and Flickinger (1984), Willis et al. (1990), and Gabelhouse et al. (1995) for further information on sport-fish management.

While impoundments often provide excellent opportunities to enhance sport fisheries, some fish species can present problems for managing other plants and wildlife. Common carp are typically viewed by biologists as a detriment in waters managed for waterfowl production. The direct cause-and-effect relationship between common carp abundance and reduction in abundance of submerged aquatic plants has not been clearly established, and the concept does remain a point of discussion among fishery and wetland biologists. However, there is a substantial body of evidence indicating that common carp and perhaps black bullheads can reduce the abundance of aquatic plants (Ricker and Gottschalk 1940, Chamberlain 1948, Anderson 1950, Cahoon 1953, Threinen and Helm 1954, Tryon 1954, Robel 1961, King and Hunt 1967, McCrimmon 1968, Crivelli 1983, Fletcher et al. 1985, Kolterman 1990). Some of these studies were observational in nature and simply reported the increase in aquatic plant abundance after removal of common carp from a water body. Others were experimental and involved the effects of common carp on vegetation in enclosures. Together, these studies provide a compelling body of evidence that where densities of common carp are high, aquatic plant communities and palustrine habitats are reduced.

Fishes can compete for invertebrates with waterfowl, especially with broods (Swanson and Nelson 1970; Bouffard and Hanson 1997). Fathead minnows can reduce abundance and biomass of insects and crustaceans in wetlands, which reduces the suitability of these habitats as foraging areas for waterfowl (Hanson and Riggs 1995, Zimmer et al. 2000).

Fish predation can also affect other organisms living in palustrine habitats of impoundments. For example, some fishes prey extensively upon amphibians (Bouffard and Hanson 1997), and some fishes, such as northern pike, are predators of duckling broods. However, there is little direct evidence of substantial mortality to ducklings from northern pike. Stomachs of only 3 of 1,218 northern pike longer than 35 cm contained ducklings during a 90-day waterfowl brood-rearing season (Lagler 1956). Evidence is lacking to show that waterfowl avoid lakes in response to predation risk by fishes (Bouffard and Hanson 1997).

Several publications can provide information on the construction of impoundments for fish (Brown 1951; U.S. Department of Agriculture 1971, 1973; Ayers et al. no date), but fisheries management may not be compatible with other wetland values.

Conclusions

Impoundments present many opportunities to enhance fish and wildlife habitat. It generally is not possible to maximize more than one management strategy on a single impoundment. However, it is possible to include multiple strategies in a management plan that encompasses the landscape if managers are realistic in their goals for specific populations. Cautions must be observed in development of nonnative wildlife or fish communities. For example, some fish species could eliminate amphibians, and nonnative species could move into natural systems. While much is known about fish and wildlife, much remains to be learned about herpetofaunal relationships in impoundments and their interactions with fish and other wildlife in the Intermountain West.

Literature Cited

Adamus, P. R. 1993. Irrigated wetlands of the Colorado Plateau: information, synthesis, and habitat evaluation method. U.S. Environmental Protection Agency EPA/600/R-93/071, Corvallis, Oregon, USA.

Altig, R., and M. T. Christensen. 1981. Behavioral characteristics of the tadpoles of *Rana hecksheri.* Journal of Herpetology 15:151–154.

Anderson, J. 1950. Some aquatic vegetation changes following fish removal. Journal of Wildlife Management 14:206–209.

Anderson, M. T., and C. L. Hawkes. 1985. Water chemistry of northern Great Plains strip mine and livestock water impoundments. Water Resources Bulletin 21:499–505.

Anderson, R. O. 1978. New approaches to recreational fishery management. Pages 73–78 in G. D. Novinger and J. G. Dillard, editors. Special Publication Number 5. North Central Division, American Fisheries Society, Bethesda, Maryland, USA.

Anderson, S. A., M. McKinstry, and K. Shelley. 1994. Reclaiming minelands to benefit wildlife. Transactions of North American Wildlife and Natural Resource Conference 59:303–308.

Ayers, H. D., H. R. McCrimmon, and A. H. Berst. No date. The construction and management of farm ponds in Ontario. Ontario Department of Agriculture Publication 515, Toronto, Canada.

Bakke, E. 1984. Specific guidelines for increasing certain species of wildlife. Pages 1C-39C in F. R. Henderson, editor. Guidelines for increasing wildlife on farms and ranches with ideas for supplemental income sources for rural families. Great Plains Agricultural Council, Wildlife Resources Committee and Kansas State University, Manhattan, Kansas, USA.

Ball, I. J., R. L. Eng, and S. K. Ball. 1995. Population density and productivity of ducks on large grassland tracts in northcentral Montana. Wildlife Society Bulletin 23:767–773.

Ball, J. P., and T. D. Nudds. 1989. Mallard habitat selection: an experiment and implications for management. Pages 659–671 in R. R. Sharitz and J. W. Gibbons, editors. Freshwater wetlands and wildlife. U.S. Department of Energy Office of Scientific and Technical Information Symposium Series Number 61.

Behenke, R. J. 1992. Native trout of western North America. Monograph 6. American Fisheries Society, Bethesda, Maryland, USA.

Bellrose, F. C. 1978. Ducks, geese, and swans of North America. Second edition. Stackpole Books, Harrisburg, Pennsylvania, USA.

Bjugstad, A. J., M. A. Rumble, R. A. Olson, and W. T. Barker. 1983. Prairie pond morphometry and aquatic plant zonation—northern high plains. Proceedings of Biennial Plains Aquatic Research Conference 3:101–111.

Boggess, E. 1984. Mink. Pages 161C–163C in F. R. Henderson, editor. Guidelines for increasing wildlife on farms and ranches with ideas for supplemental income sources for rural families. Great Plains Agricultural Council, Wildlife Resources Committee, and Kansas State University, Manhattan, Kansas, USA.

Bouffard, S. H., and M. A. Hanson. 1997. Fish in waterfowl marshes: waterfowl managers' perspective. Wildlife Society Bulletin 25:146–157.

Brewster, W. G., J. M. Gates, and L. D. Flake. 1976. Breeding waterfowl populations and their distribution in South Dakota. Journal of Wildlife Management 40:50–59.

Brodie, E. D. Jr. 1987. Antipredator mechanism of larval anurans: protection of palatable individuals. Herpetologica 43:369–373.

Brönmark, C., and P. Edenhamn. 1994. Does the presence of fish affect the distribution of tree frogs (*Hyla arborea*)? Conservation Biology 8:841–845.

Brown, C. J. D. 1951. Ranch fish ponds in Montana: their construction and management. Agricultural Experiment Station Bulletin 480, Montana State College, Bozeman, Montana, USA.

Brown, M., and Dinsmore. 1986. Implications of marsh size and isolation for marsh bird management. Journal of Wildlife Management 50:392–397.

Bultsma, P. M. 1976. Use of stockponds for nesting by giant Canada geese. Thesis, South Dakota State University, Brookings, South Dakota, USA.

Cahoon, W. G. 1953. Commercial carp removal at Lake Mattamuskeet, North Carolina. Journal of Wildlife Management 17:312–317.

Chamberlain, E. B. 1948. Ecological factors influencing the growth and management of certain waterfowl food plants on Back Bay National Wildlife Refuge. Transactions North American Wildlife Conference 13:347–356.

Collins, J. P. 1981. Distribution, habitats, and life history variation in the tiger salamander, *Ambystoma tigrinum*, in east-central and southeast Arizona. Copeia 1981:666–675.

Conover, M. R., and G. G Chasko. 1985. Nuisance Canada goose populations in the eastern United States. Wildlife Society Bulletin 13:228–233.

Cowardin, L. M., V. Carter, F. C. Golet, and E. T. LaRoe. 1979. Classification of wetlands and deepwater habitats of the United States. U.S. Fish and Wildlife Service FWS/OBS-79/31.

———, T. L. Shaffer, and K. M. Kraft. 1995. How much habitat management is needed to meet mallard production objectives? Wildlife Society Bulletin 23:48–55.

Crivelli, A. J. 1983. The destruction of aquatic vegetation by carp. Hydrobiologia 106:37–41.

Degenhardt, W. G., C. W. Painter, and A. H. Price. 1996. Amphibians and reptiles of New Mexico. University of New Mexico Press, Albuquerque, New Mexico, USA.

DeGraff, R. M., V. E. Scott, R. H. Hamre, L. Ernst, and S. H. Anderson. 1991. Forest and rangeland birds of the United States. U.S. Department of Agriculture Forest Service Handbook 688.

Dole, J. W. 1965. Summer movement of adult leopard frogs, *Rana pipiens* Schreber, in northern Michigan. Ecology 46:236–255.

———. 1968. Homing in leopard frogs, *Rana pipiens*. Ecology 49:386–399.

Eberhardt, R. T. 1973. Some aspects of mink and waterfowl relationships on prairie wetlands. Prairie Naturalist 5:19.

Emery, A. R., A. H. Berst, and K. Kodaira. 1972. Under-ice observations of wintering sites of leopard frogs. Copeia 1972:123–126.

Eng, R. L., J. D. Jones, and F. M. Gjersing. 1979. Construction and management of stock ponds for waterfowl. U.S. Department of the Interior Bureau of Land Management Technical Note Number 327.

Evans, C. D., and K. E. Black. 1956. Duck production studies on the prairie potholes of South Dakota. U.S. Fish and Wildlife Service Science Report Wildlife 32.

Evans, K. E., and R. R. Kerbs. 1977. Avian use of livestock watering ponds in western South Dakota. U.S. Department of Agriculture Forest Service General Technical Report RM-35.

Fletcher, A. R., A. K. Morrison, and D. J. Hume. 1985. Effects of carp, *Cyprinus carpio* L., on communities of aquatic vegetation and turbidity of water bodies in the lower Goulburn River Basin. Australian Journal of Marine and Freshwater Research 36: 311–327.

Forman, K. J., C. R. Madsen, and M. J. Hogan. 1996. Creating multiple purpose wetlands to enhance livestock grazing distribution, range condition, and waterfowl production in western South Dakota. Pages 185–192 *in* Jerry Schaack and Susan Anderson, editors. Water for agriculture and wildlife and the environment win-win opportunities. U.S. Committee on Irrigation and Drainage, Denver, Colorado, USA.

Gabelhouse, D. W. Jr. 1984. An assessment of crappie stocks in small midwestern private impoundments. North American Journal of Fisheries Management 4:371–384.

———, R. L. Hager, and H. E. Klaassen. 1995. Producing fish and wildlife from Kansas ponds. Third edition. Kansas Department of Wildlife and Parks, Pratt, Kansas, USA.

Gehlbach, F. R. 1965. Herpetology of the Zuni Mountains region, northwestern New Mexico. Proceedings of the U.S. National Museum 116:243–332.

Gibbons, J. W., D. E. Scott, T. J. Ryan, K. A. Buhlmann, T. D. Tuberville, B. S. Metts, J. L. Greene, T. Mills, Y. Leiden, S. Poppy, and C. T. Winne. 2000. The global decline of reptiles, déjà vu amphibians. Bioscience 50:653–666.

Gibbs, James P. 1993. Importance of small wetlands for the persistence of local populations of wetland associated animals. Wetlands 13:25–31.

Gjersing, F. M. 1975. Waterfowl production in relation to rest-rotation grazing. Journal of Range Management 28:37–42.

Gurtin, S. D., M. L. Brown, and C. G. Scalet. 1996. Dynamics of sympatric northern pike and largemouth bass in small prairie impoundments. Pages 64–72 *in* R. Soderberg, editor. 1996 warmwater workshop proceedings: esocid management and culture. Mansfield University, Mansfield, Pennsylvania, USA.

Guy, C. S., and D. W. Willis. 1990. Structural relationships of largemouth bass and bluegill populations in South Dakota ponds. North American Journal of Fisheries Management 10:338–343.

———, and———. 1991. Evaluation of largemouth bass-yellow perch communities in small South Dakota impoundments. North American Journal of Fisheries Management 11:43–49.

Hammerson, G. A. 1999. Amphibians and reptiles in Colorado. University Press of Colorado, Niwot, Colorado, USA.

Hanson, M. A., and M. R. Riggs. 1995. Potential effects of fish predation on wetland invertebrates: a comparison of wetlands with and without fathead minnows. Wetlands 15:167–175.

Hecnar, S. J., and R. T. M'Closkey. 1997. The effects of predatory fish on amphibian species richness and distribution. Biological Conservation 79:123–131.

Hews, D. K., and A. R. Blaustein. 1985. An investigation of the alarm response of *Bufo boreas* and *Rana cascadae* tadpoles. Behavioral Neurobiology 43:47–57.

Hobaugh, W. C., J. G. Teer. 1981. Waterfowl use characteristics of flood-prevention lakes in north-central Texas. Journal of Wildlife Management 45:16–26.

Hop, K. D., K. F. Higgins, and D. E. Nomsen. 1989. Vertebrate wildlife use of highway borrow pit wetlands in South Dakota. Proceedings of the South Dakota Academy of Sciences 68:47–54.

Johnson, N. F. 1984. Muskrat. Pages 156C–160C *in* F. R. Henderson, editor. Guidelines for increasing wildlife on farms and ranches with ideas for supplemental income sources for rural families. Great Plains Agricultural Council, Wildlife Resources Committee, and Kansas State University, Manhattan, Kansas, USA.

Johnson, R. R., and J. J. Dinsmore. 1986. Habitat use by breeding Virginia rails and for soras. Journal of Wildlife Management 50:387–392.

Kaminski, R. M., and H. H. Prince. 1981*a*. Dabbling duck and aquatic macroinvertebrate responses to manipulated wetland habitat. Journal of Wildlife Management 45:1–15.

——, and ——. 1981*b*. Dabbling duck activity and foraging response to aquatic macroinvertebrates. Auk 98:115–126.

——, and H. H. Prince. 1984. Dabbling duck-habitat associations during spring in Delta Marsh, Manitoba. Journal of Wildlife Management 48:37–50.

King, D. R., and G. S. Hunt. 1967. Effect of carp on vegetation in a Lake Erie marsh. Journal of Wildlife Management 31:181–188.

Kolterman, B. F. 1990. Effects of common carp and black bullheads on sago pondweed. Thesis, South Dakota State University, Brookings, South Dakota, USA.

Krapu, G. L. 1974. Foods of breeding pintails in North Dakota. Journal of Wildlife Management 38:408–417.

——. 1979. Nutrition of female dabbling ducks during reproduction. Pages 59–70 *in* T. A. Bookhout, editor. Waterfowl and wetlands—an integrated review. La Crosse Printing, La Crosse, Wisconsin, USA.

——, and G. A. Swanson. 1975. Some nutritional aspects of reproduction in prairie nesting pintails. Journal of Wildlife Management 39:156–162

Krull, J. N. 1970. Aquatic plant-macroinvertebrate associations and waterfowl. Journal of Wildlife Management 34:707–718.

Lagler, K. F. 1956. The pike, *Esox lucius* Linnaeus, in relation to waterfowl on the Seney National Wildlife Refuge, Michigan. Journal of Wildlife Management 20:114–124.

Larson, K. 1997. Faunal diversity and richness of natural, restored, dam-created, and borrow-pit wetlands in the prairie pothole region of eastern South Dakota. Thesis, South Dakota State University, Brookings, South Dakota, USA.

Lee, F. B. 1984. Waterfowl: goose populations in the Great Plains. Pages 42C–43C *in* F. R. Henderson, editor. Guidelines for increasing wildlife on farms and ranches with ideas for supplemental income sources for rural families. Great Plains Agricultural Council, Wildlife Resources Committee and Kansas State University, Manhattan, Kansas, USA.

——, C. H. Schroeder, T. L. Kuck, L. J. Schoonover, M. A. Johnson, H. K. Nelson, and C. A. Beauduy. 1984. Rearing and restoring giant Canada geese in the Dakotas. North Dakota Game and Fish Department, Bismarck, North Dakota, USA.

Leschisin, D. A., G. L. Williams, and M. W. Weller. 1992. Factors affecting waterfowl use of constructed wetlands in northwestern Minnesota. Wetlands 12:178–183.

Licht, L. E. 1969. Palatability of *Rana* and *Hyla* eggs. American Midland Naturalist 82:296–298.

Lokemoen, J. T. 1973. Waterfowl production on stock-watering ponds in the northern plains. Journal of Range Management 26:179–184.

——, F. B. Lee, H. F. Dubbert, and G. A. Swanson. 1984. Aquatic habitats—waterfowl. Pages 161B–176B *in* F. R. Henderson, editor. Guidelines for increasing wildlife on farms and ranches with ideas for supplemental income sources for rural families. Great Plains Agricultural Council, Wildlife Resources Committee and Kansas State University, Manhattan, Kansas, USA.

Lott, J. P., D. W. Willis, and D. O. Lucchesi. 1996. Relationship of food habits to yellow perch growth and population structure in South Dakota lakes. Journal of Freshwater Ecology 11:27–37.

Mack, G. D., and L. D. Flake. 1980. Habitat relationships of waterfowl broods on South Dakota stock ponds. Journal of Wildlife Management 44:695–700.

Marriage, L. D., A. E. Borrell, and P. M. Scheffer. 1971. Trout ponds for recreation. U.S. Department of Agriculture Farmers' Bulletin Number 2249.

McCrimmon, H. R. 1968. Carp in Canada. Fisheries Research Board of Canada Bulletin 165.

McEnroe, M. R. 1976. Factors influencing habitat use by breeding waterfowl in South Dakota. Thesis, South Dakota State University, Brookings, South Dakota, USA.

McKinstry, M. C., and S. H. Anderson. 1995. Wetlands created in association with bentonite mining activities in northeast Wyoming: their effectiveness at providing habitat for waterfowl. Pages 86–100 in D. P. Young Jr., R. Vinzant, and M. D. Strickland, editors. Proceedings of the second wildlife water development symposium. University of Wyoming, Laramie, Wyoming, USA.

———, and———. 2002. Creating wetlands for waterfowl in Wyoming. Ecological Engineering 18:293–304.

Monda, M. J., and J. T. Ratti. 1988. Niche overlap and habitat use by sympatric duck broods in eastern Washington. Journal of Wildlife Management 52:95–103.

Mundinger, J. G. 1976. Waterfowl response to rest-rotation grazing. Journal of Wildlife Management 40:60–68.

Naugle, David E., Jeffrey S. Gleason, Jonathan A. Jenks, Kenneth F. Higgins, Paul W. Mammenga, and Sarah M. Nusser. 1997. Factors influencing wetland use by Canada geese. Wetlands 17:552–558.

Novinger, G. D., and R. E. Legler. 1978. Bluegill population structure and dynamics. Pages 37–49 in G. D. Novinger and J. G. Dillard, editors. New approaches to the management of small impoundments. Special Publication Number 5. North Central Division, American Fisheries Society, Bethesda, Maryland, USA.

Nudds, T. D. 1983. Niche dynamics and organization of waterfowl guilds in variable environments. Ecology 64:319–330.

Olson, R. A. 1981. Wetland vegetation, environmental factors, and their interaction in strip mine ponds, stockdams, and natural wetlands. U.S. Department of Agriculture Forest Service General Technical Report RM-85.

Patterson, J. H. 1976. Role of environmental heterogeneity in the regulation of duck populations. Journal of Wildlife Management 40:22–32.

Petranka, J. W. 1998. Salamanders of the United States and Canada. Smithsonian Institution Press, Washington, D.C., USA.

Regier, H. A. 1963. Ecology and management of largemouth bass and golden shiners in farm ponds in New York. New York Fish and Game Journal 10:139–169.

Richter, K. O., and A. L. Azous. 1995. Amphibian occurrence and wetland characteristics in the Puget Sound basin. Wetlands 15:305–312.

Ricker, W. E., and J. Gottschalk. 1940. An experiment in removing coarse fish from a lake. Transactions of the American Fisheries Society 70:382–390.

Ringleman, J. K. 1991. Evaluating and managing waterfowl habitat: a general reference guide on the biological requirements and management of ducks and geese common to Colorado. Colorado Division of Wildlife Division Report Number 16.

Robel, R. J. 1961. The effect of carp populations on the production of waterfowl plant foods on a western waterfowl marsh. Transactions North American Wildlife Conference 26:147–159.

Rumble, M. A. 1989. Surface mine impoundments as wildlife and fish habitat. U.S. Department of Agriculture Forest Service General Technical Report RM-183.

———, and L. D. Flake. 1983. Management considerations to enhance use of stock ponds by waterfowl broods. Journal of Range Management 36:691–694.

———, M. T. Anderson, and C. L. Hawkes. 1985. Morphometry of coal and bentonite surface mine and livestock impoundments in the northern high plains. Reclamation and Revegetation Research 3:293–300.

Rundle, W. D., and L. H. Fredrickson. 1981. Managing seasonally flooded impoundments for migrant rails and shorebirds. Wildlife Society Bulletin 9:80–87.

Ruwaldt, J. J., L. D. Flake, and J. M. Gates. 1979. Waterfowl pair use of natural and manmade wetlands in South Dakota. Journal of Wildlife Management 43:375–383.

Saffel, P. D., C. S. Guy, and D. W. Willis. 1990. Population structure of largemouth bass and black bullheads in South Dakota ponds. Prairie Naturalist 22:113–118.

Sanderson, G. C. 1977. Management of migratory shore and upland game birds in North America. International Association of Fish and Wildlife Agencies, Washington, D.C., USA.

Satterfield, J. R. Jr., and S. A. Flickinger. 1984. Colorado warmwater pond handbook. Fisheries Bulletin Number 1. Colorado State University, Fort Collins, Colorado, USA.

———, and K. D. Koupal. 1995. Splake as a control agent for brook trout in small impoundments. Pages 431–436 in H. L. Schramm Jr. and R. G. Piper, editors. Use and effects of cultured fishes in aquatic ecosystems. American Fisheries Society Symposium 15, Bethesda, Maryland, USA.

Sayre, M. W., and W. D. Rundle. 1984. Comparison of habitat use by migrant soras and Virginia rails. Journal of Wildlife Management 48:599–605.

Scalet, C. G., and T. Modde. 1984. Pond fish species and management. Pages 5C–35C in F. R. Henderson, editor. Guidelines for increasing wildlife on farms and ranches with ideas for supplemental income sources for rural families. Great Plains Agricultural Council, Wildlife Resources Committee, and Kansas State University, Manhattan, Kansas, USA.

Semlitsch, R. D. 2000a. Size does matter: the value of small isolated wetlands. National Wetlands Newsletter, January–February 2000:5–13.

———. 2000b. Principles for management of aquatic-breeding amphibians. Journal of Wildlife Management 64:615–631.

———, and J. R. Bodie. 1998. Are small, isolated wetlands expendable? Conservation Biology 12:1129–1133.

Smith, A. G. 1969. Waterfowl habitat relationships on the Lousana, Alberta, waterfowl study area. Pages 116–122 in Saskatoon wetlands seminar. Canadian Wildlife Service Report Series 6.

Stebbins, R. C., and N. W. Cohen. 1995. A natural history of amphibians. Princeton University Press, Princeton, New Jersey, USA.

Stiefel, D. M. 1980. Nesting giant Canada geese in western South Dakota. Thesis, South Dakota State University, Brookings, South Dakota, USA.

Stone, C. C., and T. Modde. 1982. Growth and survival of largemouth bass in newly stocked South Dakota ponds. North American Journal of Fisheries Management 2: 326–333.

Storer, R. W., and G. L. Nuechterlein. 1992. Stern grebe and Clark's grebe. Pages 1–22 in A. Poole, P. Settenheim, and F. Gill, editors. The birds of North America Number 26. Philadelphia, Pennsylvania, USA.

Sudgen, L. G. 1973. Feeding ecology of pintail gadwall, American wigeon, and lesser scaup ducklings in southern Alberta. Canadian Wildlife Service Report 24.

Swanson, G. A., and M. I. Meyer. 1973. The role of invertebrates in the feeding ecology of Anatinae during the breeding season. Pages 143–165 in Waterfowl habitat symposium. Moncton, New Brunswick, Canada.

——, ——, and J. R. Serie. 1974. Feeding ecology of breeding blue-winged teal. Journal of Wildlife Management 38:396–407.

——, and H. K. Nelson. 1970. Potential influence of fish rearing programs on waterfowl breeding habitat. Pages 65–71 in E. Schneberger, editor. A symposium on the management of midwestern winterkill lakes. Special Publication. North Central Division, American Fisheries Society, Bethesda, Maryland, USA.

——, and A. B. Sargent. 1972. Observation of nighttime feeding behavior of ducks. Journal of Wildlife Management 36:959–961.

Tacha, T. C., and C. E. Braun, editors. 1994. Migratory shore and upland game bird management in North America. International Association of Fish and Wildlife Agencies, Washington, D.C., USA.

Threinen, C. W., and W. T. Helm. 1954. Experiments and observations designed to show carp destruction of aquatic vegetation. Journal of Wildlife Management 18: 247–254.

Tilton, D. L., and D. L. Denison. 1992. Colonization of restored wetlands by invertebrates, fish, amphibians, and reptiles studied (Michigan). Restoration and Management Notes 10:187.

Tryon, C. A. Jr. 1954. The effect of carp exclosures on growth of submerged aquatic vegetation in Pymatuning Lake, Pennsylvania. Journal of Wildlife Management 18:251–254.

Uresk, D. W., and K. E. Severson. 1988. Waterfowl and shorebird use of surface-mined and livestock watering impoundments on the northern Great Plains. Great Basin Naturalist 48:353–357.

U.S. Department of Agriculture. 1971. Ponds for water supply and recreation. U.S. Department of Agriculture Handbook Number 387.

——. 1973. Building a pond. U.S. Department of Agriculture Farmers' Bulletin Number 2256.

Webb, R. G. 1969. Survival adaptations of tiger salamanders (Ambystoma tigrinum) in the Chihuahuan Desert. Pages 143–147 in C. C. Hoff and M. L. Riedesel, editors. Physiological systems in semiarid environments. University of New Mexico Press, Albuquerque, New Mexico, USA.

Webb, R. G., and W. Roueche. 1971. Life history aspects of the tiger salamander (Ambystoma tigrinum mavortium) in the Chihuahuan Desert. Great Basin Naturalist 31:193–212.

Weller, M. W., and C. S. Spatcher. 1965. Role of habitat in the distribution and abundance of march birds. Special Report Number 43. Agricultural and Home Economics Experiment Station, Iowa State University, Ames, Iowa, USA.

Willis, D. W, M. D. Beem, and R. L. Hanten. 1990. Managing South Dakota ponds for fish and wildlife. South Dakota Department of Game, Fish, and Parks, Pierre, South Dakota, USA.

Yoakum, J., W. P. Dasmann, H. R. Sanderson, C. M. Nixon, and H. S. Crawford. 1980. Habitat improvement techniques. Pages 329–403 *in* S. D. Schmenitz, editor. Wildlife techniques manual. Wildlife Society, Washington, D.C., USA.

Zimmer, K. D., M. A. Hanson, and M. G. Butler. 2000. Factors influencing invertebrate communities in prairie wetlands: a multivariate approach. Canadian Journal of Fisheries and Aquatic Sciences 57:76–85.

CHAPTER 11

Management of Created Palustrine Wetlands

STEPHEN A. TESSMANN

Introduction

Since settlement, created palustrine wetlands have been coincidental and intentional products of human activities throughout the Intermountain West. Most commonly, they have been by-products of developments built for other purposes, such as livestock watering ponds, spring developments, windmill basins, produced water from oil and gas wells, canal seeps, return flows from irrigation, highway ditches, borrow pits, reservoir backwaters, wastewater discharge sites, abandoned mine workings, sediment retention basins, and industrial settling ponds. Wetlands that were purposely created have included habitat development projects on public and private lands, mitigation projects, mined-land reclamation, and wetland systems designed to treat wastewater. Created wetlands can form in excavated or subsided basins, behind dikes, dams, or spoil banks on poorly drained ground, or in areas of enhanced surface water or groundwater.

Several factors can constrain practical options for managing wetlands, such as water availability, funding, regulatory issues, chemical contaminants, or physical limitations. The overriding advice to those contemplating wetland construction or rehabilitation is to design and build systems that can persist in a productive and dynamic state at low cost with little or no human intervention.

This chapter describes management practices that have the potential for widespread application to improve the ecological condition or targeted functions of created palustrine wetlands throughout the Intermountain West. The focus is on waterfowl habitat, wildlife diversity, and ecological sustainability. Several authors caution against management that emphasizes selected wetland functions or wildlife species because this approach could potentially conflict with other functions' or species' requirements (Stearns 1978; Weller 1978, 1987; Fredrickson and Reid 1986; Preston and Bedford 1988; Marble 1992). However, most wetland functions are accommodated by management strategies intended to sustain or enhance the diversity of wetland-associated wildlife.

Ideally, management follows these steps: (1) develop a functional understanding or working hypothesis about how a wetland system works, including how it responds to internal and external influences; (2) identify conditions or trends within the system that do not meet management expectations; (3) determine quantitative goals for improving the system; (4) formulate actions that can be implemented to meet the goals; (5) identify measurable success criteria; (6) monitor and assess the effectiveness of management actions; and (7) adjust management actions based on how the system responds.

In practice, managers seldom have the time or resources to rigorously follow these steps. Wetland management is more likely to be prescriptive, consisting of an ocular assessment of condition, identification of one or more factors impairing key wetland functions, and implementation of management strategies that are based on experience, professional judgment, and the literature. Follow-up monitoring is also likely to be an ocular assessment. The prescriptive approach is satisfactory so long as experienced persons perform the assessment and there is flexibility to adjust management practices that do not achieve desired results. More intensive data collection, analysis, and monitoring may be necessary if critical chemical or physical uncertainties cannot be discerned through ocular assessment.

Two approaches, direct manipulation and management of surrounding land uses, are applied to manage created palustrine wetlands. Direct treatments traditionally have received greater attention but can be expensive, may impart artificial appearances, and often are short-lived or unsuccessful (Weller 1978, 1990; Miller 1987). A more effective way to restore or enhance wetland functions is to improve management of surrounding land uses (Bue et al. 1964, Fredrickson and Reid 1986). This process of stewardship is intended primarily to manage land uses in a sustainable and ecologically compatible manner. Better stewardship requires continuing reforms in policies, practices, and politics on the part of federal and state land management agencies and private landowners.

Land Use Management in Wetlands and Watersheds

Land use practices within watersheds can profoundly affect the ecological functions of both natural and created wetlands. Bue et al. (1964) were among the first to generalize that good range management is good waterfowl management. Fredrickson and Reid (1986) similarly concluded that manipulation of the surrounding uplands is a more economical approach to managing wetlands for nongame species. Furthermore, costly "in-basin" treatments are likely to be short-lived in a poorly managed watershed. Watershed management has by far the greatest potential to improve the ecological condition of natural and created wetlands throughout the Intermountain West.

Grazing management

Improper grazing may be the dominant factor leading to the loss and deterioration of wetland margins and other riparian systems in the Intermountain West (U.S. General Accounting Office 1988, U.S. Department of the Interior 1994; see also Chapters 5 and 8 of this volume). More than half of existing riparian habitats are in fair to poor condition (Jensen and Platts 1990). Much of this can be traced to inadequacies in federal grazing programs. In the 11 western states, 48% of the land surface is federally owned, and 75% of that is grazed (U.S. Department of the Interior 1994). Literature on grazing in western riparian systems provides useful insights regarding strategies for managing watersheds and margins or riparian zones of created wetlands.

REGULATION OF GRAZING DISTRIBUTION AND INTENSITY

Federal agencies have held the viewpoint that riparian systems are too isolated and dispersed to be managed effectively as separate units (Melton et al. 1987, Chaney et al. 1993, U.S. Department of the Interior 1994). However, uncontrolled livestock spend a disproportionate time within wetland margins and other riparian areas where they find water, succulent forage, and favorable microclimates with shade, wind reduction, and higher humidity (Eng et al. 1979, Skovlin 1984, Clary and Webster 1989, U.S. Department of the Interior 1994). Cattle may occupy riparian areas 5 to 30 times more frequently than upland areas (Clary and Webster 1989). For these reasons, regardless of stocking rates, the risk of damage to wetlands and riparian areas is high, particularly under season-long grazing strategies (Clary and Webster 1989, Chaney et al. 1993, U.S. Department of the Interior 1994).

Maintaining wetland margins and other riparian areas in good condition requires close regulation of cattle stocking rates, distribution, and season of use (Clary and Webster 1989, Chaney et al. 1993, U.S. Department of Agriculture Natural Resource Conservation Service 1997c). Several practices, including spring grazing, herding, and proper placement of salt blocks, shelters, and supplemental food and water sources, can encourage better distribution of cattle use between wetland margins and upland areas (Clary and Webster 1989, Chaney et al. 1993). Various adaptations of a system known as "intensive grazing management"

(Smith et al. 1986) have been advocated recently to achieve more uniform and efficient grazing. Under this system, high densities of livestock are rotated (or herded) among smaller pasture units where they are permitted to graze for a very short duration (approximately 5 days in each location). At high densities, grazing animals interact spatially and distribute their use of forage plants more evenly. The short duration prevents animals from overusing preferred plants. In arid and semiarid climates, a sufficient growing season must remain after livestock are removed to allow preferred plants to recover. Pasture units can be grazed once during the dormant season, provided sufficient residual cover is retained. Properly applied, this grazing system offers a promising means to rehabilitate and maintain wetland margins and other riparian communities. In addition, range condition, forage production, and profitability can be enhanced. However, as the name implies, this form of management requires a strong commitment on the part of the land manager in order to make it work.

RIPARIAN GRAZING SYSTEMS

No single grazing prescription fits all locations or year-to-year climatic variations (Dwyer et al. 1984, Clary and Webster 1989, Chaney et al. 1993). Grazing must be monitored and adjusted based on vegetation response. Carefully monitored grazing during the spring growing period is generally compatible with riparian functions (Elmore and Beschta 1987, Clary and Webster 1989, Chaney et al. 1993, Brockmann 1993). Livestock disperse more evenly between riparian vegetation and uplands, and sufficient growing season remains after livestock are removed for vegetation to recover. Possible disadvantages of spring grazing include hoof damage to saturated soils and stress upon preferred plants that grow from root reserves at that time of year. In addition, concentrated use by cattle can harm ground-nesting birds (Molini 1977, Kirsch et al. 1978, Bowen and Kruse 1993), but light to moderate grazing is probably not detrimental. Spring grazing should not begin until high water levels have subsided and soil firmness is adequate to avoid hoof damage.

Late fall is the season next preferred for grazing riparian pastures (Kauffman et al. 1982, Clary and Webster 1989). By fall, energy reserves have been transferred to root systems, and low-lying areas are drier and less susceptible to mechanical damage. However, excessive fall and winter grazing can have a negative impact on woody vegetation (Chaney et al. 1993). It also can eliminate residual herbaceous cover that buffers runoff prior to regrowth the following spring (Clary and Webster 1989), provides cover for early-season ground-nesting birds (Weller 1987, Payne 1992, Chaney et al. 1993), and is important thermal cover for terrestrial wildlife during winter. Summer or season-long grazing strategies are most difficult to manage because livestock concentrate near wetlands and water sources during hot weather (Chabreck et al. 1989, Clary and Webster 1989, Meyers 1989, Platts 1989, Brockmann 1993, Chaney et al. 1993).

Compliance with allotment plans and grazing standards must be monitored and enforced. Even a few stray or trespass cattle can severely damage a wetland margin during summer months. Summer grazing should be practiced only where residual stubble height standards can be met through tightly controlled livestock distribution (Clary and Webster 1989) or to accomplish localized habitat treatments (to be discussed later).

Moderate, short-duration grazing is preferable to light grazing over a longer period because it prevents animals from selecting and depleting preferred plant species. A grazing duration of 2 to 3 weeks between late May and early July is usually acceptable; however, it is important to remove livestock when stubble height criteria are met.

Various standards have been suggested to gauge when acceptable plant utilization has occurred and cattle should be removed. Standards are especially important for riparian communities in good to excellent condition (Clary and Webster 1989, Chaney et al. 1993), but recovery of degraded riparian systems can require 1 to 15 years of total rest. A residual stubble height of 15 cm is recommended to maintain the ecological functions of riparian ecosystems (Clary and Webster 1989). When residual stubble height has decreased to 7.5 cm, cattle preference will change and unacceptable grazing will begin (Hall and Bryant 1995).

In general, a three-pasture rest-rotation system (spring/summer/rest) can achieve satisfactory results in riparian pastures (Chaney et al. 1993), provided livestock grazing intensity is uniform and residual cover is maintained for soil stabilization and nest concealment the following spring. However, proper stocking rates and livestock distributions are more important than the particular system used. Appropriate stocking rates vary regionally (Dwyer et al. 1984, Payne 1992). Strategic placement of water sources, salt blocks, shade, shelter, and supplemental feed help achieve uniform grazing distributions. In some areas, riders may be necessary to move cattle around a pasture.

WETLAND FENCING

Fencing riparian and wetland areas can be an effective way to achieve satisfactory distribution of grazing and is often the only way to rehabilitate damaged areas (Bue et al. 1964, Clary and Webster 1989, Weller 1990, Chaney et al. 1993, U.S. Department of the Interior 1994, U.S. Department of Agriculture Natural Resource Conservation Service 1997*c*). The size, width, and shape of fenced wetland areas depend on management objectives, the configuration of the wetland or riparian feature, surrounding topography, land uses, soil characteristics, and climatic considerations. Riparian units can range from buffer strips a few meters wide (Hamor et al. 1968; Marble 1992; Payne 1992; U.S. Department of Agriculture Natural Resource Conservation Service 1997*a,b*, 1998; Greer undated) to larger blocks encompassing the wetland and a portion of the surrounding watershed (Atlantic Waterfowl Council 1972, Nelson and Duebbert 1974, Dillard 1982, Petersen et al. 1982, Piehl 1986, Sempek and Johnson 1987, Weller 1990, Payne 1992). In general, the narrower filter strips are intended to protect emergent vegetation and enough transition or upland vegetation to dissipate incoming runoff. Fairly narrow strips (>7 m) have been found effective for removing sediments, nutrients, and toxicants contained in agricultural runoff on moderate slopes (Marble 1992; U.S. Department of Agriculture Natural Resource Conservation Service 1997*a,b*, 1998).

However, Chaney et al. (1993) cautioned that exclosure fences must be set back far enough to restore ecological function. Wildlife habitat functions within wetland or riparian management units can include forage; water; hiding, escape, thermal, and nesting cover; brood-rearing habitat; and special habitat features such as snags, nest cavities, and rock and brush piles. Fenced exclosures should contain mesic and transitional vegetation in the wetland margin and some upland vegetation as well. Grazing management within the exclosure must be based upon utilization of the mesic (riparian) plant species, not the upland species (Clary and Webster 1989, Chaney et al. 1993). In the glaciated prairie region where waterfowl nesting is a management priority, fenced units should be approximately 4 times the surface area of the wetland or water surface being protected (Nelson and Duebbert 1974, Petersen et al. 1982, Piehl 1986).

Exclosure fencing should be adequate to control livestock but should not impede wildlife movement. Native ungulates do not concentrate within riparian habitats to the extent domestic livestock do; therefore it is not necessary to control their distribution. The following fence design is recommended in Wyoming where cattle and big game are present: 3-strand fence, overall height 96 cm, smooth bottom wire, and wire spacing from ground up that is 41, 25, and 30 cm (U.S. Department of the Interior Bureau of Land Management 1986). Where domestic sheep must be controlled, the recommended design is a 4-strand fence of overall height 96 cm and smooth bottom wire 20–30 cm above the ground (Wyoming Department of Environmental Quality 1982). Other designs can be compatible with wildlife use, given the following guidance: Where pronghorn are present, a ground clearance of 38 cm is needed, and the bottom wire should be smooth (ground clearance should never be <25 cm). Where deer are present, the overall height may be 96 cm but should never exceed 107 cm, and the top two wires should be spaced 30 cm apart to reduce the risk of leg entanglements by animals attempting to jump the fence. One- and 2-strand electric fences provide additional alternatives that are compatible with wildlife movements and allow easy relocation of fenced areas. Woven wire, 5- and 6-strand designs, and fences with wire stays should not be used for exclosure fencing. Fences should be set back from open water areas to prevent collisions by water birds. In particular, fences should not be placed on high banks or hilltops immediately next to wetlands where they must be cleared by birds taking off.

Water gaps can be included to allow livestock access to water (Brockmann 1993). Gaps should be constructed in a location where the pond bottom is firm and can withstand livestock traffic. If boggy conditions exist, it may be possible to deposit a sand or gravel foundation so livestock do not become mired. The fence should extend far enough into the water to prevent livestock from wading around the end. Since the water gap will receive heavy livestock use, that section of shoreline is likely to become barren and vulnerable to erosion. Erosion can be reduced by placing the gap in a sheltered location in which heavy surface runoff is not anticipated. Livestock should not be permitted on dams or dikes because grazing and trampling may destabilize these structures and lead to failure (Nelson et al. 1978). An alternative to water gaps is to siphon water to a tank below the impoundment elevation.

Livestock trailing along wetland margins and riparian corridors can damage soil and vegetation and are difficult to control. Brockmann (1993) suggested placing log barriers at right angles to riparian corridors at 90 m intervals to discourage this behavior. Log barriers or wing fences could be placed along wetland margins to encourage livestock to walk outside the saturated zone.

Use of prescribed fire in wetlands and watersheds

Prior to settlement, periodic range and forest fires sustained productive, subclimax conditions throughout much of the Intermountain West. It is logical to assume wetlands and riparian habitats burned intermittently (Davis 1979, Weller 1987). Prescribed burning may benefit wetland margins and riparian vegetation by cycling nutrients and retarding succession. However, burning may not be a practical management tool within most created palustrine wetlands due to their typically small sizes, isolation, narrow emergent fringes, and slow accumulation of organic substrate. The capability to regulate water levels is essential for effective burning within created wetland basins (Green et al. 1964, U.S. Fish and Wildlife Service 1964, Smith and Kadlec 1985, Mallic and Wein 1986).

In the Intermountain West, prescribed burning is a rangeland treatment commonly employed to rejuvenate overmature shrub communities and to control nuisance weeds. Burning may have some utility from the standpoint of watershed improvement, grazing redistribution, and management of nesting cover. Wetland burning can potentially be a useful treatment within some of the larger, diked marsh units.

PRESCRIBED FIRE TREATMENTS WITHIN WETLAND BASINS

Burning is one of the least expensive tools to attain large-scale alterations of marsh vegetation (Uhler 1944, Linde 1985), and considerable literature has been published on the topic (e.g., Uhler 1944, U.S. Fish and Wildlife Service 1964, Nelson and Dietz 1966, Vogl 1967, Ward 1968, Linde 1969, Messinger 1974, Kaiser et al. 1979, Hackney and de la Cruz 1981, Wright and Bailey 1982, Linde 1985, Kantrud 1986, Mallik and Wein 1986, Smith and Kadlec 1986, Young 1986, Weller 1987, Gordon et al. 1989, Marble 1992).

Objectives may include thinning emergent vegetation, increasing light penetration, stimulating growth of food-producing plants and invertebrates, maintaining plant vigor, increasing production, improving protein and nutrient content and palatability, increasing plant structural diversity, maintaining a mosaic of vegetation in various ecological stages, reducing litter buildup, recycling organically bound nutrients, lowering the elevation of organic marsh floors to create deeper open water areas, controlling invasion by woody plants, exposing roots and tubers attractive to geese in late summer and fall, creating open resting and loafing areas for ducks and geese along densely vegetated shorelines, and creating ash by-products to increase pH and enrich the water (Green et al. 1964, Vogl 1977).

There are basically two kinds of marsh burns: cooler "cover" burns applied to vegetation on saturated soils, frozen ground, or ice, and very hot "root" burns conducted during a drought or when the marsh has been drained and thoroughly dried (U.S. Fish and Wildlife Service 1964, Yancey 1964). Cover burns can open up dense stands of cattails, bulrushes, sedges, or other emergents within managed marsh units. Emergent vegetation is effectively killed by burning over ice or frozen ground during low water (fall or winter), then reflooding prior to regrowth in the spring (Nelson and Dietz 1966, Linde 1985, Smith and Kadlec 1985, Payne 1992). Flooding severed or burned stems disrupts oxygen transmission to the roots that is essential for regeneration (Nelson and Dietz 1966, Linde 1969, Beule 1971, Beule and Janisch 1973, Kaminski and Prince

1981). However, if stubble ends are not reflooded after burning, emergents will rapidly regenerate from the roots.

In some circumstances, cover burns are useful to remove patches of thick shoreline vegetation to create feeding, loafing, and resting areas for waterfowl and shorebirds (Grange 1949, Hovind 1949, Yancey 1964, Linde 1969, Wright and Bailey 1982, Gordon et al. 1989). However, vegetation should not be burned on shoreline segments that are exposed to wind and wave action unless regrowth will occur prior to flooding.

Created palustrine wetlands in the Intermountain West generally do not accumulate sufficient organic substrate to sustain hot root burns. Exceptions may include some older, diked marsh units that have been managed under shallow-water regimes for many decades. Habitat function is impaired by dense, monotypic emergent stands growing through saturated mats of dead plant parts. In such cases, hot root burns can be a useful restoration method provided the marsh unit can be drained and dried sufficiently. Once organic sediments have dried to a depth of 8–15 cm, root burns will kill emergent vegetation if there is enough dry plant litter to sustain a hot fire (Uhler 1944, Beule 1979).

PRESCRIBED FIRE TREATMENTS FOR NESTING COVER MANAGEMENT

Ducks tend to nest within 400 m of wetland margins (Moyle 1964). A minimum buffer area suggested for nesting cover extends 90 m from the wetland margin (Atlantic Waterfowl Council 1972:122). These distances might also comprise suitable unit boundaries for managing nesting cover and for watershed protection.

Prescribed fires are used to maintain native prairie and dense nesting cover in the northern plains region (Ohlsson et al. 1982, Owensby 1984, Fredrickson and Reid 1986, Higgins et al. 1989, Kjellsen and Higgins 1990). Mosaic-patterned burns should be conducted in rotation so adequate nesting cover is always available. For ducks, suitable nesting cover should remain in blocks of at least 15 ha and preferably of 30–40 ha to avoid concentrating predator activity (Nelson and Duebbert 1974, Petersen et al. 1982). On the other hand, structural diversity beneficial to small mammal and passerine species is often defined in much smaller units (Feldhamer 1979, O'Farrell 1980, Rotenberry and Wiens 1980, Ryder 1980), although some grassland birds select larger patch sizes. In native grasslands, burning intervals of about 3 to 5 years are recommended (Tester and Marshal 1962, Young 1986). Somewhat longer intervals (e.g., 5 to 7 years) may be reasonable to maintain larger contiguous areas of suitable nesting cover.

It is less clear whether burning native shrub communities is beneficial to nesting ducks. Herbaceous understory is important concealment for sage grouse nests (Crawford et al. 1992, Gregg et al. 1994, Heath et al. 1997) and probably serves a similar function for ducks nesting in shrub communities near created wetlands. Where the proportion of ground occupied by big sagebrush exceeds 12–15% in drier climates, cover by grass and other herbaceous understory declines due to competition with root systems of shrubs (Winward 1991, Crawford et al. 1992, Goodrich et al. 1999). Thus, shrub thinning may be beneficial to ducks in some circumstances. A vigorous herbaceous understory also stabilizes soils better than a monotypic shrub stand. Burning is one tool that can be used to open up dense shrub communities and may be appropriate on a limited scale within wetland watersheds. Natural burn intervals in sagebrush-steppe ecosystems varied from 10 to 110 years depending on sagebrush subspecies and other ecological characteristics (Champlin and Winward 1982, Hironaka et al. 1983, Crane and Fisher 1986, Bunting et al. 1987, Winward 1991, Tart 1996). To avoid erosion problems and to maintain adequate blocks of habitat, no more than one-third of an upland management unit dominated by shrubs should be burned in any 20-year increment. Desirable patchy burns are accomplished during cool spring months, while burning during late summer frequently produces hot, complete burns.

Wetland Mitigation Projects

Various human actions affect natural and created wetlands. Where required, mitigation must compensate unavoidable, adverse impacts to wetlands in accordance with section 404 of the Clean Water Act, the Environmental Protection Agency's 404(b)(1) guidelines, the National Environmental Policy Act, the Fish and Wildlife Coordination Act, the Surface Mining Control and Reclamation Act, Federal Highway Administration Mitigation Policy, Executive Order 11990, and other agency mandates (see Chapter 1). Efforts to mitigate wetland impacts have achieved varied success and could be improved with better preconstruction evaluation, postconstruction monitoring, and management (see Chapter 9).

Highway projects are a major source of impacts to wetlands throughout the Intermountain West. Road widening and realignment projects often encroach on jurisdictional wetlands in borrow ditches, streams, and oxbows or in wetlands that were crossed by road construction prior to regulation under section 404. Other substantial impacts have accrued from large impoundments, canals and diversions, irrigation projects, agricultural conversions, residential housing developments, utilities and communications lines, pipelines, oil and gas developments, surface mines, and other industrial projects.

A common mitigation strategy is to create wetlands by modifying or converting remnant project features including mine pits, sand and gravel pits, borrow sites, sediment retention ponds, diversion ponds, and drainage systems. Often these features are less than ideal foundations, but their use for wetland basins saves cost in terms of land acquisition, equipment transport, excavation, and disposal of fill. Wetland basins may also be dug, graded, diked, or dammed on backfilled materials or native surfaces. Other mitigation strategies can employ rehabilitation of impaired wetlands, restoration of drained or breached wetland sites, or actions undertaken to enhance 1 or more functions within existing wetlands. Wetland mitigation is often integrated with project construction to take advantage of heavy equipment and engineering expertise available on the construction site. Not uncommonly, wetland mitigation projects fail or only partially succeed for any of the following reasons (Golet 1986, Miller 1987, D'Avanzo 1990, Erwin 1990, Kruczynski 1990, Levine and Willard 1990, McKinstry and Anderson 1994): insufficient preconstruction evaluation; inappropriate or ecologically degraded sites used for wetland construction; biological design concepts misunderstood or misapplied by project managers, field engineering staff, or equipment operators; failure to consult experienced biologists during final grading to help guide contouring operations; overestimation of constructed habitat values from design plans; inaccurate hydrologic predictions; improper management of land uses during or following wetland establishment; erosion control problems; lack of follow-up monitoring; inadequate length of evaluation period; damage or destruction by weather anomalies (e.g., heavy precipitation events, drought); lack of an enforceable commitment to correct failures; and lack of a long-term conservation agreement with a surface owner or another designated steward.

In most situations, application of standardized designs and management practices is a reasonable approach. However, some project managers lack experience to fully appreciate the functional interrelationships of wetland features or how local conditions can modify the performance of specific design elements. For this reason, involvement by an experienced biologist is essential during both the design and construction phases. The biologist should have the ability to make site-specific adjustments to the plan and to adapt construction procedures based on field conditions encountered during excavation and grading.

Wetlands built for mitigation, once established, should be low-maintenance, sustainable systems (Erwin 1990). The following procedures are recommended:

1. Mitigation objectives should be based on restoration of key ecological functions such as habitats of important species (Larson 1987).

2. The plan should incorporate proven, ecologically sound designs (Reimold and Cobler 1986), modified as necessary to address unique problems or conditions encountered at the mitigation site.

3. As a general rule, assume that engineering designs overestimate wetland attributes, particularly size.

4. To the extent practical, salvage wetland topsoil from affected sites and respread at mitigation sites.

5. Use local propagules to establish wetland plants (Reimold and Cobler 1986). If other wetlands exist nearby, natural seed dispersal will probably be sufficient to colonize the created wetland (Reinartz and Warne 1993). The process can be accelerated by obtaining substrate from existing wetlands to provide a seed and invertebrate inoculum for the created wetland (Dunn and Best 1983, Erwin and Best 1985, Erwin 1990).

6. The mitigation plan should stipulate success criteria or performance standards that must be met (Kruczynski 1990).

7. The parties responsible for mitigation must be identified in the plan, they must accept responsibility for success of the project, and they must agree to perform any remedial action necessary to correct problems or failures. This obligation must not be discharged except upon final inspection and clearance by the regulatory authority.

8. A stewardship agreement should be developed and included in the mitigation plan (Erwin 1990, Jensen and Platts 1990, Levine and Willard 1990, Lowry 1990). The agreement should identify parties responsible for maintenance (e.g., fence, dike repair) and management of land uses (e.g., grazing), it should set forth permissible land use practices in and near the wetland, and it should specify the condition in which the wetland must be maintained (Jensen and Platts 1990). Mitigation wetlands should be protected with a perpetual conservation easement if retained in private ownership, or they should be transferred to ownership by a governmental institution (Golet 1986, Erwin 1990) or a land trust organization.

9. As soon as final grading is complete, the mitigation site should be inspected for compliance with topographic design criteria. Vegetation should be inspected after the first growing season, then subsequently to verify successful establishment. During and after the first precipitation season, the site should be inspected for compliance with hydrologic criteria and for erosion stability.

10. A site could potentially be released from the contractor's responsibility after 2 growing seasons if basic design criteria have been met, hydrology and vegetation establishment are on track, and the site has a low risk for failure. A higher-risk site may require an evaluation period of up to 10 years. In some cases, it may be appropriate to require a per-

formance bond. If basic design criteria have been met, the site is stable, and hydrology is established, succession will generally produce wetland soils and vegetation.

Intensive Wetland Management Practices

Intensive management includes direct manipulations of wetland hydrology, chemistry, vegetation, or substrate and construction of special habitat features. Such activities are usually intended to maintain or enhance waterfowl and wading bird habitat. Intensive management can also include remedial actions to correct contamination or erosion problems, restoration of drained or degraded wetlands, and conversion of basins formed coincidentally by mining or other surface excavations (e.g., gravel pits). While intensive management can be extremely beneficial on a local scale, the techniques are too costly or otherwise impractical to apply on a large scale throughout the Intermountain West. Intensive wetland management is appropriate on state and federal habitat units and some privately managed areas, provided there is a long-term commitment of personnel and funding and a reliable water supply.

Water level management

Hydrology is the principal driving force behind wetland formation and function (Fredrickson and Taylor 1982; Larson 1982, 1987; U.S. Fish and Wildlife Service 1989; Marble 1992; Payne 1992). Accordingly, many authors advocate regulation of water level as a primary means to maintain and enhance habitat in created wetlands (Fredrickson and Reid 1986, Larson 1987, McMullen 1987, Sempek and Johnson 1987, Kadlec and Smith 1989, Reinecke et al. 1989, Merendino et al. 1990, Merendino and Smith 1991, Marble 1992, Payne 1992). Objectives can include controlling composition and distribution of marsh vegetation, moist soil management, stimulation of reproduction of submersed aquatic vegetation, aerobic decomposition and nutrient cycling, improvement of water quality, preparation of basins for prescribed burning or discing, consolidation of fine sediments to reduce turbidity, provision of access for maintenance and habitat development, and control of muskrats and rough fish.

Three features are imperative to manage water levels: a properly engineered water control structure, a dependable water supply, and a commitment of personnel. Most created wetland systems in the Intermountain West lack these features. Control structures are costly to install and maintain and require a long-term commitment of personnel to monitor and operate. Most impoundments also lack a dependable water supply, particularly during late summer and fall. Consequently, they cannot be refilled on demand. Hydrology of most western wetlands is predominantly weather-dependent and driven by watershed runoff (see Chapters 2, 3, and 9).

Impoundments with uncertain refilling capability should be managed as close to full pool as possible (Linde 1969, Payne 1992). Normal evaporative losses and periodic droughts are sufficient to draw water levels down and expose organic substrates, enabling aerobic decomposition to take place. Impoundments should be sized to maintain water quality and to completely fill and spill over most years to ensure that the water level is restored to the same elevation during most springs. Periodic flushing is an important process for diluting and removing accumulated salts and toxins (Green et al. 1964, Eisenlohr 1969, Nelson et al. 1978, Bachman 1988; also see Chapter 6). An oversized impoundment will fill to varying elevations, depending on precipitation, and this may retard establishment of emergent and wet-meadow margins. In addition, evaporative losses each season will concentrate salts, leading to water quality deterioration.

Green et al. (1964) suggested maintaining water depths between 15 and 45 cm in at least half of the impoundment basin, and the Atlantic Waterfowl Council (1972) recommended a basin gradient of <1% (<1 m elevation per 100 m horizontal) so up to 75% of the basin can be flooded <60 cm deep. Reimold and Cobler (1986) suggested a maximum basin gradient of 1:15. This would provide a zone 12 m wide between normal pool elevation and the 75 cm tolerance limit of deep-marsh plants.

Weller (1987) provides the following guidance for managing water levels consistently with habitat functions in mid-latitude states: constant, high-water levels are maintained to gradually reduce excessive emergent coverage; complete drawdowns are used where large portions of a marsh have become devoid of vegetation and extensive plant recovery is needed; partial drawdowns are used when vegetation needs to be encouraged; partial drawdowns reduce water levels to meadow-like depths in early summer to encourage germination and growth of emergent and submersed plants, especially at the marsh perimeter; water levels are maintained low in late summer and returned to normal levels in fall, prior to the hunting season; in some cases, winter drawdowns can be effective and will not interfere with hunting, although muskrats are adversely affected; and reflooding should be a gradual process to avoid flotation of dead emergents, scouring of other plants, and excessive turbidity. As vegetation recovers, the water regime should be adjusted to maintain a desired plant community structure. The appropriate length of drawdown in any particular situation varies and is determined through monitoring. Substrate drying and breakdown of plant litter and organic sediments may require most of the growing season.

Nelson et al. (1978) recommended the following water level regime to improve western reservoirs: (1) raise water levels to maximum capacity from 1 March to mid-May, (2) maintain stable water levels from mid-May to July, (3) abruptly reduce water levels during the first 2 weeks of July, (4) raise water levels again beginning in October to flood feeding areas for migratory waterfowl, and (5) lower water levels to minimum pool from late October through December. This manipulation will produce maximum wetland vegetation diversity and production while enhancing nutrient cycling.

If alternative wetland habitats are available nearby, partial or complete drawdowns are recommended every 2 to 5 years to maintain wetland productivity (Harris and Marshall 1963; Linde 1969, 1971; Whitman 1974). Ideally, several (5–7) diked marsh units should be built and managed in rotation to maintain different stages of succession (Weller 1978, Fredrickson and Reid 1986, Reinecke et al. 1989). Discing or tilling is sometimes done in conjunction with controlled drawdowns. This practice fractures the soil, increases its reactive surface, facilitates aeration, releases bound nutrients, and may be used to control emergents (Linde 1969, Curry 1977, Taylor 1977, Fredrickson and Reid 1986, Payne 1992, U.S. Department of Agriculture Soil Conservation Service 1992). Wetland substrates containing concentrations of dissolved toxins should probably not be tilled. However, tilling has been found effective for redistributing lead shot from the top 6 cm of wetland soil to depths where it is not accessible to waterfowl (Fredrickson et al. 1977, Peters and Afton 1993, Thomas et al. 1999).

Moist-soil management

Moist-soil management is a technique used to encourage growth of waterfowl food plants on diked, nearly level marsh units. Moist-soil plants also decompose readily and provide a source of detritus for invertebrates after reflooding in the fall (Godshalk and Wetzel 1978). Accurate water level control in 2.5–7.5 cm increments is essential for effective moist soil management (Fredrickson and Taylor 1982, Sempek and Johnson 1987, Weller 1987, Payne 1992). The stop-log control structure is a dependable, relatively inexpensive device for achieving precise water level manipulations (Fredrickson and Taylor 1982, Payne 1992).

Water levels are reduced in mid- to late summer to encourage germination of wet-meadow plants including smartweed, sedges, dock, pigweed, rice cutgrass, sprangletop, and beggerticks; then the area is flooded incrementally during fall (Hamor et al. 1968, Fredrickson and Taylor 1982, Weller 1987, Kierstead undated). Another strategy is to reflood substrates, then slowly lower water levels to expose new foods for migrating and wintering waterfowl. Water level management for shorebirds and wading birds involves dropping water levels slowly through the fall migration period to expose mud flats and concentrate prey items (Frederickson and Reid 1986). Moist-soil water regimes are generally incompatible with waterfowl breeding and brood-rearing functions. In locations where waterfowl production is a priority, moist-soil management could be practiced on 1 or 2 units within a complex of diked marsh units. In northern climates and higher elevations, mid- to late-summer drawdowns are not considered an effective strategy because the amount of food production is negligible (Linde 1969). Growing seasons are shorter, and consequently early season drawdowns (May, June) are needed to maximize germination and to allow maturation of food plants before reflooding (Meeks 1969, Beule 1979, Merendino et al. 1990, Merendino and Smith 1991). However, it is unwise to sacrifice brood production to attract migrating ducks during the brief period prior to freeze-up.

Emergent vegetation management

Two distinct patterns of emergent vegetation grow in created wetlands throughout the Intermountain West. The more common is a relatively narrow emergent fringe along shorelines of steeper basins such as abandoned mine pits or borrow sites and most livestock ponds. The less common pattern is emergent growth throughout shallow basins such as diked marshes or reservoir backwaters. Although management approaches are different, the objective in both cases is to increase or decrease emergent coverage to optimum ranges for target species.

DEEP WETLANDS

It is common for created palustrine wetlands to have deep central areas and sloped margins that support narrow emergent fringes. This kind of topography occurs in stock ponds, borrow pits, and abandoned mine ponds. Strips of shoreline vegetation are essential brood cover (Lokemoen 1973, Evans and Kerbs 1977, Hudson 1983, Belanger and Couture 1988, Marble 1992) and protect banks from wave erosion, especially where longer wind fetch exists (Weller 1987, Foote and Kadlec 1988, Levine and Willard 1990, Marble 1992). McKinstry and Anderson (2002) recommended 15–30% emergent cover to provide waterfowl habitat in wetlands predominantly of this configuration in northeast Wyoming.

Waterfowl and shorebirds prefer shallow, open segments of shore for feeding and loafing (Hamor et al. 1968, Linde 1969, Lokemoen 1973), but several species also require vegetated shore segments for cover and concealment. Controlled grazing can be applied to produce lengths of open, grassy shoreline (Bosenmaier 1964, Bue et al. 1964, Hamor et al. 1968, Kantrud and Stewart 1984, Kantrud 1986). In larger impoundments, open segments of shore should be located on the upwind side and should alternate with intact strips of emergents. Alternate intervals of open shoreline and emergent strips 6–12 m in length are a good mix.

Cattle should not be permitted to completely strip vegetation or trample the shoreline. Root mats should remain intact. Cattle should be removed when residual stubble is 2.5–5.0 cm in cleared sections of shoreline in order to maintain stable banks.

SHALLOW WETLANDS

Shallow marshes covered by dense stands of emergent plants are poor habitat for waterfowl and wading birds (Evans and Black 1956, Linde 1969, Smith 1969, Beule and Janisch 1973, Beule 1979, Reid et al. 1989, Payne 1992). At the opposite extreme, turbid conditions and scouring from wind action can suppress productivity in wetlands that lack emergent vegetation (Marble 1992). The most productive marshes contain interspersed patches of emergent vegetation, open shallow (<45 cm) water, and permanent deeper (>75 cm) water. Stands of emergent vegetation form "baffles" that moderate wind, current, and wave influences but permit circulation and export organic detritus to the open-water phase of the marsh system. Dabbling ducks and wading birds obtain most of their food in shallow pockets of open water <45 cm deep. These semi-protected areas support submersed aquatic vegetation, benthic and epiphytic invertebrate populations, and seed-producing emergent plants (see Chapters 6 and 9 of this volume).

Waterfowl managers recommend maintaining stands of emergent vegetation interspersed throughout 30–70% of a wetland basin, with 50% considered an optimal "hemi-marsh" condition (Patterson 1976; Voigts 1976; Whitman 1976; Weller 1978, 1987; Kaminski and Prince 1981; Fredrickson and Reid 1986; Belanger and Couture 1988; Bookhout et al. 1989; Pederson et al. 1989; Payne 1992). Sizes and arrangements of emergent and open-water patches should vary. Patches ranging from 0.1 to 0.2 ha have been suggested, with some open-water patches up to 4 ha in larger marsh units (Ambrose et al. 1983). Diving ducks are attracted to more open wetlands. For example, canvasbacks prefer wetlands with <33% emergent cover (Stoudt 1982), although they will often nest on densely vegetated ponds. Canada geese prefer wetlands with approximately 10% emergent cover (Ringelman 1990). However, the hemi-marsh condition supports a maximum diversity of avian species.

Raising the water level and maintaining a depth >61 cm gradually opens up dense stands of emergents and produces lakelike conditions

(Weller 1978, 1987; Kantrud and Stewart 1984). Maintaining water depth >110 cm will kill most emergent plants in a single growing season (Weller 1990). Where predominantly open water has developed, recovery of emergent plants can be stimulated by early to mid-summer draw-downs, which expose mud flats and shallows for seed germination and rhizomatous sprouting (Rundle and Fredrickson 1981, Merendino et al. 1990, Merendino and Smith 1991, Marble 1992). Such areas are re-flooded to shallow (15–45 cm) depths the following spring. This process may have to be repeated several years to achieve recovery. Fluctuating water depths of 15–45 cm provide ideal habitat for waterfowl but may eventually lead to encroachment by dense emergent stands. As this happens, treatments are required to restore a satisfactory interspersion of the open-water phase. Salinity issues (see Chapter 6) and colonization by undesirable plants may also need to be addressed.

The most foolproof way to achieve a long-term mosaic of shallow, open-water, and emergent patches is by varying the basin elevations during initial construction of an impoundment (Weller 1978, Marble 1992). After a wetland has become established, reshaping its basin can be a very costly project and may require draining and drying the wetland unit. After drying, heavy equipment can be used to deepen portions of the basin (Weller 1987, Payne 1992), to grade mounds that rise to within 30 cm below the normal pool elevation (Payne 1992), and to form small islands. In some circumstances, a floating dredge can be used or a dragline can be walked down dikes to accomplish limited work within range of the boom.

METHODS FOR CONTROLLING EMERGENT VEGETATION

Excessive emergent coverage can be reduced by a variety of techniques in addition to, or in place of, water level manipulation. Muskrat herbivory is an invaluable natural process. Not only do muskrats clear openings in dense emergent stands, but their lodges also provide loafing and nesting islands for waterfowl (Payne 1992). When muskrat populations exceed carrying capacity of a marsh, "eat-outs" can lead to nearly complete removal of emergent plants (Dozier 1953, Payne 1992). Excessive muskrat populations can be controlled by trapping and by over-winter drawdowns, but trapping may not be feasible, depending on pelt prices and trapper interest.

An effective mechanical treatment to clear openings is to cut emergent plant stems close to the ground or ice during low water, usually late fall or winter. Once cut stems are flooded, the plants fail to resprout the following spring. Stem severing methods include burning (Linde 1985, Smith and Kadlec 1985, Weller 1987, Mensik 1990), mowing and cutting

(Linde 1969, Weller 1975, 1987), discing (Fredrickson and Reid 1986, Mensik 1990), crushing (Beule and Janisch 1973), or grazing and trampling (Bosenmaier 1964, Kantrud 1986). Cutting emergents with tools or equipment can be labor-intensive, but this method allows greater control over the location, arrangement, and size of openings. If cattails are mowed, nesting islands can be created by baling cut emergent stems and leaving the bales in place.

Some investigators advocate herbicides (e.g., 2,4-D, Dalapon, Roundup) to control emergent plants (Rollings and Warden 1964, Beule and Janisch 1973), but their application to aquatic systems can be risky. Nontarget species can be killed directly or damaged by sublethal effects (Engel 1990, Payne 1992). For general control of emergent plants, muskrat herbivory, water level manipulations, or mechanical treatments are recommended. Herbicide application is an effective way to remove woody vegetation from dikes or islands where it is not wanted (Rollings and Warden 1964, Linde 1969) and to control invasive species.

Transplants

Emergent and submersed plants readily colonize new wetlands without assistance unless the site is extremely isolated from other established wetlands (Eng et al. 1979, Levine and Willard 1990, Payne 1992, Reinartz and Warne 1993). A viable seed bank persists for decades in most wetland soils after draining. Therefore, wetland restoration projects seldom need to be seeded (Weller 1987, Payne 1992). It can also be costly and ineffective to plant preferred wildlife forage in wetlands unless the plants are a dominant species in that particular environment or the site can be managed actively to sustain them (Odum 1987, Weller 1987). Areas that tend to remain open are difficult locations in which to establish emergents (Weller 1978, 1990).

Transplanting emergent vegetation to created wetlands can be useful in two situations: to colonize a new wetland built in an extremely isolated location (Eng et al. 1979, McKinstry and Anderson 2002) and to help stabilize erosive shorelines, provided wave energy can be dissipated with a temporary structure (Berge 1987). It is more effective to transplant emergents from established wetlands in the surrounding region than to obtain nursery stock (Levine and Willard 1990, Payne 1992). An effective transplanting technique is to dig up plants, then wrap their root masses in pieces of cheesecloth or burlap weighted with a stone or nail (Addy and MacNamara 1948, Berge 1987, Levine and Willard 1990). The weighted transplants are deposited in protected, shallow water, where roots grow through the fabric and anchor the plants. After clumps of vegetation are transplanted, it is important that they remain at suitable water depth throughout the growing season.

Another effective method to accelerate colonization by locally adapted plants and invertebrates is to "inoculate" new wetlands with substrate obtained from established wetlands in the region (Miller 1987, U.S. Department of Agriculture Soil Conservation Service 1992). Submersed plants, particularly those drifted into windrows, can be collected with a rake or grappling hook (Erickson 1964). If the new wetland is a mitigation site, development of wetland features can be greatly accelerated by dressing the basin with 15–30 cm of soil salvaged from a donor wetland (Lokemoen 1973, Lowry 1990, Marble 1992, Payne 1992, U.S. Department of Agriculture Soil Conservation Service 1992).

Where wave action prevents establishment of emergent plants, particularly on downwind shorelines, a floating log boom or tire barrier can be placed to buffer wave action temporarily (Allen and Klimas 1986, Foote and Kadlec 1988, Weller 1990, Payne 1992). Floating booms consist of logs attached end to end with a chain and held at least 1.8 m offshore by perpendicular logs anchored between the boom and shore.

Wetland deepening

Two methods commonly used to deepen wetlands are level ditching and pothole blasting. Level ditches are linear excavations dug in shallow marshes, wet meadows, or areas where the permanent water table is within 40 cm of the surface (Atlantic Waterfowl Council 1972, Johnson 1984, Payne 1992). This practice requires a dragline and is impractical except on large, intensively managed wetland units. The purposes of level ditches are to improve the interspersion ratio of open water to emergent vegetation, improve habitat for waterfowl and furbearers, provide access corridors and circulation throughout a marsh, and provide nesting islands comprised of spoil banks (Mathiak and Linde 1956, Atlantic Waterfowl Council 1972, Broschart and Linder 1986, Hoffman 1988). Level ditches improve circulation of water, oxygen, and nutrients and permit export of organic detritus from emergent stands to open-water zones, thereby enhancing production of invertebrates and submersed plants. They also provide growing sites for submersed aquatic plants. Weller (1978) questioned the aesthetic characteristics (e.g., spoil banks) of level ditches. However, this is a reasonable, cost-effective method for establishing relatively long-lasting open-water areas, particularly within marsh units where sediment accumulation has impaired function, in units that are too shallow for vegetation treatments to have a persistent effect, and where manipulating water level is not an option. The functional life of ditches is about 30 years (Hammond and Lacy 1959).

In marshes with an elevation gradient, level ditches must be oriented along contours. Otherwise, improper ditching could desiccate large portions of the marsh. On flat marshes, level ditches should be dug in 30–90 m segments configured in a 10–30° zigzagged pattern and oriented perpendicularly to prevailing winds (Atlantic Waterfowl Council 1972). Ditches should be spaced 60–120 m apart and 2–4 m deep and should be 3–9 m wide. One side of the ditch should be sloped at 5:1 (horizontal: vertical), with the other side 2:1 in most soil types. Segments of spoil banks should be offset 1 m from the ditch. They should be approximately 1.5 m high, 12 m long, flat on top, placed on alternating sides of the ditch, and spaced 3 m apart (end to end). A grass and legume mix should be seeded to stabilize spoil banks and provide dense nesting cover.

Potholes are shallow depressions that contain open water and provide breeding territories, brood habitat, and feeding areas for ducks (Atlantic Waterfowl Council 1972). They are constructed in similar situations and provide similar functions as level ditches, except that they do not provide access or circulation throughout a marsh. Potholes may be excavated with equipment or blasted. Excavated potholes last longer; however, blasted potholes are less costly to build. Specific prescriptions for blasting potholes vary depending on substrate and desired results. Hopper (1971) determined that three 23 kg charges of ammonium nitrate and fuel oil planted 4.5 m apart produced the best results. The most efficient charge was a single 34 kg charge, on average, producing a 53 m^2 pothole of 8.2 m diameter when detonated in a charge hole 75 cm deep (Hopper 1972).

Islands and peninsulas

Islands provide secure loafing, resting, and nesting locations for many water birds; they increase the productive shoreline interface; and they help buffer larger wetlands from excessive wind and wave action (Giroux 1981, Lokemoen et al. 1984, Hoffman 1988, Marble 1992, Payne 1992, Lokemoen and Messmer 1993, 1994). Building islands is accomplished most efficiently during the initial construction of a wetland. However, many created wetlands in the Intermountain West—stock ponds and mine pits, for example—are not suitable for island construction due to steep basin slopes and deep water. Construction and maintenance costs can become excessive where normal water depth exceeds 0.6–0.9 m (Jones 1975, Lokemoen and Messmer 1993). Better opportunities for island construction exist in diked marsh units, backwaters of shallow reservoirs, and some wetland mitigation projects.

Where island construction is feasible, several small (0.04–0.08 ha) islands are better than a single large island, to discourage mammalian predators, and they are less expensive to build (Hoffman 1988, Payne 1992, Lokemoen and Messmer 1993). In wetlands >4 ha, islands can be located closer to the upwind side to reduce erosion problems (Eng et al 1979). Lokemoen and Messmer (1993) indicated that the most effective islands for waterfowl nest success are 100–450 m from shore, but this is impractical in most created wetlands. Other authors recommend locating islands at least 9 m from shore (Eng et al. 1979, Marble 1992). Normal water depth should be 0.50–0.75 m between the island and shore (Hammond and Mann 1956, Jones 1975). Placing islands in wetlands <0.6 ha is not recommended. Large islands should also not be built in small wetlands (Payne 1992).

Constructing peninsulas in existing wetlands has limited application due to the volume of earth moving required. Consequently, this feature has greater potential if considered in design plans for new wetlands. Marble (1992), Payne (1992), and Lokemoen and Messmer (1994) discussed peninsula design and engineering considerations.

Wetland enlargement

As a general rule, larger impoundments receive more waterfowl use and are more likely to retain water through the summer for brood rearing (Lokemoen 1973, Mack and Flake 1980, Hudson 1983, Belanger and Couture 1988, Leschisin et al. 1992, Marble 1992, McKinstry et al. 2001, McKinstry and Anderson 2002). However, complexes that include wetlands as small as 0.05 ha can be important for maintenance and dispersal of wetland-dependent species with limited mobility, such as amphibians and aquatic reptiles (Gibbs 1993).

Minimum management units for seasonal and semipermanent wetlands were assumed to be 0.04 and 0.8 ha, respectively (Payne 1992). Hudson (1983) determined that impoundments <0.5 ha received limited use by duck broods. Lokemoen (1973) recommended a minimum effective impoundment size of 0.6 ha. McKinstry and Anderson (2002) recommended that wetlands constructed for waterfowl be at least 1 ha. Species richness increases in wetlands <4 ha (Williams 1985, Brown and Dinsmore 1986).

Isolated wetlands should be larger and deeper. Raising the dike or outflow structure can increase the size of an existing wetland, provided the water supply is adequate (Weller 1990). Adjacent contours that will form the backwaters of the enlarged wetland should be considered in planning the water level to maximize shallow zonation and shoreline diversity.

Wetland complexes

Complexes of several wetland types in close proximity increase wildlife diversity and waterfowl production (Stoudt 1971; Kantrud and Stewart 1977; Ruwaldt et al. 1979; Swanson et al. 1979; Mack and Flake 1980; Kantrud and Stewart 1984; Williams 1985; Brown and Dinsmore 1986; Weller 1987; Fredrickson and Reid 1988; McKinstry and Anderson 1994, 2002). Proctor et al. (1983a,b,c) recommended a pond density of at least 1/km². McKinstry and Anderson (2002) recommended at least 5 wetlands within a 1 km² area to create functional complexes of wetlands on reclaimed land. Complexes of shallow, seasonal, or intermittent wetlands can be developed by constructing low dikes within tributary drainages <0.8 km from an existing wetland or stock pond (Linde 1969, Lokemoen 1973), provided the runoff they intercept does not adversely affect the water budget of the existing impoundment or wetland. A shallow basin could also be excavated or impounded below the outlet structure of an existing impoundment (Gabelhouse et al. 1982).

Artificial nest structures

Artificial nest structures can increase nest success in localized areas (Burger and Webster 1964, Doty et al. 1975, Payne 1992). However, Weller (1978) commented that nest structures are an intensive, species-oriented approach that accounts for a very small fraction of annual recruitment and cannot be justified where natural habitat alternatives exist. Many artificial nest structures are aesthetically unappealing. Where there is local public participation or where a budget has been set aside for construction and maintenance of nest structures, this practice can have some value.

GOOSE NEST STRUCTURES

Nest structures are commonly erected to increase production of Canada geese. Canada geese are an important source of recreation, but dense populations can become a nuisance in urban areas and can depredate agricultural crops. These concerns are not as prevalent in the Intermountain West as elsewhere but should be considered before erecting large numbers of structures in specific locations. To be effective, structures should be placed only near suitable brood-rearing habitat, which includes relatively large, permanent wetlands, rivers, or lakes. The most common and least expensive structure is the "missile" type—a single post mounted with a plywood platform and discarded tire (Ball 1990). Steel posts about 3.0 m long are driven 1–2 m into the mud to prevent ice damage. Steel fins can be welded to the base to increase stability. Initially, structures should be located at least 15 m off shore and at least 1 m above the water (Ball et al. 1988). Structures in shallow water or on land are less susceptible to ice damage. Structures can be moved closer to shore and onto dry land as geese become accustomed to using them. Nest platforms should be spaced at least 90 m apart. Structures on land should elevate platforms 2 m above ground level to deter predators. The tire must be bedded annually with hay or other suitable nesting material. Payne (1992) described more aesthetically acceptable structures, but their cost is much higher. A commitment of time and resources to annually repair and maintain nest structures must also be included in an effective program.

DUCK NEST STRUCTURES

Cavity-nesting species including wood duck, bufflehead, goldeneye, merganser, and others can be encouraged by a variety of nest box designs (see Payne 1992). Predation is reduced by erecting nest boxes in at least 0.6 m of water, or at least 3–6 m above ground if placed on land. Nest boxes can be also affixed to trees in suitable locations.

Doty (1979) described an inexpensive and effective nest structure for mallards and other puddle ducks. A long cone with one end open and the other nearly closed is fashioned of 1.3 cm hardware mesh and mounted horizontally on a steel post 6 cm in diameter. The open end of the cone is 35 cm in diameter. Total length is 80 cm. An overhead shelter made of sheet aluminum or asphalt roofing paper is installed inside the mesh to provide concealment from avian predators. Cones are mounted approximately 1 m above water and bedded with straw. In windy regions, the mesh cone may require reinforcement with heavy-gauge wire or a wood frame (also see Ball et al. 1988).

Simple, inexpensive nesting islands for both ducks and geese can be created by depositing large round or square hay bales in water <0.6 m deep within a managed marsh unit (Ball et al. 1988). These are positioned on ice during winter in locations where ice drift is not a problem. Once in place, hay bales will last up to 5 years. Decomposing hay also provides a supplemental source of detritus that increases invertebrate populations (Street 1982, Green and Salter 1987).

Conclusion and Recommendations

Created palustrine wetlands are valuable resources throughout the Intermountain West. However, the ecological condition of too many wetlands is impaired and could be improved with better management. Despite the national attention given to wetlands, public and private organizations responsible for or interested in better stewardship of created wetlands are faced with many challenges. Some of the more serious challenges include insufficient funding and personnel to carry out management, failure to make effective use of available institutions and regulatory programs, lack of resources to monitor and document problems, and social and political resistance to reformation of land use policies and traditions.

Any created wetland, especially those built for mitigation, should be designed and constructed such that the least amount of maintenance is required. Wetland systems that rely on dikes, levees, or other water control structures, or that receive heavy public use, will require periodic maintenance. Payne (1992) described procedures for repairing dikes, stabilizing shorelines, managing vegetation, controlling nuisance species, and other aspects of marsh maintenance. Where maintenance is necessary, a mechanism assuring permanent funding and assignment of maintenance responsibility should accompany the mitigation agreement (Levine and Willard 1990, Lowry 1990).

Various public and private funding sources are available to support facets of wetland management. One of the more prolific sources is the North American Wetland Conservation Act (NAWCA), administered through numerous joint venture organizations. Most of the Intermountain West is within the administrative boundary of the Intermountain West Joint Venture. Other major funding initiatives for wetland acquisition, restoration, and improvements are: the U.S. Fish and Wildlife Service's Partners for Wildlife, Landowner Incentive Program, Private Stewardship Grants, Federal Aid, and Duck Stamp programs; federal farm bill provisions including the Wetland Reserve Program, Wildlife Habitat Incentive Program, and Environmental Quality Incentive Program; the Abandoned Mine Lands Fund administered through the Federal Office of Surface Mining; the Transportation Equity Act administered by the Federal Highway Administration; the Land and Water Conservation Fund administered through four federal agencies—the U.S. Forest Service, National Park Service, U.S. Fish and Wildlife Service, and Bureau of Reclamation; and mitigation funds available through the Central Utah Project. A plethora of private granting institutions also fund conservation projects that may include various aspects of wetland creation, acquisition, and improvement. Ducks Unlimited is perhaps the foremost privately funded organization with a wetland conservation mission. The Environmental Data Research Institute periodically publishes a comprehensive directory of granting institutions (Environmental Data Research Institute 2001).

Public involvement processes associated with agency actions at local, state, and national levels afford innumerable opportunities to improve management of created wetlands and watersheds (see Chapter 1). The effectiveness of participation is increased by a thorough understanding of the legal and regulatory provisions under which agency actions are conducted, by sound technical knowledge of wetland processes and management practices, and by affiliation with organizations or agencies having acknowledged conservation credentials. Many actions affecting wetlands are open to public scrutiny. These range from small, individually permitted projects to major land use and resource management plans, entire agency programs, policies, and legislation. The sphere of influence by a person or organization can increase dramatically through active involvement in public comment processes of the major agencies that fund, permit, or authorize actions affecting wetlands. Within the Intermountain West, the major land, resource management, and regulatory agencies include the U.S. Forest Service, Bureau of Land Management, Bureau of Reclamation, National Park Service, U.S. Fish and Wildlife Service, Environmental Protection Agency, Federal Office of Surface Mining, Army Corps of Engineers, Natural Resources Conservation Service, Federal Highway Administration, and Federal Housing Administration. Many state governments also administer state primacy programs under various authorities granted by these agencies, and some counties and local governments have progressive public involvement processes with respect to local zoning and permitting decisions.

Additional research and inventory data are a legitimate need in some circumstances. Fundamental concepts and principles of wetland management have been thoroughly studied and are largely transferable to the Intermountain West. New research should be problem-solving in nature and designed to address unique management issues encountered in the Intermountain West. Examples include research to develop techniques for dealing with excessive salinity, acid-forming materials, colloidal suspension, and difficult plant establishment. In some cases, the effectiveness of management can be improved with better site information, especially regarding abiotic factors. However, pragmatic managers generally recognize that available resources accomplish greater benefit if used to implement prescriptive strategies, especially in low-risk sites and noncontroversial situations. More intensive data collection and research can be necessary to address problem sites and situations in which mitigation or management recommendations are likely to become controversial.

Literature Cited

Addy, C. E., and L. G. MacNamara. 1948. Waterfowl management on small areas. Wildlife Management Institute, Washington, D.C., USA.

Allen, H., and C. V. Klimas. 1986. Reservoir shoreline revegetation guidelines. U.S. Army Engineering Waterways Experiment Station Technical Report E-86-13.

Ambrose, R. E., C. R. Hinkle, and C. R. Wenzel. 1983. Practices for protecting and enhancing fish and wildlife on coal surface-mined land in the south-central U.S. U.S. Fish and Wildlife Service FWS/OBS-83/11.

Atlantic Waterfowl Council. 1972. Techniques handbook of waterfowl habitat and management. Second edition. Atlantic Waterfowl Council. Bethany Beach, Delaware, USA.

Bachman, V. C. 1988. Acquisition, design, and development strategies utilized on the Weber delta unit of Ogden Bay waterfowl management area. Pages 162-168 in K. M. Mutz, D. J. Cooper, M. L. Scott, and L. K. Miller, technical coordinators. Restoration, creation, and management of wetland and riparian ecosystems in the American West. Proceedings of the symposium of the Rocky Mountain Chapter of Wetland Scientists 14-16 November 1988. Denver, Colorado, USA.

Ball, I. J. 1990. Artificial nest structures for Canada geese. Pages 1-8 in D. H. Cross, compiler. Waterfowl management handbook. U.S. Fish and Wildlife Service Fish and Wildlife Leaflet 13.2.12.

————, S. K. Ball, and F. B. Lee. 1988. Artificial nest structures for mallards and Canada geese: a handbook. U.S. Fish and Wildlife Service Technical Report.

Belanger, L., and R. Couture. 1988. Use of man-made ponds by dabbling duck broods. Journal of Wildlife Management 52:718-723.

Berge, D. A. 1987. Native plants, fish introduced in a lake restoration effort (Wisconsin). Note Number 30. Restoration Management Notes 5(1):35.

Beule, J. D. 1971. Evaluation of wetland impoundments on state-owned wildlife areas. Progress Report, Project Number W-141-R-7, Study Number 304. Wisconsin Department of Natural Resources, Madison, Wisconsin, USA.

————. 1979. Control and management of cattails in southeastern Wisconsin wetlands. Wisconsin Department of Natural Resources Technical Bulletin 112.

————, and T. Janisch. 1973. Experimental wetland management on state-owned wildlife areas. Progress Report, Bureau Research Project Number W-141-R-8, Study Number 309. Madison, Wisconsin. Wisconsin Department of Natural Resources.

Bookhout, T. A., K. E. Bednarik, and R. W. Kroll. 1989. The Great Lakes marshes. Pages 131-156 in L. M. Smith, R. L. Pederson, and R. M. Kaminski, editors. Habitat management for migrating and wintering waterfowl in North America. Texas Tech University Press, Lubbock, Texas, USA.

Bosenmaier, E. F. 1964. Cows and cutter bars. Pages 627-634 in J. P. Linduska, editor. Waterfowl tomorrow. U.S. Fish and Wildlife Service. Washington D.C., USA.

Bowen, B. S., and A. D. Kruse. 1993. Effects of grazing on nesting by upland sandpipers in south-central North Dakota. Journal of Wildlife Management. 57:291-301.

Brockmann, S. 1993. Grazing management for streamside areas. Habitat Extension Bulletin Number 47. Wyoming Cooperative Fish and Wildlife Research Unit, University of Wyoming, Laramie, Wyoming, and Wyoming Game and Fish Department, Cheyenne, Wyoming, USA.

Broschart, M. R., and R. L. Linder. 1986. Aquatic invertebrates in level ditches and adjacent emergent marsh in a South Dakota wetland. Prairie Naturalist. 18:167-178.

Brown, M., and J. J. Dinsmore. 1986. Implications of marsh size and isolation for marsh bird management. Journal of Wildlife Management. 50:392-397.

Bue, I. G., H. G. Uhlig, and F. D. Smith. 1964. Stock ponds and dugouts. Pages 391-

398 *in* J. P. Linduska, editor. Waterfowl tomorrow. U.S. Fish and Wildlife Service, Washington D.C., USA.

Bunting, S. C., B. M. Kilgore, and C. L. Bushey. 1987. Guidelines for prescribed burning sagebrush-grass rangelands in the northern Great Basin. U.S. Forest Service Intermountain Research Station General Technical Report INT-231.

Burger, G. V., and C. G. Webster. 1964. Instant nesting habitat. Pages 655–666 *in* J. P. Linduska, editor. Waterfowl tomorrow. U.S. Fish and Wildlife Service, Washington, D.C., USA.

Chabreck, R. H., T. Joanen, and S. L. Paulus. 1989. Southern coastal marshes and lakes. Pages 249–277 *in* L. M. Smith, R. L. Pederson, and R. M. Kaminski, editors. Habitat management for migrating and wintering waterfowl in North America. Texas Tech University Press, Lubbock, Texas, USA.

Champlin, M. R., and A. H. Winward. 1982. The effect of simulated fire on emergence of seeds found in the soil of big sagebrush communities. Abstracts of Papers. Society of Rangeland Management. Calgary, Alberta, Canada.

Chaney, E., W. Elmore, and W. S. Platts. 1993. Managing change: livestock grazing on western riparian areas. U.S. Environmental Protection Agency, Denver, Colorado, USA.

Clary, W. P., and B. F. Webster. 1989. Managing grazing of riparian areas in the intermountain region. U.S. Forest Service General Technical Report INT-263.

Crane, M. F., and W. C. Fisher. 1986. Fire ecology of the forest habitat types of central Idaho. U.S. Forest Service Intermountain Research Station General Technical Report INT-218, Ogden, Utah, USA.

Crawford, J. A., M. A. Gregg, M. S. Drut, and A. K. DeLong. 1992. Habitat use by female sage grouse during the breeding season in Oregon. Final report submitted to the Bureau of Land Management Department of Fisheries and Wildlife, Oregon State University, Corvallis, Oregon, USA.

Curry, R. L. 1977. Reinhabiting the earth: life support and the future primitive. Pages 1–24 *in* J. Cairns Jr., K. L. Dickson, and E. E. Herricks. Recovery and restoration of damaged ecosystems. University Press of Virginia, Charlottesville, Virginia, USA.

D'Avanzo, C. 1990. Long-term evaluation of wetland creation projects. Pages 487–496 *in* J. A. Kusler and M. E. Kentula, editors. Wetland creation and restoration: the status of the science. Island Press, Covelo, California, USA.

Davis, A. M. 1979. Wetland succession, fire, and the pollen record: a midwestern example. American Midland Naturalist. 102:86–94.

Dillard, J. G. 1982. Missouri pond handbook. Missouri Department of Conservation, Jefferson City, Missouri, USA.

Doty, H. A. 1979. Duck nest structure evaluations in prairie wetlands. Journal of Wildlife Management 43:976–979.

———, F. B. Lee, and A. D. Kruse. 1975. Use of elevated nest baskets by ducks. Wildlife Society Bulletin 3:68–73.

Dozier, H. L. 1953. Muskrat production and management. U.S. Fish and Wildlife Service Circular 18.

Dunn, W. J., and G. R. Best. 1983. Enhancing ecological succession: 5. Seed bank survey of some Florida marshes and role of seed banks in marsh reclamation. Pages 365–370 *in* Proceedings of the 1983 symposium on surface mining, hydrology, sedimentology, and reclamation. University of Kentucky, Lexington, Kentucky, USA.

Dwyer, D. D., J. C. Buckhouse, and W. S. Huey. 1984. Impacts of grazing intensity and specialized grazing systems on use and value of rangeland: summary and recommendations. Pages 867–884 *in* Developing strategies for rangeland management. Westview Press. Boulder, Colorado, USA.

Eisenlohr, W. S. Jr. 1969. Hydrology of small water areas in the prairie pothole region. Pages 35–39 *in* Saskatoon wetlands seminar. Canadian Wildlife Service Report Series Number 6. Ottawa, Ontario, Canada.

Elmore, W., and R. L. Beschta. 1987. Riparian areas: perceptions in management. Rangelands. 9:260–265.

Eng, R. L., J. D. Jones, and F. M. Gjersling. 1979. Construction and management of stockponds for waterfowl. U.S. Bureau of Land Management Technical Bulletin 170.

Engel, S. 1990. Ecosystem responses to growth and control of submerged macrophytes: a literature review. Wisconsin Department of Natural Resources Technical Bulletin 170.

Environmental Data Research Institute. 2001. Environmental Grantmaking Foundations. Environmental Data Resources, Rochester, New York, USA.

Erickson, R. C. 1964. Planting and misplantings. Pages 579–592 *in* J. P. Linduska, editor. Waterfowl tomorrow. U.S. Fish and Wildlife Service, Washington, D.C., USA.

Erwin, K. L. 1990. Freshwater marsh creation and restoration in the southeast. Pages 233–265 *in* J. A. Kusler and M. E. Kentula, editors. Wetland creation and restoration: the status of the science. Island Press, Covelo, California, USA.

————, and G. R. Best. 1985. Marsh community development in a central Florida phosphate surface-mined reclaimed wetland. Wetlands. 5:155–166.

Evans, C. D., and K. E. Black. 1956. Duck production studies on the prairie potholes of South Dakota. U.S. Fish and Wildlife Service Special Science Report-Wildlife Number 32.

Evans, K. E., and R. R. Kerbs. 1977. Avian use of livestock watering ponds in western South Dakota. U.S. Forest Service General Technical Report RM-35, Saint Paul, Minnesota, USA.

Feldhamer, G. A. 1979. Vegetation and edaphic factors affecting abundance and distribution of small mammals in southeast Oregon. Great Basin Naturalist. 39:207–218.

Foote, A. L., and J. A. Kadlec. 1988. Effects of wave energy on plant establishment in shallow lacustrine wetlands. Journal Freshwater Ecology 4:523–532.

Fredrickson, L. H., T. S. Baskett, G. K. Brakhage, and V. C. Cravens. 1977. Evaluating cultivation near duck blinds to reduce lead poisoning hazard. Journal of Wildlife Management 41:624–631.

————, and F. A. Reid. 1986. Wetland and riparian habitats: a nongame management overview. Pages 59–96 *in* J. B. Hale, L. B. Best, and R. L. Clawson, editors. Management of nongame wildlife in the midwest: a developing art. Proceedings of the 47th Midwest Fish and Wildlife Conference, Grand Rapids, Michigan, USA.

————, and T. S. Taylor. 1982. Management of seasonally flooded impoundments for wildlife. U.S. Fish and Wildlife Service Resource Publication 148.

Gabelhouse, D. W. Jr., R. L. Hagen, and H. E. Klaasen. 1982. Producing fish and wildlife from Kansas ponds. Kansas Fish and Game Commission, Pratt, Kansas, USA.

Gibbs, J. P. 1993. Importance of small wetlands for the persistence of local populations of wetland-associated animals. Wetlands 13:25–31.

Giroux, J. F. 1981. Use of artificial islands by nesting waterfowl in southeastern Alberta. Journal of Wildlife Management 45:669–679.

Godshalk, G. L., and R. G. Wetzel. 1978. Decomposition in the littoral zone of lakes. Pages 131–143 *in* R. E. Good, D. F. Whigham, and R. L. Simpson, editors. Freshwater wetlands, ecological processes and management potential. Academic Press, New York, New York, USA.

Golet, F. C. 1986. Critical issues in wetland mitigation: a scientific perspective. National Wetlands News. 8(5):3–6.

Goodrich, S., D. Nelson, and N. Gale. 1999. Some features of Wyoming big sagebrush communities on gravel pediments of the Green River in Daggett County, Utah. General Technical Report U.S. Forest Service, Rocky Mountain Research Station, Ogden, Utah, USA.

Gordon, D. H., B. T. Gray, R. D. Perry, M. B. Prevost, T. H. Strange, and R. K. Williams. 1989. South Atlantic Coastal Wetlands. Pages 57–92 in L. M. Smith, R. L. Pederson, and R. M. Kaminski, editors. Habitat management for migrating and wintering waterfowl in North America. Texas Tech University Press, Lubbock, Texas, USA.

Grange, W. B. 1949. The way to game abundance. Charles Scribner and Sons, New York, New York, USA.

Green, J. E., and R. E. Salter. 1987. Methods for reclamation of wildlife habitat in the Canadian prairie provinces. Environment Canada, Edmonton, Alberta, Canada.

Green, W. E., L. G. MacNamara, and F. M. Uhler. 1964. Water off and on. Pages 557–568 in J. P. Linduska, editor. Waterfowl tomorrow. U.S. Fish and Wildlife Service, Washington, D.C., USA.

Greer, R. Undated. Duck habitat needs and development. Habitat Extension Bulletin Number 4. Wyoming Cooperative Fish and Wildlife Research Unit, University of Wyoming, Laramie, Wyoming, and Wyoming Game and Fish Department, Cheyenne, Wyoming, USA.

Gregg, M. A., J. A. Crawford, M. S. Drut, and A. K. Delong. 1994. Vegetational cover and predation of sage grouse nests in Oregon. Journal of Wildlife Management 58: 162–166.

Hackney, C. T., and A. A. de la Cruz. 1981. Effects of fire on brackish marsh communities: management implications. Wetlands 1:75–86.

Hall, F. C., and L. Bryant. 1995. Herbaceous stubble height as a warning of impending cattle grazing damage to riparian areas. U.S. Forest Service Technical Report PNW-GTR-362.

Hammond, M. C., and C. H. Lacy. 1959. Artificial potholes and ditches as wildlife habitat. Paper presented at 21st Midwest Wildlife Conference, Minneapolis, Minnesota, USA.

———, and G. E. Mann. 1956. Waterfowl nesting islands. Journal of Wildlife Management 20:345–352.

Hamor, W. H., H. G. Uhlig, and L. V. Compton. 1968. Ponds and marshes for wild ducks on farms and ranches in the northern plains. U.S. Department of Agriculture Farmer's Bulletin Number 2234.

Harris, S. W., and W. H. Marshall. 1963. Ecology of water-level manipulations on a northern marsh. Ecology 44:331–343.

Heath, B. J., R. Straw, S. H. Anderson, and J. Lawson. 1997. Sage grouse productivity, survival, and seasonal habitat use near Farson, Wyoming. Completion Report. Wyoming Game and Fish Commission, Cheyenne, Wyoming, USA.

Higgins, K. F., A. D. Kruse, and J. L. Piehl. 1989. Prescribed burning guidelines in the Northern Great Plains. EC 760. Wildlife Fisheries Science Department, South Dakota State University, Brookings, South Dakota, USA.

Hironaka, M., M. A. Fosberg, and A. H. Winward. 1983. Sagebrush-grass habitat types of southern Idaho. University of Idaho Forest, Wildlife, and Range Experimental Station. Bulletin Number 35. Moscow, Idaho, USA.

Hoffman, R. D. 1988. Ducks Unlimited's United States construction program for enhancing waterfowl production. Pages 109–113 in J. Zelazny and J. S. Feierabend, editors. Increasing our wetland resources. National Wildlife Federation, Washington, D.C., USA.

Hopper, R. M. 1971. Use of ammonium nitrate–fuel oil mixtures in blasting potholes for wildlife. Colorado Department of Natural Resources Game Information Leaflet 85.

———. 1972. Waterfowl use in relation to size and cost of potholes. Journal of Wildlife Management 36:459–468.

Hovind, R. B. 1949. Controlled burning of public hunting grounds. Wisconsin Conservation Bulletin 14:13–15.

Hudson, M. S. 1983. Waterfowl production on three age-classes of stock ponds in Montana. Journal of Wildlife Management 47:112–117.

Jensen, S. E., and W. S. Platts. 1990. Restoration of degraded riverine/riparian habitat in the Great Basin and Snake River regions. Pages 367–404 in J. A. Kusler and M. E. Kentula. Wetland creation and restoration: the status of the science. Island Press, Covelo, California, USA.

Johnson, N. F. 1984. Muskrat. Pages 156C–160C in F. R. Henderson, editor. Guidelines for increasing wildlife on farms and ranches. Kansas State University Cooperative Extension Service, Manhattan, Kansas, USA.

Jones, J. D. 1975. Waterfowl nesting island development. U.S. Bureau of Land Management Technical Note 260.

Kadlec, J. A., and L. M. Smith. 1989. The Great Basin marshes. Pages 451–474 in L. M. Smith, R. L. Pederson, and R. M. Kaminski, editors. Habitat management for migrating and wintering waterfowl in North America. Texas Tech University Press, Lubbock, Texas, USA.

Kaiser, P. H., S. S. Berlinger, and L. H. Fredrickson. 1979. Response of blue-winged teal to range management on waterfowl production areas in southeastern South Dakota. Journal of Range Management 32:295–298.

Kaminski, R. M., and H. H. Prince. 1981. Dabbling duck and aquatic macroinvertebrate responses to manipulated wetland habitat. Journal of Wildlife Management 45:1–15.

Kantrud, H. A. 1986. Effects of vegetation manipulation on breeding waterfowl in prairie wetlands: a literature review. U.S. Fish and Wildlife Service Technical Report 3.

———, and R. E. Stewart. 1977. Use of natural basin wetlands by breeding waterfowl in North Dakota. Journal of Wildlife Management 41:243–253.

———, and———. 1984. Ecological distribution and crude density of breeding birds on prairie wetlands. Journal of Wildlife Management 48:426–437.

Kauffman, J. B., W. C. Krueger, and M. Vavra. 1982. Impacts of a late season grazing scheme on nongame wildlife in Wallowa Mountain riparian ecosystem. Pages 208–220 in J. M. Peek, and P. D. Dalke, editors. Proceedings of the wildlife-livestock relationships symposium. University of Idaho Forestry, Wildlife, and Range Experimental Station, Moscow, Idaho, USA.

Kierstead, M. W. Undated. Wetlands creation and management. Pages 1–57 in Community wildlife involvement program field manual. Ontario Ministry of Natural Resources, Toronto, Ontario, Canada.

Kirsch, L. M., H. F. Duebbert, and A. D. Kruse. 1978. Grazing and haying effects of upland nesting birds. Transactions of the North American Wildlife Research Conference 43:486–497.

Kjellsen, M. L., and K. F. Higgins. 1990. Grasslands: benefits of management by fire. FS 857. U.S. Fish and Wildlife Service and Cooperative Extension, South Dakota State University, Brookings, South Dakota, USA.

Kruczynski, W. L. 1990. Options to be considered in preparation and evaluation of mitigation plans. Pages 555–570 in J. A. Kusler and M. E. Kentula, editors. Wetland creation and restoration: the status of the science. Island Press, Covelo, California, USA.

Larson, J. S. 1982. Understanding the ecological values of wetlands. Pages 108–118 in W. T. Mason Jr. and S. Iker, editors. Research on fish and wildlife habitat. Office of Research and Development, U.S. Environmental Protection Agency, Washington, D.C., USA.

———. 1987. Wetland creation and restoration: an outline of the scientific perspective. Pages 73–79 in J. Zelazny and J. S. Feierabend, editors. Increasing our wetland resources: proceedings of a conference. National Wildlife Federation, Washington, D.C., USA.

Leschisin, D. A., G. L. Williams, and M. W. Weller. 1992. Factors affecting use of constructed wetlands in northwestern Minnesota. Wetlands. 12:178–183.

Levine, D. A., and D. E. Willard. 1990. Regional analysis of fringe wetlands in the midwest: creation and restoration. Pages 299–326 in J. A. Kusler and M. E. Kentula, editors. Wetland creation and restoration: the status of the science. Island Press, Covelo, California, USA.

Linde, A. F. 1969. Techniques for wetland management. Report 45. Wisconsin Department of Natural Resources, Madison, Wisconsin, USA.

———. 1971. Evaluation of wetland impoundments on state-owned wildlife areas. Progress Report, Project W-141-R-6, Study Number 304. Wisconsin Department of Natural Resources, Madison, Wisconsin, USA.

———. 1985. Vegetation management in water impoundments: alternatives and supplements to water-level control. Pages 51–60 in M. D. Knighton, compiler. Water impoundments for wildlife: a habitat management workshop. U.S. Forest Service General Technical Report NC-100.

Lokemoen, J. T. 1973. Waterfowl production on stock-watering ponds in the northern plains. Journal of Range Management. 26:179–184.

———, F. B. Lee, H. F. Duebbert, and G. A. Swanson. 1984. Aquatic habitats—waterfowl. Pages 161B–176B in F. R. Henderson, editor. Guidelines for increasing wildlife on farms and ranches. Kansas State University Cooperative Extension Service, Manhattan, Kansas, USA.

———, and T. A. Messmer. 1993. Locating, constructing, and managing islands for nesting waterfowl. Utah State University Cooperative Extension Service Publication. Berryman Institute, Logan, Utah, USA.

———, and———. 1994. Locating and managing peninsulas for nesting ducks. Utah State University Cooperative Extension Service Publication. Berryman Institute, Logan, Utah, USA.

Lowry, D. H. 1990. Restoration and creation of palustrine wetlands associated with riverine systems of the glaciated northeast. Pages 267–280 in J. A. Kusler and M. E. Kentula, editors. Wetland creation and restoration: the status of the science. Island Press, Covelo, California, USA.

Mack, G. D., and L. D. Flake. 1980. Habitat relationships of waterfowl broods on South Dakota stock ponds. Journal of Wildlife Management 44(3):695–699.

Mallic, A. V., and R. W. Wein. 1986. Response of a *Typha* marsh community to draining, flooding, and seasonal burning. Canadian Journal of Botany 64:2136–2143.

Marble, A. D. 1992. A guide to wetland functional design. Lewis Publishers, Boca Raton, Florida, USA.

Mathiak, H. A., and A. F. Linde. 1956. Studies on level ditching for marsh management. Wisconsin Conservation Department Technical Bulletin 12.

McKinstry, M. C., and S. H. Anderson. 1994. Evaluation of wetland creation and waterfowl use in conjunction with abandoned mine lands in northeast Wyoming. Wetlands 14(4):284–292.

———, and———. 2002. Creating wetlands for waterfowl in Wyoming. Ecological Engineering 18:293–304.

———, P. Caffrey, and S. H. Anderson. 2000. The importance of beaver to duck populations in Wyoming. Pages 95–100 in P. J. Wiggington and R. Beschta, editors. Riparian ecology and management in multi-land use watersheds. American Water Resources Association. Middleburg, Virginia, USA.

———, T. A. Richmond, and S. H. Anderson. 2001. Wetland enhancement and creation on reclaimed abandoned mine lands in northeast Wyoming. American Society for Surface Mining and Reclamation. 18:348–355.

McMullen, J. M. 1987. Selection of plant species for use in wetlands creation and restoration. Pages 333–337 in J. Zelazny and J. S. Feierabend, editors. Increasing our wetland resources, proceedings of a conference. National Wildlife Federation, Washington, D.C., USA.

Meeks, R. L. 1969. The effect of drawdown date on wetland plant succession. Journal of Wildlife Management 33(4):817–821.

Melton, B. L., R. L. Hoover, R. L. Moore, and D. J. Pfankuch. 1987. Aquatic and riparian wildlife. Pages 260–301 in R. L. Hoover and D. L. Wills, editors. Managing forested lands for wildlife. Colorado Division of Wildlife and U.S. Forest Service, Denver, Colorado, USA.

Mensik, G. 1990. Managing emergent cover. California Waterfowl summer: 30–31.

Merendino, M. T., and L. M. Smith. 1991. Influence of drawdown date and reflood depth on wetland vegetation establishment. Wildlife Society Bulletin 19:143–150.

———, and———, H. R. Murkin, and R. L. Pederson. 1990. The response of prairie wetland vegetation to seasonality of drawdown. Wildlife Society Bulletin 18:245–251.

Messinger, R. D. 1974. Effects of controlled burning on waterfowl nesting habitat in northwest Iowa. Thesis, Iowa State University, Ames, Iowa, USA.

Meyers, L. H. 1989. Grazing and riparian management in southwestern Montana. Pages 117–120 in R. E. Gresswell, B. A. Barton, and J. L. Kershner, editors. Practical approaches to riparian resource management. Proceedings of a workshop 8–11 May, Billings, Montana. U.S. Department of Interior Bureau of Land Management.

Miller, T. S. 1987. Techniques used to enhance, restore, or create freshwater wetlands in the Pacific northwest. Pages 116–121 in K. M. Mutz and L. C. Lee, technical coordinators. Wetland and riparian ecosystems of the American west: eighth annual meeting of the Society of Wetland Scientists. Society of Wetland Scientists, Wilmington, North Carolina, USA.

Molini, W. A. 1977. Livestock interactions with upland game, nongame, and waterfowl in the Great Basin. A workshop synopsis. Transactions of California-Nevada Wildlife 1977:97–103.

Moyle, J. F., editor. 1964. Ducks and land use in Minnesota. Minnesota Department of Conservation Technical Bulletin Number 8.

Nelson, H. K., and H. F. Duebbert. 1974. New concepts regarding the production of waterfowl and other game birds in areas of diversified agriculture. International Congress of Game Biologists 11:385–394.

Nelson, N. F., and R. H. Dietz. 1966. Cattail control methods in Utah. Utah Department of Fish and Game Publication Number 66–2.

Nelson, R. W., G. C. Horak, and J. E. Olson. 1978. Western reservoir and stream habitat improvements handbook. U.S. Fish and Wildlife Service FWS/OBS-78/56.

Odum, W. E. 1987. Predicting ecosystem development following creation and restoration of wetlands. Pages 67–70 in J. Zelazny and J. S. Feierabend, editors. Increasing our wetland resources: proceedings of a conference. National Wildlife Federation, Washington, D.C., USA.

O'Farrell, M. J. 1980. Spatial relationships of rodents in a sagebrush community. Journal of Mammalogy 61:589–605.

Ohlsson, K. E., A. E. Robb Jr., C. E. Guindon Jr., D. E. Samuel, and R. L. Smith. 1982. Best current practices for fish and wildlife on surface-mined land in the northern Appalachian coal region. U.S. Fish and Wildlife Service FWS/OBS-81/45.

Owensby, C. 1984. Prescribed or controlled burning. Pages 47B–54B in F. R. Henderson, editor. Guidelines for increasing wildlife on farms and ranches. Kansas State University Cooperative Extension Service, Manhattan, Kansas, USA.

Patterson, J. 1976. The role of environmental heterogeneity in the regulation of duck populations. Journal of Wildlife Management 40:22–32.

Payne, N. F. 1992. Techniques of wildlife habitat management of wetlands. McGraw-Hill, New York, New York, USA.

Pederson, R. L., D. G. Jorde, and S. G. Simpson. 1989. Northern Great Plains. Pages 281–310 in L. M. Smith, R. L. Pederson, and R. M. Kaminski, editors. Habitat management for migrating and wintering waterfowl in North America. Texas Tech University Press, Lubbock, Texas, USA.

Peters, M. S., and A. D. Afton. 1993. Effects of deep tillage on redistribution of lead shot and chufa flatsedge at Catahoula Lake, Louisiana. Wildlife Society Bulletin 21:471–479.

Petersen, L. R., M. A. Martin, J. M. Cole, J. R. March, and C. M. Pils. 1982. Evaluation of waterfowl production areas in Wisconsin. Wisconsin Department of Natural Resources Bulletin 135.

Piehl, J. 1986. Restoration of drained wetlands. Pages 33–37 in J. L. Piehl, editors. Wetland restoration: a techniques workshop. Minnesota Chapter of the Wildlife Society, Fergus Falls, Minnesota, USA.

Platts, W. S. 1989. Compatibility of livestock grazing strategies with fisheries. Pages 103–110 in R. E. Gresswell, B. A. Barton, and J. L. Kershner, editors. Practical approaches to riparian resource management: an educational workshop. U.S. Bureau of Land Management, Billings, Montana, USA.

Preston, E. M., and B. L. Bedford. 1988. Evaluating cumulative effects on wetland functions: a conceptual overview and generic framework. Environment Management 12(5):565–583.

Proctor, B. R., R. W. Thompson, J. E. Bunin, K. W. Fucik, G. R. Tamm, and E. G. Wolf. 1983a. Practices for protecting and enhancing fish and wildlife on coal mined land in the Green River–Hams Fork region. U.S. Fish and Wildlife Service FWS/OBS-83/09.

————, ————, ————, ————, ————, and————. 1983*b*. Practices for protecting and enhancing fish and wildlife on coal mined land in the Uinta–southwestern Utah region. U.S. Fish and Wildlife Service FWS/OBS-83/12.

————, ————, ————, ————, ————, and————. 1983*c*. Practices for protecting and enhancing fish and wildlife on coal mined land in the Powder River–Fort Union region. U.S. Fish and Wildlife Service. FWS/OBS-83/10.

Reid, F. A., J. R. Kelley Jr., T. S. Taysor, and L. H. Fredrickson. 1989. Upper Mississippi Valley wetlands—refuges and moist-soil impoundments. Pages 181–202 *in* L. M. Smith, R. L. Pederson, and R. M. Kaminski, editors. Habitat management for migrating and wintering waterfowl in North America. Texas Tech University Press, Lubbock, Texas, USA.

Reimold, R. J., and S. A. Cobler. 1986. Wetland mitigation effectiveness. U. S. Environmental Protection Agency, Boston, Massachusetts, USA.

Reinartz, J. A., and E. L. Warne. 1993. Development of vegetation in small created wetlands in southeastern Wisconsin. Wetlands 13:153–164.

Reinecke, K. J., R. M. Kaminski, D. J. Moorhead, J. D. Hodges, and J. R. Nassar. 1989. Mississippi alluvial valley. Pages 203–247 *in* L. M. Smith, R. L. Pederson, and R. M. Kaminski, editors. Habitat management for migrating and wintering waterfowl in North America. Texas Tech University Press, Lubbock, Texas, USA.

Ringelman, J. K. 1990. Habitat management for molting waterfowl. Pages 1–6 *in* D. H. Cross, compiler. Waterfowl management handbook. U.S. Fish and Wildlife Service Fish and Wildlife Leaflet 13.

Rollings, C. T., and R. L. Warden. 1964. Weedkillers and waterfowl. Pages 588–593 *in* J. P. Linduska, editor. Waterfowl tomorrow. U.S. Fish and Wildlife Service, Washington, D.C., USA.

Rotenberry, J. T., and J. A. Wiens. 1980. Habitat structure, patchiness, and avian communities in North American steppe vegetation: a multivariate analysis. Ecology 61:1228–1250.

Rundle, W. D., and L. H. Fredrickson. 1981. Managing seasonally flooded impoundments for migrant rails and shorebirds. Wildlife Society Bulletin 9:80–87.

Ruwaldt, J. J. Jr., L. D. Flake, and J. M. Gates. 1979. Waterfowl pair use of natural and man-made wetlands in South Dakota. Journal of Wildlife Management 43:375–383.

Ryder, R. A. 1980. Effects of grazing on bird habitats. Pages 51–66 *in* Management of western forests and grasslands for non-game birds. U.S. Forest Service Federal Technical Report INT-88.

Sempek, J. E., and C. W. Johnson. 1987. Wetlands enhancement at the Ogden Nature Center in Ogden, Utah. Pages 161–165 *in* K. M. Mutz and L. C. Lee, technical coordinators. Wetland and riparian ecosystems of the American west: eighth annual meeting of the Society of Wetland Scientists. Society of Wetland Scientists, Wilmington, North Carolina, USA.

Skovlin, J. M. 1984. Impacts of grazing on wetlands and riparian habitat: a review of our knowledge. Pages 1001–1103 *in* Developing strategies for rangeland management. Westview Press. Boulder, Colorado, USA.

Smith, A. G. 1969. Waterfowl-habitat relationships on the Lousana, Alberta Waterfowl Study Area. Pages 116–122 *in* Saskatoon wetlands seminar. Canadian Wildlife Service Report Series Number 6, Ottawa, Ontario, Canada.

Smith, B., P. Leung, and G. Love. 1986. Intensive grazing management: forage, animals, men, profits. The Graziers Hui. Yu Luen Offset Printing, Hong Kong.

Smith, L. M., and J. A. Kadlec. 1985. The effects of disturbance on marsh seed banks. Canadian Journal of Botany 63:2133–2137.

———, and———. 1986. Habitat management for wildlife in marshes of Great Salt Lake. Transactions of the North American Wildlife Natural Resource Conference 51:222–231.

Stearns, F. 1978. Management potential summary and recommendations. Pages 357–363 in R. Good, D. Whigham, and R. Simpson, editors. Freshwater wetlands. Academic Press, New York, New York, USA.

Stoudt, J. H. 1971. Ecological factors affecting waterfowl production in the Saskatchewan parklands. U.S. Fish and Wildlife Service Publication 99.

———. 1982. Habitat use and productivity of canvasbacks in southwestern Manitoba, 1961–72. U.S. Fish and Wildlife Service Special Science Report-Wildlife 248.

Street, M. 1982. The use of waste straw to promote the production of invertebrate food for waterfowl in man-made wetlands. Pages 98–103 in D. A. Scott, editor. Managing wetlands and their birds. Proceedings of the third technical meeting on western palearctic migratory bird management. International Waterfowl Research Bureau, Slimbridge, Gloucester, England.

Swanson, G. A., G. L. Krapu, and J. R. Serie. 1979. Foods of laying female dabbling ducks on the breeding grounds. Pages 47–57 in T. A. Bookhout, editor. Waterfowl and wetlands—an integrated review. Wildlife Society, Bethesda, Maryland, USA.

Tart, D. L. 1996. Big sagebrush plant associations of the Pinedale Ranger District. U.S. Forest Service, Bridger-Teton National Forest, Pinedale, Wyoming, USA.

Taylor, T. S. 1977. Avian use of moist soil impoundments in southeastern Missouri. Thesis, University of Missouri, Columbia, Missouri, USA.

Tester, J. R., and W. H. Marshall. 1962. Minnesota prairie management techniques and their wildlife implications. Transactions of the North American Wildlife Natural Resource Conference 27:267–287.

Thomas, C. M., J. G. Mensik, and C. L. Feldheim. 1999. Tillage effects on lead shot distribution in wetland sediments. Final Report. U.S. Fish and Wildlife Service Ecological Services. Sacramento, California, USA.

Uhler, F. M. 1944. Control of undesirable plants in waterfowl habitats. Transactions of the North American Wildlife Conference 9:295–303.

U.S. Department of Agriculture Natural Resource Conservation Service. 1997a. Field borders. U.S. Department of Agriculture Natural Resource Conservation Service Conservation Practice Job Sheet Number 386.

———. 1997b. Filter strips. U.S. Department of Agriculture Natural Resource Conservation Service Conservation Practice Job Sheet Number 393.

———. 1997c. Riparian areas: implications for management. Natural Resource Conservation Service Issue Brief 13.

———. 1998. Riparian forest buffer. Conservation Practice Job Sheet Number 391.

U.S. Department of Agriculture Soil Conservation Service. 1992. Wetland restoration, enhancement, or creation. Pages 13–77 in Engineering field handbook. 210–EFH, 1/92.

U.S. Department of the Interior. 1994. The impact of federal programs on wetlands. Volume 2. A report to Congress by the Secretary of the Interior, Washington, D.C., USA.

———, Bureau of Land Management. 1986. Bureau of Land Management fence standards for livestock and wildlife. Guideline H-1741–1–Fencing. Bureau of Land Management Manual 1–1452. Washington, D.C., USA.

U.S. Fish and Wildlife Service. 1964. Managing wetlands for wildlife. Pages 219–231 *in* L. Hoffman, compiler. The conservation and management of temperate marshes, bogs, and other wetlands. Volume 1 of Proceedings of the MAR Conference. IUCN Publication New Series 3.

———. 1989. National wetlands priority conservation plan. U.S. Fish and Wildlife Service, Washington, D.C., USA.

U.S. General Accounting Office. 1988. Public rangelands: some riparian areas restored, but widespread improvements will be slow. GAO/RCED-88-105. U.S. General Accounting Office, Washington, D.C., USA.

Vogl, R. J. 1967. Controlled burning for wildlife in Wisconsin. Proceedings of the Annual Tall Timbers Fire Ecology Conference 6:47–96.

———. 1977 Fire: a destructive menace or a natural process? Pages 261–289 *in* J. Cairns Jr., K. L. Dickson, and E. E. Herricks, editors. Recovery and restoration of damaged ecosystem. University Press, Charlottesville, North Carolina, USA.

Voigts, D. K. 1976. Aquatic invertebrate abundance in relation to changing marsh vegetation. American Midland Naturalist 95:313–322.

Ward, P. 1968. Fire in relation to waterfowl habitat of the Delta Marshes. Proceedings of the annual Tall Timbers fire ecology conference 8:255–268.

Weller, M. W. 1975. Studies of cattail in relation to management for marsh wildlife. Iowa State Journal of Science 49:393–412.

———. 1978. Management of freshwater marshes for wildlife. Pages 267–284 in R. Good, D. Whigham, and R. Simpson, editors. Freshwater wetlands. Academic Press, New York, New York, USA.

———. 1987. Freshwater marshes: ecology and wildlife management. Second edition. University of Minnesota Press, Minneapolis, Minnesota, USA.

———1990. Waterfowl management techniques for wetland enhancement, restoration, and creation useful in mitigation procedures. Pages 528–577 in J. A. Kusler and M. E. Kentula, editors. Wetland creation and restoration: the status of the science. Island Press, Covelo, California, USA.

Whitman, W. R. 1974. The response of macro-invertebrates to experimental marsh management. Dissertation, University of Maine, Orono, Maine, USA.

———. 1976. Impoundments for waterfowl. Canadian Wildlife Service Occasional Paper 22.

Williams, G. L. 1985. Classifying wetlands according to relative wildlife value: application to water impoundments. Pages 110–119 *in* M. D. Knighton, compiler. Water impoundments for wildlife: a habitat management workshop. U.S. Forest Service General Technical Report NC-100.

Winward, A. H. 1991. Management in the sagebrush steppe. Agricultural Experimental Station, Oregon State University Special Report 880.

Wright, H. A., and A. W. Bailey. 1982. Fire ecology, United States and southern Canada. Wiley, New York, New York, USA.

Wyoming Department of Environmental Quality. 1982. Wyoming state coal progress guideline 5—fencing. Wyoming Department of Environmental Quality Land Quality Division, Cheyenne, Wyoming, USA.

Yancey, R. K. 1964. Matches and marshes. Pages 619–626 *in* J. P. Linduska, editor. Waterfowl tomorrow. U.S. Fish and Wildlife Service, Washington, D.C., USA.

Young, R. P. 1986. Fire ecology and management in plant communities of Malheur National Wildlife Refuge, southeastern Oregon. Dissertation, Oregon State University, Corvallis, Oregon, USA.

CHAPTER 12

Classification, Assessment, Monitoring, and Evaluation of Riverine and Palustrine Wetland Ecosystems

PAUL ADAMUS

Introduction

Scientists, planners, and managers of public and private lands frequently find it useful to classify, assess, monitor, and evaluate riparian and wetland ecosystems. Classification is the process of organizing information into classes, groups, or categories that are intended to be relatively discrete and internally homogeneous. Assessment is the detailed and systematic measurement or estimation of attributes or characteristics, e.g., a landscape's species, functions, or physical characteristics. Monitoring is assessment conducted recurrently. Evaluation is the process of assigning relative or absolute value, where value is commonly expressed as scores, ranks, dollars, or qualitative categories based on criteria or models. For example, evaluation is involved in describing habitat suitability, ecological integrity, soil erosion potential, invasibility of native plant communities, and forage value. Classification normally precedes assessment and evaluation to simplify these tasks by stratifying the resource into categories, thus reducing variability. However, assessment data are sometimes collected first and then analyzed to examine the variability within a tentative classification, thus defining or providing a basis for refinements in the classification.

In the Intermountain West, some of the reasons for classifying, assessing, or evaluating riparian and wetland ecosystems are to: (1) assess and evaluate functions, ecological integrity, condition, or health; (2) assess past effects of natural or human alteration; (3) predict or assess risks of future natural or human-related changes; (4) assess sustainability of habitats or their species and functions; (5) prioritize sites or categories for restoration, remediation, acquisition, or other management activities; and (6) facilitate understanding and communication regarding the resource.

A need for credible methods of riparian and wetland classification, assessment, and evaluation is created by many legal mandates and agency policies, and also by numerous voluntary programs for managing wetland and riparian ecosystems. To assess, classify, and evaluate a resource, people typically develop and apply methods—variously termed procedures, protocols, tools, schemes, techniques, or approaches. Methods may be implicit and informal, as in the case of a person visiting a site and mentally assigning it to a category, or they may be explicit and standardized. Standardization is commonly a carefully structured series of questions that were developed prior to a site visit using the same suite of variables. A persistent dilemma concerns the desirable level of standardization of methods. Standardization can foster increased objectivity and repeatability of methods. For this reason, standardization is viewed favorably by scientists and the courts. Standardization also is a way of efficiently disseminating scientific knowledge and complex judgment. For example, resource agencies often cannot exercise the luxury of having a multidisciplinary team of seasoned experts assess every situation. Standard methods are developed to encode and reflect the knowledge of experts so that users with less expertise will reach the same conclusions. Despite these assets, standardization forces a disciplined approach upon users. Consequently, some users become uneasy with a perception that their personal knowledge is subordinated or not fully utilized. Standardization also can create situations that do not allow for flexibility and adaptation of methods to address idiosyncratic situations or new knowledge. Resource managers are continually seeking an acceptable balance as they attempt to develop methods that are standardized and consistent but adaptive and flexible. The balancing points frequently depend on the particular objectives and intended uses of a method.

Classifications

Many classification schemes have been devised for describing the Intermountain West's riparian and wetland ecosystems (Gebhardt et al. 1990, Maxwell et al. 1995). Reviewing or even listing all of these is beyond the scope of this chapter, so a few examples are provided. Most commonly, classifications are based on characteristics of vegetation, geomorphology, hydrology, water chemistry, or some combination. All classifications represent some compromise between specificity (splitting the resource into many classes and subclasses) and generality (lumping the resource into a few broad classes). Statistical methods such as Cluster Analysis (in combination with Analysis of Variance, ANOVA) and Multi-Response Permutation Procedures (MRPP) can be used to recommend the fewest number of statistically significant splits of a data set (i.e., the fewest supportable subclasses). When tempered with expert knowledge, such results may provide a systematic objectivity that sometimes is lacking in classifications based solely on expert knowledge.

Vegetation-based classifications

Classifications of riparian and wetland vegetation sometimes have been derived by using statistical tools (e.g., Cluster Analysis, Principal Components Analysis, Canonical Correspondence Analysis), by using more intuitive approaches, or by employing a combination of approaches. Depending on perceived interactions among species, their environment, and the spatial and temporal scales being considered, the collection of plant species within a vegetation class may be called a community, assemblage, or association. Spatially, vegetation classifications may be designed to operate at a landscape scale (e.g., classification of stand types and patch types spanning many square kilometers) or at a finer scale (e.g., classification of species assemblages within plots of $1\ m^2$). On a vertical scale, they may consider overstory, understory, or both. Temporally, vegetation classifications may or may not include seral stages as discrete classes. Many classification schemes seek to address vegetation at multiple scales in a hierarchical manner, often in combination with geomorphic attributes. Also, some vegetation-based classifications use information on the physical form or life history of vegetation (e.g., shrub versus tree, evergreen versus deciduous, annual versus perennial; see Friedman et al. 1996) rather than plant species composition. Finally, some classifications consider current vegetation (plant species and communities presently at a site), whereas others consider potential vegetation (plant species and communities that would become established naturally through succession and disturbance, given particular climatic and geomorphic criteria and assumptions about the spatial and temporal occurrence of those factors at the site). In many wetland systems, potential vegetation or a related concept, site potential, is quite difficult to predict (Bedford 1996).

In the Intermountain West, wetlands have been classified most often using the scheme of Cowardin et al. (1979), a hierarchical classification that at its initial levels is based mainly on vegetation form. The popularity of the Cowardin et al. (1979) classification is partially attributable to the fact that it is used for mapping by the National Wetland Inventory (NWI) of the U.S. Fish and Wildlife Service. Although not comprehensive, NWI maps are the single largest regionwide source of spatial data on wetland and riparian areas. Also, modifications of the Cowardin et al. (1979) scheme are being used for mapping riparian areas and waterfowl habitat. As applied in the Intermountain West, the Cowardin et al. (1979) scheme categorizes wetlands at a system level as riverine, palustrine (small and without flowing water), or lacustrine (larger and lakelike). Subsystems are recognized for riverine wetlands (upper perennial, lower perennial, intermittent) and lacustrine (limnetic, littoral). At a tertiary level, broad substrate and vegetation classes are recognized (emergent, scrub-shrub, forested, aquatic bed, moss-lichen, rock bottom, unconsolidated bottom, unconsolidated shore). At finer levels, the classification defines 8 modifiers for water regime, 4 for salinity, 3 for pH, 2 for soil, and 6 for human alterations. In the region's flatter terrain, the hydrology-based wetland classification of Stewart and Kantrud (1972) has been used. Another classification proposed by Windell et al. (1986) has received limited use for subalpine and montane wetlands in Colorado. It recognizes the following classes: bog, fen, marsh, meadow, carr, and shrub wetland.

Among the region's many other vegetation-based schemes used to classify wetland and riparian systems, an example is Crowe and Clausnitzer's (1997), which describes more than 100 plant associations and community types in northeastern Oregon. A classification of the riparian and wetland resources of Montana, focusing largely on vegetation form, was developed and applied by Hansen et al. (1995), and classifications developed by Youngblood et al. (1985) and Padgett et al. (1989) have been used by the U.S. Forest Service. Vegetation has also been used to classify wetland (Carsey et al. 2001) and riparian (Kittel et al. 1999) habitats in Colorado. Vegetation-based classifications are being developed and refined by state heritage programs, many of which are using the hierarchical classification scheme proposed nationally by The Nature Conservancy (Anderson et al. 1998) as a framework.

Classifications based on geomorphic, hydrologic, and chemical characteristics

Vegetation can be a useful classifier and integrator of a site's condition, but usually it is not as fundamentally strong and stable a determinant of a site's many functions as are geomorphic factors. Elmore et al. (1994: 88) noted that "not all questions about a piece of land can be answered by a plant association classification. Therefore, geomorphic classification must be considered to effectively describe and manage riparian ecosystems." Perhaps the most popular geomorphic classification in the Intermountain West is that of Rosgen (1994), which is relevant to wetland and riparian resources to the extent that it focuses on channels and their floodplains. The classification identifies the following categories:

Type A. Steep, highly entrenched channels containing step pool systems with high sediment transport potential;

Type B. Moderate gradient channels that are moderately entrenched in gentle to moderately steep terrain, have low sinuosity, and are riffle-dominated;

Type C. Low gradient channels, moderately high sinuosity, pool-riffle bedform with well-developed floodplains;
Type D. Braided channels with moderate channel slope;
Type E. Very low gradient, highly sinuous channel; and
Type F. Highly entrenched channel.

Hydrogeomorphic processes have been used as a basis for classifying channels (Frissell et al. 1986) and wetlands (Brinson 1993). Brinson's hydrogeomorphic (HGM) classification scheme for wetlands is being adapted by some western states that regulate development and restoration of wetlands. At the national level, it defines 7 classes (Table 12.1).
    A study of Colorado wetlands (Noe et al. 1998) used an analysis of field data to propose splits for some national HGM classes and identified reference sites in Colorado for each subclass (Table 12.2). Soils and other geomorphic features have been associated with vegetation in classifications developed and applied to riparian systems in Nevada (Swanson et al. 1988, Jensen et al. 1989), central Oregon (Kovalchik and Chitwood

Table 12.1. Hydrogeomorphic (HGM) classes of wetlands relevant to the Intermountain region (selected from Smith et al. 1995, based on classification developed by Brinson 1993)

Hydrogeomorphic Class	Dominant Water Sources	Water Flow Direction
Riverine	Channel flow and overbank flow from channel	Unidirectional (channels) and bidirectional (floodplain)
Depressional	Return flow from interflow, groundwater discharge	Vertical (seepage)
Mineral soil flats	Direct precipitation	Vertical (seepage)
Organic soil flats	Direct precipitation	Vertical (seepage)
Slope	Groundwater discharge	Unidirectional, horizontal
Lacustrine fringe	Overbank flow from lake	Bidirectional, horizontal
Estuarine fringe	Overbank flow from estuary	Bidirectional, horizontal

Table 12.2. Subclasses proposed for Colorado riverine, slope, and depressional wetlands (Noe et al. 1998)

Riverine Wetland Subclasses

R1 Steep gradient, low-order streams and springs on coarse-textured substrate. Very common in the subalpine zone but also occur on the plains.

R2 Moderate gradient, low- to mid-order streams on coarse- and fine-textured substrates. Typically dominated by willow thickets.

R3 Mid-elevation, moderate gradient reaches along small and mid-order streams. Dominated by tall shrubs (alder) and trees (cottonwood, spruce).

R4 Low-elevation canyons in mountain foothills and plateaus along larger rivers. Generally with steep gradients, coarse soils, and woody vegetation (boxelder, tamarisk) predominating.

R5 Low-elevation floodplains along mid- to high-order streams with fine-textured substrate. Most have perennial flow, but a few may be intermittent. Highly manipulated.

Slope Wetland Subclasses

S1 Alpine and subalpine fens and wet meadows on non-calcareous, organic, or non-organic substrates.

S2 Subalpine and montane fens and wet meadows on calcareous, organic, or non-organic substrates. Typically saturated for long duration of each growing season.

S3 Mid-elevation wet meadows with a seasonally high water table, sometimes sustained partly by irrigation runoff and seepage.

S4 Low-elevation meadows with a seasonal high water table, sometimes sustained partly by irrigation runoff and seepage. May occur on floodplains or at springs.

Depressional Wetland Subclasses

D1 Mid- to high-elevation basins with peat soils and lake fringe wetlands with or without peat soils.

D2 Low-elevation basins, permanently or semipermanently flooded. Includes wetlands along the fringe of reservoirs and ponds. Water levels fluctuate noticeably.

D3 Low-elevation basins, flooded only seasonally.

D4 Low-elevation basins, flooded only temporarily (short durations during spring and early summer). May include some abandoned beaver ponds and small irrigation ponds.

D5 Low-elevation basins, flooded intermittently (not annually). May include some barren playas.

1990), western Wyoming and eastern Idaho (Youngblood et al. 1985), and southern parts of the Intermountain West (Brown 1978). Another classification developed in Idaho is noteworthy in its attempt to integrate wetlands with adjoining terrestrial habitats (Haufler et al. 1996). There have been few attempts to use geomorphic features to classify floodplains that sometimes fall outside of existing classification schemes for wetlands and channels. Concepts described by Mertes (1997) might provide one basis.

Statistical analyses of chemical and biological data can be used to classify wetlands, as was done for a series of 80 depressional wetlands in Montana (Apfelbeck 1997):

I. Permanently Flooded Basins
  A. Small Watershed
    1. Dilute (pH <7)
    2. Recharge (pH 7–9)
    3. Alkaline (pH >9)
  B. Large Watershed
    1. Fresh (conductivity <20,000 uS/cm)
    2. Saline (conductivity >20,000 uS/cm)
II. Ephemerally Flooded Basins

Assessment and Evaluation Methods

Assessment begins with determining the location of wetland and riparian areas. This is accomplished through inventories or surveys that use some combination of vegetation, hydrologic, and soil features—observable in aerial photographs or during site visits—to define the landward limits of wetland and riparian sites. In the Intermountain West, preliminary maps of wetland and riparian systems are available from the National Wetlands Inventory of the U.S. Fish and Wildlife Service (U.S. Fish and Wildlife Service 1997), from some national forests, and sometimes from other federal, state, and local agencies. Most such maps do not adequately show wetlands that contain water for only short periods, such as vernal pools amid agricultural lands or small wooded seeps beneath a forest canopy.

Once sites have been delineated, assessment focuses on collecting information that may be used to evaluate the sites. Wetland sites commonly are evaluated to determine (1) if they are in a desirable ecological condition as required by the federal Clean Water Act, (2) the potential consequences of actions proposed by applicants for wetland alteration permits (see Chapter 1 of this volume), and (3) whether created or restored wetland or riparian sites are successful as compared to wetland and riparian systems of the same type (see Chapter 9).

Before evaluation begins, decisions must be made regarding an appropriate and feasible level of effort for achieving evaluation objectives. For reconnaissance or planning-level objectives, data collection might focus mainly on variables (characteristics) that can be estimated using commonly available data sources, such as topographic and soils maps, augmented by perhaps a single brief visit to a site. Methods used for such objectives are often called rapid assessment methods (reviewed by Adamus 1992, Bartoldus 1999) and can be applied by persons with basic training in environmental sciences. In contrast, if information is required to predict ecosystem processes or impacts to highly sensitive species or areas, persons with advanced training might be needed and data collection might demand greater quantification of variables, typically using costly equipment to measure variables during multiple visits to a site.

The sampling design also should be geared to assessment objectives. Stratification, randomization, and sample size requirements are especially important in assessments that may be subject to intense scientific and legal scrutiny or that involve sensitive resources, spatial or temporal extrapolation, initial calibration and validation of models, or measurement of trends.

One of the first rapid assessment methods was developed for systematic assessment of wildlife habitat (U.S. Fish and Wildlife Service, 1981). Called the Habitat Evaluation Procedures (HEP), it has found wide application for assessing possible consequences of altering riparian and wetland habitat. During each application, users select a few species as indicators of habitat suitability of an area and then propose models containing variables that are both important to the species and readily observable. The variables are assessed at a site by a team of biologists. During the evaluation stage, the data are converted to habitat suitability scores. The application of HEP to wetland and riparian habitats of the Intermountain West has been constrained partly by a scarcity of validated (or even unvalidated) models that link individual species to habitat variables. To overcome some of these limitations, an Avian Richness Evaluation Method (AREM) was developed for use in assessing wetland and riparian habitat of the Colorado Plateau (Adamus 1993). Subsequent testing of the method showed that its variables were successful in predicting the relative species richness of a series of 70 wetland and riparian sites (Adamus 1995). At this writing, the computerized model (arem.exe) and its manual (arem_man) can be downloaded from http://www.epa.gov/owow/wetlands/wqual/.

Although the first rapid assessment methods focused primarily on habitat, successive methods sought to address a wider range of wetland

and riparian functions. For example, the Wetland Evaluation Technique, WET (Adamus 1983, Adamus et al. 1987), which was developed for nationwide use, came to be used by many agencies and consultants. However, its ability to detect differences in function among sites in the Intermountain West sometimes does not meet user expectations (Dougherty 1989). Several users have suggested improvements to WET to increase its usefulness in Colorado (Cooper et al. 1990) and Montana (Berglund 1996).

More recently, some state and federal agencies have shown interest in developing rapid assessment methods based on the HGM classification. To develop such methods, variables deemed important to local wetland functions are estimated or measured at a series of wetlands belonging to a particular hydrogeomorphic subclass and spanning a gradient of human-related disturbance (Smith et al. 1995, Brinson 1996). The wetlands do not have to be in pristine condition. The data are then used to calibrate the variables in simple models that produce scores reflective of a site's potential capacity to provide each of several named functions. Within the Intermountain West, function assessment methods that use components of the HGM approach have been prepared for playa wetlands generally (Natural Resources and Conservation Service 1999) and for other wetland types in Colorado (Noe et al. 1998), Montana (Hauer and Smith 1998), Idaho (Natural Resources and Conservation Service 1998), Utah (Nancy Keate, Utah Governor's Office of Planning and Budget, personal communication), Washington (Hruby et al. 2001), and Oregon (Adamus and Field 2001).

The rapid assessment method that is used most often in wetlands and riparian systems of the Intermountain West is the Proper Functioning Condition (PFC) method (Pritchard 1994, 1998). As of 1998, the PFC method had been used to categorize the functionality of wetlands in Colorado, Utah, Wyoming, Montana, and Idaho (E. Luce, U.S. Bureau of Land Management, Washington, D.C., personal communication). The PFC method was designed primarily for prioritizing restoration activities at a site level and for suggesting design features for such projects. Although not based on a statistical sample of all wetland or riparian sites, statewide tabulations of PFC results provide a first-cut, approximate picture of the condition of wetland and riparian resources, mainly on public land, at watershed, state, and regional scales.

The PFC method allows users to assign a site to 1 of 4 categories: (1) Proper Functioning Condition, (2) Functional–At Risk, (3) Nonfunctional, or (4) Unknown. The method does not include an explicit model for processing the estimates of variables. Rather, users record on a checklist "yes," "no," or "not applicable" to describe the condition of 20 easily observed variables in 3 categories (hydrologic, vegetation, and soils-erosion), and they must decide in which of the categories their responses would collectively place the site. Decisions should be made by a 3-person multidisciplinary team during a site visit. Sites are stream reaches at least 400 m in length or discrete lentic wetlands. Lentic sites are assigned the Proper Functioning Condition designation when users have judged there to be "adequate vegetation, landform, and debris" to dissipate energies associated with wind action, wave action, and overland flow from adjacent sites, thereby reducing erosion and improving water quality; to filter sediment and aid floodplain development; to improve floodwater retention and groundwater recharge; to develop root masses that stabilize islands and shoreline features against cutting action; to restrict water percolation; to develop diverse ponding characteristics to provide the habitat and water depth, duration, and temperature necessary for fish production, waterbird breeding, and other uses; and to support greater biodiversity (Pritchard 1994).

A Functional–At Risk designation means a 25- to 30-year flood event would likely cause a site to lose existing habitat. The PFC guidance cautions that just because a site is considered to be in proper functioning condition does not mean that conditions are optimal for all functions and species. Users are instructed to view PFC results as the minimum condition needed before efforts can be made to attain more rigorous water quality and biological objectives. Users have the option of using other methods to define higher goals and objectives, such as Desired Future Condition (DFC). That is particularly appropriate because the PFC method does not directly or explicitly assess vegetation or fish and wildlife habitat.

Methods and models such as PFC, HEP, WET, and HGM have been widely used because of diminishing budgets of resource agencies and related demands that assessments be conducted rapidly (often within hours). These methods have been thoroughly peer-reviewed, but like all models, they are at best only as strong as available research data allow. Few tests of their consistency (repeatability among users) or accuracy (congruence with more rigorous measures of the functions they are intended to assess rapidly) have been published. This may or may not be a concern, depending on the situations in which the methods are being used. Managers may choose to use methods that are less rapid but more consistent and accurate. Indeed, dozens of time-intensive protocols have been developed for making detailed measurements of variables thought to characterize riparian and wetland functions in the Intermountain West. These include methods for measuring resources or particular functions indirectly (e.g., fish habitat inventory methods) or directly (e.g., survey techniques for riparian birds).

Indirect methods infer species presence or absence, populations, or habitat suitability based on variables thought to comprise habitat for particular species. Predictive variables are measured using transects, quadrats, or aerial imagery. For example, users might measure a variable such as canopy closure at several points along a riparian transect using a spherical densiometer. Or they might use a computerized geographical information system (GIS) to measure the connectedness of wooded riparian patches at a landscape scale. The information on connectedness or canopy closure is input into models that may infer, for example, bird richness or species presence. Those models can be fairly simple, such as those used by statewide Gap Analysis projects (Flather et al. 1997). Or they can attempt to account for complex conditional relationships among variables (expert systems) or can be deterministic (based on fundamental principles and proven interactions among variables), such as some spatially explicit demographic and climate models. They can make predictions on a regional or landscape scale (such as the models just mentioned) or on a site-specific scale, such as the instream incremental flow models of the U.S. Fish and Wildlife Service (Bovee 1982). Or the method may include no evaluation model at all, if the intent is only to provide measured assessment data. Examples of methods or compilations of methods developed for stream or riparian areas are shown in Table 12.3.

Wetland and riparian species and functions also can be surveyed directly. For example, information relevant to designing and conducting surveys of vertebrates and their habitat is presented in Cooperrider et al. (1986). Methods applicable specifically to wetlands are summarized by Adamus and Brandt (1990) and Adamus et al. (2001). Methods used to measure functions of some Colorado wetlands are reported by Noe et al. (1998).

Organisms that live in wetland and riparian ecosystems of the Intermountain West are exposed to a wide variety of stresses, both natural and human-related (Table 12.4). A challenge is how to interpret plant and animal species data in a manner that tells something about the condition, integrity, or health of a landscape or site. To meet this challenge, stream biologists over many decades have developed, refined, and regionalized indices of biotic integrity (IBI). Data from fish and aquatic invertebrate samples are summarized in terms of species composition, richness, dominance, physical deformities, and other parameters. These metrics are combined to yield an IBI score that represents the ecological condition of a site (Karr 1981, Karr and Chu 1998). However, IBIs may be customized by region and ecosystem type. Doing so requires an initial sampling of a dozen or more sites picked to represent the range of expected environmental impact or stress from humans (least- to most-disturbed sites). Data from these samples are used to calibrate IBI models, which then can be applied elsewhere. An IBI development also requires understanding of the life histories of individual species and their relative tolerances

Table 12.3. Examples of methods or compilations of methods developed for stream or riparian areas

Method	Reference
Methods to estimate aquatic habitat variables	Hamilton and Bergersen 1981
Methods for evaluating stream, riparian, and biotic conditions	Platts et al. 1983
Methods for evaluating riparian habitats with applications to management	Platts et al. 1987
Integrated riparian evaluation guide	Burton et al. 1992
Procedures for Ecological Site Inventory (ESI) —with special reference to riparian-wetland sites	Leonard et al. 1992a,b
Greenline riparian-wetland monitoring	Cagney 1993
Use of aerial photography to manage riparian-wetland areas	Clemmer 1994
Observing physical and biological change through historical photographs	Hindley 1996
Monitoring the vegetation resources in riparian areas	Winward 2000

to various types of stressors. A species database that catalogs North American literature on effects of hydrologic alteration and nutrients on wetland invertebrates and plants is available for this purpose (Adamus and Gonyaw 2001a,b). Although IBIs have been developed and validated in many stream environments, state-level efforts to develop IBIs for assessing wetland and riparian areas have been initiated only in the past few years (see www.epa.gov/owow/wetlands/wqual/bio_fact). Montana's wetland IBI effort (Apfelbeck 1997) is noteworthy.

Another approach to assessing the ecological condition of wetland or riparian ecosystems is to assess the condition of individuals or populations of a few target species. The target species are usually selected because they are known or assumed to be particularly sensitive to chemical contamination or other human-related stresses. Physiological condition, survival rates, population age structure, growth rates, fecundity (or seed germination), or morphology may be measured, and tissue analysis may be used to detect bioaccumulation of contaminants. Models describing foodweb linkages and predicting species exposure levels to contaminants can be hypothesized and compared with field data. This approach

Table 12.4. Types of stressors to natural wetland and riparian areas

Stressor	Definition	Typical Causes or Associated Activities
Enrichment/eutrophication	Increases in concentration or availability of nitrogen and phosphorus	Fertilizer application, cattle, ineffective wastewater treatment systems, fossil fuel combustion, urban runoff
Organic loading and depleted dissolved oxygen	Increases in carbon to the point that an increased biological oxygen demand reduces dissolved oxygen in sediments and the water column and increases toxic gases (e.g., hydrogen sulfide, ammonia)	Ineffective waste treatment systems, urban runoff
Contaminant toxicity	Increases in concentration, availability, and/or toxicity of metals and synthetic organic substances	Agriculture (pesticide applications), aquatic weed control, mining, urban runoff, landfills, hazardous waste sites, fossil fuel combustion, wastewater treatment systems, and other sources
Acidification	Increases in acidity (decreases in pH)	Mining, fossil fuel combustion
Salinization	Increases in dissolved salts, particularly chloride, and related parameters such as conductivity and alkalinity	Geothermal exploration, road salt used for winter ice control, irrigation return waters, and domestic/industrial wastes (see Chapter 6)

continued

Table 12.4 *continued*

Sedimentation/burial	Increases in deposited sediments, resulting in partial or complete burial of organisms and alteration of substrate	Agriculture, disturbance of stream flow regimes, urban runoff, ineffective waste treatment, deposition of dredged or other fill material, erosion from mining and construction sites
Turbidity/shade	Reductions in solar penetration of waters as a result of blockage by suspended sediments and/or overstory vegetation or other physical obstructions	Agriculture, disturbance of stream flow regimes, urban runoff, ineffective waste-water treatment plants, and erosion from mining and construction sites, as well as from natural succession, placement of bridges and other structures, and resuspension by fish (e.g., common carp) and wind.
Vegetation removal and thermal alteration	Defoliation and possibly reduction of vegetation through physical removal, with concomitant increases in solar radiation	Grazing, logging, other agricultural and silvicultural activities, aquatic weed control, fire or fire suppression, channelization, bank stabilization, urban development, defoliation from airborne contaminants and concentrated herbivory (e.g., from muskrat, geese, insects), disease, and fire (see Ehrhart this volume)

Dehydration and restriction of animal movements	Reductions in wetland water levels and/or increased frequency, duration, or extent of desiccation of wetland sediments	Ditching, channelization of nearby streams, invasion of wetlands by highly transpirative plant species, outlet widening, subsurface drainage, global climate change, and groundwater or surface water withdrawals for agricultural, industrial, or residential use
Inundation and connecting of hydrologically isolated basins	Increases in wetland water levels and/or increase in the frequency, duration, or extent of saturation of wetland sediments	Impoundments (e.g., for flood control, water supply, waterfowl management) or changes in watershed land use that result in more runoff being provided to wetlands under a different seasonal schedule (see Tessman, Chapter 11 of this volume)
Invasion by widespread, generalist species	Increase in dominance of usually nonnative species	Any of the above stressors
Other human presence	Alteration of wild animal behavior in response to human or domestic animal presence	Hiking, water sports, other outdoor activities, livestock, house pets

has been used to assess the biological condition of some riparian and wetland areas in the Intermountain West exposed to contamination from mine wastes or irrigation return water (e.g., Lambing et al. 1988; Pascoe et al. 1994*a,b*; LeJeune et al. 1996). Depending on time, budgets, and objectives, this approach can be used in lieu of or in addition to other approaches described above.

Conclusion

Data need to be collected routinely from riparian and wetland ecosystems to classify, assess, monitor, and evaluate the ecological condition of these areas. Such data may be useful for prioritizing sites (or categories of sites or landscapes) for restoration, remediation, acquisition, or other management activities. Some ongoing issues surrounding data collection concern the optimal balance between standardization and flexibility and of method, speed, consistency, and accuracy.

For classification of Intermountain West wetlands, the Cowardin et al. (1979) scheme is used most frequently. A new hydrogeomorphic classification scheme developed at a national level for wetlands shows promise when adapted for regional conditions. Channels and floodplains associated with riparian systems have been classified using Rosgen's scheme, but many other classifications using vegetation, geomorphology, or both have been developed and used within the region.

Methods for assessment and evaluation can be categorized as rapid or detailed. Rapid methods used most frequently in the Intermountain West are PFC, HEP, and WET. Methods based on the HGM classification and developed by individual states for application to specific wetland classes may eventually be useful but are in the early stages of development, calibration, and testing. For more detailed and quantified assessment and evaluation of wetland and riparian areas, a large variety of methods are available. Some detailed methods measure functions and species indirectly, whereas others are more direct. Data on community structure and other characteristics of communities, species, and populations can be interpreted using indices of biotic integrity (IBI) to yield estimates of the relative condition or health of an area, once such indices have been calibrated and tested. Many models are available to assess exposure of wetland and riparian communities to contaminants and other stressors.

Literature Cited

Adamus, P. R. 1983. A method for wetland functional assessment. Federal Highway Administration Report FHWA-IP-82–24.

———. 1992. Data sources and evaluation methods for addressing wetland issues. Pages 171–224 *in* Statewide wetlands strategies. World Wildlife Fund and Island Press, Washington, D.C., USA.

———. 1993. Irrigated wetlands of the Colorado Plateau: information synthesis and habitat evaluation method. U.S. Environmental Protection Agency Report EPA/600/R-93/071.

———. 1995. Validating a habitat evaluation method for predicting avian richness. Wildlife Society Bulletin 23:743–749.

———, and K. Brandt. 1990. Impacts on quality of inland wetlands of the United States: a survey of indicators, techniques, and applications of community level biomonitoring data. U.S. Environmental Protection Agency Report EPA/600/3–90/073.

———, E. J. Clairain, R. D. Smith, and R. E. Young. 1987. Methodology. Volume 2 of Wetland Evaluation Technique (WET). U.S. Army Corps of Engineers Waterways Experiment Station, Vicksburg, Mississippi, USA.

———, T. J. Danielson, and A. Gonyaw. 2001. Indicators for monitoring biological integrity of inland freshwater wetlands: a survey of North American technical literature (1990–2000). U.S. Environmental Protection Agency Report EPA 843–R-01 at *www.epa.gov/owow/wetlands/bawwg/monindicators.pdf*

———, and D. Field. 2001. Assessment methods. Volume 1A of Guidebook for hydrogeomorphic (HGM)-based assessment of Oregon wetland and riparian sites. I. Willamette Valley ecoregion, riverine impounding and slope/flat subclasses. Oregon Division of State Lands, Salem, Oregon, USA.

———, and A. Gonyaw. 2001a. National database of wetland invertebrate sensitivities to enrichment and hydrologic alteration. U.S. Environmental Protection Agency, at *www.epa.gov/owow/wetlands/bawwg/publicat.html*

———, and———. 2001b. National database of wetland plant tolerances to enrichment and hydrologic alteration. U.S. Environmental Protection Agency, at *www.epa.gov/owow/wetlands/bawwg/publicat.html*

Anderson, M., P. Bourgeron, M. T. Bryer, R. Crawford, L. Engelking, D. Faber-Langendoen, K. Gallyoun, K. Goodin, D. H. Grossman, S. Landall, K. Metzler, K. D. Patterson, M. Pyne, M. Reid, L. Sneddon, and A. S. Weakley. 1998. International classification of ecological communities: terrestrial vegetation for the United States. Nature Conservancy, Arlington, Virginia, USA.

Apfelbeck, R. 1997. Developing preliminary bioassessment protocols for Montana wetlands. Montana Department of Environmental Quality, Helena, Montana, USA.

Bartoldus, C. C. 1999. A comprehensive review of wetland assessment procedures: a guide for wetland practitioners. Environmental Concern. Edgewater, Maryland, USA.

Bedford, B. L. 1996. The need to define hydrologic equivalence at the landscape scale for freshwater wetland mitigation. Ecological Applications 6:57–68.

Berglund, J. 1996. Montana wetland field evaluation form and instructions. Montana Department of Transportation, Helena, Montana, USA.

Bovee, K. D. 1982. A guide to stream habitat analysis using the instream flow incremental methodology. U.S. Fish and Wildlife Service Report FWS/OBS-82/26.

Brinson, M. M. 1993. A hydrogeomorphic classification of wetlands. U.S. Army Corps of Engineers Technical Report WRP-DE-11.

———. 1996. The HGM approach explained. National Wetlands Newsletter 17(6): 7–16.

Brown, D. E. 1978. Southwestern wetlands—their classification and characterization. Pages 269–282 in U.S. Forest Service General Technical Report WO-12.

Burton, T., N. Bare, G. Ketcheson, H. Hudak, W. Little, W. Grow, T. M. Collins, A. H. Winward, D. Duff, and H. Forsgren. 1992. Integrated riparian evaluation guide, intermountain region. U.S. Forest Service Intermountain Research Station, Ogden, Utah, USA.

Cagney, J. 1993. Riparian area management: greenline riparian-wetland monitoring. U.S. Bureau of Land Management Technical Report 1737-8.

Carsey, K., D. Cooper, K. Decker, and G. Kittel. 2001. Comprehensive statewide wetlands classification and characterization: wetland plant associations of Colorado. Colorado Natural Heritage Program, Fort Collins, Colorado, USA.

Clemmer, P. 1994. The use of aerial photography to manage riparian-wetland areas. U.S. Bureau of Land Management Technical Reference 1737-10.

Cooper, D., K. Mutz, B. Van Haveren, A. Allen, and G. Jacob. 1990. Intermountain riparian lands evaluation method. U.S. Environmental Protection Agency, Office of Policy Analysis, and Office of Wetlands Protection, Washington, D.C., USA.

Cooperrider, A. Y., R. J. Boyd, and H. R. Stuart, editors. 1986. Inventory and monitoring of wildlife habitat. U.S. Bureau of Land Management, Washington, D.C., USA.

Cowardin, L. M., V. Carter, F. C. Golet, and E. T. LaRoe. 1979. Classification of wetlands and deepwater habitats of the United States. U.S. Fish and Wildlife Service Report FWS-OBS 79-31.

Crowe, E. A., and R. R. Clausnitzer. 1997. Mid-montane wetland plant associations of the Malheur, Umatilla, and Wallowa-Whitman National Forests. Report R6 ECOL TP 22 97. U.S. Forest Service, Wallowa-Whitman National Forest, Baker City, Oregon, USA.

Dougherty, S. T. 1989. Evaluation of the applicability of the Wetland Evaluation Technique (WET) to high elevation wetlands in Colorado. Pages 415–427 in D. W. Fish, editor. Wetlands concerns and successes. American Water Resources Association, Minneapolis, Minnesota, USA.

Elmore, D. W., B. L. Kovalchik, and L. D. Jurs. 1994. Restoration of stressed sites and processes. Volume 4 of Restoration of riparian ecosystems. Pages 87–92 in Eastside forest ecosystem health assessment. U.S. Forest Service General Technical Report PNW-GTR-330.

Flather, C. H., K. R. Wilson, D. J. Dean, and W. C. McComb. 1997. Identifying gaps in conservation networks: of indicators and uncertainty in geographic-based analyses. Ecological Applications 7:531–542.

Friedman, J. M., W. R. Osterkamp, and W. M. Lewis Jr. 1996. Channel narrowing and vegetation development following a Great Plains flood. Ecology 77:2167–2181.

Frissell, C. A., W. J. Liss, C. E. Warren, and M. D. Hurley. 1986. A hierarchical framework for stream habitat classification: viewing streams in a watershed context. Environmental Management 10:199–214.

Gebhardt, K., S. Leonard, G. Staidl, and D. Prichard. 1990. Riparian area management: riparian and wetland classification review. U.S. Bureau of Land Management Report TR 1737-5.

Hamilton, K., and E. P. Bergersen. 1981. Methods to estimate aquatic habitat variables. Colorado Cooperative Fishery Research Unit, Colorado State University, Fort Collins, Colorado, USA.

Hansen, P. L., R. D. Pfister, K. Boggs, B. J. Cook, J. Joy, and D. K. Hinckley. 1995. Classification and management of Montana's riparian and wetland sites. Miscellaneous

Publications Number 54. Montana Forest and Conservation Experiment Station, School of Forestry, University of Montana, Missoula, USA.

Hauer, F. R., and R. D. Smith. 1998. The hydrogeomorphic approach to functional assessment of riparian wetlands: evaluating impacts and mitigation on river floodplains in the USA. Freshwater Biology 40:517–530.

Haufler, J. B., C. A. Mehl, and G. J. Roloff. 1996. Using a coarse filter approach with species assessment for ecosystem management. Wildlife Society Bulletin 24:200–208.

Hindley, E. 1996. Observing physical and biological change through historical photographs. U.S. Bureau of Land Management Technical Reference 1737-13.

Hruby, T., S. Stanley, T. Granger, T. Duebendorfer, R. Fiez, B. Lang, B. Leonard, K. March, and A. Wald. 2001. Assessment methods. Part 1 of Depressional wetlands in the Columbia Basin of eastern Washington. Washington Department of Ecology Publication Number 00-06-47.

Jensen, S., R. Ryel and W. S. Platts. 1989. Classification of riverine, riparian habitat and assessment of nonpoint source impacts: North Fork Humboldt River, Nevada. U.S. Forest Service Intermountain Research Station Fisheries Unit, Boise, Idaho, USA.

Karr, J. R. 1981. Assessment of biotic integrity using fish communities. Fisheries 6: 21–27.

———, and E.W. Chu. 1998. Restoring life in running waters: better biological monitoring. Island Press, Covelo, California, USA.

Kittel, G. M., E. VanWie, M. Damm, R. J. Rondeau, S. Kettler, A. McMullen, and J. Sanderson. 1999. Classification of riparian wetland plant associations of Colorado. Colorado Natural Heritage Program, Fort Collins, Colorado, USA.

Kovalchik, B. L., and L. A. Chitwood. 1990. Use of geomorphology in the classification of riparian plant associations in mountainous landscapes of central Oregon, USA. Forest Ecology and Management 33/34:405–418.

Lambing, J. H., W. E. Jones, and J. W. Sutphin. 1988. Reconnaissance investigation of water quality, bottom sediment, and biota associated with irrigation drainage in Bowdoin National Wildlife Refuge and adjacent areas of the Milk River Basin, northeastern Montana. U.S. Geological Survey Water Resources Investigations Report 87-4243.

LeJeune, K., H. Galbraith, J. Lipton, and L. Kapustka. 1996. Effects of metals and arsenic on riparian communities in southwest Montana. Ecotoxicology 5:297–312.

Leonard, S. G., G. J. Staidl, K. A. Gebhardt, and D. E. Pritchard. 1992a. Viewpoint: Range site/ecological site information requirements for classification of riverine riparian systems. Journal of Range Management 45:431–435.

———,———, J. Fogg, K. Gebhardt, W. Hagenbuck, and D. Pritchard. 1992b. Procedures for ecological site inventory—with special reference to riparian-wetland sites. U.S. Bureau of Land Management Technical Reference 1737-7.

Maxwell, J. R., C. J. Edwards, M. E. Jensen, S. J. Paustian, H. Parrott, and D. M. Hill. 1995. A hierarchical framework of aquatic ecological units in North America (Nearctic zone). U.S. Forest Service General Technical Report NC-176.

Mertes, L. A. K. 1997. Documentation of the significance of the perirheic zone on inundated floodplains. Water Resources Research 33: 1749–62.

Natural Resources and Conservation Service. 1998. Draft interim functional assessment method for Idaho, at *www.pwrc.usgs.gov/wlistates/idaho.htm.*

———. 1999. Interim functional assessment method for playa wetlands, at *www.pwrc .usgs.gov/wlistates/playas2.htm.*

Noe, D. C., K. Kolm, J. Emerick, and D. Cooper. 1998. Characterization and functional assessment of reference wetlands in Colorado. Colorado Geological Survey, Department of Natural Resources, Denver, Colorado, USA.

Padgett, W. G., A. P. Youngblood, and A. H. Winward. 1989. Riparian community type classification of Utah and southeastern Idaho. U.S. Forest Service Report R4-Ecol-89-01.

Pascoe, G. A., R. J. Blanchet, and G. Linder. 1994a. Bioavailability of metals and arsenic to small mammals at a mining waste-contaminated wetland. Archives of Environmental Contamination and Toxicology 27:44–50.

——, ——, ——, D. Palawski, W. G. Brumbaugh, T. J. Canfield, N. E. Kemble, C. G. Ingersoll, A. Farag, and J. A. DalSoglio. 1994b. Characterization of ecological risks at the Milltown Reservoir–Clark Fork River sediments Superfund site, Montana. Environmental Toxicology and Chemistry 13:2043–2058.

Platts, W., W. F. Megahan, and G. W. Minshall. 1983. Methods for evaluating streams, riparian and biotic conditions. U.S. Forest Service General Technical Report INT-138.

——, C. Amour, G. D. Booth, M. Bryant, J. L. Buford, P. Cuplin, S. Jensen, G. W. Lienkaemper, W. G. Minshall, and S. B. Monsen. 1987. Methods for evaluating riparian habitats with applications to management. U.S. Forest Service General Techical Report INT-221.

Pritchard, D., coordinator. 1994. Process for assessing proper functioning condition for lentic riparian-wetland areas. U.S. Bureau of Land Management Technical Reference 1737-11.

——. 1998. A user guide to assessing proper functioning condition and the supporting science for lotic areas. U.S. Bureau of Land Management Technical Reference 1737-15.

Rosgen, D. L. 1994. A classification of natural rivers. Catena 22:169–199.

Smith, R. D., A. Ammann, C. Bartoldus, and M. M. Brinson. 1995. An approach for assessing wetland functions using hydrogeomorphic classification, reference wetlands, and functional indices. U.S. Army Corps of Engineers Technical Report WRP-DE-9.

Stewart, R. E., and H. A. Kantrud. 1972. Classification of natural ponds and lakes in the glaciated prairie region. U.S. Fish and Wildlife Service Research Publication 92.

Swanson, S., R. Miles, S. Leonard, and K. Genz. 1988. Classifying rangeland riparian areas: the Nevada Task Force approach. Journal of Soil and Water Conservation 43:3.

U.S. Fish and Wildlife Service. 1981. Habitat Evaluation Procedures (HEP). U.S. Fish and Wildlife Service, Washington, D.C., USA.

——. 1997. A system for mapping riparian areas in the western United States. U.S. Fish and Wildlife Service, National Wetlands Inventory, Washington, D.C., USA.

Windell, J. T., B. E. Willard, D. J. Cooper, S. Q. Foster, C. F. Knud-Hansen, L. P. Rink, and G. N. Kiladis. 1986. An ecological characterization of Rocky Mountain montane and subalpine wetlands. U.S. Fish and Wildlife Service Biological Report 86(11).

Winward, A. H. 2000. Monitoring the vegetation resources in riparian areas. U.S. Forest Service Report RMRS-GTR-47.

Youngblood, A. P., W. G. Padgett, and A. H. Winward. 1985. Riparian community type classification of eastern Idaho–western Wyoming. U.S. Forest Service Report R4-Ecol-85-01.

Conclusions and Future Directions

MARK C. MCKINSTRY

Overview

The United States has an abundant supply of water, but most of the water is in the coastal regions and east of the 100th meridian. Few areas of the Intermountain West have excess water, and many areas are considered deserts. Precipitation within the Intermountain West from the Rocky Mountains to the Sierra Nevada and Cascade Mountains varies from <15 cm/year in the desert basins to >140 cm in the mountains and originates primarily from spring storms (Kadlec and Smith 1989). While mountainous areas contain valuable wetland and riparian areas, most of these habitats are in the alluvial valleys between mountain ranges. In mountainous areas, precipitation from rain and snow are greater than losses and wetlands rarely go dry, but in basin areas, evapotranspiration can be 3 to 4 times greater than inflows, and many of these areas are dry by late summer. Furthermore, evaporation can increase dissolved solids in wetlands, dramatically altering salinity levels and subsequent biological function (Kadlec and Smith 1989; also see Chapter 6 of this volume).

However, despite the lack of abundant precipitation across much of the Intermountain West, there are numerous and varied wetland and riparian areas within the region. And although these habitats may be scattered and imperceptible, their worth is disproportionate to their areal extent. Wetland and riparian habitats comprise <2% of the land area in the Intermountain West yet provide habitat for >80% of wildlife species, as well as having incalculable value to farmers and ranchers (Johnson and Jones 1977, Vavra et al. 1994, Rich 2002). Wetland and riparian areas of the Intermountain West are unique areas that are valuable biologically, economically, and socially; they could be termed "keystone habitats" because they help drive ecosystem form and function, and they structure biotic communities far beyond their areal extent.

Many human uses for water require that its physical occurrence be altered. Farmers, ranchers, industrial users, municipalities, and government agencies all divert water in the Intermountain West for a multi-tude of purposes. All of the uses have utility, but not all can be protected by law and given the status of "water right" (Trelease and Gould 1986). Laws governing water use in the Intermountain West are based on prior appropriation, where the first user to put the water to a beneficial use is the first to get the appropriation (see Chapter 1 of this volume). The courts generally do not define beneficial use, except that instream uses (e.g., for fish and wildlife habitat) are either not supported or are subor-dinate to other uses. This view is changing in some western states as the importance of fish and other water-dependent species is recognized, but there is much progress to be made in this arena.

Since water is a limited resource in the Intermountain West, the de-mands for it are high and constantly increasing. The major impact on wetland and riparian areas in the western United States has been from the development and subsequent depletion of water resources for en-ergy, agricultural, industrial, and domestic use (Kadlec and Smith 1989). Water diversions for irrigation account for >85% of the water use in the western United States (National Research Council 1982); however, irri-gated lands are decreasing as water use shifts from agricultural to indus-trial and domestic use, especially in areas with increasing urban popu-lations. This pattern is widespread throughout the Intermountain West and is expected to increase as the population expands. James Lovvorn and Andrew Hart, in Chapter 6 of this volume, describe the importance of irrigation to wetlands of the Intermountain West and illustrate how cumulative impacts from irrigation affect consumers, both human and wildlife. Few studies have been completed on the impacts of irrigation and water diversions to wetland and riparian habitats and, more impor-tantly, on the subsequent impacts that various uses have on the alter-ation of fish and wildlife habitat. Because many streams and wetlands de-pend upon return flows from irrigated lands, especially for late-summer water levels, changes in water use can have dramatic effects on wetland and riverine species that use these areas, including many that are con-sidered endangered, further complicating management and policies that govern these habitats. As land use patterns shift from predominantly agricultural to industrial or urban, managers will need to take a multi-disciplinary (i.e., legal, ecological, and social) approach in dealing with these issues.

Riparian Habitats

Riparian areas are among the most ecologically productive and diverse environments in the world (Johnson and Jones 1977, Gregory et al. 1991). Some examples of the important and diverse functions that riparian habitats provide include food, water, and shelter for wildlife and live-stock; migratory corridors for birds and mammals; breeding areas for am-phibians and reptiles; nutrient cycling and foodweb support; and recre-ational areas for humans. Despite their ecological importance, riparian areas of the Intermountain West have been the subject of little research and certainly of no data collection at a scale approaching the entire re-gion (Kondolf et al. 1996). Gaps in knowledge for riparian systems iden-tified by authors in this volume include: (1) hydrologic needs of plants, especially minimum groundwater depths and duration of flooding to sustain species, (2) instream flow needs and how to develop and improve instream flow policies within the various states, (3) management tech-niques to limit the spread and growth of invasive plants, especially tam-arisk, (4) formulation of effective management plans to protect native species including plants, invertebrates, reptiles, amphibians, fish, birds, and mammals, and (5) techniques that successfully restore the structure and function of affected habitats. Some progress has been made in under-standing the ecological importance of riparian habitats, but much re-mains to be done (Kauffman et al. 1997).

Palustrine Habitats

Palustrine habitats in the Intermountain West are highly dispersed and tend to be associated with lacustrine (open water) habitats, unlike more typical palustrine wetlands in the Great Plains and Prairie Pothole re-gion (Ringelman et al. 1989). Management of palustrine wetlands in the Intermountain West is complicated by diverse ownership patterns, al-though this problem may be less severe than in other areas of the United States where land ownership is even more fractious. The importance of palustrine habitats to wildlife in the Intermountain West cannot be over-emphasized. As James Gammonley points out in Chapter 7, palustrine habitats in the Intermountain West serve as critical habitat for hundreds of species, especially waterbirds. Furthermore, these areas can have high densities of wildlife (Gilbert et al. 1996; see also Chapters 7 and 10) with productivity rates for nesting birds (especially waterfowl) exceeding those found in other regions (Ball et al. 1995). Created palustrine wet-lands number more than 1 million in the Intermountain West (Modde 1980) and add significantly to a limited resource. Because these wetlands are usually created incidental to other activities, they are often over-looked for their importance in providing habitat and hence have escaped much attention from research. Productive areas for future work on both created and natural palustrine wetlands include (1) the importance of substrate conditions and how they can structure aquatic plant commu-nities, (2) identification of ecological processes that occur in palustrine wetlands and how they can be managed for a desired outcome, (3) the importance of water quality (especially salinity) in structuring plant and animal communities, (4) factors affecting colloidal suspension and sedimentation and development of techniques to minimize them, (5) techniques for the establishment of aquatic plants, and (6) techniques to restore impacted and degraded wetlands. Both created and natural palustrine habitats support a wide array of ecological processes, and research has only scratched the surface in defining their importance in structuring biotic communities in the Intermountain West.

Livestock Grazing

Livestock grazing and its impact on wetland and riparian areas of the Intermountain West is clearly a focal point in this book, with several authors addressing its importance as well as offering recommendations to minimize its effects. I highlight grazing again in this section because of its importance in land management in the Intermountain West and because I feel that, in general, the research on grazing has been ambiguous (Vavra et al. 1994) and has not led to large improvements in land management. Belsky et al. (1999) and Donahue (1999) examined more than 150 peer-reviewed articles, government reports, and other documents relating to the impacts of grazing to western rangelands, especially riparian areas, and concluded that no study has documented an ecological benefit from livestock grazing. However, this is contradicted by several authors in Vavra et al. (1994) who cited the benefits of grazing and its role in improving ecosystem health. Many grazing strategies continue to rely upon age-old practices and conventions that undoubtedly are not beneficial to wetland and riparian plant communities (Belsky et al. 1999). However, western rangelands and riparian areas evolved with extensive grazing communities, and no evidence suggests that these areas cannot support grazing if it mimics evolutionary patterns (as reviewed in Vavra et al. 1994).

Land managers are unsure how to regulate grazing, especially under existing sociological, ecological, economical, and political constraints. Due in part to variation in habitats and precipitation, it will be difficult to develop grazing strategies that are effective and prescriptive across large regions. However, little information exists that land managers can use to improve productivity of Intermountain West wetland and riparian areas with concurrent grazing, and this needs to change if grazing is to continue to be one of the primary activities in these habitats. One method to achieve better management is to develop monitoring techniques that allow managers to target specific results in conjunction with grazing strategies. Developing effective grazing strategies will not be easy and may be hampered by social and political pressures, but as several authors point out in this volume, there is obviously a need for multidisciplinary studies to determine the role of livestock grazing and its future in managing wetland and riparian areas of the Intermountain West.

Monitoring

Monitoring programs are especially important in assessing wetland and riparian mitigation, restoration, and enhancement efforts. Paul Adamus, in Chapter 12 of this volume, offers guidance on assessment methods and how they can be used in a world of shrinking agency budgets that demands quick results, especially from development interests. But while these methods are quick to apply and can yield useful results to help guide management and mitigation, they have often not been tested for accuracy, precision, or consistency. Furthermore, very few of these methods have incorporated vegetative or wildlife value/habitat measurements into their protocols. Keddy (1999) suggested that identifying critical indicators (e.g., water and salinity levels) of wetland function and setting acceptable and desired levels for them is required for maintaining ecosystem integrity. To be effective these indicators must be ecologically meaningful, applicable to a macro scale, pragmatic, sensitive, and simple to use (Keddy 1999). Determining critical indicators and incorporating them into management schemes will not be easy or without controversy. However, approaches like this that give managers the tools to set goals and reach them by controlling limiting factors while minimizing extraneous noise are desirable and necessary if management is to keep pace with increasing demands on the resource.

Conclusions

Clearly more work is needed concerning wetland and riparian habitats of the Intermountain West. One glaring take-home message from this book is the scarcity of recent information and research, as illustrated by the limited number of citations within the past 10 years. Most of the literature cited in this book was published prior to 1980, and few studies were cited that had incorporated new techniques important to research in other regions of the country. Furthermore, as the editors mention in the introduction, much of the cited research is from studies outside of the Intermountain West region and may have limited applicability to this region. Shrinking agency budgets and increased demands from other issues have led to declining emphasis on research and management programs. However, increasing pressures from development and extractive industries as well as burgeoning human populations and associated impacts will put added pressures and demands on an already limited resource. Adopting adaptive management strategies (Walters and Hollings 1990) in which research and management are explicitly linked to identify uncertainty and determine cause and effect relationships may be the best approach to solving problems that continue to frustrate managers.

In conclusion, perpetuation of healthy wetland and riparian areas of the Intermountain West will depend upon research, conservation education, and wise use through proper management. Successful long-term research and management programs will require concerted efforts from different agencies and levels of government as well as from private stakeholders. Finding support for these programs will be a daunting task for managers and researchers, but these areas are too valuable to relegate to haphazard management that relies on outdated information and untested dogma.

Literature Cited

Ball, I. J., R. L. Eng, and S. K. Ball. 1995. Population density and productivity of ducks on large grassland tracts in northcentral Montana. Wildlife Society Bulletin 23: 767–773.

Belsky, A. J., A. Matzke, and S. Uselman. 1999. Survey of livestock influences on stream and riparian ecosystems in the western United States. Journal of Soil and Water Conservation 54:419–431.

Donahue, D. L. 1999. The western range revisited: removing livestock from public lands to conserve native biodiversity. University of Oklahoma Press, Norman, Oklahoma, USA.

Gilbert, D. W., D. R. Anderson, J. K. Ringelman, and M. R. Szymczak. 1996. Response of nesting ducks to habitat and management on the Monte Vista National Wildlife Refuge, Colorado. Wildlife Monographs 131:1–44.

Gregory, S. V., F. J. Swanson, W. A. McKee, and K. W. Cummins. 1991. An ecosystem perspective of riparian zones. BioScience 41: 540–551.

Johnson, R. R., and D. A. Jones, technical coordinators. 1977. Importance, preservation, and management of riparian habitat: a symposium. U.S. Department of Agriculture Forest Service General Technical Report RM-GTR-43.

Kadlec, J. A., and L. M. Smith. 1989. The Great Basin marshes. Pages 451–474 in L. Smith, R. L. Pedersen, and R. M. Kaminski, editors. Habitat management for migrating and wintering waterfowl in North America. Texas Tech University Press, Lubbock, Texas, USA.

Kauffman, J. B., R. L. Beschta, N. Otting, and D. Lytjen. 1997. An ecological perspective of riparian and stream restoration in the western United States. Fisheries 22(5): 12–24.

Keddy, P. 1999. Wetland restoration: the potential for assembly rules in the service of conservation. Wetlands 19:716–732.

Kondolf, G. M., R. Kattelmann, M. Embury, and D. C. Erman. 1996. Assessments and scientific basis for management options. Volume 2 of Status of riparian habitat. Sierra Nevada Ecosystem Project: Final report to Congress. Centers for Water and Wildland Resources, University of California, Davis, California, USA.

Modde, T. 1980. State stocking policies for small warmwater impoundments. Fisheries 5(5):14–17

National Research Council. 1982. Impacts of emerging agricultural trends on fish and wildlife habitat. National Academic Press, Washington, D.C., USA.

Rich, T. D. 2002. Using breeding land birds in the assessment of western riparian systems. Wildlife Society Bulletin 30:1128–1139.

Ringelman, J. K., W. E. Eddleman, and H. W. Miller. 1989. High plains and sloughs. Pages 311–340 *in* L. Smith, R. L. Pedersen, and R. M. Kaminski, editors. Habitat management for migrating and wintering waterfowl in North America. Texas Tech University Press, Lubbock, Texas, USA.

Trelease, F. J., and G. A. Gould. 1986. Water law: cases and materials. Fourth edition. West Publishing, Saint Paul, Minnesota, USA.

Vavra, M., W. A. Laycock, and R. D. Pieper, editors. 1994. Ecological implications of livestock herbivory in the west. Society for Range Management, Denver, Colorado, USA.

Walters, C. J., and C. S. Hollings. 1990. Large-scale management experiments and learning by doing. Ecology 7:2060–2068.

Common and Scientific Names of Mammals, Birds, Amphibians and Reptiles, Fish, and Plants Used in Text

Mammals	Scientific Name
beaver	*Castor canadensis*
black bear	*Ursus americanus*
bobcat	*Lynx rufus*
brown bear	*Ursus arctos*
cattle	*Bos* spp.
deer mice	*Peromyscus maniculatus*
eastern cottontail	*Sylvilagus floridanus*
elk	*Cervus elaphus*
ermine	*Mustela erminea*
fisher	*Martes pennanti*
lynx	*Lynx lynx*
mink	*Mustela vison*
moose	*Alces alces*
mule deer	*Odocoileus hemionus*
muskrat	*Ondatra zibethicus*
opposum	*Didelphis virginiana*
pronghorn	*Antilocapra americana*
raccoon	*Procyon lotor*
ringtail	*Bassariseus astutus*
river otter	*Lutra canadensis*
shrew	*Sorex cinereus, S. monticolus*
snowshoe hare	*Lepus americanus*
striped skunk	*Mephitis mephitis*
vole	*Microtus longicaudus, M. ochrogaster*
water shrew	*Sorex palustris*
water vole	*Microtus richardsonii*
western spotted skunk	*Spilogale gracilis*
white-tail deer	*Odocoileus virginianus*

Birds	Scientific Name
American avocet	*Recurvirostra americana*
American bittern	*Botaurus lentiginosus*
American coot	*Fulica americans*
American dippers	*Cinclus mexicanus*
American white pelican	*Pelicanus erythrorhynchos*
American wigeon	*Anas americana*
Barrows goldeneye	*Bucephala islandica*
belted kingfisher	*Ceryle alcyon*
black-crowned night heron	*Nycticorax nycticax*
black tern	*Chlidonias niger*
blue-winged teal	*Anas discors*
bufflehead	*Bucephala albeola*
California gull	*Larus californicus*
Canada goose	*Branta canadensis*
canvasback	*Aythya valisineria*
cinnamon teal	*Anas cyanoptera*
Clark's grebe	*Aechmophorus clarkii*
common gadwall	*Anas strepera*
common goldeneye	*Bucephala clangula*
common moorhen	*Porphyrula martinca*
common snipe	*Gallinago gallinago*
common tern	*Sterna hirundo*
dabbling duck	*Anas* spp.
diving duck	Aythyini
double-crested cormorant	*Phalacrocrax auritus*
eared grebe	*Podiceps nigricolis*
Forster's tern	*Sterna forsteri*
Franklin's gull	*Larus pipixcan*
great blue heron	*Ardea herodias*
green-backed heron	*Butorides striatus*
green-winged teal	*Anas crecca*
horned grebe	*Podiceps auritus*
killdeer	*Charadrius vociferus*
lesser scaup	*Anas affinis*
long-billed curlew	*Numenius americanus*
mallard	*Anas platyrhynchos*
marbled godwit	*Limosa fedoa*
marsh wren	*Cistothorus palustris*
merganser	*Mergus* spp.
northern harrier	*Circus cyaneus*
northern shoveler	*Anas clypeata*

pied-billed grebe	*Podilymbus podiceps*
pintail	*Anas acuta*
redhead	*Aythya americana*
ring-billed gull	*Larus delawarensis*
ring-necked duck	*Anas collaris*
red-winged blackbird	*Agelaius phoeniceus*
ruddy duck	*Oxyura jamaicensis*
sage grouse	*Centrocercus urophasianus*
sandhill crane	*Grus canadensis*
sea duck	Mergerini
short-eared owl	*Asio flammeus*
snowy egrets	*Egretta thula*
snowy plover	*Charadrius alexandrinus*
song sparrow	*Melospiza melodia*
sora rail	*Porzana Carolina*
spotted sandpiper	*Actitus macularia*
stiff-tailed duck	Oxyurini
trumpeter swan	*Cygnus buccinator*
Virginia rail	*Rallis limicola*
western grebe	*Aechmophorus occidentalis*
white-faced ibis	*Plegadis chihi*
whooping crane	*Grus americana*
willet	*Catoptrophorus semipalmatus*
willow flycatcher	*Empidonax traillii*
Wilson's phalarope	*Phalaropus tricolor*
wood duck	*Aix sponsa*
yellow warbler	*Dendroica petechia*
yellow-headed blackbird	*Xanthocephalus xanthocephalus*

Amphibians and Reptiles	**Scientific Name**
Armagosa toad	*Bufo nelsoni*
arroyo toad	*Bufo microscaphus californicus*
bullfrog	*Rana catesbeiana*
Chiricahua leopard frog	*Rana chiricahuensis*
chorus frog	*Pseudacris triseriata*
garter snake	*Thamnophis* spp.
Great Plains toad	*Bufo cognatus*
green frog	*Rana clamitans*
lowland leopard frog	*Rana yavapaiensis*
mountain yellow-legged frog	*Rana muscosa*
northern leopard frog	*Rana pipiens*

northwestern pond turtle	*Clemmys marmorata*
painted turtle	*Chrysemys picta*
pickerel frog	*Rana palustris*
plains leopard frog	*Rana blairi*
plains spadefoot	*Spea bombifrons*
red-spotted toad	*Bufo punctatus*
ringneck snake	*Diadophis* spp.
slider	*Pseudomys scripta*
snapping turtle	*Chelydra serpentina*
Sonoran mud turtle	*Kinostrnon sonoriense*
spadefoot toad	*Scaphiopus* spp.
spiny softshell	*Trionyx spiniferus*
spotted frog	*Rana pretiosa*
Tarahumara frog	*Rana tarahumarae*
Texas spiny softshell	*Trionyx spiniferus*
tiger salamander	*Ambystoma tigrinis*
western box turtle	*Terrapene ornata*
western or boreal toad	*Bufo boreas boreas*
Woodhouse's toad	*Bufo woodhousei*
Wyoming toad	*Bufo hemiophrys baxteri*
yellow mud turtle	*Kinosternon flavescens*

Fish	**Scientific Name**
black bullhead	*Ameiurus melas*
black crappie	*Pomoxis nigromaculatus*
bluegill	*Lepomis macrochirus*
brook trout	*Salvelinus fontinalis*
brown trout	*Salmo trutta*
channel catfish	*Ictalurus punctatus*
Colorado pikeminnow	*Ptychocheilus lucius*
common carp	*Cyprinus carpio*
cutthroat trout	*Oncorhynchus clarki*
fathead minnow	*Pimephales promelas*
golden shiner	*Notemigonus crysoleucas*
grass carp	*Ctenopharyngodon idella*
lake trout	*Salvelinus namaycush*
largemouth bass	*Micropterus salmoides*
northern pike	*Esox lucius*
rainbow trout	*Oncorhnychus mykiss*
smallmouth bass	*Micropterus dolomieu*
trout	Salmonidae

walleye	*Sander vitreus*
white crappie	*Pomoxis annularis*
yellow perch	*Perca flavescens*

Plants	**Scientific Name**
alder	*Alnus* spp.
alkali bulrush	*Scirpus paludosus*
alkali cordgrass	*Spartina gracilis*
alkali sacaton	*Sporobolus airoides*
American bulrush	*Scirpus americanus*
American pondweed	*Potamogeton nodusos*
arrowhead	*Sagittaria* spp.
ash	*Fraxinus* spp.
aspen	*Populus tremuloides*
baby pondweed	*Potamogeton pusillus*
Baltic rush	*Juncus balticus*
barnyard grass	*Echinochloa* spp.
basin wildrye	*Elymus cinereus*
beaked sedge	*Carex rostrata*
beggertick	*Bidens* spp.
big sagebrush	*Artemisia tridentata*
bitterbrush	*Purshia* spp.
black greasewood	*Sarcobatus vermiculatus*
black sagebrush	*Artemesia nova*
bladderwort	*Utricularia* spp.
bluegrass	*Poa* spp.
boxelder	*Acer negundo*
bullwhip	*Scirpus californicus*
bulrush	*Scirpus* spp.
burreed	*Sparganium* spp.
cattail	*Typha* spp.
Chara	*Chara globularis*
cheatgrass	*Bromus tectorum*
common bladderwort	*Utricularia vulgaris*
common cattail	*Typha latifolia*
common duckweed	*Lemna minor*
common hornwort	*Ceratophyllum demersum*
common marestail	*Hippuris vulgaris*
common reed	*Phragmites communis*
common spikerush	*Eleocharis palustris*
common widgeonweed	*Ruppia maritima*

common winterfat	*Eurotia lanata*
cottonwood	*Populus* spp.
cowlily	*Nuphar* spp.
creeping spikerush	*Eleocharis palustris*
curly dock	*Rumex crispus*
curlyleaf pondweed	*Potamageton crispus*
dogwood	*Cornus* spp.
Douglas rabbitbrush	*Chrysothamnus viscidiflorus*
Douglas sedge	*Carex douglasii*
dwarf spikerush	*Eleocharis parvula*
enteromorpha	*Enteromorpha* spp.
European water plantain	*Alisma plantago-aquatica*
evening primrose	*Oenothera boothii*
fennelleaf pondweed	*Potamogeton pectinatus*
few-flowered panicum	*Panicum oligosanthes*
field horsetail	*Equisetum arvense*
fireweed summercypress	*Kochia scoparia*
floating knotweed	*Polygonum natans*
foxtail barley	*Hordeum jubatum*
giant burreed	*Sparganium eurycarpum*
giant reed	*Phragmites australis*
goosefoot	*Chenopodium* spp.
green algae	*Chlorophyta* spp.
hairgrass	*Deschampsia* spp.
hardstem bulrush	*Scirpus acutus*
hawthorn	*Crataegus* spp.
horned pondweed	*Zannichellia palustris*
Indian ricegrass	*Oryzopsis hymenoides*
inland rush	*Juncus interior*
inland saltgrass	*Distichlis stricta*
iodine bush	*Allenrolfia occidentalis*
juncus	*Juncus arcticus*
lambsquarters goosefoot	*Chenopodium album*
lanceleaf cottonwood	*Populus acuminata*
lemon scurfpea	*Psoralea lanceolata*
longspike spikerush	*Eleocharis macrostachya*
mannagrass	*Glyceria* spp.
mentzelia	*Mentzelia torreyi*
mesquite	*Prosopis* spp.
mud plantain	*Heteranthera limosa*
muhly	*Muhlenbergia* spp.
muskgrass	*Chara* spp., *C. golbularis,* *C. aspera, C. longifolia*

narrowleaf burreed	*Sparganium angustifolium*
narrow-leaf cattail	*Typha angustifolia*
narrowleaf cottonwood	*Populus angustifolia*
narrowleaved water plantain	*Alisma gramineum*
Nebraska sedge	*Carex nebraskensis*
needle spikerush	*Eleocharis acicularis*
Nevada club rush	*Scirpus nevadensis*
northern mannagrass	*Glyceria borealis*
northern meadow barley	*Hordeum brachyantherum*
Nuttall saltbush	*Atriplex nuttallii*
oak	*Quercus* spp.
olney bulrush	*Scirpus olneyi*
painted cowlily	*Nymphaea variegatum*
pale sedge	*Carex canescens*
peachleaf willow	*Salix amygdaloides*
pickleweed	*Salicornia rubra, S. pacifica*
pigweed	*Amaranthus* spp.
pine	*Pinus* spp.
plains cottonwood	*Populus sargentii*
plantain	*Plantago patogonica*
pondweed	*Potamogeton pusillus*
pondweed	*Potamogeton* spp.
poplar	*Populus* spp.
purple loosestripe	*Lythrum salicaria*
quillwort	*Isoetes* spp.
rabbitbrush	*Chrysothamnus* spp.
rabbitfoot grass	*Polypogon monspeliensis*
redtop bentgrass	*Agrostis alba*
reedgrass	*Calamagrostis* spp.
rice cutgrass	*Leersia oryzoides*
river bulrush	*Scirpus lacustris*
rosette grass	*Poa acuminatum*
rubber rabbitbrush	*Chrysothamnus nauseosus*
rush	*Juncus* spp.
sagebrush	*Artemisia* spp.
sago pondweed	*Potamogeton pectinatus*
saltbush	*Atriplex* spp.
salt cedar	*Tamarix chinensis*
salt grass	*Distichlis spicata*
sedge	*Carex* spp.
shadscale	*Atriplex confertifolia*
shortawn foxtail	*Alopecurus aequalis*
shrubby cinquefoil	*Potentilla fruticosa*

slender naiad	*Najas flexilis*
slender pondweed	*Potamogeton filiformis*
smartweed	*Polygonum* spp.
softstem bulrush	*Scirpus validus*
spiked watermilfoil	*Myriophyllum exalbescens*
spikerush	*Eleocharis* spp.
spiny hopsage	*Grayia spinosa*
sprangletop	*Leptochloa fascicularis*
star duckweed	*Lemna trisulca*
stonewort	*Nitella* spp.
Torrey's rush	*Juncas torreyi*
tule bulrush	*Scirpus acutus*
veiny dock	*Rumex venosus*
water ladysthumb	*Polygonum amphibium*
watercress	*Rorippa sphaerocarpa*
watercrowfoot buttercup	*Ranunculus aquatilis*
waterlily	*Nymphaea tetragona*
watermilfoil	*Myriophyllum exalbescens*
white buttercup	*Ranunculus trichophyllus*
widgeon grass	*Ruppia maritima*
wildrye	*Elymus* spp.
willow	*Salix* spp.
winterfat	*Eurotia lanata*
wooly sedge	*Carex lanuginosa*
yellow pondlily	*Nuphar luteum*

CONTRIBUTORS

Paul Adamus, Department of Fisheries and Wildlife, Oregon State University, Corvallis, Oregon

Michael A. Bozek, University of Wisconsin, Stevens Point, Wisconsin

Robert C. Ehrhart, Department of Rangeland Resources, Oregon State University, Bend, Oregon

James H. Gammonley, Colorado Division of Wildlife, Fort Collins, Colorado

Paul L. Hansen, Bitterroot Restoration, Corvallis, Montana

E. Andrew Hart, Department of Zoology and Physiology, University of Wyoming, Laramie, Wyoming

Wayne A. Hubert, U.S. Geological Survey, Wyoming Cooperative Fish and Wildlife Research Unit, University of Wyoming, Laramie, Wyoming

Murray K. Laubhan, Biological Resources Division, U.S. Geological Survey, Fort Collins, Colorado

Kirk Lohman, Department of Fish and Wildlife Resources, University of Idaho, Moscow, Idaho

James R. Lovvorn, Department of Zoology and Physiology, University of Wyoming, Laramie, Wyoming

Mark C. McKinstry, Wyoming Cooperative Fish and Wildlife Research Unit, Laramie, Wyoming

Neal D. Niemuth, College of Natural Resources, University of Wisconsin, Stevens Point, Wisconsin

Richard A. Olson, Department of Renewable Resources, University of Wyoming, Laramie, Wyoming

Neil F. Payne, College of Natural Resources, University of Wisconsin, Stevens Point, Wisconsin

Mark A. Rumble, U.S. Department of Agriculture, Forest Service, Rocky Mountain Research Station, Rapid City, South Dakota

Maureen Ryan, University of Toledo College of Law, Toledo, Ohio

Brian E. Smith, U.S. Geological Survey, Northern Prairie Wildlife Research Center, Jamestown, North Dakota

Mark Squillace, University of Toledo College of Law, Toledo, Ohio

Stephen A. Tessmann, Wyoming Game and Fish Department, Cheyenne, Wyoming

David W. Willis, Department of Wildlife and Fisheries Sciences, South Dakota State University, Brookings, South Dakota

INDEX